MODERN RUSSIAN

AN ADVANCED GRAMMAR COURSE

DEREK OFFORD

Bristol Classical Press

First published in 1993 by
Bristol Classical Press
an imprint of
Gerald Duckworth & Co. Ltd
61 Frith Street
London W1D 3JL
e-mail: inquiries@duckworth-publishers.co.uk
Website: www.ducknet.co.uk

Reprinted 1994, 1995, 1997, 1998, 1999 (twice), 2001, 2002

A catalogue record for this book is available from the British Library

ISBN 1-85399-361-1

Printed in Great Britain by
Antony Rowe Ltd

CONTENTS

Foreword

This book has been written primarily for students in higher education who have prior knowledge of Russian. Such students nowadays fall into two categories: firstly, those who come to university with a pass at A-level Russian or equivalent qualification; and secondly, those who have already proceeded beyond a preliminary-year or first-year *ab initio* course (in which they may have built on a qualification at GCSE level). The book is not designed for beginners, or for pupils learning Russian at school.

The purpose of the book is to provide students with the solid grammatical foundation which I think is essential if they are to go on to read, write and speak Russian well. It therefore deals thoroughly and systematically with, and provides copious exercises on, such subjects as declension of nouns (Lessons 2-6); conjugation of verbs (7-12); use of cases (15-27); the forms and use of adjectives (28-33), pronouns (34-36), numerals (37-42), and verbs of motion (44-45); prefixes (46-49); aspects (50-54); and gerunds and participles (57-60).

With this purpose in mind the book is conceived as a basis for part of a student's first-year and second-year (or in the case of *ab initio* students, second-year) language work. The material has been divided into portions which it is hoped are manageable at a sitting. The teacher might outline or highlight the main points in each lesson in class, and will no doubt discuss the exercises, but it is intended that students themselves should also study each lesson in their own time and independently work through the exercises on it. The book might also serve final-year students as a basis for revision of topics which continue to give them difficulty.

The justification for a book such as this is twofold. Firstly, it is my conviction that without a sound grammatical framework a student at the higher-education level encounters increasing difficulty in all aspects of the use of such a highly inflected, and generally grammatically complex, language as Russian. Ability even to develop a good reading comprehension, let alone to master the spoken language, is greatly impeded by inattention to basic grammar. Secondly, there is a perennial need for students of Russian to revise and build on the basic grammar they have already learned at school or on an intensive *ab initio* course. From the point of view of the student who is a qualified entrant to higher education, this need would seem to have increased in recent years inasmuch as the linguistic syllabus in British schools has tended to place less emphasis than was formerly the case on the importance of the early acquisition of a sound grammatical framework. At the same time students in higher education who have completed an *ab initio* course, having tried to absorb much difficult material very quickly, are likely as a rule to feel that their grasp of that material is rather weak and to welcome early consolidation and extension of their knowledge.

In insisting on the importance of a thorough grounding in Russian grammar I am not at all advocating an exclusively grammatical approach to the teaching of the language. Study of grammar must of course go together with acquisition of vocabulary, translation from and into Russian, composition, development of oral and aural skills, and exercises in pronunciation and intonation. Use of coursebooks such as this one should be backed up by the exploitation of such aids as language laboratories, satellite television, and computer-assisted language-learning materials. ("Russian Morphological Routines" prepared by the Russian Department and the Centre for Computer-Based Learning of the University of Birmingham are a useful back-up to the lessons on declension and conjugation in this book.) Most important of all, perhaps, a student requires a prolonged period of study in Russia on one or more of the courses that have become available there over the past two decades. I merely contend that the teaching of grammar does have an essential place in the early part of a Russian course at tertiary level, and it is my hope that this coursebook will help to fill what I see as a gap in this area.

I have taken pains to conform in this book to actual current linguistic practice. Such practice may on occasion differ from the usage prescribed in the most authoritative works of reference available to the English-speaking student. In some areas this approach may lead to simpler or less strict rules than those frequently offered to the student or to departures from the usage described by previous authors.

In the hope of achieving a description of the language that is accurate and up-to-date I have had this book read at various stages by native speakers who were brought up in the USSR, including native speakers who are still resident in Russia. I have also drawn some 500 examples from the recent Soviet/Russian media. Many of the sentences in the exercises are also taken from the press or based on material found there. The main papers and journals I have used, in alphabetical order, are *Говорит и показывает Москва* (now renamed *Семь дней*), *Голос родины*, *Известия*, *Крокодил*, *Литературная газета*, *Огонёк*, and *Советская женщина* (now renamed *Мир женщины*). All examples culled from these publications are from numbers that have come out since 1989. The Soviet/Russian press has of course become a much more useful linguistic tool for the foreign student in recent years, and study of the examples drawn from it should not only help students to understand the grammatical points it is hoped to illustrate but also introduce them to much useful contemporary vocabulary on topics such as politics, economics, social problems, ecology, medicine, and cultural and military affairs.

Bristol, March 1993

Acknowledgements

Several colleagues, both Russian and British, have helped in the compilation of this book and in the improvement of the several versions that have preceded this one. My special thanks are due to Anna Nikolaevna Darmodekhina of the Kuban State University, Krasnodar; Yury Aleksandrovich Dubovsky of Pyatigorsk State Pedagogical Institute of Foreign Languages; Peter Mayo of the Russian Department of the University of Sheffield; and two members of my own Department at the University of Bristol, Michael Basker and Gordon McVay. All these colleagues have at one time or another read the coursebook with much care and have made very numerous corrections, amendments and suggestions, both linguistic and editorial. I am much indebted for technical advice and assistance – and for further linguistic suggestions – to Geoffrey Rolfe, head of Russian at Abingdon School, who has transferred the material from my own Amstrad files to an Apple Macintosh from which it has been reproduced on a laser printer. I also gratefully acknowledge receipt of a grant from the Ford Foundation towards the cost of this operation. For all mistakes and imperfections which remain in the book I myself, of course, am solely responsible.

Bibliographical note

I have consulted many earlier works on Russian grammar which remain useful, especially: B.O.Unbegaun, *Russian Grammar*, Oxford University Press, 1957; *Forbes' Russian Grammar*, 3rd ed., revised and enlarged by J.C.Dumbreck, Oxford University Press, 1964; Dennis Ward, *The Russian Language Today*, Hutchinson University Library, 1965; F.M.Borras and R.M.Christian, *Russian Syntax*, 2nd ed., Oxford University Press, 1971; I.M.Pulkina, *A Short Russian Reference Grammar*, translated from the Russian by V.Korotky, 7th ed., Russky Yazyk, Moscow, 1984; and Terence Wade, *A Comprehensive Russian Grammar*, Blackwell, Oxford, 1992. I have also drawn on the following monographs (in the order of the lessons in this book to which they relate): R.M.Davison, *The Use of the Genitive in Negative Constructions*, Cambridge University Press, 1967; М.В. Всеволодова, «Употребление кратких и полных прилагательных» (*Русский язык за рубежом*, 1971, no. 3, pp. 65-8 and 1972, no. 1, pp. 59-64); О.П.Рассудова, *Употребление видов глагола*, Moscow University Press, 1971; I.M.Foote, *Verbs of Motion*, Cambridge University Press, 1967; James Forsyth, *A Grammar of Aspect: Usage and Meaning in the Russian Verb*, Cambridge University Press, 1970; and W.Harrison, *The Expression of the Passive Voice*, Cambridge University Press, 1967.

Note on conventions and use of the book

Space does not permit translation of all possible English versions of Russian words given, especially of Russian verbs given in lists.

From Lesson 14 on, whenever verbs appear in lists both members of an aspectual pair (i.e. imperfective and perfective forms, e.g. пыта́ться/ попыта́ться) are generally given. However, only one form is given if the verb has a perfective that is rarely used (e.g. боя́ться, горди́ться), or if the prefix which occurs in the commonest perfective form of the verb is used in that form to modify the meaning of the basic verb (e.g. сме́яться, whose perfective засме́яться, means *to start laughing*).

When both members of an aspectual pair are given, the first member is invariably imperfective.

In the translation of some of the examples given in the lessons some material is inserted in square brackets. Such material may either be an explanatory interpolation of my own (in which case it is in Roman font), or it may help to clarify the meaning of the original by adding words which although not actually stated in the Russian are implicit in it (in which case the material is in italics, like the rest of the translation).

The vocabulary on pp. 403-433 gives Russian translations of all the English words used in the exercises, unless the Russian word required in the exercise is specifically examined in the lesson to which the exercise relates. However, when doing the English-Russian exercises, particularly those in the first half of the book, the student is advised also to consult the sections on personal pronouns (Lesson 34, Sections 1-2), possessive pronouns (35.1-2), the use of свой (35.3), the table of cardinal numerals (37.1), and the index showing sections in the book which deal with the rendering of English prepositions into Russian (pp.434-436). These subjects arise frequently in the exercises and are the source of many mistakes.

List of abbreviations

acc.	accusative	imp.	imperative
act.	active	impers.	impersonal
adj.	adjective	impf.	imperfective
adv.	adverb	indic.	indicative
coll.	colloquial	infin.	infinitive
comp.	comparative	instr.	instrumental
dat.	dative	intrans.	intransitive
fem.	feminine	irreg.	irregular
fut.	future	lit.	literally
gen.	genitive	loc.	locative

masc.	masculine
neut.	neuter
nom.	nominative
part.	participle
pass.	passive
pers.	person
pf.	perfective
pl.	plural
poss.	possessive
prep.	prepositional
pres.	present
refl.	reflexive
sb.	somebody
sing.	singular
sthg.	something
sup.	superlative
trans.	transitive
vulg.	vulgar

LESSON 1

HARD AND SOFT CONSONANTS; SPELLING RULES

It is important at the outset to understand the Russian system of hard and soft consonants and to master a few basic rules concerning spelling. In the light of these rules much of the apparent complexity of the declension of Russian nouns and adjectives and the conjugation of Russian verbs disappears. The most important points to which reference will repeatedly be made are the following.

§1. Hard and soft consonants

Russian has ten letters which represent vowel sounds: **а, е, ё, и, о, у, ы, э, ю, я**. These letters may be divided into two categories, viz.

col. 1	col. 2
а	я
о	ё
у	ю
ы	и
э	е

The letters in column 2 (with the exception of **и**) represent iotised variants of the corresponding vowel in column 1. That is to say the vowels they represent are pronounced with an initial *y* sound (or in phonetic transcription [j]). These iotised vowels, unlike the vowels represented by the letters in column 1, have the effect of softening a preceding consonant. Compare for example the pronunciation of **л** in the following words:

пила́	*saw*	земля́	*earth*
ло́дка	*boat*	лёд	*ice*
лук	*onion*	люк	*hatch*
лы́жа	*ski*	ли́ния	*line*

It follows that letters in column 1, such as **а**, **у** and **ы**, which frequently occur in standard declensional endings, are replaced by letters in column 2 (**я, ю** and **и** respectively) in endings which follow a soft consonant. Compare for example the endings of пила́, *saw*, which has a hard **л**, with the endings of земля́, *land, earth,* which has a soft **л**, in the accusative, genitive, and instrumental singular cases:

пилу́ зе́млю
пилы́ земли́
пило́й землёй

§2. The sibilants

Note however that the consonants **ч** and **щ** are always soft (e.g. чай, *tea*, in which the vowel **а** is pronounced with an initial *y* [j] sound) and that the consonants **ж**, **ц** and **ш**, on the other hand, are always hard (e.g. жёсткий, *hard, tough*; центр, *centre*; шесть, *six*, in which the vowel does not have an initial *y* [j] sound).

§3. Use of и after velars and sibilants

After the three velars **г**, **к**, and **х**, and after the four sibilants **ж**, **ч**, **ш** and **щ** the letter **ы** cannot occur (except in a very small number of words, especially names, of foreign origin). It must be replaced, in those endings where it would be expected, by the letter **и**, e.g. ру́сский, ти́хий, as opposed to кра́сный.

Both **и** and **ы** may occur after the sibilant **ц** however, e.g. цирк, *circus*, but цыга́н, *gipsy*. (But **и** is pronounced as **ы** when it follows **ц**, as it is after the other hard sibilants **ж** and **ш**.)

§4. Use of а and у after velars and sibilants

The letters **я** and **ю** do not occur either after the velars **г**, **к**, **х**, or after any of the sibilants **ж**, **ц**, **ч**, **ш**, and **щ**, except in a few words, especially proper nouns, of foreign origin (e.g. Гю́го, *Hugo*; Кюрасо́, *Curaçao*; жюри́, *jury*; Цю́рих, *Zürich*). They must be replaced, in those endings where they would be expected, by **а** and **у** respectively. Thus the normal endings for the 1st person singular and the 3rd person plural of second-conjugation verbs (-ю and -ят respectively) are replaced by -у and -ат after sibilants, e.g. говорю́ and говоря́т, but лежу́ and лежа́т.

§5. Impossibility of unstressed о after sibilants

Unstressed **о** is not found after the sibilants **ж**, **ц**, **ч**, **ш**, or **щ** and is replaced by **е** after these letters, e.g. in the ending of the neuter nominative singular adjectival form хоро́шее (cf. the normal ending for this form, as in кра́сное, ру́сское).

§6. Stressed ё

The letter **ё** is always stressed, e.g. in полёт, *flight*. It follows that **ё** cannot normally occur if the stress in a word is on any other syllable.

§7. Punctuation

Note that in Russian a subordinate clause must always be separated from the main clause by a comma or commas, e.g.

main clause	subordinate clause	
Я зна́ю,	что он умён.	*I know he is intelligent.*
Мы поговори́м,	когда́ вы придёте.	*We shall have a chat when you come.*
Я не вы́йду,	е́сли не прекрати́тся дождь.	*I shall not go out if the rain does not stop.*
Он не вы́шел,	потому́ что бы́ло по́здно.	*He did not go out because it was late.*
Сев на велосипе́д,	она́ отпра́вилась по у́лице.	*Having got on her bicycle, she set off down the street.* (Press)
Объе́кт,	слегка́ напомина́ющий ба́мпер автомоби́ля,	*The object, which was slightly reminiscent of the bumper of a car, was captured on video by the astronauts.* (Press)
был засня́т на видеоплёнку астрона́втами.		

LESSON 2

THE BASIC DECLENSIONS OF THE NOUN

For the purposes of this course Russian nouns will be treated as divisible into ten basic declensions (three masculine, three neuter and four feminine). Groups of nouns which do not fall into these declensions will be dealt with separately in the following lessons (3-6), as will the phenomenon of mobile vowels (Lesson 3) and the use of the cases (Lessons 15-27). Note that in many instances the differences between one declension and another are explained merely by the fact that in one declension the stem of the noun ends in a hard consonant whereas in another it ends in a soft consonant.

Many of the nouns which have been chosen to illustrate the various declensional types and whose paradigms are given below have fixed stress. However, it should be noted that the stress patterns of Russian nouns are extremely complex, and in several of the declensional categories nouns of various stress patterns are to be found.

§1. Masculine nouns ending in a hard consonant

Nouns of this type, e.g. автóбус, *bus*, decline as follows:

	sing.	pl.
nom.	автóбус	автóбусы
acc.	автóбус	автóбусы
gen.	автóбуса	автóбусов
dat.	автóбусу	автóбусам
instr.	автóбусом	автóбусами
prep.	автóбусе	автóбусах

Note the following points about nouns in this declension:

i. in accordance with one of the basic spelling rules (see 1.3), nouns of this declension have nominative/accusative plural in -и, not -ы, if the stem ends in one of the velars or sibilants **г**, **к**, **х**, **ж**, **ч**, **ш**, **щ**, e.g.

враги́	*enemies*
сóки	*juices*
петухи́	*cockerels*
ножи́	*knives*
врачи́	*doctors*

карандаши́ *pencils*
плащи́ *cloaks*

ii. in accordance with the rule in 1.5, nouns of this type which end in one of the sibilants **ж, ц, ч, ш, щ** have instrumental singular in -ем if the stress is on the stem (though they retain -ом if the stress is on the ending), e.g.

	му́жем	from муж, *husband*
but	ножо́м	from нож, *knife*

iii. nouns in **ж, ч, ш,** and **щ** (but not **ц**) also have genitive plural in -ей, not -ов, e.g.

ноже́й
враче́й
карандаше́й
плаще́й

§2. Masculine nouns ending in -й
Nouns of this type, e.g. трамва́й, *tram*, decline as follows:

	sing.	pl.
nom.	трамва́й	трамва́и
acc.	трамва́й	трамва́и
gen.	трамва́я	трамва́ев
dat.	трамва́ю	трамва́ям
instr.	трамва́ем	трамва́ями
prep.	трамва́е	трамва́ях

Note that nouns of this type follow precisely the same pattern as the masculine nouns ending in a hard consonant, but the letters **а, о, у, ы** have been replaced by **я, е, ю, и** respectively.

§3. Masculine nouns ending in a soft sign
Nouns of this type, e.g. автомоби́ль, *car*, decline as follows:

	sing.	pl.
nom.	автомоби́ль	автомоби́ли
acc.	автомоби́ль	автомоби́ли
gen.	автомоби́ля	автомоби́лей
dat.	автомоби́лю	автомоби́лям
instr.	автомоби́лем	автомоби́лями
prep.	автомоби́ле	автомоби́лях

Note that these nouns have genitive plural in -ей, and that in other respects their endings are the same as those for the nouns in -й (see §2 above).

Nouns of this type which have stressed endings have instrumental singular in -ём, e.g. рублём.

§4. Neuter nouns ending in -о

Nouns of this type, e.g. сло́во, *word*, decline as follows:

	sing.	pl.
nom.	сло́во	слова́
acc.	сло́во	слова́
gen.	сло́ва	слов
dat.	сло́ву	слова́м
instr.	сло́вом	слова́ми
prep.	сло́ве	слова́х

These nouns conform to the same basic pattern as the masculine nouns ending in a hard consonant, except that in the genitive plural there is a zero ending, i.e. no ending is added to the stem.

Note that the stress in neuter nouns in -о will usually fall on different syllables in singular and plural forms. This difference may be explained by the need for distinctive forms: the nominative/ accusative plural would be identical with the genitive singular were it not for the difference in stress.

§5. Neuter nouns in -е

Nouns of this type, e.g. по́ле, *field*, decline as follows:

	sing.	pl.
nom.	по́ле	поля́
acc.	по́ле	поля́
gen.	по́ля	поле́й
dat.	по́лю	поля́м
instr.	по́лем	поля́ми
prep.	по́ле	поля́х

As with the masculine nouns ending in -й and masculine nouns ending in a soft sign, these nouns differ from nouns of the same gender which have stems in a hard consonant (i.e. nouns in -о) by virtue of the fact that endings in -а, -у, and -о are replaced by endings in -я, -ю, and -е respectively.

Nouns in -е preceded by one of the sibilants **ж, ц, ч, ш, щ**, have instrumental singular in -ем, but in other cases spelling rules (see 1.4) dictate the use of the vowels **а** and **у** instead of **я** and **ю**. Thus кла́дбище, *cemetery*, has the following paradigm:

	sing.	pl.
nom.	кла́дбище	кла́дбища
acc.	кла́дбище	кла́дбища
gen.	кла́дбища	кла́дбищ
dat.	кла́дбищу	кла́дбищам
instr.	кла́дбищем	кла́дбищами
prep.	кла́дбище	кла́дбищах

§6. Neuter nouns in -ие

Nouns of this type, e.g. зда́ние, *building*, decline as follows:

	sing.	pl.
nom.	зда́ние	зда́ния
acc.	зда́ние	зда́ния
gen.	зда́ния	зда́ний
dat.	зда́нию	зда́ниям
instr.	зда́нием	зда́ниями
prep.	зда́нии	зда́ниях

Nouns of this type are identical with neuter nouns in -е, except in the prepositional singular and genitive plural cases.

Stress in nouns in -ие is invariably on the same syllable throughout.

§7. Feminine nouns in -а

Nouns of this type, e.g. газе́та, *newspaper*, decline as follows:

	sing.	pl.
nom.	газе́та	газе́ты
acc.	газе́ту	газе́ты
gen.	газе́ты	газе́т
dat.	газе́те	газе́там
instr.	газе́той	газе́тами
prep.	газе́те	газе́тах

Note the following points about nouns of this type:

i. they have an accusative singular form that is different from the nominative form;

ii. like the masculine nouns with a stem in a hard consonant (see §1.i above), they will have endings in -и rather than -ы, in accordance with the spelling rule (see 1.3), after one of the velars or sibilants **г**, **к**, **х**, **ж**, **ч**, **ш**, **щ**, i.e. in the genitive singular and nominative/accusative plural, e.g.

		gen. sing.	nom./acc. pl.
нога́	*leg, foot*	ноги́	но́ги
рука́	*arm, hand*	руки́	ру́ки
да́ча	*dacha*	да́чи	да́чи
ро́ща	*copse*	ро́щи	ро́щи

iii. as in masculine nouns with stems ending in a sibilant (see §1.ii above), the vowel in the ending of the instrumental singular will vary depending on the stress. Thus nouns in -жа, -ца, -ча, -ша, -ща have instrumental singular in -ей, if the stem is stressed, but -о́й if the ending is stressed, e.g.

	больни́ца	*hospital*	has	больни́цей
	пи́ща	*food*	has	пи́щей
but	душа́	*soul*	has	душо́й

iv. as with neuter nouns in -о (see §4 above) stress change may take place in these nouns in order to distinguish their genitive singular form from their nominative/accusative plural forms (as in нога́, рука́ above);

v. an instrumental singular form in -ою is also found (e.g. газе́тою), but in the modern language this form is used mainly in literary contexts or in poetry where the metre requires an additional syllable.

§8. Feminine nouns in -я

Nouns of this type, e.g. неде́ля, *week*, decline as follows:

	sing.	pl.
nom.	неде́ля	неде́ли
acc.	неде́лю	неде́ли
gen.	неде́ли	неде́ль
dat.	неде́ле	неде́лям
instr.	неде́лей	неде́лями
prep.	неде́ле	неде́лях

These nouns follow the same pattern as those in -а, except that as in the masculine nouns with stems in soft consonants (see §3 above) the endings -а, -о, -у, and -ы have been replaced by -я, -е, -ю, and -и respectively.

Note that an instrumental singular ending in -ею may also be found, in the same circumstances as -ою (see §7.v above).

The zero ending which occurs in the genitive plural of nouns in -а is in effect retained, the soft sign merely serving to denote that the consonant remains soft in this case just as it is when followed by any of the vowels used in the other endings of this declension.

§9. Feminine nouns in -ия

Nouns of this type, e.g. фами́лия, *surname*, decline as follows:

	sing.	pl.
nom.	фами́лия	фами́лии
acc.	фами́лию	фами́лии
gen.	фами́лии	фами́лий
dat.	фами́лии	фами́лиям
instr.	фами́лией	фами́лиями
prep.	фами́лии	фами́лиях

These nouns follow a similar pattern to those in -я, except in the dative singular, prepositional singular, and genitive plural. The endings in two of these cases, the prepositional singular and the genitive plural, are the same as for neuter nouns in -ие (see §6 above).

§10. Feminine nouns in a soft sign

Nouns of this type, e.g. кость, *bone*, decline as follows:

	sing.	pl.
nom.	кость	ко́сти
acc.	кость	ко́сти
gen.	ко́сти	косте́й
dat.	ко́сти	костя́м
instr.	ко́стью	костя́ми
prep.	ко́сти	костя́х

Note the following points about nouns of this type:

i. the spelling rule (1.4) dictates that nouns ending in a soft sign preceded by one of the sibilants **ж**, **ч**, **ш**, **щ**, must have the letter **а** rather than **я** in their dative/instrumental/prepositional plural forms, e.g. ночь, *night*, has ноча́м, ноча́ми, ноча́х; вещь, *thing*, has веща́м, веща́ми, веща́х;

ii. unlike all other types of feminine noun they do not have a distinctive accusative singular form;

iii. the soft sign that occurs in the nominative/accusative singular is not retained in any of the oblique cases except the instrumental singular;

iv. feminine nouns ending in a soft sign differ from masculine nouns ending in a soft sign in the genitive, dative, instrumental and prepositional singular cases.

§11. Gender

It is much simpler to determine the gender of Russian nouns than of French or German nouns.

All nouns ending in a hard consonant or in -й are masculine.

The great majority of nouns ending in -о or -е are neuter.

Most nouns ending in -а or -я are feminine. However, a few nouns in -а or -я which denote male persons, including the diminutive forms of many Christian names, are masculine, e.g. слуга́, *servant*; дя́дя, *uncle*; Са́ша (diminutive of Алекса́ндр, *Alexander*). Any adjectives qualifying these nouns and verbs in the past tense of which they are the subject will have masculine forms, e.g. ста́рый дя́дя был..., *the old uncle was...*

The gender of nouns ending in a soft sign is not so obviously apparent as is the gender of the vast majority of other Russian nouns. Some rules may be given, however:

i. if the noun refers to a male or female being then it is masculine or feminine accordingly, e.g. зять, *son-in-law*, is masculine, but мать, *mother*, is feminine;

ii. nouns with the suffix -тель which denote people or things who/which do something (e.g. чита́тель, *reader*; громкоговори́тель, *loudspeaker*) are invariably masculine, even though many of them may refer to people of either sex;

iii. if the soft sign is preceded by one of the sibilants **ж, ч, ш, or щ** then the noun is feminine, e.g. рожь, *rye*; ночь, *night*; мышь, *mouse*; вещь, *thing*;

iv. nouns ending in -ость or -есть are feminine, e.g. мо́лодость, *youth*; хра́брость, *bravery*; све́жесть, *freshness*.

Exercises

1. *Give the accusative singular of:* балко́н, биоло́гия, ка́рта, ту́фля, фи́зика.

2. *Give the genitive singular of:* боль (fem.), де́вушка, земля́, лист, май, ма́льчик, мо́ре, портфе́ль (masc.), стекло́, стена́, трево́га, упражне́ние, Фра́нция, хра́брость (fem.).

3. *Give the dative singular of:* дверь (fem.), де́рево, ла́мпа, ле́кция, пиджа́к, профе́ссор, семья́, соба́ка, спа́льня, сталь (fem.), стиль (masc.), тротуа́р, урожа́й, чте́ние.

4. *Give the instrumental singular of:* áрмия, багáж (end stress), внимáние, глáсность (fem.), доскá, достопримечáтельность (fem.), клей, кремль (masc.; end stress), лентя́й, мéсто, мост, пáрта, рубль (masc.; end stress), указáтель (masc.).

5. *Give the prepositional singular of:* дом, желéзо, заключéние, конвóй, нéбо, реáкция, рубáшка, руль (masc.), самолёт, спинá, тетрáдь (fem.).

6. *Give the nominative plural of:* авáрия, бáня, борьбá, глу́пость (fem.), дя́дя, корóль (masc.), музéй, пáмятник, собрáние, чáйка.

7. *Give the genitive plural of:* вагóн, кирпи́ч, маши́на, мышь (fem.), попугáй, приключéние, пу́ля, ры́ба, ситуáция, стáдо, стару́ха, учи́тель (masc.).

8. *Give the dative plural of:* аудитóрия, восклицáние, копéйка, лóшадь (fem.), ня́ня, преподавáтель (masc.), сарáй, шля́па, экзáмен.

9. *Give the instrumental plural of:* воскресéнье, зéркало, карандáш, секретáрь (masc.), телефóн, вещь (fem.).

10. *Give the prepositional plural of:* бáшня, влия́ние, гáлстук, плóщадь (fem.), пу́говица.

LESSON 3

MOBILE VOWELS; NOUNS WITH PLURAL FORM ONLY; INDECLINABLE NOUNS

§1. Mobile vowels

Many masculine nouns have a mobile vowel (sometimes called a 'fleeting vowel'), i.e. **о** or **е** or **ё** which is found in the last syllable of the nominative singular form but which disappears in all other cases, e.g.

nom. sing.		gen. sing.	gen. pl.	dat. pl.
за́мок	*castle*	за́мка	за́мков	за́мкам
ко́готь	*claw*	ко́гтя	когте́й	когтя́м
кусо́к	*piece*	куска́	куско́в	куска́м
лоб	*forehead*	лба	лбов	лбам
ло́коть	*elbow*	ло́ктя	локте́й	локтя́м
но́готь	*fingernail*	но́гтя	ногте́й	ногтя́м
ого́нь	*fire*	огня́	огне́й	огня́м
посо́л	*ambassador*	посла́	посло́в	посла́м
потоло́к	*ceiling*	потолка́	потолко́в	потолка́м
прила́вок	*counter*	прила́вка	прила́вков	прила́вкам
у́гол	*corner*	угла́	угло́в	угла́м
ве́тер	*wind*	ве́тра	ве́тров	ве́трам
дворе́ц	*palace*	дворца́	дворцо́в	дворца́м
день	*day*	дня	дней	дням
ка́мень	*stone*	ка́мня	камне́й	камня́м
коне́ц	*end*	конца́	концо́в	конца́м
ко́рень	*root*	ко́рня	корне́й	корня́м
оте́ц	*father*	отца́	отцо́в	отца́м
у́зел	*knot*	узла́	узло́в	узла́м
козёл	*he-goat*	козла́	козло́в	козла́м
шатёр	*tent*	шатра́	шатро́в	шатра́м

When a mobile **е** follows the letter **л** it must be replaced by **ь** in order to indicate that the **л** remains soft, e.g.

лев	*lion*	льва	львов	львам
па́лец	*finger*	па́льца	па́льцев	па́льцам

The feminine nouns вошь, *louse*; ложь, *lie*; любо́вь, *love*, and рожь, *rye*, lose their о in all oblique cases except the instrumental singular. Thus вошь has genitive/dative/prepositional singular вши; nominative plural вши; accusative/genitive plural вшей; dative plural вшам, etc., but instrumental singular во́шью.

§2. Nouns with plural form only

Many nouns exist only in a plural form, at least when they have certain meanings, e.g. the word for *a clock* is часы́ (genitive часо́в). There are many common nouns of this type. Some of them correspond to nouns which are also plural in English, e.g.

nom. pl.		gen. pl.
брю́ки	*trousers*	брюк
ве́сы	*scales*	весо́в
кавы́чки	*quotation marks*	кавы́чек
кани́кулы	*holidays*	кани́кул
коньки́	*skates*	коньков
ку́дри	*curls*	кудре́й
лю́ди	*people*	люде́й
но́жницы	*scissors*	но́жниц
очки́	*spectacles*	очко́в
перегово́ры	*talks, negotiations*	перегово́ров
стихи́	*verses*	стихо́в
хло́поты	*efforts, trouble*	хлопо́т
хло́пья	*snowflakes*	хло́пьев

Others correspond to a noun which is singular in English, e.g.

nom. pl.		gen. pl.
воро́та	*gate*	воро́т
вы́боры	*election*	вы́боров
де́ньги	*money*	де́нег
джу́нгли	*jungle*	джу́нглей
дрова́	*firewood*	дров
духи́	*scent*	духо́в
носи́лки	*stretcher*	носи́лок
обо́и	*wallpaper*	обо́ев
пери́ла	*handrail*	пери́л
по́хороны	*funeral*	похоро́н
са́ни	*sledge*	сане́й
сли́вки	*cream*	сли́вок

сýмерки	*twilight*	сýмерек
сýтки	*day* (24-hour period)	сýток
счёты	*abacus*	счётов
черни́ла	*ink*	черни́л
шáхматы	*chess*	шáхмат
щи	*cabbage soup*	щей
я́сли	*crèche*	я́слей

It will be noted that many of the nouns which in Russian have only a plural form denote objects that have two parts (e.g. *two blades of scissors*), or objects that exist in pairs (e.g. *skates*), or occasions or ceremonies that consist of several elements (e.g. *funeral*).

§3. Indeclinable nouns

Russian also has quite a large number of common nouns that are indeclinable, most of them fairly recent borrowings from other languages that do not easily fit into the Russian declensional pattern. Indeclinable nouns are generally neuter, unless they denote male or female persons (in which case they are masculine or feminine accordingly). Indeclinable nouns denoting birds or animals, however, tend to be masculine. The following list gives some of the commoner nouns that are indeclinable:

атташé (masc.)	*attaché*
бюрó	*office*
ви́ски	*whisky*
гéтто	*ghetto*
депó	*depot*
желé	*jelly*
жюри́	*judges* (of competition)
интервью́	*interview*
какáо	*cocoa*
кафé	*café*
кенгурý (masc.)	*kangaroo*
кинó	*cinema*
клишé	*cliché*
коли́бри (masc.)	*humming-bird*
коммюникé	*communiqué*
кóфе (masc.)	*coffee*
купé	*compartment*
меню́	*menu*
метрó	*underground*
пальтó	*overcoat*

пари́	*bet*
пиани́но	*upright piano*
плато́	*plateau*
резюме́	*résumé*
такси́	*taxi*
шимпанзе́ (masc.)	*chimpanzee*
шоссе́	*highway*

Exercise

Translate into Russian: (1) A cup of coffee; (2) a bottle of whisky; (3) in quotation marks; (4) after the interview; (5) a bottle of scent; (6) a lot of money; (7) the end of the day; (8) on the counter; (9) on the ceiling; (10) the ambassador's house; (11) in the café; (12) the lion's claws; (13) pieces of bread; (14) in the compartment; (15) to look at the clock; (16) with love; (17) red wallpaper; (18) the beginning of the holidays; (19) out of the jungle; (20) after the talks; (21) the price of cocoa; (22) on a stretcher; (23) under the gate; (24) in the castle; (25) in the crèche.

LESSON 4

IRREGULAR DECLENSION PATTERNS

§1. Neuter nouns in -мя.
There is a small group of nouns ending in -мя which are neuter and which have a stem in **н** in their oblique cases in the singular and throughout the plural, e.g. и́мя, *name*:

	sing.	pl.
nom.	и́мя	имена́
acc.	и́мя	имена́
gen.	и́мени	имён
dat.	и́мени	имена́м
instr.	и́менем	имена́ми
prep.	и́мени	имена́х

Like и́мя are the following nouns:

бре́мя	*burden*
вре́мя	*time*
вы́мя	*udder*
зна́мя	*flag*
пла́мя	*flame*
пле́мя	*tribe*
се́мя	*seed*
стре́мя	*stirrup*
те́мя	*crown of the head*

Note the following points though:

i. се́мя and стре́мя have genitive plural семя́н and стремя́н respectively;

ii. зна́мя has nominative/accusative plural знамёна; genitive plural знамён; dative plural знамёнам, etc.;

iii. бре́мя, вы́мя, пла́мя, and те́мя do not have plural forms. For a plural form of пла́мя use instead the expression языки́ пла́мени, *tongues of flame*, putting язы́к in the case appropriate in the context.

§2. Declension of мать *(mother)* and дочь *(daughter)*
These two nouns have a stem in **р** in all oblique cases in the singular and throughout the plural:

	sing.	pl.	sing.	pl.
nom.	мать	ма́тери	дочь	до́чери
acc.	мать	матере́й	дочь	дочере́й
gen.	ма́тери	матере́й	до́чери	дочере́й
dat.	ма́тери	матеря́м	до́чери	дочеря́м
instr.	ма́терью	матеря́ми	до́черью	дочерьми́*
prep.	ма́тери	матеря́х	до́чери	дочеря́х

* See also 5.11 below.

§3. Nouns ending in -нин

Nouns in -нин, e.g. англича́нин, *Englishman*, are regular in the singular but do not conform to the normal pattern in the plural. The last two letters -ин are removed to form the stem for the plural forms, to which are added the endings -е, for the nominative; zero ending, for the accusative and genitive (all these nouns are animate, and their accusative form is therefore the same as their genitive [see 16.2 below]); and -ам, -ами, -ах for the dative, instrumental and prepositional respectively:

nom. pl.	англича́не
acc./gen. pl.	англича́н
dat. pl.	англича́нам
instr. pl.	англича́нами
prep. pl.	англича́нах

Like англича́нин are many other nouns which indicate male persons from a certain place or of a certain status, e.g.

nom. sing.		nom. pl.
горожа́нин	*towndweller*	горожа́не
граждани́н	*citizen*	гра́ждане
датча́нин	*Dane*	датча́не
дворяни́н	*nobleman*	дворя́не
киевля́нин	*Kievan*	киевля́не
крестья́нин	*peasant*	крестья́не
марсиа́нин	*Martian*	марсиа́не
минча́нин	*person from Minsk*	минча́не
мусульма́нин	*Moslem*	мусульма́не
островитя́нин	*islander*	островитя́не
славяни́н	*Slav*	славя́не
христиани́н	*Christian*	христиа́не

The nouns бо́лга́рин, *Bulgarian*, and тата́рин, *Tartar*, also follow this pattern, except that they have nominative plural in -ы rather than -е, i.e. болга́ры, болга́р, болга́рам, etc., and тата́ры, тата́р, тата́рам, etc.).

The noun цыга́н, *gipsy*, has plural forms цыга́не, цыга́н, цыга́нам, etc. in the modern language, but nominative plural цыга́ны in the 19th century (e.g. in the title of Pushkin's narrative poem).

Note also the plural forms of хозя́ин, *landlord, host*, and господи́н, *master, gentleman, Mr*:

nom. pl.	хозя́ева	господа́
acc./gen. pl.	хозя́ев	госпо́д
dat. pl.	хозя́евам	господа́м
instr. pl.	хозя́евами	господа́ми
prep. pl.	хозя́евах	господа́х

It should be remembered that all the nouns in this section depart from the normal pattern only in their plural forms. In the singular they decline in exactly the same way as regular masculine nouns of the animate category ending in a hard consonant.

§4. Declension of nouns in -ёнок

Nouns in -ёнок, e.g. телёнок, *calf*, are regular in the singular (except that they have a mobile о which is lost in the oblique cases), but in the plural they lose this whole suffix and have the endings -я́та, for the nominative; -я́т, for the accusative and genitive (all these nouns are animate and their accusative form is therefore the same as their genitive); and -я́там, -я́тами, -я́тах for the dative, instrumental and prepositional plural respectively:

	sing.	pl.
nom.	телёнок	теля́та
acc./gen.	телёнка	теля́т
dat.	телёнку	теля́там
instr.	телёнком	теля́тами
prep.	телёнке	теля́тах

Like телёнок are many other nouns which indicate the young of some creature, e.g.

nom. sing.		nom. pl.
жеребёнок	*foal, colt*	жеребя́та
котёнок	*kitten*	котя́та
львёнок	*lion-cub*	львя́та
поросёнок	*piglet*	порося́та
тигрёнок	*tiger-cub*	тигря́та
цыплёнок	*chick*	цыпля́та
ягнёнок	*lamb*	ягня́та

The noun ребёнок, *child*, does have a plural of this type (ребя́та, etc.), but this is a more colloquial word for *children* than де́ти (see 5.11 below), and it is also used in the sense of *lads*.

§5. Declension of certain nouns in -ей

Note the declension of the masculine noun воробе́й, *sparrow*:

	sing.	pl.
nom.	воробе́й	воробьи́
acc./gen.	воробья́	воробьёв
dat.	воробью́	воробья́м
instr.	воробьём	воробья́ми
prep.	воробье́	воробья́х

Like воробе́й are мураве́й, *ant*; солове́й, *nightingale*; and руче́й, *stream*, though руче́й, being inanimate, has accusative singular руче́й and accusative plural ручьи́.

§6. Declension of путь *(way, path)*

Note that although путь is a masculine noun it declines in the genitive, dative and prepositional singular like a feminine noun:

	sing.	pl.
nom.	путь	пути́
acc.	путь	пути́
gen.	пути́	путе́й
dat.	пути́	путя́м
instr.	путём	путя́ми
prep.	пути́	путя́х

§7. Declension of surnames

Russian surnames in -ов, -ев, -ёв, -ин, and -ын decline like nouns ending in a hard consonant in the accusative/genitive, dative and prepositional singular, and in the nominative plural, but in the remaining cases they have adjectival endings:

	sing.	pl.	sing.	pl.
nom.	Че́хов	Че́ховы	Пу́шкин	Пу́шкины
acc./gen.	Че́хова	Че́ховых	Пу́шкина	Пу́шкиных
dat.	Че́хову	Че́ховым	Пу́шкину	Пу́шкиным
instr.	Че́ховым	Че́ховыми	Пу́шкиным	Пу́шкиными
prep.	Че́хове	Че́ховых	Пу́шкине	Пу́шкиных

Note though that foreign surnames ending in -ов and -ин have instrumental singular in -ом, e.g. Да́рвином.

Women's surnames in -ова, -ева, -ёва, -ина, and -ына have accusative singular in -у (e.g. Ивано́ву), and the ending -ой in all the oblique cases in the singular (e.g. Ивано́вой).

Note though that surnames ending in a hard consonant do not decline when a woman is denoted, e.g. the forms Ку́чер, Тэ́тчер *(Mrs Thatcher)* are used for all cases.

Surnames in -ский decline in exactly the same way as adjectives of this type (see 28.4 below).

Surnames ending in -их, -ых, -ово, -аго, -енко (e.g. Долги́х, Черны́х, Дурново́, Жива́го, Евтуше́нко) are indeclinable.

Exercise

Translate into Russian: (1) White kittens; (2) Danes drink beer. (3) Moslems don't drink. (4) Our hosts are Bulgarians. (5) He killed the calves*. (6) mothers and daughters; (7) We went to the cinema with the Ivanovs. (8) a lot of time; (9) red flags; (10) The English are islanders. (11) on the way; (12) He knows the Lukashins* and the Petrovs*. (13) You can see lion-cubs* and tiger-cubs* at the zoo. (14) out of the flames; (15) The Russians are Slavs. (16) Nightingales are singing. (17) pretty names; (18) Irina Ivanova's birthday; (19) a lot of seeds; (20) Mrs Thatcher's hat.

* See 16.2 below on case of animate object.

LESSON 5

NOUNS WITH IRREGULAR PLURAL FORMS

§1. Masculine nouns with nominative plural in -á
Many masculine nouns ending in a hard consonant have nominative plural (and accusative plural too if they are inanimate) not in -ы or -и, but in -á. The ending is always stressed in such nouns. Nouns with this ending fall into three groups.

i. Some of these nouns denote objects which, when spoken of in the plural, usually exist in pairs, e.g.

nom./acc. sing.		nom./acc. pl.
бéрег	*bank* (of river)	берегá
бок	*side*	бокá
глаз	*eye*	глазá
рог	*horn*	рогá
рукáв	*sleeve*	рукавá

These forms have their origin in the dual category that existed in Common Slavonic and Old Russian. It is by analogy with these nouns that the nouns in the following two groups also have nominative plural in -á in modern Russian.

ii. Some nouns in -ор which have been borrowed in fairly recent times from Western European languages, especially German, e.g.

nom. sing.		nom. pl.
дирéктор	*manager, headmaster*	директорá
дóктор	*doctor*	докторá
инспéктор	*inspector*	инспекторá
профéссор	*professor*	профессорá

Note however that there are also animate nouns in -ор which have a regular plural in -ы, e.g.

администрáтор	*administrator*	администрáторы
сенáтор	*senator*	сенáторы

and yet others for which either plural form may be found. In any case usage is changing and varies depending on who is speaking.

Note also that as the nouns given above are animate, their accusative form in both singular and plural coincides with the genitive.

iii. Many miscellaneous nouns, of which the following are among the more common:

nom. sing.		nom./acc. pl.
áдрес	*address*	адресá
бег	*race*	бегá
вéчер	*evening*	вечерá
гóлос	*voice*	голосá
гóрод	*town*	городá
дом	*house*	домá
кáтер	*launch* (boat)	катерá
кóлокол	*church bell*	колоколá
лес	*forest*	лесá
луг	*meadow*	лугá
мáстер	*master, skilled workman*	мастерá (nom. only)
нóмер	*number, hotel room*	номерá
óкруг	*district*	округá
óстров	*island*	островá
пáрус	*sail*	парусá
пáспорт	*passport*	паспортá
пóвар	*cook*	поварá (nom. only)
пóгреб	*cellar*	погребá
пóезд	*train*	поездá
сорт	*sort*	сортá
стóрож	*watchman*	сторожá (nom. only)
том	*volume*	томá
чéреп	*skull*	черепá

Note that it is only in the nominative/accusative plural that the nouns in the three groups set out above depart from the usual pattern followed by masculine nouns ending in a hard consonant (see 2.1 above).

§2. Masculine nouns with nominative plural in -я́

A few masculine nouns ending in a soft sign, or in -й, by analogy with those nouns with a plural in -á, have nominative plural (and accusative plural too if they are inanimate) in -я́, e.g.

nom. sing.		nom./acc. pl.
тóполь	*poplar tree*	тополя́
учи́тель	*teacher*	учителя́ (nom. only)
я́корь	*anchor*	якоря́
край	*edge, region*	края́

§3. Masculine nouns with two nominative plural forms

A number of masculine nouns ending in a hard consonant have two different forms in the nominative plural (and accusative plural too if they are inanimate), i.e. one form in -ы or -и and another in -á. These plural forms are not interchangeable, but are used to distinguish different meanings which the noun may have, e.g.

nom. sing.	nom. pl. in -ы/-и		nom. pl. in -á	
ко́рпус	ко́рпусы	*torsos, hulls*	корпуса́	*blocks*
мех	мехи́	*bellows*	меха́	*furs*
о́браз	о́бразы	*images*	образа́	*icons*
о́рден	о́рдены	*monastic orders*	ордена́	*medals*
по́яс	по́ясы	*belts* (geographical)	пояса́	*belts* (clothing)
про́пуск	про́пуски	*omissions*	пропуска́	*passes, permits*
счёт	счёты	*abacus*	счета́	*bills*
тон	то́ны	*tones* (sound)	тона́	*tones* (colour)

The noun цвето́к, *flower*, has nominative/accusative plural цветы́, while цвет, *colour*, has nominative/accusative plural цвета́.

Similarly the soft masculine noun ла́герь, *camp*, has both ла́гери (when the noun is used in a figurative sense, e.g. *political camps*) and лагеря́ (when it is used literally, i.e. to mean *holiday camps, military camps, prison camps*).

§4. Masculine and neuter nouns with plural in -ья, etc.

A few masculine nouns which end in a hard consonant and a few neuter nouns which end in -о have regular endings for nouns of this type in the singular but have nominative/accusative plural forms in -ья; genitive plural in -ьев; and dative/instrumental/prepositional plural in -ьям, -ьями, -ьях respectively, e.g. стул, *chair*, and де́рево, *tree*:

nom./acc. pl.	сту́лья	дере́вья
gen. pl.	сту́льев	дере́вьев
dat. pl.	сту́льям	дере́вьям
instr. pl.	сту́льями	дере́вьями
prep. pl.	сту́льях	дере́вьях

Like стул and де́рево are:

		nom./acc. pl.	gen. pl.
кол	*stake*	ко́лья	ко́льев
ком	*lump*	ко́мья	ко́мьев
прут	*twig*	пру́тья	пру́тьев
звено́	*link* (in chain)	зве́нья	зве́ньев

крыло́	*wing*	кры́лья	кры́льев
перо́	*feather*	пе́рья	пе́рьев
поле́но	*log*	поле́нья	поле́ньев

The noun брат, *brother*, declines in exactly the same way, except that, being animate, it has accusative plural бра́тьев.

The noun лист declines like стул when it means *leaf* (i.e. foliage), but it declines like a regular masculine noun of the same type as авто́бус when it means *sheet of paper.*

The noun сук, *branch, bough*, declines like стул, but the к of the stem changes to ч in the plural, thus су́чья, су́чьев, су́чьям, etc.

It is important to remember that it is only in the plural that any of the nouns dealt with in this section departs from the pattern of авто́бус (see 2.1 above).

§5. The nouns друг *(friend)* and сын *(son)*

These nouns require special attention. They are similar to стул and перо in §4 above, but it should be noted firstly that the stem for their plural forms is not the same as that for their singular forms, and secondly that they have accusative/genitive plural in -е́й:

nom. pl.	друзья́	сыновья́
acc./gen. pl.	друзе́й	сынове́й
dat. pl.	друзья́м	сыновья́м
instr. pl.	друзья́ми	сыновья́ми
prep. pl.	друзья́х	сыновья́х

The noun сын also has a regular plural (сыны́, сыно́в, сына́м, сына́ми, сына́х) when it has a figurative sense, as in сыны́ оте́чества, *sons of the fatherland.*

The nouns князь, *prince*, and муж, *husband*, have plural endings similar to those of друг:

nom. pl.	князья́	мужья́
acc./gen. pl.	князе́й	муже́й
dat. pl.	князья́м	мужья́м
instr. pl.	князья́ми	мужья́ми
prep. pl.	князья́х	мужья́х

§6. Neuter nouns with plural in -и, etc.

A few neuter nouns in -o indicating parts of the body have irregular plural forms (which are derived, like the masculine plurals глаза́ etc., from the old dual forms). The nouns in question are плечо́, *shoulder*; коле́но, *knee*; and у́хо, *ear*:

nom./acc. pl.	плéчи	колéни	ýши
gen. pl.	плеч	колéней	ушéй
dat. pl.	плечáм	колéням	ушáм
instr. pl.	плечáми	колéнями	ушáми
prep. pl.	плечáх	колéнях	ушáх

The noun колéно does have other plural forms, when it means not *knee* but *joint* in a technical sense, e.g. in a pipe (колéнья, колéньев, колéньям, etc.) or *bend* in a river (колéна, колéн, колéнам, etc.).

§7. Plural of neuter nouns in -ко

Most neuter nouns ending in -ко, including diminutives of this type, have nominative/accusative plural in -и, e.g. вéко, *eyelid*; я́блоко, *apple*; окóшко, *little window* (e.g. in ticket office):

nom./acc. pl..	вéки	я́блоки	окóшки
gen. pl.	век	я́блок	окóшек
dat. pl.	вéкам	я́блокам	окóшкам
instr. pl.	вéками	я́блоками	окóшками
prep. pl.	вéках	я́блоках	окóшках

§8. Plural of сосéд *(neighbour)* and чёрт *(devil)*

Note the irregular plural forms (i.e. with soft endings) of these two masculine nouns:

nom. pl.	сосéди	чéрти
acc./gen.pl.	сосéдей	чертéй
dat. pl.	сосéдям	чертя́м
instr. pl.	сосéдями	чертя́ми
prep. pl.	сосéдях	чертя́х

Both these nouns are regular in the singular (e.g. accusative/genitive singular сосéда).

§9. Declension of цéрковь *(church)*

Note the instrumental singular and the hard endings in the dative/instrumental/prepositional plural forms of the feminine noun цéрковь, *church*, which declines in the following way:

	sing.	pl.
nom./acc.	цéрковь	цéркви
gen.	цéркви	церквéй
dat.	цéркви	церквáм
instr.	цéрковью	церквáми
prep.	цéркви	церквáх

Forms with soft endings will also be found in the dative, instrumental, and prepositional plural in the modern spoken language (церквя́м, церквя́ми, and церквя́х respectively).

§10. Plural of не́бо *(sky, heaven)* and чудо *(miracle, wonder)*

Note the irregular plural forms of these neuter nouns:

nom./acc. pl.	небеса́	чудеса́
gen. pl.	небе́с	чуде́с
dat. pl.	небеса́м	чудеса́м
instr. pl.	небеса́ми	чудеса́ми
prep. pl.	небеса́х	чудеса́х

The consonant **с** with which the stem of the plural forms of these nouns ends also occurs in the adjectives formed from the same roots, небе́сный, *heavenly*, and чуде́сный, *marvellous, wonderful*.

§11. Nouns with instrumental plural forms in -ьми́

A very small number of nouns have instrumental plural in -ьми́. This form is a relic of the Old Russian declensional system, which was more complex than the modern Russian system. The nouns in question are:

nom. pl.		instr. pl.
де́ти	*children*	детьми́
ло́шади	*horses*	лошадьми́
лю́ди	*people*	людьми́

The feminine noun дверь, *door*, has both дверьми́ and дверя́ми, and дочь, *daughter*, has both дочерьми́ and (as a more colloquial form) дочеря́ми.

The noun кость, *bone*, normally has костя́ми, but the archaic form костьми́ is found in the expression лечь костьми́, *to lay down one's life* (in battle).

Note that all the nouns dealt with in this section have regular endings in the dative and prepositional plural forms, e.g. де́тям, де́тях; дочеря́м, дочеря́х; лошадя́м, лошадя́х, etc.

Exercises

A. *Write out the nominative plural of:* apples, brothers, ears, eyes, friends, horns, husbands, islands, knees, logs, neighbours, omissions, passes, shoulders, sons *(in its literal meaning)*, teachers, towns, trains, trees, voices.

B. *Translate into Russian:* (1) The names of my brothers; (2) the banks of the river; (3) the sleeves of his shirt; (4) the addresses of our friends; (5) on the leaves of the trees; (6) sheets of paper; (7) birds' wings; (8) on the chairs; (9) in the churches; (10) together with their children; (11) bright colours; (12) a few twigs; (13) She bought the flowers. (14) In his suitcase they found passports and bills. (15) The pilot could see the forests, meadows, islands, towns and even the houses.

LESSON 6

IRREGULARITIES IN THE GENITIVE PLURAL OF NOUNS

§1. Insertion of о or е in genitive plural of feminine and neuter nouns

There are many feminine and neuter nouns which require the insertion of **о** or **е** before the final consonant in the genitive plural, that is to say when the final **а** or **о** of the nominative singular form disappears to leave a zero ending, e.g.

nom. sing.		gen. pl.
бе́лка	*squirrel*	бе́лок
ви́лка	*fork*	ви́лок
доска́	*board, blackboard*	досо́к
ла́вка	*small shop*	ла́вок
ло́дка	*small boat*	ло́док
окно́	*window*	о́кон
про́бка	*cork, plug, traffic jam*	про́бок
ска́зка	*fairy-tale*	ска́зок
таре́лка	*plate*	таре́лок
де́вочка	*small girl*	де́вочек
дере́вня	*village*	деревéнь
земля́	*earth, land*	земе́ль
кни́жка	*booklet*	кни́жек
ко́шка	*cat*	ко́шек
кре́сло	*armchair*	кре́сел
ла́сточка	*swallow*	ла́сточек
метла́	*broom*	мётел
овца́	*sheep*	ове́ц
па́чка	*packet*	па́чек
пе́тля	*buttonhole, hinge, stitch, loop, noose*	пе́тель
сосна́	*pine-tree*	со́сен
ча́шка	*cup*	ча́шек

§2. Change of ь to е in genitive plural of feminine and neuter nouns

Where the first of two consonants preceding the final **а** or **о** of a feminine or neuter noun is soft, the vowel inserted before the final consonant in the genitive plural form is **е**, e.g.

nom./acc. sing.		gen. pl.
письмо́	*letter*	пи́сем
сва́дьба	*wedding*	сва́деб

судьба́	*fate, destiny*	су́деб
тюрьма́	*prison*	тю́рем

The noun про́сьба, *request*, however, has про́сьб.

§3. Change of й to е in genitive plural of feminine nouns in -ка

This change affects a number of nouns, e.g.

nom. sing.		gen. pl.
балала́йка	*balalaika*	балала́ек
га́йка	*nut*	га́ек
дво́йка	*two*	дво́ек
ко́йка	*bunk, berth*	ко́ек
копе́йка	*kopeck*	копе́ек
ле́йка	*watering-can*	ле́ек
ча́йка	*seagull*	ча́ек
ша́йка	*gang*	ша́ек

§4. Masculine nouns with zero ending in genitive plural

A few masculine nouns ending in a hard consonant have a zero ending in the genitive plural where one would expect an ending in -ов, e.g. раз, *time, occasion*, has genitive plural раз. Like раз in this respect are

вольт	*volt*
глаз	*eye*
грузин	*Georgian*
партиза́н	*guerrilla*
сапо́г	*boot*
солда́т	*soldier*
ту́рок	*Turk*
чуло́к	*stocking*

The noun грамм (*gramme*) has genitive plural грамм as well as the more formal гра́ммов.

The noun челове́к, *person*, also has genitive plural челове́к, though in most contexts the genitive plural of лю́ди, люде́й, is used instead (see 41.4 ii below).

The noun во́лос, *hair*, has genitive plural воло́с. This noun is always used in the plural form (nominative/accusative во́лосы) in the sense of *hair on one's head.*

§5. Genitive plural of о́блако

The neuter noun о́блако, *cloud*, has genitive plural облако́в, but in all other cases conforms to the same pattern as standard neuter nouns in -о, as in 2.4 above.

§6. Genitive plural of nouns in -це and -цо

Nouns of this type generally have genitive plural forms in -ец, e.g.

nom. sing.		gen. pl.
полоте́нце	*towel*	полоте́нец
се́рдце	*heart*	серде́ц
кольцо́	*ring*	коле́ц
крыльцо́	*porch*	крыле́ц

Note though that яйцо́, *egg*, has яиц.

§7. Genitive plural of neuter nouns in -ье and -ьё

Nouns of this type generally have genitive plural forms in -ий, e.g.

nom. sing.		gen. pl.
уще́лье	*gorge*	уще́лий
копьё	*spear*	ко́пий

Note though that пла́тье, *dress*, has пла́тьев; ружьё, *gun*, has ру́жей; у́стье, *mouth of river*, has у́стьев; and the noun подмасте́рье, *apprentice*, which in spite of its ending is masculine, has подмасте́рьев.

§8. Genitive plural of certain nouns in -жа, -ча, -ша, -ща

Some nouns of this type have genitive plural forms in -ей, e.g.

nom. sing.		gen. pl.
ханжа́	*sanctimonious person*	ханже́й
левша́	*left-handed person*	левше́й
ю́ноша	*youth*	ю́ношей

§9. Nouns in -я with genitive plural in -ей

Although most nouns in -я have genitive plural in a soft consonant (see 2.8 above), some have genitive plural in -ей, e.g.

nom. sing.		gen. pl.
дя́дя	*uncle*	дя́дей
ноздря́	*nostril*	ноздре́й
тётя	*aunt*	тётей

§10. Nouns in -ня with genitive plural in -н

Many nouns in -ня preceded by another consonant have a zero ending with a hard consonant rather than the soft ending that is normal for nouns in -я, e.g.

nom. sing.		gen. pl.
ба́сня	*fable*	ба́сен
ба́шня	*tower*	ба́шен
ви́шня	*cherry-tree*	ви́шен
пе́сня	*song*	пе́сен
со́тня	*hundred* (collective word)	со́тен
спа́льня	*bedroom*	спа́лен
ста́вня	*shutter*	ста́вен
тамо́жня	*customs* (at frontier post)	тамо́жен
чита́льня	*reading-room*	чита́лен

Note though that дере́вня, *village*, has дереве́нь, and ку́хня, *kitchen*, has ку́хонь.

§11. Genitive plural of nouns in -ая, -ея, -уя

Nouns of this type have genitive plural forms in -ай, -ей, -уй respectively, e.g.

nom. sing.		gen. pl.
ста́я	*flock, shoal*	стай
иде́я	*idea*	иде́й
ста́туя	*statue*	ста́туй
струя́	*jet, stream*	струй

§12. Genitive plural of nouns in -ья́

Nouns in stressed -ья́ have genitive plural in -е́й, e.g.

nom. sing.		gen. pl.
свинья́	*pig*	свине́й
семья́	*family*	семе́й
статья́	*article*	стате́й
судья́	*judge, referee*	суде́й

Exercises

A. *Translate into Russian:* (1) The colour of clouds; (2) a lot of soldiers; (3) the price of dresses; (4) a group of Turks; (5) They love cats. (6) out of the windows; (7) a lot of forks and plates and cups; (8) a flock of sheep; (9) several letters; (10) There are no requests. (11) twenty kopecks; (12) thousands of seagulls; (13) a hundred volts; (14) six eggs; (15) the colour of his hair; (16) a gang of youths; (17) hundreds of cherry trees; (18) the names of her uncles and aunts; (19) a lot of families; (20) a few songs.

B. Revision exercise on Lessons 2-6 (declension of nouns).

1. *Give the genitive singular of:* англича́нин, Горбачёв, дочь, ию́ль (masc.), маши́на, нога́, окно́, па́ртия, трамва́й, упражне́ние.

2. *Give the instrumental singular of:* автомоби́ль (masc.), же́нщина, кусо́к, лев, мать, по́езд, рука́, телефо́н, тетра́дь (fem.), Че́хов.

3. *Give the prepositional singular of:* ба́бушка, зда́ние, земля́, карти́на, магази́н, оле́нь (masc.), пло́щадь (fem.), посо́л, студе́нт, электрифика́ция.

4. *Give the nominative plural of:* бе́рег, брат, вещь, вре́мя, граждани́н, де́рево, дом, и́мя, ла́мпа, лес, не́бо, оте́ц, плечо́, про́пуск (in the sense of 'pass'), рог, стул, сын, тигрёнок, у́хо, язы́к.

5. *Give the genitive plural of:* ба́шня, друг, Ивано́в, кость, крыло́, ли́ния, мо́ре, музе́й, мусульма́нин, неде́ля, нож, о́блако, письмо́, пле́мя, потоло́к, сло́во, таре́лка, телёнок, сочине́ние, фа́брика.

6. *Give the instrumental plural of:* авто́бус, де́ти, ло́шадь, пло́щадь, стул.

LESSON 7

CONJUGATION 1A

§1. The conjugation system

Russian verbs may be divided into two broad conjugations.

Verbs of the first conjugation have endings that are characterised by the vowel **е** (or **ё** under stress) in the 2nd and 3rd persons singular and the 1st and 2nd persons plural (i.e. ты, он, онá, мы, вы forms).

The first conjugation may be subdivided into two types, which will be referred to as 1a and 1b, according to whether the stem of the present/future tense is derived from the infinitive simply by omitting the final -ть (1a verbs) or in some other way (1b verbs). The type 1b may itself be subdivided into four sub-types, according to whether stress is on the stem or the ending and whether the stem ends in a vowel or a consonant.

Verbs of the second conjugation have endings that are characterised by the vowel **и** in the 2nd and 3rd persons singular and the 1st and 2nd persons plural (i.e. ты, он, онá, мы, вы forms).

In the second conjugation the 1st person singular and the 3rd person plural (i.e. я and они́ forms) are modified in certain verbs in accordance with basic spelling rules (see 1.4 above). Moreover, in the 1st person singular certain consonants at the end of the present/future tense stem have to be changed or require the insertion after them of the letter -л-).

The endings of verbs in the two conjugations are as follows:

	1st conjugation	2nd conjugation
1st pers. sing.	-ю (-у after consonant*)	-ю (-у in some verbs)
2nd pers. sing.	-ешь (-ёшь under stress)	-ишь
3rd pers. sing.	-ет (-ёт under stress)	-ит
1st pers. pl.	-ем (-ём under stress)	-им
2nd pers. pl.	-ете (-ёте under stress)	-ите
3rd pers. pl.	-ют (-ут after consonant*)	-ят (-ат in some verbs)

* Except л and sometimes р.

§2. Aspects of the verb

The vast majority of Russian verbs have two aspects, imperfective and perfective. The forms and use of these aspects will be dealt with at length later in the course (in Lessons 50-54 inclusive). It is however essential that from the outset the student note the aspect, imperfective or perfective, of every verb form encountered.

All the verbs examined in this lesson, in §3 below, are imperfective verbs.

§3. First conjugation: verbs of type 1a

Verbs of this type have an infinitive in -ать, -ять, -еть, or -уть, and their present/future tense stem is formed simply by removing the final -ть of the infinitive. To the resultant vowel stem are added the unstressed endings -ю, -ешь, -ет, -ем, -ете, -ют, e.g.

рабо́тать (*to work*; stem рабо́та-)	теря́ть (*to lose*; stem теря́-)
рабо́таю	теря́ю
рабо́таешь	теря́ешь
рабо́тает	теря́ет
рабо́таем	теря́ем
рабо́таете	теря́ете
рабо́тают	теря́ют

уме́ть (*to know how to*; stem уме́-)	дуть (*to blow*; stem ду́-)
уме́ю	ду́ю
уме́ешь	ду́ешь
уме́ет	ду́ет
уме́ем	ду́ем
уме́ете	ду́ете
уме́ют	ду́ют

There are very many verbs of the 1a type with present/future tense stem in **а**, like рабо́тать, e.g.

де́лать	*to do, make*	открыва́ть	*to open*
за́втракать	*to have breakfast*	отпира́ть	*to unlock*
закрыва́ть	*to close*	покупа́ть	*to buy*
запира́ть	*to lock*	получа́ть	*to get, obtain*
знать	*to know*	понима́ть	*to understand*
игра́ть	*to play*	принима́ть	*to receive*
конча́ть	*to finish*	продолжа́ть	*to continue*
начина́ть	*to begin*	раздева́ть	*to undress*
обе́дать	*to have dinner*	у́жинать	*to have supper*
одева́ть	*to dress*	улучша́ть	*to improve*

Similarly there are very many verbs of the 1a type with present/future tense stem in **я**, like теря́ть, e.g.

меня́ть	*to change*	проверя́ть	*to check*
объясня́ть	*to explain*	расширя́ть	*to broaden, extend*
ослабля́ть	*to weaken*	стреля́ть	*to shoot*
ослепля́ть	*to blind*	удлиня́ть	*to lengthen*
поправля́ть	*to correct*	уточня́ть	*to make more precise*

There are also many verbs of the 1a type with present/future tense stems in **е**, like уме́ть, a large proportion of them intransitive verbs derived from adjectival roots, e.g.

бedне́ть	*to grow poor*	красне́ть	*to go red, blush*
беле́ть	*to look white*	сине́ть	*to look blue*
богате́ть	*to get rich*	слабе́ть	*to grow weak*
греть	*to warm*	сметь	*to dare*
желте́ть	*to look yellow*	толсте́ть	*to grow fat*
зелене́ть	*to look green*	худе́ть	*to get thin*
име́ть	*to have*	черне́ть	*to look black*

Very few verbs in -уть belong to the 1a type. The most common is дуть, *to blow*.

Note that there are also many verbs in -ать, -ять, -еть which do not belong to the 1a type but to the 1b type or the second conjugation. These will be dealt with in the following lessons.

Exercise

Write out the present tense of the following 1a verbs: име́ть, копа́ть, красне́ть, лома́ть, меня́ть, надева́ть, объясня́ть, ослабля́ть, ослепля́ть, открыва́ть, слабе́ть, сметь, снима́ть, толсте́ть, чита́ть.

LESSON 8

1B VERBS WITH VOWEL STEMS AND UNSTRESSED ENDINGS

§1. Verbs of type 1b: stems and sub-groups
The common characteristic of 1b verbs is that the stem of the present/future tense cannot be found simply by removing the -ть of the infinitive. Indeed there are many Russian verbs which have an infinitive ending in some combination other than vowel + ть (viz. verbs in -зти, -зть, -сти, -сть, and -чь; also идти́ and all its derivatives). With the exception of the thoroughly irregular verb есть, *to eat*, all such verbs, as well as a large number which do end in vowel + ть, belong to the 1b type.

At first sight the 1b conjugation presents a bewildering multitude of present/future tense stems and patterns, but when all verbs within the conjugation are classified and when copious examples of all the different types are given it may be seen that 1b verbs are less idiosyncratic, and therefore easier to learn, than might otherwise seem to be the case.

It is best to subdivide the conjugation into four sub-groups, characterised by type of present/future tense stem (vowel or consonant) and type of ending (unstressed or stressed), viz.

(a) vowel stem and unstressed ending, e.g. мо́-ю (1bi)*
(b) vowel stem and stressed ending, e.g. да-ю́ (1bii)*
(c) consonant stem and unstressed ending, e.g. ре́ж-у (1biii)
(d) consonant stem and stressed ending, e.g. жив-у́ (1biv)

* Strictly speaking verbs of these types too may be said to have a consonant stem (moj-, daj-), but the distinction made here seems a good one for practical purposes.

Each of these four groups will be dealt with in a separate lesson. 1b verbs with vowel stems in the present/future tense are less numerous than those with consonant stems in these tenses and will be dealt with first.

The lists of verbs belonging to the various 1b categories which are given in this and the following lessons are not exhaustive but they do contain a large proportion of all the simple verbs in these categories. By 'simple verb' is meant a basic verb (e.g. знать, *to know*; писа́ть, *to write*) from which compound verbs are derived by means of the use of prefixes and suffixes (see 46-49 and 51 below).

§2. Verbal forms and aspect

It is worth noting at this point that most simple verbs which are imperfective (e.g. крыть, *to cover*; знать, *to know*; писа́ть, *to write*; мести́, *to sweep*) become perfective – and may change their meaning – when a prefix is added to them (e.g. покры́ть, perfective of крыть, *to cover*; откры́ть, *to open*; узна́ть *to find out*; подписа́ть, *to sign*; смести́, *to sweep off*). Imperfectives from the same root which retain the prefix (and the meaning implicit in the prefix) almost always belong to a different conjugation or type. Thus perfective откры́ть is 1b, but imperfective открыва́ть is 1a; perfective узна́ть is 1a, but imperfective узнава́ть is 1b; perfective подписа́ть is 1b, but imperfective подпи́сывать is 1a; and perfective смести́ is 1b, but imperfective смета́ть is 1a. This subject will be covered in much greater detail in later lessons on aspectual pairs (50-51).

§3. Verbs of type 1b with vowel stems and unstressed endings in the present/future tense

Verbs of this type have the endings -ю, -ешь, -ет, -ем, -ете, -ют. They fall into a number of categories, which are dealt with below. All verbs given in this lesson are imperfective unless otherwise stated, though some verbs in -овать, e.g. организова́ть, may also be used as perfectives.

§4. Monosyllabic verbs in -ыть

There are five monosyllabic verbs in -ыть which have a present/future tense stem in о and unstressed endings, e.g. мыть (*to wash*; stem мо́-):

мо́ю
мо́ешь
мо́ет
мо́ем
мо́ете
мо́ют

Like мыть are the following verbs:

infin.		1st pers. sing.	2nd pers. sing.
выть	*to howl*	во́ю	во́ешь
крыть	*to cover*	кро́ю	кро́ешь
ныть	*to ache*	но́ю	но́ешь
рыть	*to dig*	ро́ю	ро́ешь

Also like мыть are all the perfective derivatives of these verbs, e.g. смыть, *to wash off*; закры́ть, *to close*; накры́ть, *to lay* (table); откры́ть, *to open*; раскры́ть, *to reveal*; скрыть, *to conceal*; подры́ть, *to undermine*, etc.

Stress is fixed throughout the present/future tense in all these verbs.

§5. Verbs in -овать

The vast majority of verbs in -овать have present/future tense stems in **у** and unstressed endings, e.g. организова́ть (*to organise*; stem организу́-):

организу́ю
организу́ешь
организу́ет
организу́ем
организу́ете
организу́ют

These verbs are very numerous and important, because the suffix -овать is an active suffix in modern Russian, being the suffix that is most commonly used for the formation of new verbs, especially verbs based on foreign words, e.g.

аплоди́ровать	*to applaud*	ликвиди́ровать	*to liquidate*
бесе́довать	*to chat*	парализова́ть	*to paralyse*
бойкоти́ровать	*to boycott*	сове́товать	*to advise*
волнова́ть	*to agitate*	существова́ть	*to exist*
жа́ловаться	*to complain*	эваку́ировать	*to evacuate*
импорти́ровать	*to import*	эксплуати́ровать	*to exploit*
интересова́ть	*to interest*	экспорти́ровать	*to export*

Also in this category are verbs in a sibilant + -евать, e.g. танцева́ть, *to dance* (танцу́ю, танцу́ешь, etc.). Most other verbs in -евать, however, have endings in -юю, -юешь, etc., e.g. воева́ть, *to wage war* (вою́ю, вою́ешь, etc.).

Stress is fixed throughout the present/future tense in all these verbs.

§6. Verbs in -а́ять and -е́ять

There are a few verbs with these endings which have present/future tense stems in **а** and **е** respectively, e.g. ла́ять (*to bark*; stem ла́-), and се́ять (*to sow;* stem се́-):

ла́ю	се́ю
ла́ешь	се́ешь
ла́ет	се́ет
ла́ем	се́ем
ла́ете	се́ете
ла́ют	се́ют

Similarly та́ять, *to melt, thaw*; ве́ять, *to blow, flutter* (intrans.); наде́яться, *to hope*.

Stress is fixed throughout the present/future tense in all these verbs.

§7. Брить *(to shave)*
This verb conjugates as follows:

брéю
брéешь
брéет
брéем
брéете
брéют

§8. Verbs in -óть
The small number of verbs with this ending have a present/future tense stem in one of the liquid consonants л or р, but conjugate in the same way as 1b verbs with vowel stems, e.g. колóть, *to prick*, *to chop*; борóться, *to fight*, *struggle*:

колю́	борю́сь
кóлешь	бóрешься
кóлет	бóрется
кóлем	бóремся
кóлете	бóретесь
кóлют	бóрются

Like колóть and борóться are:

infin.		1st pers. sing.	2nd pers. sing.
полóть	*to weed*	полю́	пóлешь
порóть	*to thrash, unstitch*	порю́	пóрешь

The verb молóть, *to grind*, belongs in this category but the vowel in its present/future tense stem changes from о to е (мелю́, мéлешь, мéлет, мéлем, мéлете, мéлют). The verb is used in a literal sense (e.g. молóть кóфе, *to grind coffee*), but is probably more common nowadays in figurative phrases such as молóть вздор, *to talk nonsense*.

It should be noted that in all verbs in -óть stress is on the ending of the 1st person singular but on the stem in all other persons in the present/future tense.

§9. Verbs in -бать, -мать and -пать
Some, but not all, verbs with these endings have present/future tense stems in бл-, мл- and пл- respectively, e.g. колебáться (*to hesitate*; stem колéбл-):

колéблюсь
колéблешься
колéблется
колéблемся
колéблетесь
колéблются

Like колебáться are:

infin.		1st pers. sing.	2nd pers. sing.
дремáть	*to doze*	дремлю́	дрéмлешь
сы́пать	*to pour* (solids)	сы́плю	сы́плешь
трепáть	*to tousle, dishevel*	треплю́	трéплешь
щипáть	*to nip, pinch*	щиплю́	щи́плешь

It should be noted that in many verbs of this type the stress is on the ending of the 1st person singular, but in all other persons it is on the stem.

Exercise

Write out the present tense (or, in the case of perfective verbs, the future tense) of the following verbs: бомбардировáть, волновáть, иллюстри́ровать, инспири́ровать, крыть, откры́ть, подры́ть, проколóть, растáять, смолóть, спосóбствовать, сы́пать, торговáть, трéбовать, умы́ть.

LESSON 9

1B VERBS WITH VOWEL STEMS AND STRESSED ENDINGS

§1. Endings and stress

Verbs of type 1b with vowel stems in the present/future tense and stressed endings have the endings -ю́, -ёшь, -ёт, -ём, -ёте, -ю́т. Verbs of this type fall into several categories, which are dealt with separately below. In all verbs of all categories stress is fixed on the ending throughout the present/future tense. All verbs given in this lesson are imperfective.

§2. Verbs in -ава́ть

These have a present/future tense stem in **а**, e.g. дава́ть (*to give*; stem да-):

даю́
даёшь
даёт
даём
даёте
даю́т

Like дава́ть are (i) all its compounds; (ii) all the imperfective verbs in -знава́ть which are derived from the simple verb знать, *to know*, with the help of a prefix; and (iii) some other common verbs consisting of a prefix and the root -става́ть, e.g.

infin.		1st pers. sing.	2nd pers. sing.
задава́ть	*to set, pose*	задаю́	задаёшь
издава́ть	*to publish*	издаю́	издаёшь
отдава́ть	*to give back*	отдаю́	отдаёшь
передава́ть	*to pass, transfer*	передаю́	передаёшь
подава́ть	*to serve, hand*	подаю́	подаёшь
придава́ть	*to impart, attach*	придаю́	придаёшь
продава́ть	*to sell*	продаю́	продаёшь
раздава́ть	*to give out*	раздаю́	раздаёшь
создава́ть	*to create*	создаю́	создаёшь
признава́ть	*to acknowledge, admit*	признаю́	признаёшь
сознава́ть	*to acknowledge, realise*	сознаю́	сознаёшь
узнава́ть	*to recognise, discover*	узнаю́	узнаёшь
встава́ть	*to get up*	встаю́	встаёшь
застава́ть	*to find*	застаю́	застаёшь

остава́ться	*to stay, remain*	остаю́сь	остаёшься
перестава́ть	*to stop* (doing sthg.)	перестаю́	перестаёшь
расстава́ться	*to part (with)*	расстаю́сь	расстаёшься
устава́ть	*to become tired*	устаю́	устаёшь

§3. Verbs in -ова́ть or -ева́ть

The vast majority of such verbs have unstressed endings in the present/ future tense, like организова́ть (see 8.5 above). However, there are a few verbs with these infinitive endings which have stressed endings after a vowel, e.g. плева́ть (*to spit*; stem плю-):

плюю́
плюёшь
плюёт
плюём
плюёте
плюю́т

Like плева́ть are клева́ть, *to peck* (клюю́, клюёшь, etc.); кова́ть, *to forge* (кую́, куёшь, etc.); and a few others.

§4. Miscellaneous verbs

The verbs петь (*to sing*; stem по-) and смея́ться (*to laugh*; stem сме-) also belong in this category:

пою́	смею́сь
поёшь	смеёшься
поёт	смеётся
поём	смеёмся
поёте	смеётесь
пою́т	смею́тся

§5. Monosyllabic verbs in -ить

There are five important monosyllabic verbs with present/future tense stems ending not in a vowel but in a soft consonant, e.g. пить (*to drink*; stem пь-), which also belong in this category:

пью
пьёшь
пьёт
пьём
пьёте
пьют

Like пить are:

infin.		1st pers. sing.	2nd pers. sing.
бить	*to beat, strike*	бью	бьёшь
вить	*to wind*	вью	вьёшь
лить	*to pour* (liquids)	лью	льёшь
шить	*to sew*	шью	шьёшь

and all perfective compounds of these monosyllabic verbs.

§6. Слать, *to send*
This verb has a consonant stem (шл-), but conjugates шлю, шлёшь, шлёт, шлём, шлёте, шлют.

Exercise

Write out the present tense (or, in the case of perfective verbs, the future tense) of the following verbs: зави́ть, застава́ть, кова́ть, нали́ть, напе́ть, остава́ться, проби́ть, продава́ть, раздава́ть, узнава́ть.

LESSON 10

1B VERBS WITH CONSONANT STEMS AND UNSTRESSED ENDINGS

§1. Endings, stress, and types of present/future tense stem
Verbs of this type have the endings -у, -ешь, -ет, -ем, -ете, -ут.

It will be noted that the stress is often on the ending in the infinitive and the 1st person singular of verbs of this type, but is always on the stem throughout the remaining persons of the present/future tense.

Verbs of this type fall into many different groups, and may be classified according to the consonant with which the present/future tense stem ends. Apart from a few miscellaneous verbs which will be dealt with at the end of the lesson, verbs of this type have stems in one of the sibilants **ж**, **ч**, **ш**, **щ** or **м** or **н**.

§2. Verbs in -зать with present/future tense stem in ж
There are several important verbs of this type, e.g. ре́зать (*to cut*; stem ре́ж-):

ре́жу
ре́жешь
ре́жет
ре́жем
ре́жете
ре́жут

Like ре́зать are all its perfective compounds and some other imperfective verbs with infinitives in -зать, and their compounds, e.g.

infin.		1st pers. sing.	2nd pers. sing.
вяза́ть	*to tie, knit*	вяжу́	вя́жешь
завяза́ть	*to tie up*	завяжу́	завя́жешь
развяза́ть	*to untie*	развяжу́	развя́жешь
связа́ть	*to link, connect*	свяжу́	свя́жешь
каза́ться	*to seem*	кажу́сь	ка́жешься
доказа́ть	*to prove*	докажу́	дока́жешь
заказа́ть	*to reserve, order*	закажу́	зака́жешь
наказа́ть	*to punish*	накажу́	нака́жешь
отказа́ться	*to refuse*	откажу́сь	отка́жешься
показа́ть	*to show*	покажу́	пока́жешь

приказа́ть	*to order*	прикажу́	прика́жешь
рассказа́ть	*to relate*	расскажу́	расска́жешь
указа́ть	*to indicate*	укажу́	ука́жешь
сказа́ть	*to say, tell*	скажу́	ска́жешь
ма́зать	*to smear, oil*	ма́жу	ма́жешь

§3. Verbs in -кать and -тать with present/future tense stem in ч
Common verbs of this type include пла́кать (*to cry, weep*; stem пла́ч-) and шепта́ть (*to whisper*; stem шепч-):

пла́чу	шепчу́
пла́чешь	ше́пчешь
пла́чет	ше́пчет
пла́чем	ше́пчем
пла́чете	ше́пчете
пла́чут	ше́пчут

Like пла́кать and шепта́ть are a number of other verbs in -кать and -тать, e.g. the following imperfectives:

infin.		1st pers. sing.	2nd pers. sing.
скака́ть	*to gallop*	скачу́	ска́чешь
бормота́ть	*to mutter*	бормочу́	бормо́чешь
пря́тать	*to hide*	пря́чу	пря́чешь
топта́ть	*to trample*	топчу́	то́пчешь
хохота́ть	*to guffaw*	хохочу́	хохо́чешь
щекота́ть	*to tickle*	щекочу́	щеко́чешь

§4. Verbs in -сать and -хать with present/future tense stem in ш
Common among verbs of this type are писа́ть (*to write*; stem пиш-) and маха́ть (*to wave*; stem маш-):

пишу́	машу́
пи́шешь	ма́шешь
пи́шет	ма́шет
пи́шем	ма́шем
пи́шете	ма́шете
пи́шут	ма́шут

Like писа́ть and маха́ть are all their imperfective compounds and a number of other imperfective verbs in -сать and -хать, e.g.

infin.		1st pers. sing.	2nd pers. sing.
записа́ть	*to note down*	запишу́	запи́шешь
описа́ть	*to describe*	опишу́	опи́шешь
подписа́ть	*to sign*	подпишу́	подпи́шешь
чеса́ть	*to comb, scratch*	чешу́	че́шешь
колыха́ть	*to sway*	колы́шу	колы́шешь
паха́ть	*to plough*	пашу́	па́шешь

§5. Verbs in -скать, -стать and -тать with present/future tense stem in щ

Examples of this type are иска́ть (*to look for*; stem ищ-), свиста́ть *(to whistle*; stem свищ-), and трепета́ть (*to tremble*; stem трепещ-):

ищу́	свищу́	трепещу́
и́щешь	сви́щешь	трепе́щешь
и́щет	сви́щет	трепе́щет
и́щем	сви́щем	трепе́щем
и́щете	сви́щете	трепе́щете
и́щут	сви́щут	трепе́щут

Like иска́ть, свиста́ть and трепета́ть are a number of other imperfective verbs in -скать, -стать, and -тать, e.g.

infin.		1st pers. sing.	2nd pers. sing.
плеска́ть	*to splash*	плещу́	пле́щешь
полоска́ть	*to rinse*	полощу́	поло́щешь
хлеста́ть	*to lash*	хлещу́	хле́щешь
ропта́ть	*to grumble*	ропщу́	ро́пщешь

§6. Verbs with present/future tense stem in м

There is a small group of perfective verbs with the basic meaning of *to take* which have a stem in м and unstressed endings, e.g. приня́ть (*to receive*; stem прим-):

приму́
при́мешь
при́мет
при́мем
при́мете
при́мут

Other verbs of this type include:

infin.		1st pers. sing.	2nd pers. sing.
обня́ть	*to embrace*	обниму́	обни́мешь
отня́ть	*to take away*	отниму́	отни́мешь
подня́ть	*to lift*	подниму́	подни́мешь
снять	*to take off*	сниму́	сни́мешь

Note, however, that a few other verbs from the same root, and which also have **м** stems in the future tense, have stressed endings throughout. These are dealt with in 11.3 below.

§7. Verbs in -нуть with present/future tense stem in н

Russian has a very large number of verbs with infinitives in -нуть, some of which have unstressed endings and some of which have stressed endings (the latter are dealt with in the following lesson).

Many verbs of this type which have unstressed endings denote change of state, e.g. гло́хнуть (*to go deaf*; stem гло́хн-):

гло́хну
гло́хнешь
гло́хнет
гло́хнем
гло́хнете
гло́хнут

The following is a far from exhaustive list of other imperfective verbs in -нуть, which denote change of state and conjugate like гло́хнуть:

infin.		1st pers. sing.	2nd pers. sing.
блёкнуть	*to fade*	блёкну	блёкнешь
ки́снуть	*to go sour*	ки́сну	ки́снешь
мёрзнуть	*to freeze* (intrans.)	мёрзну	мёрзнешь
мо́кнуть	*to get wet*	мо́кну	мо́кнешь
сле́пнуть	*to go blind*	сле́пну	сле́пнешь
со́хнуть	*to dry up*	со́хну	со́хнешь

There is a very large number of other common verbs in -нуть which conjugate in the same way, including many semelfactive verbs, i.e. verbs denoting an instantaneous single action, e.g. the following perfectives:

infin.		1st pers. sing.	2nd pers. sing.
вспы́хнуть	*to flare up*	вспы́хну	вспы́хнешь
дви́нуть	*to move*	дви́ну	дви́нешь
кри́кнуть	*to give a shout*	кри́кну	кри́кнешь
пры́гнуть	*to jump, leap*	пры́гну	пры́гнешь

Many verbs in -нуть which have unstressed endings are derived from the following roots: -бег-, -верг-, -вык-, -ник-, -стиг-, -тих-, -чез-, e.g. the following perfectives:

infin.		1st pers. sing.	2nd pers. sing.
прибе́гнуть	*to resort (to)*	прибе́гну	прибе́гнешь
опрове́ргнуть	*to refute*	опрове́ргну	опрове́ргнешь
све́ргнуть	*to overthrow*	све́ргну	све́ргнешь
привы́кнуть	*to get used/ grow accustomed to*	привы́кну	привы́кнешь
возни́кнуть	*to arise*	возни́кну	возни́кнешь
прони́кнуть	*to penetrate*	прони́кну	прони́кнешь
дости́гнуть	*to attain*	дости́гну	дости́гнешь
зати́хнуть	*to die down, abate*	зати́хну	зати́хнешь
исче́знуть	*to disappear*	исче́зну	исче́знешь

§8. Verbs in -стать and other verbs with present/future tense stem in н

The perfective verb стать, the principal meaning of which is *to become*, conjugates as follows:

ста́ну
ста́нешь
ста́нет
ста́нем
ста́нете
ста́нут

A number of important perfective verbs are derived from стать:

infin.		1st pers. sing.	2nd pers. sing.
встать	*to get up*	вста́ну	вста́нешь
заста́ть	*to find*	заста́ну	заста́нешь
оста́ться	*to remain*	оста́нусь	оста́нешься
переста́ть	*to stop* (doing sthg.)	переста́ну	переста́нешь
уста́ть	*to get tired*	уста́ну	уста́нешь

These verbs all have a corresponding imperfective in -ава́ть which also belongs to the 1b conjugation but has a vowel stem and stressed ending in the present tense (see 9.2 above).

§9. Derivatives of деть

Another small group of verbs with present/future tense stem in **н** is that derived from the simple verb деть, *to put*, which itself is not much used but which occurs in very common compounds, all of which are perfective, e.g. одéть, *to dress*, stem одéн-:

одéну
одéнешь
одéнет
одéнем
одéнете
одéнут

Like одéть are:

infin.		1st pers. sing.	2nd pers. sing.
надéть	*to put on* (clothes)	надéну	надéнешь
переодéться	*to change* (one's clothes)	переодéнусь	переодéнешься
раздéться	*to get undressed*	раздéнусь	раздéнешься

§10. Быть *(to be)*, éхать *(to go [by transport])*, сесть *(to sit down)*

These three very important verbs all have a present/future tense stem in **д** and unstressed endings:

бýду	éду	ся́ду
бýдешь	éдешь	ся́дешь
бýдет	éдет	ся́дет
бýдем	éдем	ся́дем
бýдете	éдете	ся́дете
бýдут	éдут	ся́дут

Note that бýду, etc. is the future tense of быть, there being no present tense of this verb in modern Russian. Éхать is imperfective; сесть is perfective.

§11. Лечь *(to lie down)*, мочь *(to be able)*

These two very common verbs are exceptional in that, unlike all other verbs in -чь, they have unstressed endings. They conjugate as follows:

ля́гу	могý
ля́жешь	мóжешь

ля́жет	мо́жет
ля́жем	мо́жем
ля́жете	мо́жете
ля́гут	мо́гут

Note the fact that two different consonants appear in the present/future tense stem, a velar in the 1st person singular and the 3rd person plural and a sibilant in the other four persons. This feature is characteristic of all verbs in -чь (see also 11.13-14 below). Лечь is perfective; мочь is imperfective .

§12. Лезть *(to climb)*

This imperfective verb conjugates ле́зу, ле́зешь, etc.

Exercise

Write out the present tense (or, in the case of perfective verbs, the future tense) of the following verbs: влезть, встать, доказа́ть, замёрзнуть, запла́кать, иска́ть, исче́знуть, маха́ть, наде́ть, написа́ть, пересе́сть, подня́ть, помо́чь, почеса́ть, протяну́ть, пря́тать, связа́ть, сказа́ть, снять, уе́хать.

LESSON 11

IB VERBS WITH CONSONANT STEMS AND STRESSED ENDINGS

§1. Endings, present/future tense stems and stress

Verbs of this type have the endings -ý, -ёшь, -ёт, -ём, -ёте, -ýт. They fall into several different categories. There are some verbs with infinitive in vowel + ть and which have present/future tense stems in **в**, **м**, **н**, or **р**. There are also almost all verbs which end in some combination other than vowel + ть, viz. verbs with infinitive in -зти or -зть (which have stems in **з**), verbs with infinitive in -сти or -сть (which have present/future tense stems in **б**, **д**, **с**, or **т**), and verbs with infinitive in -чь (which have present/future tense stems in **г****ж** or **к****ч**). There are also a few verbs which do not fit into any of these categories.

Stress in all verbs of all categories is fixed on the ending throughout the present/future tense.

All forms given in this lesson are imperfective unless otherwise indicated.

§2. Verbs with present/future tense stem in в

Perhaps the most important verb of this category is жить (*to live*; stem жив-):

живý
живёшь
живёт
живём
живёте
живýт

Like жить are two verbs in -ыть and two in whose infinitive form the consonant **в** is already apparent:

infin.		1st pers. sing.	2nd pers. sing.
плыть	*to swim, sail*	плывý	плывёшь
слыть	*to be reputed to be*	слывý	слывёшь
звать	*to call*	зовý	зовёшь
рвать	*to tear*	рву	рвёшь

§3. Verbs with present/future tense stem in м

There are a few common perfective verbs in -нять which have a stem in м, e.g. поня́ть (*to understand*; stem пойм-):

пойму́
поймёшь
поймёт
поймём
поймёте
пойму́т

Like поня́ть are:

infin.		1st pers. sing.	2nd pers. sing.
взять	*to take*	возьму́	возьмёшь
заня́ть	*to occupy, borrow*	займу́	займёшь
наня́ть	*to hire*	найму́	наймёшь

See 10.6 above though for verbs in -ять which have a stem in м and unstressed endings.

Also with a stem in м are the imperfective verb жать, *to press, squeeze* (жму, жмёшь, etc.) and all its perfective compounds.

§4. Verbs in -нуть with present/future tense stem in н and stressed endings

There are many verbs of this type, e.g. гнуть (*to bend*; stem гн-):

гну
гнёшь
гнёт
гнём
гнёте
гнут

Among the many verbs like гнуть are the following perfectives:

infin.		1st pers. sing.	2nd pers. sing.
косну́ться	*to touch, concern*	косну́сь	коснёшься
махну́ть	*to wave*	махну́	махнёшь
улыбну́ться	*to smile*	улыбну́сь	улыбнёшься

§5. Verbs in -ать and -ять with present/future tense stem in н and stressed endings

Also with a stem in **н** is the perfective verb начáть, *to begin*:

начнý
начнёшь
начнёт
начнём
начнёте
начнýт

Likewise the following imperfectives:

infin.		1st pers. sing.	2nd pers. sing.
жать*	*to reap*	жну	жнёшь
мять	*to crumple*	мну	мнёшь

* This verb should not be confused with the verb жать meaning *to press* (see §3 above).

There is also one verb in -сть which has a present/future tense stem in **н**, клясть, *to swear* (клянý, клянёшь, etc.).

§6. Verbs in -ерéть

There is a small but important group of verbs of this type, in which the present/future tense stem contracts, e.g. perfective умерéть (*to die*; stem умр-):

умрý
умрёшь
умрёт
умрём
умрёте
умрýт

Like умерéть are the colloquial verb перéть, *to go, make one's way, drag*; терéть, *to rub*; and all their perfective compound forms, e.g.

infin.		1st pers. sing.	2nd pers. sing.
заперéть	*to lock*	запрý	запрёшь
отперéть	*to unlock*	отопрý	отопрёшь*
терéть	*to rub*	тру	трёшь
стерéть	*to wipe off*	сотрý	сотрёшь*

* Note the buffer vowel **o** in indicative forms of these verbs.

§7. Other verbs with present/future tense stem in р and stressed endings

Also with a stem in р is the imperfective verb брать, *to take*:

беру́
берёшь
берёт
берём
берёте
беру́т

The verb драть, *to fleece*, and its reflexive дра́ться, *to fight*, conjugate in precisely the same way as брать (деру́, дерёшь, etc., and деру́сь, дерёшься, etc.).

The verb врать, *to lie (to tell a lie / lies)* has similar endings, but does not have **е** in its present/future tense stem (вру, врёшь, etc.).

§8. Verbs in -зти with present/future tense stem in з

There are two important verbs of this type, везти́ (*to take* [by transport]; stem вез-); and ползти́ (*to crawl*; stem полз-):

везу́	ползу́
везёшь	ползёшь
везёт	ползёт
везём	ползём
везёте	ползёте
везу́т	ползу́т

The verb грызть, *to gnaw*, conjugates in the same way (грызу́, грызёшь, etc.).

§9. Verbs in -сти with present/future tense stem in б

There are two verbs of this type, грести́ (*to row*; stem греб-), and скрести́ (*to scrape*; stem скреб-):

гребу́	скребу́
гребёшь	скребёшь
гребёт	скребёт
гребём	скребём
гребёте	скребёте
гребу́т	скребу́т

§10. Verbs in -сти and -сть with present/future tense stem in д

This is an important category which includes the verbs вести́ (*to take* [on foot, i.e. *to lead*]; stem вед-) and класть (*to put*; stem клад-):

веду́	кладу́
ведёшь	кладёшь
ведёт	кладёт
ведём	кладём
ведёте	кладёте
веду́т	кладу́т

Like вести́ are a few other verbs in -сти and a few in -сть, e.g.

infin.		1st pers. sing.	2nd pers. sing.
блюсти́	*to observe*	блюду́	блюдёшь
красть	*to steal*	краду́	крадёшь
прясть	*to spin* (cloth)	пряду́	прядёшь
упа́сть (pf.)	*to fall*	упаду́	упадёшь

§11. Verbs in -сти with present/future tense stem in с

The most common verb of this type is нести́ (*to carry*; stem нес-):

несу́
несёшь
несёт
несём
несёте
несу́т

Similarly:

infin.		1st pers. sing.	2nd pers. sing.
спасти́ (pf.)	*to save*	спасу́	спасёшь
трясти́	*to shake*	трясу́	трясёшь

§12. Verbs in -сти and -сть with present/future tense stem in т

This type includes the verb мести́ (*to sweep*; stem мет-):

мету́
метёшь
метёт
метём
метёте
мету́т

Similarly:

infin.		1st pers. sing.	2nd pers. sing.
изобрести́ (pf.)	*to invent*	изобрету́	изобретёшь
приобрести́ (pf.)	*to acquire*	приобрету́	приобретёшь
плести́	*to plait*	плету́	плетёшь
цвести́	*to flourish*	цвету́	цветёшь
проче́сть (pf.)	*to read*	прочту́	прочтёшь*
счесть (pf.)	*to count, reckon*	сочту́	сочтёшь*

* Note the loss of the vowel **е** in the stem of these verbs and the need for a buffer vowel in сочту́ etc.

§13. Verbs in -чь with present/future tense stem in г\ж

Verbs of this type have a stem with the velar consonant in the 1st person singular and the 3rd person plural and with a sibilant in the remaining four persons. In most cases the vowel preceding -чь is retained in the present/future tense, e.g. in бере́чь (*to guard, look after*; stem берег-), but in the common verb жечь (*to burn*; stem жг-) the vowel disappears:

берегу́	жгу
бережёшь	жжёшь
бережёт	жжёт
бережём	жжём
бережёте	жжёте
берегу́т	жгут

Like бере́чь are a few other verbs in -ечь, -ичь, and -ячь:

infin.		1st pers. sing.	2nd pers. sing.
пренебре́чь (pf.)	*to ignore, neglect*	пренебрегу́	пренебрежёшь
стричь	*to cut* (hair)	стригу́	стрижёшь
запря́чь (pf.)	*to harness*	запрягу́	запряжёшь

One verb which does not end in -чь, лгать, *to lie* (i.e. *to tell a lie*), conjugates in the same way as verbs of this type (лгу, лжёшь, лжёт, лжём, лжёте, лгут).

§14. Verbs in -чь with present/future tense stem in к\ч

Verbs of this type also have a stem with a velar consonant in the 1st person singular and the 3rd person plural and with a sibilant in the remaining four persons. Some verbs ending in -ечь and most verbs ending in -очь belong to this type, e.g. печь (*to bake*; stem пек-):

пеку́
печёшь
печёт
печём
печёте
пеку́т

Like печь are a few other verbs in -ечь and -очь and all the perfective compound forms of these verbs, e.g.

infin.		1st pers. sing.	2nd pers. sing.
влечь	*to draw, drag*	влеку́	влечёшь
привле́чь	*to attract*	привлеку́	привлечёшь
сечь	*to cut*	секу́	сечёшь
отсе́чь	*to cut off*	отсеку́	отсечёшь
пересе́чь	*to cross, intersect*	пересеку́	пересечёшь
течь	*to flow*	теку́	течёшь
уте́чь	*to leak*	утеку́	утечёшь
воло́чь	*to drag*	волоку́	волочёшь

§15. Ждать *(to wait)* and идти́ *(to go on foot)*

These two verbs conjugate as follows:

жду	иду́
ждёшь	идёшь
ждёт	идёт
ждём	идём
ждёте	идёте
ждут	иду́т

§16. Miscellaneous verbs with consonant stems and stressed endings in the present/future tense

The following verbs, for one reason or another, do not fit neatly into any of the categories dealt with above:

infin.		1st pers. sing.	2nd pers. sing.
ошиби́ться (pf.)	*to be mistaken*	ошибу́сь	ошибёшься
ушиби́ть (pf.)	*to knock, bruise*	ушибу́	ушибёшь
еба́ть or еть (vulg.)	*to fuck*	ебу́	ебёшь
расти́	*to grow* (intrans.)	расту́	растёшь
соса́ть	*to suck*	сосу́	сосёшь
ткать	*to weave*	тку	ткёшь

Exercise

Write out the present tense (or, in the case of perfective verbs, the future tense) of the following verbs: брать, ввести́, взять, войти́, заже́чь, изобрести́, испе́чь, назва́ть, нача́ть, отсе́чь, пережи́ть, плыть, подмести́, помя́ть, привезти́, привле́чь, принести́, провести́, согну́ть, соскрести́, трясти́, укра́сть, умере́ть, упа́сть, уте́чь.

LESSON 12

VERBS OF THE SECOND CONJUGATION AND FOUR IRREGULAR VERBS

§1. Present/future tense stems and endings

The second conjugation comprises the vast majority of verbs that have an infinitive ending in -ить and some verbs which have an infinitive ending in -еть, -ать, or -ять. The stem of the present or future tense of these verbs is found by removing this infinitive ending (i.e. vowel + **ть**). The endings to be added to this stem are -ю, (or in some verbs -у), -ишь, -ит, -им, -ите, -ят (or in some verbs -ат), e.g. говори́ть (*to speak*; stem говор-):

говорю́
говори́шь
говори́т
говори́м
говори́те
говоря́т

All the forms given in this lesson are imperfective unless otherwise indicated.

§2. Second-conjugation verbs in -еть

The following common verbs with infinitive in -еть belong to the second conjugation (for the 1st person singular forms of most of them see §§6 and 7 below):

infin.		3rd pers. sing.	3rd pers. pl.
боле́ть	*to hurt*	боли́т	боля́т
верте́ть	*to turn*	ве́ртит	ве́ртят
ви́деть	*to see*	ви́дит	ви́дят
висе́ть	*to hang* (intrans.)	виси́т	вися́т
горе́ть	*to burn* (intrans.)	гори́т	горя́т
зави́сеть	*to depend*	зави́сит	зави́сят
лете́ть	*to fly*	лети́т	летя́т
ненави́деть	*to hate*	ненави́дит	ненави́дят
оби́деть	*to offend*	оби́дит	оби́дят
перде́ть(vulg.)	*to fart*	перди́т	пердя́т
свисте́ть	*to whistle*	свисти́т	свистя́т
сиде́ть	*to sit*	сиди́т	сидя́т

смотре́ть	*to look at, watch*	смо́трит	смо́трят
терпе́ть	*to bear, tolerate*	те́рпит	те́рпят

The verb блесте́ть, *to shine*, is most commonly used as a second-conjugation verb, and therefore has 3rd person singular блести́т and 3rd person plural блестя́т, though it may also be conjugated as a 1b verb with a stem in **щ** (блещу́, бле́щешь, etc.).

§3. First-person singular and third-person plural endings after sibilants

In accordance with the spelling rule that dictates that the sibilants **ж**, **ч**, **ш**, **щ** cannot be followed by **ю** or **я** (see 1.4 above), second-conjugation verbs which have a stem ending in one of these sibilants have 1st person singular in -у and 3rd person plural in -ат, e.g. лежа́ть (*to lie / be lying*; stem леж-):

лежу́
лежи́шь
лежи́т
лежи́м
лежи́те
лежа́т

Like лежа́ть are a number of other common verbs with infinitive forms in -жать, -чать, and -шать:

infin.		1st pers. sing.	3rd pers. pl.
держа́ть	*to hold*	держу́	де́ржат
дрожа́ть	*to tremble*	дрожу́	дрожа́т
принадлежа́ть	*to belong*	принадлежу́	принадлежа́т
звуча́ть	*to ring, sound*	звучу́	звуча́т
крича́ть	*to shout*	кричу́	крича́т
молча́ть	*to be silent*	молчу́	молча́т
стуча́ть	*to knock*	стучу́	стуча́т
дыша́ть	*to breathe*	дышу́	ды́шат
слы́шать	*to hear*	слы́шу	слы́шат

Note that the endings in the remaining forms of the indicative (i.e. 2nd and 3rd person singular and 1st and 2nd person plural) are unaffected by any spelling rule, e.g. де́ржишь, де́ржит, де́ржим, де́ржите.

Note also that not all verbs ending in -жать, -чать, or -шать, belong to the second conjugation. For example, дорожа́ть, *to get more expensive*, получа́ть, *to obtain*, and слу́шать, *to listen to*, all belong to type 1a, while жать, in both its meanings *(to press; to reap)*, belongs to type 1b (see 11.3 and 11.5 above).

§4. Гнать *(to chase, drive)* and спать *(to sleep)*

These two verbs in -ать also belong to the second conjugation:

гоню́	сплю*
го́нишь	спишь
го́нит	спит
го́ним	спим
го́ните	спи́те
го́нят	спят

* See §6 below for explanation of this form.

§5. Second-conjugation verbs in -ять

Two common verbs in -ять belong to the second conjugation, namely боя́ться, *to be afraid*, and стоя́ть, *to stand*:

бою́сь	стою́
бойшься	стойшь
бойтся	стойт
боймся	стойм
бойтесь	стойте
боя́тся	стоя́т

§6. Second-conjugation verbs with 1st person singular in -лю

There are certain peculiarities which affect the 1st person singular of some second-conjugation verbs. In verbs whose stem ends in one of the consonants **б, в, м, п**, for example, it is necessary to insert the consonant -л- between the present/future tense stem and the ending, e.g.

infin.		1st pers. sing.
люби́ть	*to love*	люблю́
ста́вить	*to put*	ста́влю
корми́ть	*to feed*	кормлю́
купи́ть (pf.)	*to buy*	куплю́
спать	*to sleep*	сплю

The so-called epenthetic -л- is also required after the consonant **ф** (e.g. графлю́, from графи́ть, *to rule* [paper]), but there are few second-conjugation verbs in the modern language with this present/future tense stem.

Note that the epenthetic -л- is inserted only in the 1st person singular. Thus the remaining forms of люби́ть are лю́бишь, лю́бит, лю́бим, лю́бите, лю́бят.

§7. Second-conjugation verbs with 1st person singular stem in a sibilant

A further peculiarity affecting the 1st person singular of second-conjugation verbs is the transformation of certain consonants and the combination **ст** into sibilants, viz.

д	>	ж
з	>	ж
с	>	ш
т	>	ч
ст	>	щ

Thus:

infin.		1st pers. sing.
ви́деть	*to see*	ви́жу
вози́ть	*to transport*	вожу́
носи́ть	*to carry*	ношу́
лете́ть	*to fly*	лечу́
чи́стить	*to clean*	чи́щу

Note that verbs which undergo this consonant change in the 1st person singular have the ending -у as a result of the fact that the stem in this person ends in one of the sibilants **ж**, **ч**, **ш**, **щ**.

Note also that these consonant changes affect only the 1st person singular form. Thus the remaining forms of ви́деть are ви́дишь, ви́дит, ви́дим, ви́дите, ви́дят.

§8. Other second-conjugation verbs with 1st person singular in -щу

In some second-conjugation verbs with a present/future tense stem ending in **т** this consonant changes not into **ч**, as in лете́ть, but into **щ**. This change takes place only in those verbs in -тить which are perfective forms of verbs in -щать, e.g.

infin.		1st pers. sing.	impf. form
запрети́ть	*to forbid*	запрещу́	запреща́ть
защити́ть	*to defend*	защищу́	защища́ть
обогати́ть	*to enrich*	обогащу́	обогаща́ть
обрати́ть	*to turn*	обращу́	обраща́ть
освети́ть	*to illuminate*	освещу́	освеща́ть
ощути́ть	*to feel*	ощущу́	ощуща́ть
укроти́ть	*to tame*	укрощу́	укроща́ть

Note that this consonant change too affects only the 1st person singular.

Thus the remaining persons of защити́ть are защити́шь, защити́т, защити́м, защити́те, защитя́т.

§9. Stress in second-conjugation verbs

Three patterns are found in second-conjugation verbs: (i) fixed stress on the ending in the infinitive and throughout the present/future tense; (ii) fixed stress on the stem in the infinitive and throughout the present/future tense; (iii) mobile stress, on the ending in the infinitive and 1st person singular and on the stem throughout the remaining persons of the present/future tense, e.g.

	infin.		1st pers. sing.	2nd pers. sing.
(i)	говори́ть	*to speak*	говорю́	говори́шь
(ii)	жа́рить	*to roast*	жа́рю	жа́ришь
(iii)	вари́ть	*to boil, cook*	варю́	ва́ришь

It should be noted that in verbs of this conjugation which have mobile stress the movement is always from the ending in the 1st person singular to the stem in all other persons, singular and plural, never in the other direction.

§10. Бежа́ть *(to run)*, дать *(to give)*, есть *(to eat)*, хоте́ть *(to want)*

These four very common verbs have a mixed conjugation, i.e. in some persons they have first-conjugation endings, in others second-conjugation endings, and indeed in the case of дать (which is perfective) and есть there are some endings that belong to neither conjugation and are found nowhere else in the modern Russian verbal system:

бегу́	дам	ем	хочу́
бежи́шь	дашь	ешь	хо́чешь
бежи́т	даст	ест	хо́чет
бежи́м	дади́м	еди́м	хоти́м
бежи́те	дади́те	еди́те	хоти́те
бегу́т	даду́т	едя́т	хотя́т

Like these verbs are all their perfective compounds, e.g. избежа́ть, *to avoid*; прода́ть, *to sell*; прое́сть, *to corrode*; захоте́ть, *to want*.

Exercise

Write out the present tense (or, in the case of perfective verbs, the future tense) of the following verbs, all of which belong to the second conjugation: включи́ть, вы́разить, гла́дить, гляде́ть, горди́ться, знако́мить, кури́ть, лови́ть, молча́ть, мстить, ненави́деть, осла́бить, ослепи́ть, отве́тить, плати́ть, поглоти́ть (impf. поглоща́ть), порази́ть, предложи́ть, предста́вить, прекрати́ть (impf. прекраща́ть), проси́ть, прости́ть, сиде́ть, терпе́ть, ходи́ть.

LESSON 13

FORMATION OF THE PAST TENSE

§1. Forms of the past tense

The past tense may be formed from verbs of either aspect. It has only four forms: masculine, feminine and neuter singular forms, and one plural form for all three genders.

The fact that the past tense makes distinctions of gender and number, but not of person, is easily explained: the forms of the past tense in modern Russian are in origin short forms of preterite participles before which, in Old Russian, an auxiliary verb (part of the verb *to be*) was used. This participle would agree in gender and number with the subject. (Compare agreement of a past passive participle with the subject of the verb after the auxiliary verbs *être* and *essere* in French and Italian respectively, e.g. *les jeunes filles sont* ***arrivées*** and *le ragazze sono* ***arrivate.***)

§2. Usual past tense forms

With few exceptions Russian verbs which have an infinitive ending in vowel + ть, irrespective of their conjugation, form their past tense by replacing the -ть with -л (masculine), -ла (feminine), -ло (neuter), and -ли (plural), e.g.

infin.		masc.	fem.	neut.	pl.
читáть	*to read*	читáл	читáла	читáло	читáли
терять	*to lose*	терял	теряла	теряло	теряли
краснéть	*to blush*	краснéл	краснéла	краснéло	краснéли
дуть	*to blow*	дул	дýла	дýло	дýли
мыть	*to wash*	мыл	мы́ла	мы́ло	мы́ли
колóть	*to prick*	колóл	колóла	колóло	колóли
говори́ть	*to speak*	говори́л	говори́ла	говори́ло	говори́ли

(The neuter forms given here and in subsequent sections are in many cases largely theoretical, since many verbs will rarely, if ever, be used with a neuter subject.)

§3. Past tense of verbs in -зти, -зть, -сти

The majority of Russian verbs have an infinitive ending in vowel + ть, but as was seen in Lesson 11 above there are also many which have some other ending. With the exception of verbs which end in -сти and which have a present/future tense stem in д or т (see §5 below on these verbs) all verbs ending in the above combinations have a masculine form in the past tense which ends in the consonant characteristic of their stem in the present/future tense. To the consonant in which the masculine form ends are added -ла, -ло, -ли for the feminine, neuter and plural forms respectively, e.g.

infin.		masc.	fem.	neut.	pl.
везти́	*to transport*	вёз	везла́	везло́	везли́
лезть	*to climb*	лез	ле́зла	ле́зло	ле́зли
грести́	*to row*	грёб	гребла́	гребло́	гребли́
нести́	*to carry*	нёс	несла́	несло́	несли́

Note that the verb расти́, *to grow* (intrans.), has past tense forms рос, росла́, росло́, росли́.

Note that whenever the endings -зти, -зть, or -сти are preceded by the vowel **е**, then this vowel (except in the case of лезть [see 10.12 above]) changes into **ё** in the masculine form of the past tense because the stress falls on it. (In the feminine, neuter and plural forms, however, **е** remains, because the stress in these forms falls on the final vowel.)

§4. Past tense of verbs in -чь

In the case of verbs in -чь which have two different consonants in their present/future tense stem (e.g. бере́чь, *to guard*; печь, *to bake*), it is the velar which occurs in the 1st person singular and 3rd person plural that appears in the past tense, e.g.

infin.		masc.	fem.	neut.	pl.
бере́чь	*to look after*	берёг	берегла́	берегло́	берегли́
лечь	*to lie down*	лёг	легла́	легло́	легли́
стричь	*to cut* (hair)	стриг	стри́гла	стри́гло	стри́гли
мочь	*to be able*	мог	могла́	могло́	могли́
печь	*to bake*	пёк	пекла́	пекло́	пекли́

The verb жечь, *to burn* (trans.), and all its compounds, belong in this category. The past tense of жечь, is жёг, жгла, жгло, жгли, and the past tense of e.g. the perfective form зажёчь, *to set light to*, is зажёг, зажгла́, зажгло́, зажгли́.

Note that whenever the ending -чь is preceded by the vowel **е**, then this vowel changes into **ё** in the masculine form of the past tense because the stress falls on it. (In the feminine, neuter and plural forms, however, **е** remains, because the stress in these forms falls on the final vowel.)

§5. Past tense of verbs in -сти and -сть with present/future tense stem in д or т

In verbs of this type (which are dealt with in 11.10 and 11.12 above), the infinitive endings -сти and -сть are merely replaced with -л, -ла, -ло, -ли, e.g.

infin.		masc.	fem.	neut.	pl.
вести́	*to lead*	вёл	вела́	вело́	вели́
мести́	*to sweep*	мёл	мела́	мело́	мели́
изобрести́ (pf.)	*to invent*	изобрёл	изобрела́	изобрело́	изобрели́
класть	*to put*	клал	кла́ла	кла́ло	кла́ли
красть	*to steal*	крал	кра́ла	кра́ло	кра́ли

Note that if the ending -сти is preceded by the vowel е, then in verbs of this type too this vowel is transformed into ё in the masculine form of the past tense because the stress falls on it. (In the feminine, neuter and plural forms, however, е remains, because the stress in these forms falls on the final vowel.)

The verb сесть, *to sit down* (see 10.10 above) has сел, се́ла, се́ло, се́ли. Есть, *to eat,* also belongs in this category, although it does not have a stem in д throughout its present tense. Its past tense is ел, е́ла, е́ло, е́ли.

§6. Идти́ *(to go [on foot])*

This verb has past tense шёл, шла, шло, шли, and with one exception all its perfective compounds (e.g. войти́, *to enter*; дойти́, *to reach*; перейти́, *to cross*; прийти́, *to arrive*; пройти́, *to pass*; уйти́, *to go away*) incorporate these forms too (thus вошёл, вошла́, вошло́, вошли́; дошёл, дошла́, дошло́, дошли́; перешёл, перешла́, перешло́, перешли́; пришёл, пришла́, пришло́, пришли́; прошёл, прошла́, прошло́, прошли́; ушёл, ушла́, ушло́, ушли́).

The one exception to this pattern is вы́йти, *to go out*. The prefix вы- always attracts the stress in perfective verbs. It follows that whenever this prefix occurs in a perfective verb the vowel ё, which itself can occur only in a stressed position, must change into е. Thus the masculine form of the past tense of вы́йти is вы́шел.

§7. Past tense of verbs in -нуть

Most verbs in -нуть have normal past tense forms, but some of those with stress on the stem lose the suffix -нуть altogether in their past tense. Among such verbs are all those verbs indicating change of state listed in 10.7 above and all of those derived from the roots -бег-, etc. also listed in that section. Like all other verbs which have a masculine past tense form ending in a consonant other than л, these verbs add -ла, -ло, -ли for their feminine, neuter and plural forms respectively. Thus:

infin.		masc.	fem.	neut.	pl.
возни́кнуть	*to arise*	возни́к	возни́кла	возни́кло	возни́кли
гло́хнуть	*to go deaf*	глох	гло́хла	гло́хло	гло́хли
дости́гнуть	*to attain*	дости́г	дости́гла	дости́гло	дости́гли
замёрзнуть	*to freeze*	замёрз	замёрзла	замёрзло	замёрзли
исчё́знуть	*to disappear*	исчё́з	исчё́зла	исчё́зло	исчё́зли

поблёкнуть	*to fade*	поблёк	поблёкла	поблёкло	поблёкли
погúбнуть	*to die, perish*	погúб	погúбла	погúбло	погúбли
прибéгнуть	*to resort (to)*	прибéг	прибéгла	прибéгло	прибéгли
привы́кнуть	*to get used (to)*	привы́к	привы́кла	привы́кло	привы́кли
промóкнуть	*to get wet*	промóк	промóкла	промóкло	промóкли
пронúкнуть	*to penetrate*	пронúк	пронúкла	пронúкло	пронúкли
свéргнуть	*to overthrow*	сверг	свéргла	свéргло	свéргли
сóхнуть	*to get dry*	сох	сóхла	сóхло	сóхли

All the above verbs are perfective except глóхнуть and сóхнуть, which themselves have perfective forms with a prefix, from which the past tense is formed in the same way: оглóх, etc., вы́сох, etc.

§8. Past tense of verbs in -ерéть

These verbs also form their past tense by dropping the ending of the infinitive form, e.g.

infin.		masc.	fem.	neut.	pl.
умерéть	*to die*	у́мер	умерлá	у́мерло	у́мерли
заперéть	*to lock*	зáпер	заперлá	зáперло	зáперли
отперéть	*to unlock*	óтпер	отперлá	óтперло	óтперли
стерéть	*to wipe off*	стёр	стёрла	стёрло	стёрли

Note also the past tense of the perfective verbs ошибúться, *to be mistaken* (ошúбся, ошúблась, ошúблось, ошúблись) and ушибúться, *to hurt oneself, bruise oneself* (ушúбся, ушúблась, ушúблось, ушúблись).

Exercises

A. *Write out the four forms (masculine, feminine, neuter and plural) of the past tense of the following verbs:* волновáть, затúхнуть, копáть, лить, молóть, напáсть (1st pers. sing. нападу́), отвлéчь (1st pers. sing. отвлеку́), перевезтú (1st pers. sing. перевезу́), подместú (1st pers. sing. подмету́), пренебрéчь (1st pers. sing. пренебрегу́), прийтú, принестú (1st pers. sing. принесу́), приобрестú (1st pers. sing. приобрету́), провестú (1st pers. sing. проведу́), съесть.

B. Revision exercise on Lessons 7-13 (verb forms).

1. *Give the first person singular of the following verbs:* вестú, давáть, дать, жечь, жить, знать, имéть, кормúть, крыть, любúть, местú, нестú, носúть, отвéтить, печь, посетúть, рабóтать, скрестú, спать, терять, умерéть, умирáть, ходúть, чúстить, эвакуúровать.

2. *Give the second person singular of the following verbs:* берéчь, брать, вставáть, говорúть, дéлать, звать, импортúровать, искáть,

краснéть, лежáть, летéть, махáть, мыть, пить, принять, рéзать, свя́зывать, стать, течь, тянýть.

3. *Give the third person plural of the following verbs:* дать, есть, молчáть, объяснйть, объясня́ть, плыть, покупáть, поня́ть, принимáть, продавáть, сечь, сидéть, сказáть, фотографйровать, хотéть.

4. *Give the masculine form of the past tense of the following verbs:* бить, везтй, говорйть, достйгнуть, закры́ть, игрáть, идтй, колóть, мочь, нестй, печь, проверя́ть, растй, умерéть, экспортйровать.

LESSON 14

REFLEXIVE VERBS

§1. The reflexive particle -ся\-сь
This particle is attached to the end of the verb, and can never be detached from it.

The full form -ся (pronounced sa) is invariably used when the preceding letter is a consonant or a soft sign. The contracted form -сь is used after vowels, except in the present and past active participles, in which -ся is used after vowels as well as consonants. Thus the verb улыба́ться, *to smile*, has the following forms:

pres. indic.	улыба́юсь
	улыба́ешься
	улыба́ется
	улыба́емся
	улыба́етесь
	улыба́ются
past tense	улыба́лся
	улыба́лась
	улыба́лось
	улыба́лись
imp.	улыба́йся
	улыба́йтесь
impf. gerund	улыба́ясь
pf. gerund	
(from pf. улыбну́ться)	улыбну́вшись
pres. act. part.	
e.g. masc. nom. sing.	улыба́ющийся
masc. gen. sing.	улыба́ющегося
fem. nom. sing.	улыба́ющаяся
fem. sing. oblique cases	улыба́ющейся
neut. nom./acc. sing.	улыба́ющееся
past act. part. impf.	
e.g. masc. gen. sing.	улыба́вшегося

§2. Common reflexive verbs without reflexive meaning
Many common verbs exist only in a reflexive form, and the reflexive particle does not bear any obviously apparent reflexive meaning, e.g.

боя́ться	*to fear, be afraid of*
горди́ться	*to be proud of*
пыта́ться\попыта́ться	*to attempt*
смея́ться	*to laugh*
стара́ться\постара́ться	*to try*
улыба́ться\улыбну́ться	*to smile*

§3. Use of reflexive verbs as intransitive verbs

The vast majority of verbs which are reflexive, though, also have non-reflexive forms, and in order to understand the difference between the non-reflexive and reflexive forms one must in most instances bear in mind the distinction between transitive and intransitive verbs.

A transitive verb is one which takes a direct object, i.e. something upon which the action of the verb is directed. In the sentence *each morning the guide assembles the tourists at nine o'clock*, for example, the verb *to assemble* is used transitively and its object is *tourists*.

An intransitive verb, on the other hand, is one which does not have a direct object, because the action is confined to the agent. In the sentence *each morning the tourists assemble at nine o'clock*, for example, the verb *to assemble* is intransitive. The meaning is complete without the inclusion of any object, because we are being told what the tourists (the subject of the sentence) do, not who or what is affected by the action indicated by the verb.

In English the form of the verb *to assemble* is the same irrespective of whether the verb is used transitively, as in the first example, or intransitively, as in the second example. In Russian, however, the different functions of the verb are made clear by the absence of the reflexive particle (in the case of the transitive verb), or its presence (in the case of the intransitive verb), e.g.

> Ка́ждое у́тро экскурсово́д собира́ет тури́стов в де́вять часо́в.
> *Each morning the guide assembles the tourists at nine o'clock.*

> Ка́ждое у́тро тури́сты собира́ются в де́вять часо́в.
> *Each morning the tourists assemble at nine o'clock.*

Note that it is not always a noun that fulfils the function of direct object. After some verbs the infinitive of another verb may be used to complete the meaning, and in those instances too the main verb in the Russian will be non-reflexive, e.g. экскурсово́д начина́ет говори́ть, *the guide begins to speak.*

The number of Russian verbs which must take the reflexive particle when they are used intransitively is very large. The following are only a few common examples:

non-reflexive forms (transitive verbs)	reflexive forms (intransitive verbs)
весели́ть\повесели́ть	весели́ться\повесели́ться
to amuse, gladden	*to enjoy oneself*
возвраща́ть\возврати́ть or верну́ть	возвраща́ться\возврати́ться or верну́ться
to return (give back)	*to return (go back)*
волнова́ть\взволнова́ть	волнова́ться\взволнова́ться
to agitate	*to be agitated*
закрыва́ть\закры́ть	закрыва́ться\закры́ться
to close (e.g. door)	*to close*
изумля́ть\изуми́ть	изумля́ться\изуми́ться
to astonish	*to be astonished*
конча́ть\ко́нчить	конча́ться\ко́нчиться
to finish	*to finish*
начина́ть\нача́ть	начина́ться\нача́ться
to begin	*to begin*
одева́ть\оде́ть	одева́ться\оде́ться
to dress	*to get dressed*
остана́вливать\останови́ть	остана́вливаться\останови́ться
to stop (e.g. bus)	*to stop (come to halt)*
открыва́ть\откры́ть	открыва́ться\откры́ться
to open (e.g. door)	*to open*
отправля́ть\отпра́вить	отправля́ться\отпра́виться
to send, dispatch	*to set off*
повыша́ть\повы́сить	повыша́ться\повы́ситься
to raise, heighten	*to rise*
поднима́ть\подня́ть	поднима́ться\подня́ться
to raise, lift	*to rise, go up*
продолжа́ть\продо́лжить*	продолжа́ться\продо́лжиться*
to continue, last	*to continue, last*
ра́довать\обра́довать	ра́доваться\обра́доваться
to gladden	*to be glad, rejoice*
раздева́ть\разде́ть	раздева́ться\разде́ться
to undress	*to undress, get undressed*
расширя́ть\расши́рить	расширя́ться\расши́риться
to broaden, extend	*to get broader, be extended*
собира́ть\собра́ть	собира́ться\собра́ться
to gather, assemble	*to gather, assemble*
увели́чивать\увели́чить	увели́чиваться\увели́читься
to increase	*to increase*
удивля́ть\удиви́ть	удивля́ться\удиви́ться
to surprise	*to be surprised*
улучша́ть\улу́чшить	улучша́ться\улу́чшиться
to improve	*to improve*

* The perfective form is rarely used (see 53.1 below).

уменьша́ть\уме́ньшить	уменьша́ться\уме́ньшиться
to reduce, lessen	*to be reduced, lessened*
успока́ивать\успоко́ить	успака́иваться\успоко́иться
to calm	*to calm down*
ухудша́ть\уху́дшить	ухудша́ться\уху́дшиться
to worsen	*to get worse*

Examples from the press:

A. non-reflexive verbs used transitively (with direct object or followed by an infinitive):

Па́спорт ему **верну́ли** с пропи́ской в Го́рьком, таки́м о́бразом как бы узако́нив его́ пребыва́ние там.
They returned his passport with a residence permit for Gorky, thus apparently legitimising his stay there.
Мы так и не **ко́нчили** э́тот спор.
We didn't finish this argument.
А вот в ма́рте 1990 го́да специали́сты **повы́сили** себе́ окла́ды.
And in March 1990 specialists went and raised their salaries.
Я **продолжа́л** слу́шать.
I carried on listening.

B. reflexive verbs used intransitively:

Верну́лась домо́й и легла́ в посте́ль.
I returned home and went to bed.
Перестре́лка **начала́сь** в по́лночь.
The exchange of fire began at midnight.
Повыша́ется у́ровень диску́ссий.
The level of debate is rising.
У меня́ был друг. Мы **познако́мились** ещё до а́рмии.
I had a friend. We had met way back before we were in the army.
Жизнь **продолжа́ется**. Мы вме́сте.
Life goes on. We are together.

§4. Reflexive verbs with strictly reflexive meaning

The number of Russian reflexive verbs in which the particle -ся has a strictly reflexive meaning (that is to say, turns the action of the verb back on the subject itself, and corresponds to the reflexive pronoun себя́, *oneself*) is relatively small. Одева́ться\оде́ться, *to dress* (*oneself*, as opposed to *someone else*) and умыва́ться\умы́ться, *to wash* (*oneself*, as opposed to *someone/ something else*) are good examples of verbs in which the particle does have strictly reflexive meaning. English may make a distinction between such reflexive forms and the corresponding transitive verb (we may say, for example, *to get dressed, to get washed*, when we intend an intransitive verb), but we may also use the same verb form, *to dress, to wash*, both transitively and intransitively.

§5. Reflexive verbs denoting reciprocal action

In some Russian reflexive verbs the function of the particle is to indicate reciprocal action, e.g. встреча́ться\встре́титься, *to meet (with one another)*, обнима́ться\обня́ться, *to embrace (one another)*; целова́ться\ поцелова́ться, *to kiss (one another)*. In these verbs the particle -ся is synonymous with the compound pronoun друг дру́га, друг с дру́гом.

§6. Reflexive verbs denoting characteristic action

Some verbs which are generally transitive and non-reflexive take the reflexive particle in contexts where they do not have any specific object but where they indicate action that is characteristic of the subject. Thus whereas in the statement *my dog is biting our neighbour* the verb has a specific direct object and would not be reflexive (моя́ соба́ка куса́ет на́шего сосе́да), in the sentence *my dog bites*, the action indicated by the verb is directed towards no particular object but is typical of the subject in question and would be described by a reflexive verb (моя́ соба́ка куса́ется). The following transitive verbs, among many others, also become reflexive when used in this way: жечь, *to burn*; ляга́ть, *to kick*; цара́пать, *to scratch*. Examples:

Крапи́ва жжётся.	*Nettles sting.*
Э́та ло́шадь ляга́ется.	*This horse kicks.*
Ко́шки цара́паются.	*Cats scratch.*

§7. Impersonal reflexive verbs

Some common verbs are used in an impersonal way, in a 3rd person singular reflexive form, to indicate the physical condition or mood of the subject, e.g.

Мне хо́чется есть.	*I am hungry.*
Нам хо́чется пить.	*We are thirsty.*
Ему́ не спи́тся.	*He can't get to sleep.*
Ей не чита́ется.	*She does not feel like reading.*

§8. Aspectual pairs with reflexive/non-reflexive forms

There are a few verbs whose imperfective forms are reflexive but whose perfective forms are not, viz.

ложи́ться\лечь	*to lie down*
ло́паться\ло́пнуть	*to burst, split* (intrans.)
сади́ться\сесть	*to sit down, get into* (means of transport)
станови́ться\стать	*to become, to stand* (i.e. to go into certain positions, e.g. станови́ться\стать на коле́ни, *to kneel;* станови́ться\стать в о́чередь, *to join a queue*; станови́ться\стать на цы́почки, *to get up on tiptoe*)

§9. Combination of reflexive particle and prefixes

Some of the prefixes that may be attached to verbs (e.g. в-, за-, на-, раз-, с-) are combined with the reflexive particle when they have certain meanings, e.g. всмотре́ться, *to look closely at*; зачита́ться, *to get engrossed in reading*; нае́сться, *to eat one's fill*; разойти́сь, *to disperse*; съе́хаться, *to come together*. Such verbs are dealt with in the lessons on prefixes (46-49).

§10. Use of reflexive verbs in passive sense

In many Russian imperfective verbs the addition of the reflexive particle serves to render the active transitive verb passive, e.g. учи́тывать\уче́сть, *to take into account*, is an active verb requiring a direct object, but учи́тываться, *to be taken into account*, is passive (see 60.4 below on this use of reflexive verbs).

Exercises

A. *The following sentences are drawn from the press, the first ten of them from horoscopes. However, in each sentence a verb has been put together in brackets with its reflexive or non-reflexive form. From the two verbs given in brackets in each sentence choose the one which is correct (non-reflexive or reflexive) in the context:* (1) Бо́лее благоприя́тный пери́од (начнёт\начнётся) по́сле 24 ию́ля. (2) По́сле 12 числа́ ва́ши ша́нсы и перспекти́вы (повыша́ют\повыша́ются). (3) Ию́ль нельзя́ назва́ть благоприя́тным, осо́бенно с 5 до 13 числа́, одна́ко он позво́лит в дальне́йшем (измени́ть\ измени́ться) ва́шу жизнь к лу́чшему. (4) По́сле 13 числа́ ситуа́ция ре́зко (изме́нит\изме́нится). (5) (Начну́т\начну́тся) пробужда́ться скры́тые си́лы. (6) По́сле 23-го (начина́ет\начина́ется) пери́од, когда́ возмо́жны встре́чи с изве́стными людьми́. (7) Рабо́та и встре́чи ию́ля позво́лят (собра́ть\собра́ться) впосле́дствии хоро́шие плоды́. (8) Напряжённый пери́од бу́дет (продолжа́ть\продолжа́ться) до 16-го ию́ля. (9) По́сле 8-го октября́ поя́вится реа́льная возмо́жность (повы́сить\повы́ситься) своё материа́льное благополу́чие. (10) Мно́гие респу́блики захотя́т (верну́ть\верну́ться) в Сою́з. (11) Ры́ночная эконо́мика (возвраща́ет\возвраща́ется) нам таки́е поня́тия, как инфля́ция, безрабо́тица. (12) За одну́ треть смерте́й от ра́ка отве́тственен таба́к, и э́та до́ля (продолжа́ет\продолжа́ется) расти́. (13) За «кру́глым столо́м» (соберу́т\соберу́тся) представи́тели Це́нтра подгото́вки ме́неджеров при Моско́вском институ́те наро́дного хозя́йства. (14) Ребя́та о́чень бы́стро (нахо́дят\нахо́дятся) о́бщий язы́к. (15) Здесь (откры́ла\откры́лась) евре́йская шко́ла. (16) В фи́льме режиссёр (собра́л\собра́лся) це́лое созве́здие знамени́тостей. (17) Простота́ и эффекти́вность ме́тода лече́ния позволя́ют в коро́ткие сро́ки (улу́чшить\улу́чшиться) состоя́ние пацие́нтов. (18) Кооперати́в приглаша́ет всех жела́ющих восстанови́ть своё здоро́вье. Опла́та за лече́ние не (увели́чила\увели́чилась). (19) Престу́пность бу́дет (продолжа́ть\продолжа́ться) расти́ и (останови́ть\останови́ться) её невозмо́жно. (20) Мо́жно наде́яться, что (начну́т\

начнýтся) (расширя́ть\расширя́ться) междунарóдные свя́зи, пойдёт процéсс постепéнного возрождéния Росси́и.

B. *Translate into Russian:* (1) She closed the window. (2) The teacher is beginning to speak. (3) The lesson begins at nine o'clock. (4) He is finishing the letter. (5) The play is ending. (6) He continued to talk. (7) The excursion lasts one hour. (8) A crowd was gathering. (9) They were gathering mushrooms in the wood. (10) The door opens inwards. (11) He is opening the door. (12) She got dressed and then undressed again. (13) He stopped a taxi in the street. (14) The bus does not stop here. (15) Prices are going up. (16) The number of accidents is increasing. (17) Dogs bite and cats scratch. (18) The suitcase is bursting. (19) I returned the book to the library. (20) We returned home early.

LESSON 15

THE PREPOSITIONAL OR LOCATIVE CASE

§1. Basic functions

The prepositional case, as its name suggests, may only be used with certain prepositions (в, на, о, по, при). It is also sometimes called the locative case, since when used with the prepositions в and на it may define location.

§2. The preposition в + prepositional case

The basic meaning of в is *in* or *at*. With the prepositional case в defines location, the place where something is situated or happening, e.g.

Он живёт в Москве́.	*He lives in Moscow.*
Мы сиди́м в спа́льне.	*We are sitting in the bedroom.*
Она́ у́чится в университе́те.	*She is studying at the university.*

Note that в cannot be used with the prepositional case if movement into a place is involved, as in the statement *he is going to Moscow* (он е́дет в Москву́), where the accusative is required.

§3. В + prepositional case in expressions of time

В may also have a temporal meaning, being used to define the month, year, decade, century, or period of one's life, or stage in a period in which an event takes place:

в январе́	*in January*
в а́вгусте	*in August*
в ты́сяча девятьсо́т во́семьдесят восьмо́м году́	*in 1988*
в про́шлом году́	*last year*
в э́том году́	*this year*
в бу́дущем году́	*next year*
в сле́дующем году́	*the following year*
в двадца́тых года́х	*in the 20s*
в двадца́том ве́ке	*in the 20th century*
в де́тстве	*in childhood*
в мо́лодости	*in youth*
в во́зрасте сорока́ лет	*at the age of 40*
в нача́ле го́да	*at the beginning of the year*

в середи́не уро́ка	*in the middle of the lesson*
в конце́ войны́	*at the end of the war*

Note also the use of в + prepositional case to translate *at* half past the hour:

в полови́не пе́рвого	*at half past twelve*
в полови́не шесто́го	*at half past five*

§4. Expressing distance

A further use of в + prepositional is to express distance:

Вокза́л нахо́дится в одно́м киломе́тре от це́нтра го́рода.
The station is a kilometre from the centre of town.
В двух шага́х отсю́да.
A stone's throw [lit. *two steps*] *from here.*
В трёх мину́тах ходьбы́ от шко́лы.
Three minutes' walk from the school.
В пяти́ часа́х езды́ от Пари́жа.
Five hours [by transport] *from Paris.*

See also 42.2 below on expression of distance.

§5. Clothing

The preposition в + prepositional case may also be used to describe what someone is wearing:

Она́ в но́вом пла́тье.	*She is wearing a new dress.*
Он был в чёрном костю́ме.	*He was wearing a black suit.*
Он в кра́сной руба́шке.	*He's got a red shirt on.*

§6. Use of в + prepositional case after certain verbs

Note the following verbs which may require в + prepositional case:

нужда́ться в (no pf.)	*to need, be in need of*
обвиня́ть\обвини́ть в	*to accuse of*
признава́ться\призна́ться в	*to confess, own up to*
сомнева́ться в (no pf.)	*to doubt, question*
уча́ствовать в (no pf.)	*to participate in, take part in*

Examples from the press:

Мы нужда́емся в передово́й техноло́гии и валю́те.
We need advanced technology and foreign currency.
Они́ име́ли по́лную возмо́жность уча́ствовать в диску́ссиях.
They had every opportunity to take part in the discussions.

§7. The preposition на + prepositional case

На is used with the prepositional case to mean *on*. Like в, when it is used with this case, на defines the place where something is located, and cannot be used if movement to the place is involved. Examples:

> Кни́га лежи́т на столе́.
> *The book is on the table.*
> Самолёт стои́т на взлётной доро́жке.
> *The plane is on the runway.*
> Спят они́ на раскладу́шке.
> *They sleep on a camp bed.* (Press)

§8. Nouns combined with на

There are many common Russian nouns which require на rather than в before them in contexts where English would have *in* or *at*. Many of these nouns denote some sort of occasion, or refer to both the place and the event or activity associated with it, e.g.

ве́чер	*party*	на ве́чере
война́	*war*	на войне́
вокза́л	*station*	на вокза́ле
вы́ставка	*exhibition*	на вы́ставке
заво́д	*factory*	на заво́де
заседа́ние	*meeting, session*	на заседа́нии
ка́федра	*department* (in higher educational institution)	на ка́федре
конгре́сс	*congress*	на конгре́ссе
конфере́нция	*conference*	на конфере́нции
конце́рт	*concert*	на конце́рте
куро́рт	*resort*	на куро́рте
курс	*year* (of course in higher educational institution)	на ку́рсе
ле́кция	*lecture*	на ле́кции
о́пера	*opera*	на о́пере
пло́щадь (fem.)	*square*	на пло́щади
по́хороны (pl.)	*funeral*	на похорона́х
по́чта	*post office*	на по́чте
предприя́тие	*enterprise*	на предприя́тии
рабо́та	*work*	на рабо́те
ры́нок	*market*	на ры́нке
сва́дьба	*wedding*	на сва́дьбе
собра́ние	*meeting, gathering*	на собра́нии
ста́нция	*station*	на ста́нции
съезд	*congress*	на съе́зде
у́лица	*street*	на у́лице
уро́к	*lesson*	на уро́ке
фа́брика	*factory*	на фа́брике

факульте́т	*faculty* (of higher educational institution)	на факульте́те
фронт	*front* (military)	на фро́нте
ша́хта	*mine*	на ша́хте
экза́мен	*examination*	на экза́мене

§9. Nouns used with both в and на

Before certain nouns, especially nouns denoting means of transport (e.g. авто́бус, автомоби́ль, маши́на, по́езд), both в and на will be found. With these nouns на tends to be used if presence in the place in question is associated with the activity for which the place is designed (e.g. е́хать на авто́бусе, *to go by bus*, where being on the bus is associated with travelling). The preposition в, on the other hand, may be preferred if the action indicated by the verb merely happens to take place in the location specified (e.g. чита́ть газе́ту в авто́бусе, *to read a newspaper on the bus*). The following examples from the press make clear the use of в in such contexts:

В по́езде Го́рький-Москва́ мне предъяви́ли о́рдер и произвели́ официа́льный о́быск.
In the Gorky-Moscow train they showed me a warrant and carried out an official search.
Когда́ больно́й не мо́жет назва́ть партнёра (случа́йная связь, ска́жем, в по́езде)...
When a patient [suffering from a sexual disease] *cannot name [his or her] partner (a casual contact, let's say in a train)...*

§10. Use of на in geographical names

The preposition на is also used with the prepositional case to translate *in* as well as (in some phrases) *on* with points of the compass, islands, peninsulas, several mountainous regions of the CIS, the word *Ukraine*, and names of streets and squares, thus:

на восто́ке	*in the east*
на за́паде	*in the west*
на се́вере	*in the north*
на ю́ге	*in the south*
на се́веро-восто́ке	*in the north-east*
на о́строве	*on the island*
на Ки́пре	*in/on Cyprus*
на Ку́бе	*in/on Cuba*
на Сахали́не	*in/on Sakhalin*
на Коре́йском полуо́строве	*on the Korean peninsula*
на Аля́ске	*in Alaska*
на Камча́тке	*in Kamchatka*
на Кавка́зе	*in the Caucasus*
на Пами́ре	*in the Pamirs*

на Ура́ле	*in the Urals*
на Украи́не	*in the Ukraine*
на Арба́те	*in the Arbat*
на Не́вском проспе́кте	*in/on Nevsky Prospect*
на Кра́сной пло́щади	*in/on Red Square*

Note, however, that в + prepositional is used in the following expressions: в А́льпах, *in the Alps*; в А́ндах, *in the Andes*; в Гимала́ях, *in the Himalayas*; в Карпа́тах, *in the Carpathians*.

§11. Miscellaneous expressions with на + prepositional case

Note also the following expressions, which indicate place or time:

на моро́зе	*in the frost*
на сквозняке́	*in a draught*
на со́лнце	*in the sun*
на рассве́те	*at dawn*
на пе́нсии	*retired* (on a pension)
на откры́том во́здухе	*in the open air*
на све́жем во́здухе	*in the fresh air*
на чи́стом во́здухе	*in the fresh air*
на бу́дущей неде́ле	*next week*
на про́шлой неде́ле	*last week*
на сле́дующей неде́ле	*the following week*
на э́той неде́ле	*this week*

§12. Use of на + prepositional case after certain verbs

The verb игра́ть is followed by на + prepositional case when it means *to play a musical instrument*, e.g.

игра́ть на гита́ре	*to play the guitar*
игра́ть на роя́ле	*to play the piano*
игра́ть на скри́пке	*to play the violin*
игра́ть на фле́йте	*to play the flute*

The verb говори́ть is followed by на + prepositional case when one is specifying in which language communication is taking place, e.g. говори́ть на ру́сском языке́, *to speak in Russian*; cf. говори́ть по-ру́сски, *to speak Russian*.

The verb жени́ться, *to get married* (of man marrying woman), is also followed by на + prepositional case, e.g. его́ оте́ц жени́лся на актри́се, *his father married an actress*.

The verb остана́вливаться\останови́ться is followed by на + prepositional case in the sense of *to dwell on* (of conversation, lecture, etc.) or *to settle on* (of gaze), e.g. ли́дер то́ри осо́бо останови́лась на пробле́ме охра́ны окружа́ющей среды́, *the leader of the Tories dwelt particularly on the problem of conservation of the environment* (Press).

The verb ска́зываться\сказа́ться, *to tell on, have an effect on*, is also followed by на + prepositional case, e.g. всё э́то па́губно ска́зывается на эконо́мике регио́нов, *all this is having a harmful effect on the economy of the regions* (Press).

Note also the expressions сосредото́чивать\сосредто́чить внима́ние на + prepositional case, *to concentrate* (attention) *on*, and быть на коро́ткой ноге́ с + instrumental, *to be on close terms with*.

§13. Nouns with prepositional forms in -у́ after в and на

Quite a large number of masculine nouns ending in a hard consonant, all of which denote inanimate objects and the vast majority of which are monosyllabic, have a prepositional singular ending in -у́ when they are used after в or на in a locative sense (i.e. when they indicate the place where something is situated or happening). The phrases below incorporate whichever preposition is more likely to be found in combination with the noun in question.

бал	*ball* (dance)	на балу́	
бе́рег	*bank, shore*	на берегу́	
бок	*side*	на боку́	
борт	*side* (of ship)	на борту́	*on board*
бред	*fever, delirium*	в бреду	
глаз	*eye*	в глазу́	
год	*year*	в году́	
жар	*heat*	в жару́	
круг	*circle*	в кругу́	
лес	*forest*	в лесу́	
лоб	*forehead*	на лбу́	
луг	*meadow*	на лугу́	
лёд	*ice*	на льду́	
мёд	*honey*	в меду́	
мех	*fur*	на меху́	*fur-lined*
мозг	*brain*	в мозгу́	
мост	*bridge*	на мосту́	
нос	*nose*	на носу́	
пол	*floor*	на полу́	
полк	*regiment*	в полку́	
порт	*port*	в порту́	
пост	*post* (position)	на посту́	
пруд	*pool, pond*	в пруду́	
рот	*mouth*	во рту́	
ряд	*row, line*	в ряду́	

сад	*garden*	в саду́	
снег	*snow*	в снегу́	
у́гол	*corner*	в углу́	
час	*hour*	в часу́	
шёлк	*silk*	на шелку́	*silk-lined*
шкаф	*cupboard*	в шкафу́	

The noun аэропо́рт, *airport*, generally has locative в аэропорту́, presumably by analogy with в порту́.

The geographical names Дон, *River Don*, and Крым, *Crimea*, also have locative forms in -у́, e.g. Росто́в-на-Дону́, *Rostov-on-Don*; в Крыму́, *in the Crimea*.

The locative ending in -у́ is also embodied in various set expressions, e.g. име́ть в виду́, *to have in mind*; в про́шлом году́, *last year*; в кото́ром часу́? *at what time?*

A few nouns in -й have analogous locative endings in -ю́, e.g.:

бой	*battle, fighting*	в бою́
край	*edge, brim*	на краю́
рай	*paradise*	в раю́
строй	*formation* (military)	в строю́

Note the following points about these forms in -у́ and -ю́:

i. the ending -у́ or -ю́ is always stressed;

ii. these endings are used only after в and на (not after the other prepositions, о, по and при, which may govern the prepositional case). Thus в лесу́ but о ле́се;

iii. even after в and на the endings in -у́ and -ю́ are used only when there is locative meaning, thus:

> Он исполня́ет роль в "Вишнёвом са́де".
> *He is playing a part in 'The Cherry Orchard'.*

iv. the noun край has locative singular in -е when it denotes an administrative region, e.g. в Ставропо́льском кра́е, *in Stavropol Region,* and ряд has ря́де when it means *series*.

§14. Feminine nouns with prepositional singular in stressed -и́

Some monosyllabic feminine nouns ending in a soft sign have a stressed prepositional singular ending after the prepositions в and на used in their locative sense, whereas in other contexts they have a prepositional singular ending in unstressed -и, viz. грудь, *chest*; грязь, *dirt, mud*; дверь, *door*; кость, *bone*; кровь, *blood*; мель, *sandbank*; печь, *stove*; пыль, *dust*; Русь, *Rus* (old name for Russia); связь, *link, communication*; степь, *steppe*; тень, *shadow*; тишь, *stillness, quiet*; цепь, *chain*; честь, *honour*. Thus на Руси́, *in Old Russia*; в степи́, *in the steppe*.

The qualifications made in §13.ii and iii above apply to these nouns too.

§15. The preposition о (об) + prepositional case

Used with the prepositional case о means *about* or *concerning*:

> Об э́том поговори́м в друго́й раз. А сего́дня - о любви́.
> *We'll talk about this on another occasion. But today [we'll talk] about love.* (Press)
> Он ду́мает о бра́те.
> *He is thinking about his brother.*
> Андре́й почти́ не пи́шет о своём состоя́нии.
> *Andrey hardly writes anything about his condition.* (Press)

The preposition о will commonly be found with the following verbs:

жале́ть\пожале́ть о	*to regret, be sorry about*
забо́титься\позабо́титься о	*to worry about, take pains over*
знать о (no pf.)	*to know about*
мечта́ть о (no pf.)	*to dream about*
расска́зывать\рассказа́ть о	*to recount, relate, tell*
слы́шать\услы́шать о	*to hear about*
сообща́ть\сообщи́ть о	*to inform about*
узнава́ть\узна́ть о	*to find out about, discover*

Examples from the press:

> Он рассказа́л мне об уби́йстве генера́ла Куте́пова.
> *He told me about the murder of General Kutepov.*
> О судьбе́ инжене́ра я узна́л, когда́ побыва́л до́ма по́сле второ́го ране́ния.
> *I learnt about the fate of the engineer when I was at home after being wounded for the second time.*

When the following noun or adjective begins with one of the vowels **а**, **о**, **у**, **э** (i.e. a vowel without an initial [j] sound), then the consonant **б** is generally added to **о** for the sake of euphony, e.g. об университе́те, об э́том (as in two of the examples given in this section). Note also the expressions обо всём, *about everything*; обо всех, *about everybody*; and обо мне, *about me*.

Note also the expression па́лка о двух конца́х, *a double-edged weapon* (lit. *a two-ended stick*).

§16. The preposition по + prepositional case

Used with the prepositional case по means *after, following,* or *on completion of*, and is most commonly found with verbal nouns. This usage is rather literary or official, e.g.

по истечéнии вúзы	*on expiry of the visa*
по окончáнии шкóлы	*on leaving school*
по окончáнии университéта	*on graduating*
по получéнии письмá	*on receipt of the letter*

§17. The preposition при + prepositional case

This preposition may only be used with the prepositional case. It means *at the time of, adjacent/attached to, in the presence of, given the availability of* or *while* something is being done, e.g.

Достоéвский нáчал писáть при Николáе пéрвом.
Dostoyevsky started writing in the reign of Nicholas I.
шкóла при университéте
a school attached to the university
ссóриться при гостя́х
to quarrel in front of the guests
Саддáм Хуссéйн я́кобы согласúтся освободúть бóльшую часть кувéйтской территóрии при трёх услóвиях.
Saddam Hussein will supposedly liberate the greater part of Kuwaiti territory given three conditions. (Press)
Хотéлось узнáть, мнóго ли мы теря́ем, пóртим продýктов при транспортирóвке.
We should have liked to have known whether we lose or spoil a lot of foodstuffs while they are being transported. (Press)

Exercises

A. *Complete the following sentences by choosing an appropriate preposition (*в, на, о, по *or* при*) and by putting the words in brackets in the form required by the context:* (1) Вы бы́ли ... (Гималáи)? (2) Онú погúбли ... (войнá). (3) ... (янвáрь) он заболéл. (4) Онú поженúлись ... (начáло) гóда. (5) Днепропетрóвск нахóдится ... (Украúна). (6) Я вы́полню вáшу прóсьбу ... (однó услóвие). (7) Шкаф стоúт ... (ýгол). (8) Он дéлает покýпки ... (ры́нок). (9) Мы встрéтились ... (аэропóрт). (10) Нáчали стрóить желéзные дорóги в Россúи ... (Николáй I). (11) Он отдыхáет ... (Крым). (12) Он мнóго лет жил ... (сéвер) страны́. (13) Онá игрáла ... (гитáра). (14) Отстáлые стрáны нуждáются ... (передовáя технолóгия). (15) ... (бýдущий год) мы проведём óтпуск ... (Кипр). (16) Он рабóтает ... (автомобúльный завóд). (17) Дом стоúт ... (бéрег) рекú. (18) Откры́ли буфéт ... (теáтр). (19) Храм «Васúлия Блажéнного» стоúт ... (Крáсная плóщадь). (20) Стадиóн нахо́дится ... (одна́ ми́ля) от ста́нции. (21) Обвини́ли его́ ... (уби́йство). (22) Самолёт разби́лся ... (взлёт). (23) Я то́лько вчера́ узна́л ... (смерть) отца́. (24) Он роди́лся ... (Ура́л). (25) Он служи́л офице́ром ... (за́падный фронт).

B. *Translate into Russian:* (1) In Moscow; (2) in the exercise-book; (3) on the table; (4) in the centre; (5) at a concert; (6) in the cupboard; (7) in the corner; (8) a kilometre from Moscow; (9) a ten-minute walk away from the school; (10) at the end of the year; (11) in December; (12) last week; (13) at half past four; (14) in the garden; (15) in France; (16) in Spain; (17) a character in 'The Cherry Orchard'; (18) all the passengers on board; (19) on arrival; (20) at an exhibition; (21) in the West; (22) a town in Cuba; (23) in Red Square; (24) a house on the bank of the river; (25) a hostel attached to the institute; (26) The manager was wearing a blue suit. (27) They were talking about the students. (28) Ivan works in a factory. (29) They are strolling in the forest. (30) She is standing on the bridge. (31) They are sitting in the classroom. (32) He works at the post office. (33) They accused him of theft. (34) They are taking part in the play. (35) The captain needs support.

LESSON 16

USE OF THE ACCUSATIVE CASE

§1. Direct object of transitive verb
The main use of the accusative case without a preposition is to express the direct object of a transitive verb, e.g.

Он лю́бит э́тот го́род.
He likes this town.
Я чита́ю кни́гу.
I am reading a book.
Он пи́шет письмо́.
He is writing a letter.
Мы зна́ем её фами́лию.
We know her surname.

§2. Animate nouns
Nouns of the animate category are those which denote people, animals, birds, insects and fish.

Nouns which end in -а or -я (most of which are feminine, but a few of which are masculine, e.g. мужчи́на, *man*; дя́дя, *uncle*) have an accusative singular form, in -у and -ю respectively, which is distinct from the nominative singular form. Thus:

Я ви́жу де́вушку/сестру́/тётю/мужчи́ну/дя́дю.
I (can) see a girl/(my) sister/(my) aunt/a man/(my) uncle.

Feminine nouns of the animate category which end in -ь (e.g. мать, *mother*) have an accusative singular form which is the same as the nominative singular form (as do feminine nouns of the inanimate category which end in -ь), e.g.

Я ви́жу мать.
I see my mother.

However, for masculine nouns of the animate category which end in a hard or soft consonant an accusative form clearly distinguishable from the nominative form is obtained by the use of the genitive flexions in both the singular and the plural. Examples:

masc. nouns (gen. endings for acc. sing. and pl.)
Я вижу бра́та/бра́тьев/отца́/отцо́в/слона́/слоно́в/оле́ня/оле́ней/орла́/орло́в/ле́бедя/лебеде́й/жука́/жуко́в/ка́рпа/ка́рпов.
I (can) see (my) brother/brothers/(my) father/fathers/an elephant/elephants/a deer/deer/an eagle/eagles/a swan/swans/a beetle/beetles/a carp/carp.

For feminine and neuter nouns of the animate category the genitive flexions are used to render the accusative in the plural only. Examples:

fem. nouns (gen. endings for acc. pl. only)
Я ви́жу де́вушек/сестёр/тётей/матере́й/соба́к/лошаде́й/ла́сточек/мух/аку́л.
I (can) see the girls/sisters/aunts/mothers/dogs/horses/swallows/flies/sharks.

neut. nouns (gen. endings for acc. pl. only)
Я ви́жу э́тих лиц/живо́тных/млекопита́ющих/пресмыка́ющихся/насеко́мых.
I (can) see these people/animals/mammals/reptiles/insects.

Note that the genitive form is also used for the accusative case of the nouns мертве́ц, *corpse*, and поко́йник, *deceased*, e.g. мы зна́ли поко́йника, *we knew the deceased.* It is presumably the fact that these nouns have the suffixes -ец and -ник respectively (suffixes which are commonly used to denote people) that accounts for their treatment as animate nouns. Contrast the treatment of труп, *dead body, corpse*, as an inanimate noun (я ви́дел труп, *I saw a corpse*).

Nouns denoting certain chessmen and playing cards are also treated as animate, e.g. ферзь (masc.), *queen* (at chess); туз, *ace*; коро́ль (masc.), *king*; валёт, *jack*.

On the other hand collective nouns referring to animate things are treated as inanimate, e.g. наро́д, *a people*; отря́д, *a detachment*; семе́йство, *a family*; табу́н, *a herd* (of horses, deer); толпа́, *a crowd*.

§3. Duration, distance covered, price and weight

The accusative case is also used without a preposition to express the duration of an action, distance covered, price, and weight. In the first two meanings it is often found after a verb with the prefix про- (if the verb is perfective), since one of the functions of this prefix is to define duration or distance (see also 49.6.i). Examples:

Рабо́та над ру́кописью продолжа́лась всю зи́му.
Work on the manuscript continued all winter. (Press)

А.В. Мень всю жизнь работал для духовного возрождения нашего отечества.
A.V. Men worked all his life for the spiritual regeneration of our fatherland. (Press)
Они проехали тысячу километров.
They travelled a thousand kilometres.
Мешок муки стоит пятьдесят-шестьдесят рублей.
A bag of flour costs 50-60 roubles. (Press)
Нет сил и средств, чтобы поднять со дна океана АПЛ, которая весит не одну тонну.
We do not have the forces or resources to raise the atomic submarine, which weighs many tonnes [lit. *not one tonne*] *from the ocean floor.* (Press)

Exercises

A. *Put the words in brackets in the following sentences in the correct form:* (1) Она читала (газета). (2) Груз весит (одна тонна). (3) Фермер продал (все свои коровы). (4) Он любит (наш дядя). (5) Комплект такой посуды стоит (тысяча) фунтов. (6) Я уважаю (свои коллеги). (7) Лампа привлекает (насекомые). (8) В этом районе разводят (свиньи). (9) Котёнок старается поймать (крысы). (10) Она раздавила (муравей).* (11) Она поцеловала (мать). (12) Он пробежал (тысяча) метров. (13) Я знал (Попов) в лицо. (14) Я изучаю (русская литература). (15) Мы проехали только (одна миля), как автобус сломался. (16) Он ест (клубника). (17) Лев поймал (олень). (18) Она купила (лошадь). (19) Он варит (капуста). (20) Местные жители охотятся на (медведь). (21) Мы встретили (учитель) на улице. (22) Я смотрел на (орлы). (23) Ящерица представляет собой (пресмыкающееся). (24) Экологисты охраняют (кит). (25) Промышленные отходы вытекают в реки и отравляют (рыбы).

* See 4.5 on declension of this noun.

B. *Translate into Russian:* (1) I am feeding the cat. (2) I fed the dogs. (3) They are feeding the tigers. (4) The hunter killed an elephant. (5) Few foreigners understand the Chinese people. (6) We have travelled just one mile. (7) The car weighs one tonne. (8) She has been reading* this book all winter. (9) He loves his sister. (10) He usually listens to this programme. (11) I hate reptiles and insects, especially spiders. (12) I love animals. (13) She is seeing the headmaster this morning. (14) The work continued all winter. (15) I caught a mouse. (16) They were listening to the chairman. (17) I saw my aunt yesterday. (18) Everybody likes the professor. (19) He is driving his son to school. (20) We invited the Nikitins.

* See 52.6 for tense.

LESSON 17

THE PREPOSITIONS В AND НА WITH THE ACCUSATIVE CASE

§1. Prepositions used with the accusative case

The following prepositions may be used with the accusative case: в, за, на, о, по, под, про, с, сквозь, чéрез. Of these про, сквозь and чéрез are used only with the accusative case. Note especially that в, за, на, and под are used with the accusative to express the concept of movement *into, behind, on to*, and *under* respectively. When on the other hand в and на are used with the prepositional case and за and под are used with the instrumental case, then they signify that the object is stationary.

For the sake of convenience the commonest of these prepositions, в and на, are dealt with separately in this lesson. The remaining prepositions which may govern the accusative case are dealt with in the following lesson.

§2. Uses of в with the accusative case

The preposition в has many meanings and functions when used with the accusative case, including the following:

i. *into, to, in*, when movement is involved, e.g.

Он вошёл в кóмнату.	*He went into the room.*
Он положи́л вéщи в чемодáн.	*He put his things in a case.*
éхать в Москвý	*to go to Moscow*

cf. в + prepositional case, see 15.2 above.

ii. *a* or *per*, e.g.

раз в год	*once a year*
два рáза в недéлю	*twice a week*
сто киломéтров в час	*a hundred kilometres per hour*

iii. *at* a time on the hour or past the hour, e.g.

в час	*at one o'clock*
в два часá	*at two o'clock*
в чéтверть пя́того	*at a quarter past four*
в двáдцать минýт шестóго	*at twenty past five*

Note also в пóлдень, *at midday*, and в пóлночь, *at midnight*.

For *half past* the hour and for times *to* the hour, though, use в + prepositional case (see 15.3 above) and без + genitive case (see 22.1 below) respectively.

В + accusative may also be used for *at* an age, as in the following examples from the press: в дéвять лет он остáлся без мáтери, *at the age of nine he was left without a mother*; её сын попáл в семнáдцать лет в тюрьмý, *her son wound up in prison at the age of seventeen*.

iv. *on* a day of the week, thus:

в понедéльник	*on Monday*
во втóрник	*on Tuesday*
в срéду	*on Wednesday*
в четвéрг	*on Thursday*
в пя́тницу	*on Friday*
в суббóту	*on Saturday*
в воскресéнье	*on Sunday*

v. to express dimension and measurement, e.g.

стол ширинóй в оди́н метр	*a table a metre wide*
дом в два этажá	*a two-storey house*
морóз в дéсять грáдусов	*a 10-degree frost*
вéтер в пять бáллов	*a force 5 wind*

See also 42.3 below on dimension and measurement.

vi. to denote pattern, e.g.

в клéточку	*check*
в крáпинку	*spotted*
в полóску	*striped*

vii. to denote change of status, promotion, in expressions such as the following (in which, it should be noted, the accusative form of the noun coincides with the nominative, in other words the genitive flexion is not used, even though the noun belongs to the animate category):

произвести́ в полкóвники	*to promote to the rank of colonel*
пойти́ в лётчики	*to become a pilot*
вы́йти в лю́ди	*to get on in the world*

§3. Use of в + accusative after certain verbs

Many common verbs are followed by в + accusative in certain meanings, e.g.

ве́рить\пове́рить в	*to believe in*
вме́шиваться\вмеша́ться в	*to interfere, intervene in*
вторга́ться\вто́ргнуться в	*to invade*
игра́ть в (no pf. in this sense)	*to play* (a game, sport)
одева́ть(ся)\оде́ть(ся) в	*to dress (oneself in)*
поступа́ть\поступи́ть в	*to enter* (institution)
превраща́ть(ся)\преврати́ть(ся) в	*to turn into, be turned into*
стреля́ть\вы́стрелить в	*to shoot at* (fixed target)

Examples:

ве́рить в бо́га
to believe in God
вме́шиваться в чужу́ю жизнь
to interfere in someone else's life
Мини́стр оборо́ны Р.Че́йни на неда́вней пресс-конфере́нции сказа́л, что америка́нцы мо́гут вто́ргнуться в Ира́к на значи́тельное расстоя́ние.
Defence Secretary Richard Cheney said at a recent press-conference that the Americans might invade Iraq to a considerable distance. (Press)
игра́ть в ка́рты, футбо́л, те́ннис
to play cards, football, tennis
Он сиде́л в своём кабине́те в о́бществе сре́дних лет же́нщины, оде́той в стро́гий костю́м.
He was sitting in his study in the company of a middle-aged woman dressed in an austere suit. (Press)
Он поступи́л в институ́т.
He entered an institute. (Press)
Ле́том со́лнце нагрева́ет во́здух до сорока́ гра́дусов, дви́гатель даёт ещё со́рок. Поэ́тому сиде́нье превраща́ется в раскалённую сковороду́.
In summer the sun warms the air up to 40 degrees and the engine [of a combine harvester] *gives off another 40. Consequently the seat turns into a scorching frying-pan.* (Press)
Не стреля́йте в наро́дных депута́тов.
Don't shoot at the people's deputies. (Press)

§4. Uses of на with the accusative case

The preposition на also has many meanings and functions when used with the accusative case, viz.

i. *on to, on,* when movement is involved, e.g.

класть\положи́ть кни́гу на стол
to put the book on the table
сади́ться\сесть на стул
to sit down on the chair

ii. *to, into* with those nouns listed in 15.8-10 above which require на + prepositional case for the translation of *in* or *at*, e.g. на ры́нок, *to the market*.

iii. *for* a period of time, when one is defining not the duration of an action (see 16.3 above) but what period an action is intended or expected to cover, e.g.

Он поéхал в Москву́ на недéлю.
He went to Moscow for a week.
Он приезжáет к нам нá год.
He is coming to us for a year.
закры́то нá зиму
closed for the winter (notice on window of Russian trains)

Hence the expression навсегдá, *for ever.*

iv. *for* a certain purpose, e.g.

тало́ны на мя́со
rationing coupons for meat
лес нá постро́йку
wood for building
обéд на пять человéк
dinner for five people
ко́мната на двои́х
a room for two
Билéты на э́ти и́гры нáчали продавáть в дéсять часо́в утрá.
They started selling tickets for these games at ten in the morning. (Press)

Hence the expressions на вся́кий слу́чай, *to be on the safe side, just in case*, and на крáйний слу́чай, *for an emergency.*

v. *by* a certain margin, e.g.

Он на два го́да стáрше брáта.
He is two years older than his brother.
Нéкоторые проду́кты подорожáли зá год на ты́сячу процéнтов.
Some products became a thousand per cent more expensive over the year. (Press)
Вы нерéдко опáздываете на два-три дня.
You are not infrequently two or three days late. (Press)

vi. Note the following expressions involving the use of на + accusative case:

на друго́е у́тро	*the next morning*
на друго́й день	*the next day*
на сле́дующее у́тро	*the next morning*
на сле́дующий день	*the next day*
на ско́рую ру́ку	*in a rough-and-ready fashion*
на чужо́й счёт	*at somebody else's expense*
в отве́т на	*in reply to*
жить на широ́кую но́гу	*to live in grand style*
гото́в на	*prepared for* (in the sense of *willing*)
похо́жий на	*like, similar to*
на всё гора́зд	*good at everything, Jack-of-all-trades*

§5. Use of на + accusative after certain verbs

Many common verbs are followed by на + accusative when they have certain meanings, e.g.

гляде́ть\погляде́ть на	*to look at*
дели́ть\раздели́ть на	*to divide into*
жа́ловаться\пожа́ловаться на	*to complain of*
наезжа́ть\нае́хать на	*to run into, run over*
напада́ть\напа́сть на	*to attack, fall upon*
ната́лкиваться\натолкну́ться на	*to run up against, come across*
натыка́ться\наткну́ться на	*to run up against, strike*
отвеча́ть\отве́тить на	*to reply to* (letter, question)
полага́ться\положи́ться на	*to count on, rely on*
серди́ться\рассерди́ться на	*to be angry at, cross with*
смотре́ть\посмотре́ть на	*to look at*
соглаша́ться\согласи́ться на	*to agree to* (but not *to agree with*)

Examples:

Учи́тель раздели́л ученико́в на две гру́ппы.
The teacher divided the pupils into two groups.
Го́сти жа́луются на плохо́й се́рвис.
The guests are complaining about the bad service.
Авто́бус нае́хал на пешехо́да.
A bus ran over the pedestrian.
Аталку́я Э. Шевардна́дзе, коали́ция генера́лов, партаппара́тчиков, «интеллектуа́лов» напада́ла на са́мом де́ле на М. Горбачёва.
In attacking E. Shevardnadze the coalition of generals, party apparatchiks and 'intellectuals' was in fact attacking M. Gorbachev. (Press)
Мы натолкну́лись на пробле́му.
We have run up against a problem.

Не́сколько мгнове́ний он ничего́ не мог отве́тить на мои́ вопро́сы.
For several moments he could not say anything in reply to my questions. (Press)
Он рассерди́лся на сестру́.
He got cross with his sister.
Она́ смо́трит на карти́ну.
She is looking at the picture.
То́лько нече́стный врач согласи́тся на таку́ю про́сьбу.
Only a dishonourable doctor will agree to such a request. (Press)

Exercises

A. *Complete the following sentences by choosing the appropriate preposition (в or на):* (1) Мы е́дем ... Кана́ду. (2) Мы е́дем ... Кавка́з. (3) Пти́цы летя́т ... юг. (4) ... суббо́ту он придёт к нам в го́сти. (5) На ней блу́зка ... клё́точку. (6) Преподава́тельница вошла́ ... аудито́рию и начала́ чита́ть ле́кцию. (7) Вы уезжа́ете ... день или ... неде́лю? (8) Она́ прие́хала ... пя́тницу, а ... друго́й день неожи́данно уе́хала. (9) ... ско́лько дней е́дете в Москву́? (10) Они́ игра́ют ... футбо́л. (11) Она́ положи́ла все ве́щи ... я́щик. (12) Что вы де́лаете ... понеде́льник? (13) Рабо́чие жа́ловались ... плоху́ю зарпла́ту. (14) Вы ве́рите ... бо́га? (15) Два ру́сских бомбарди- ро́вщика вто́рглись ... япо́нское возду́шное простра́нство. (16) Лев напа́л ... оле́ня. (17) Число́ студе́нтов увели́чилось ... де́сять проце́нтов. (18) При температу́ре ста гра́дусов по Це́льсию вода́ превраща́ется ... пар. (19) Э́та руба́шка ... поло́ску осо́бенно мне нра́вится. (20) Я отвеча́ю ... ва́ше письмо́ от двадца́того а́вгуста. (21) Ребёнок опроки́нул стака́н со́ка и оте́ц рассе́рдился ... него́. (22) В результа́те экономи́ческого кри́зиса прави́тельство ввело́ тало́ны ... все основны́е проду́кты. (23) Це́ны повы́сились ... два́дцать проце́нтов. (24) Вы уме́ете игра́ть ... ша́хматы? (25) Не вме́шивайтесь ... наш спор.

B. *Translate into Russian:* (1) He put his briefcase on the chair. (2) He came in at midday. (3) She went into the classroom. (4) I am going to Cuba on Wednesday. (5) People do not believe in communism now. (6) Soviet forces invaded Czechoslovakia in 1968.* (7) We were playing tennis on Friday. (8) She is fifteen months older than me. (9) The next day I replied to his letter. (10) I am going to Spain for a week. (11) I shall take an umbrella just in case. (12) Englishmen are always complaining about the weather. (13) He sees his father three times a year. (14) The police were shooting at the crowd. (15) He is turning into a miser.

* See 40.3.vii on rendering of date.

LESSON 18

OTHER PREPOSITIONS WITH THE ACCUSATIVE CASE

§1. Uses of за with the accusative case
The preposition за also has several meanings when used with the accusative case, viz.

i. *behind* or *beyond*, when movement into a position is involved (cf. за + instrumental; see 26.5 below), e.g.

Ма́льчик зашёл за дом.
The boy went round behind the house.
Со́лнце зашло́ за горизо́нт.
The sun set [lit. *went behind the horizon*]
Мы зае́хали за́ город.
We went into the country [lit. *beyond the town*]

This is the sense in which за is used in the following phrases:

сади́ться/сесть за стол
to sit down at table
сади́ться/сесть за за́втрак, обе́д, у́жин
to sit down to breakfast, dinner, supper
сади́ться/сесть за роя́ль
to sit down at the piano
е́хать/пое́хать за грани́цу
to go abroad
выходи́ть/вы́йти за́муж за мужчи́ну
to get married (of woman to man)
бра́ться/взя́ться за рабо́ту, де́ло, зада́чу
to get down to work, business, a task
принима́ться/приня́ться за рабо́ту, де́ло, зада́чу
to get down to work, business, a task

ii. *for*, when some sort of exchange or reciprocity is involved, e.g.

Аренда́торы пригото́вились получа́ть хоро́шие де́ньги за свою́ хоро́шую рабо́ту.
The tenants [farmers] *got ready to receive good money for their good work.* (Press)

Есть и курс неофициа́льный, по кото́рому за одну́ западногерма́нскую ма́рку даю́т 7-8 ма́рок ГДР.
There is also an unofficial rate of exchange according to which people give 7 or 8 East German marks for one West German mark. (Press)
Спаси́бо вам за мора́льную и материа́льную подде́ржку.
Thank you for [your] moral and material support. (Press)
благодари́ть/поблагодари́ть хозя́ина за гостеприи́мство
to thank the host for his hospitality
извиня́ться/извини́ться за своё поведе́ние
to apologise for one's behaviour

iii. *during, in the space of, over*, e.g.

за су́тки
in the space of 24 hours
За три дня вы́пало две ме́сячные но́рмы оса́дков.
In the space of three days there was twice the usual monthly rainfall. (Press)
Э́то мои́ заме́тки — отчёт о том, что прочёл и услы́шал за два после́дних ме́сяца.
These are my notes, an account of what I have read and heard over the last two months. (Press)

iv. *after* a period of time, or *over/beyond* a certain age, e.g.

далеко́ за́ полночь
long after midnight
Ему́ уже́ за со́рок.
He is already over 40.

v. *at* a distance in space or time, in which case за is likely to combine with the prepositions от and до respectively, e.g.

Э́то произошло́ за сто киломе́тров отсю́да.
This happened 100 kilometres from here.
за оди́н день до его́ сме́рти
a day before his death

Note the expressions задо́лго до, *long before*, and незадо́лго до, *not long before*.

vi. *by* after verbs with the sense of *taking hold of*, e.g.

брать/взять за́ руку
to take by the hand
вести́/повести́ за́ руку
to lead by the hand

держа́ть за́ руку (no pf. in this sense)
to hold by the hand
держа́ться за (e.g. пери́ла) (no pf. in this sense)
to hold on to (e.g. *the handrail*)
хвата́ть/схвати́ть за ши́ворот
to seize by the scruff of the neck

Examples from the press:

Из посо́льства вы́бежала же́нщина, взяла́ за́ руку. Милицион́ер — за другу́ю, тяну́л, не пуска́я.
A woman ran out of the embassy and took [her] by one hand. A policeman [took her] by the other and pulled, without letting go.
И схвати́ла граби́теля за́ руки, забы́в о со́бственной безопа́сности.
And she seized the robber by the arms, forgetting about her own safety.

vii. *for the sake of, in favour of* in certain contexts, e.g.

боро́ться за (no pf. in this sense)
to fight, struggle for
голосова́ть/проголосова́ть за
to vote for
дра́ться за (no pf. in this sense)
to fight for
заступа́ться/заступи́ться за
to stand up, plead, intercede for
пить/вы́пить за (e.g. здоро́вье)
to drink to (e.g. *health*)
сража́ться/срази́ться за (e.g. ро́дину)
to fight for (e.g. *one's country*)

Examples from the press:

Я боро́лась за сы́на.
I fought for my son.
Я могу́ быть уве́рен — они́ всё равно́ бу́дут голосова́ть за меня́.
I can be sure – they'll vote for me all the same.
Эй, официа́нт, ещё коньяку́! Шампа́нского! Вы́пьем за прие́зд Ма́йи Анто́новны к нам в Ерева́н!
Hey, waiter, more brandy! Champagne! Let's drink to the arrival of Maya Antonovna in Erevan!

За is one of several prepositions that attracts the stress away from the following noun in certain phrases, as may be seen in a number of the examples of its usage given above.

§2. Use of о with the accusative case

The preposition о means *against* in the sense of *in contact with* when used with the accusative case, e.g.

спотыка́ться/споткну́ться о ка́мень
to stumble against a stone
бок о́ бок
side by side
рука́ о́б руку
hand in hand
как о́б стену горо́х
like a pea against a wall (of sthg. having no effect)
би́ться как ры́ба об лёд
to fight like a fish against ice (of desperate but vain attempts)

§3. Use of по with the accusative case

The preposition по is used with the accusative case in the sense of *up to* a certain point in space or time, e.g.

Он стоя́л по коле́ни в воде́.
He was standing up to his knees in water.
Труди́сь, аренда́тор. И он вка́лывает под дыря́вой кры́шей, в грязи́ по коле́но, с ви́лами в рука́х.
Toil away, tenant [farmer]. *And he gets stuck in under a roof with holes in it, up to his knees in mud, with a pitchfork in his hands.* (Press)
по́ уши в рабо́те/в долга́х
up to the ears in work/debt
Ви́за действи́тельна по двадца́тое ма́я.
The visa is valid up until 20 May inclusive.

Note also the expression по ту сто́рону, *on the other side.*

§4. Uses of под with the accusative case

The preposition под has several meanings or functions when used with the accusative case, viz.

i. *under*, when movement into a position is involved, e.g.

Ко́шка пошла́ под крова́ть.
The cat went under the bed.
Я поста́вил пусты́е буты́лки под стол.
I put the empty bottles under the table.

ii. *towards*, in a temporal sense, or *just before*, e.g.

под ве́чер
towards evening
под Но́вый год
on New Year's Eve
Ему́ под со́рок лет.
He is getting on for 40 (cf. ему́ за со́рок, see §1.iv above).

iii. *to the accompaniment of* a sound, e.g.

петь под гита́ру
to sing to the accompaniment of the guitar
танцева́ть под му́зыку
to dance to music
писа́ть под дикто́вку
to write to dictation

iv. *in imitation of*, e.g.

стол под де́рево
an imitation wood table
ме́бель под оре́х
furniture that looks like walnut
кольцо́ под зо́лото
an imitation gold ring
писа́ть под Замя́тина
to write in the style of Zamyatin

v. note the following expressions in which под is used with the accusative case:

по́д гору
downhill
ста́вить/поста́вить под угро́зу
to threaten, imperil, jeopardise

§5. Use of про with the accusative case

The preposition про is used only with the accusative case. Its main meaning is *about* or *concerning*. (In this sense it is more or less synonymous with o + prepositional case, though it is slightly more colloquial.) It may be used with verbs such as говори́ть, ду́мать, петь, e.g.

Мне ка́жется, что про Вели́кую Оте́чественную войну́ ка́ждую неде́лю пока́зывать не на́до.
I think [films] about the Great Patriotic War [i.e. the Second World War] *should not be shown every week.* (Press)
петь про любо́вь
to sing about love

The phrase про себя́ may mean *to oneself*, e.g. ду́мать про себя́, *to think to oneself*; чита́ть про себя́, *to read to oneself*.

§6. Use of с with the accusative case

The preposition с is occasionally used with the accusative case with nouns denoting measurement, distance, time, etc. in the sense of *approximately, about*, e.g.

ве́сить с килогра́мм	*to weigh about a kilogramme*
помидо́р с кула́к	*a tomato about the size of one's fist*
Мы прошли́ с ми́лю.	*We walked about a mile.*
Я был там с неде́лю.	*I was there about a week.*

§7. Use of сквозь with the accusative case

The preposition сквозь is used only with the accusative sase. It means *through*. It may mean that an object is visible through something, but also often implies that the passage through something is difficult, e.g.

пробира́ться/пробра́ться сквозь толпу́
to force one's way through a crowd

Note the expressions:

смотре́ть/посмотре́ть сквозь па́льцы на что́-нибудь
to turn a blind eye to sthg. (lit. *to look through one's fingers at sthg.*)
смотре́ть/посмотре́ть сквозь ро́зовые очки́ на что́-нибудь
to look at sthg. through rose-tinted spectacles
смех сквозь слёзы
laughter through tears

§8. Use of че́рез with the accusative case

The preposition че́рез is also used only with the accusative case. It has two principal meanings, one spatial and one temporal.

i. *across, through*, or *over* when this preposition means *across*, e.g.

Она́ перешла́ че́рез доро́гу
She crossed over the road.
перелеза́ть/переле́зть че́рез забо́р
to climb over the fence

Note that in this meaning че́рез will often be used with a verb bearing the prefix пере-, which may also convey the meaning of *across* or *through* (see 47.1 below).

ii. *in* (a certain amount of time from the time of speaking), e.g.

Чéрез недéлю он вошёл в свой обы́чный, óчень акти́вный темп.
In a week he went into his usual very active tempo. (Press)
А молодóй человéк, отéц ребёнка, пообещáв позвони́ть чéрез три дня, исчезáет.
And the young man, the child's father, having promised to ring in three days, disappears. (Press)

It has a similar use in phrases such as чéрез две останóвки, *in three stops* (i.e. of getting out of bus or train). It may also mean:

iii. *via* a place, e.g.

Мы полетéли в Москвý чéрез Варшáву.
We flew to Moscow via Warsaw.

iv. *through* an intermediary, e.g.

Я говори́л с ни́ми чéрез переводчика.
I spoke to them through an interpreter.

v. that an action is repeated at certain intervals, e.g.

рабóтать чéрез день
to work every other day
печáтать/напечáтать чéрез строкý
to print on every other line, to double space (typing, printing)
принимáть/приня́ть лекáрство чéрез кáждые два часá
to take the medicine every two hours

Exercises

A. *Complete the following sentences by choosing the appropriate preposition (за, о, по, под, про, с, сквозь, or чéрез):* (1) Мы поéдем в Рим ... Пари́ж. (2) Я купи́л рéдкую кни́гу ... ты́сячу рублéй. (3) Он без рабóты и бы́стро идёт ... гóру. (4) Экзаменáтор попроси́л студéнта прочитáть текст ... себя́. (5) Он ýмер ... три дня до концá войны́. (6) Пострóили нóвый мост ... рéку. (7) Онá чáсто éздит ... грани́цу. (8) Он никогдá не благодари́т нас ... гостеприи́мство. (9) Они́ ýжинали ... звýки оркéстра. (10) ... оди́н мéсяц мили́ция арестовáла всех члéнов престýпной организáции. (11) Профéссор ушёл. Он подойдёт ... час. (12) Мы положи́ли свои́ вéщи ... скамéйку и сéли на неё. (13) Он заложи́л рýки ... спи́ну. (14) Друзья́ говори́ли ... футбóльный матч. (15) ... какóго кандидáта вы бýдете голосовáть? (16) Отéц смóтрит ... пáльцы на грýбости сы́на. (17) Он вы́шел, и ... пять минýт вернýлся. (18) Шахтёры борóлись ... бóлее корóткий рабóчий день. (19) Я поднимáлся по лéстнице, споткнýлся ... послéднюю ступéньку. (20) Э́то хорошó оплáчиваемая рабóта. ... оди́н день мóжно зарабóтать сто фýнтов. (21) На ней браслéт ... зóлото. (22)

Мать взяла́ до́чку ... ру́ку и повела́ её в дом. (23) Они́ лежа́ли бок ... бок на пля́же. (24) Со́лнце зашло́ ... ту́чи. (25) Его́ визи́т продолжа́ется ... двадца́тое а́вгуста.

B. *Translate into Russian:* (1) Every other page; (2) about the size of a window; (3) through a thick fog; (4) approaching thirty (years of age); (5) up to the 1st of June; (6) He paid for his lunch and thanked the waiter for the good service. (7) The children sat down to breakfast. (8) The students got down to work. (9) We thanked him for the book. (10) In the space of a week five members of the group fell ill. (11) Are you going to vote for the same party? (12) They were strolling hand in hand. (13) She took him by the arm. (14) He was standing up to his neck in water. (15) He was working to the sound of music. (16) Dostoevsky sometimes writes in the style of Gogol. (17) They were running downhill. (18) The government's policy is putting teachers' work in jeopardy. (19) She was reading the book to herself. (20) A yacht is sailing across the river. (21) He will arrive in one week. (22) He is looking through a crack in the wall. (23) I shall go to Russia via Denmark. (24) Let's speak* through an interpreter. (25) I shall go abroad.

* See 43.10 on first-person plural imperatives.

LESSON 19

USE OF THE GENITIVE CASE

§1. Basic uses of the genitive case

The fundamental use of the genitive case without a preposition is to express possession, origin, relationship of part to whole, the nature, quality, measurement, or quantity of something, i.e. to denote *of* a certain thing, e.g.

кни́га моего́ бра́та	*my brother's book*
стихи́ Пу́шкина	*Pushkin's poetry*
пе́рвый ваго́н по́езда	*the first coach of the train*
мужчи́на большо́го ро́ста	*a man of large stature*
за́пах цвето́в	*the scent of flowers*
метр тка́ни	*a metre of fabric*
литр вина́	*a litre of wine*

Note though that the genitive case is not used in a number of contexts where English has *of*, e.g.

Азо́вское мо́ре	*the Sea of Azov*
го́род Москва́	*the city of Moscow*
Ло́ндонский университе́т	*the University of London*

§2. Use of the genitive case after quantitative words

The genitive case is also required, without a preposition, after the following words indicating quantity:

ма́ло	*little, few*
мно́го	*many, much, a lot of*
немно́го	*not many, not much, a few, a little*
не́сколько	*a few, some, several*
ско́лько?	*how many? how much?*
сто́лько	*so many, so much*

Examples:

Там бы́ло ма́ло студе́нтов.
There were few students there.
мно́го рабо́ты
a lot of work

много книг
a lot of books
Остаётся немного времени.
There is not much time left.
Вот лишь несколько примеров.
Here are just a few examples. (Press)
Сколько учителей работают в школе?
How many teachers work in the school?
Эти Лищенко столько денег уже получили!
These Lishchenkos have already received so much money! (Press)

Note that after all these quantitative expressions *years* is translated by лет rather than годов. For translation of *people* after these words see 41.4 below.

§3. Use of the genitive case with partitive meaning

The genitive case without a preposition may also be used to denote a certain quantity, some of a given object. (Compare French usage: *du pain, de l'eau*, etc.) Thus:

налить молока
to pour some milk
Дома вечером Андрей ничего не ел, только выпил чая.
At home in the evening Andrey didn't eat anything, he just drank some tea. (Press)

The accusative case in such contexts would denote not some of the object but the object. Thus налить молоко would mean *to pour the* (i.e. some specific) *milk*, e.g. the milk left in the bottle, the milk on the table, the milk in the refrigerator, etc.

A genitive case with this partitive meaning will often be found after verbs bearing the prefix на- in its meaning of *a certain quantity of* (see 48.7.i below), e.g.

накупить книг	*to buy up a number of books*
наговорить чепухи	*to talk a lot of nonsense*

§4. Nouns with partitive genitive forms in -у or -ю

A small number of masculine nouns (e.g. коньяк, *brandy*; мёд, *honey*; сахар, *sugar*; сыр, *cheese*; чай, *tea*) used to have a distinctive genitive singular form in -у (rather than the normal -а) or -ю (rather than -я, in the case of nouns with a soft stem); thus коньяку, мёду, сахару, сыру, чаю. These forms would be used if a quantity of the substance in question was being specified, e.g. бутылка коньяку, *a bottle of brandy*; банка мёду, *a jar of honey* (cf. цена мёда, *the price of honey*).

The phrase стака́н ча́ю, *a glass of tea*, is still widely used as is the expression мно́го наро́ду, *a lot of people* (as well as мно́го наро́да). However, special partitive forms are for the most part rarely used, except perhaps by older speakers, in the standard modern language. The student should be aware of their existence, but there is no need to attempt to use them.

§5. Use of the genitive to express lack or absence

The genitive is also used to denote the thing lacking in constructions with нет, *there is not, there are not*; не́ было, *there was not, there were not*; and не бу́дет, *there will not be*. Note also that these three Russian expressions, when they have the meanings given above, are invariable, i.e. they remain the same irrespective of the number or gender of the thing lacking. Thus:

Хле́ба нет в магази́не.
There is no bread in the shop.
Ры́бы нет.
There is no fish.
Мя́са нет.
There is no meat.
Нет вре́мени да́же газе́ту в рука́х взять.
There isn't even time to take a newspaper in one's hands. (Press)
Сне́га не́ было.
There was no snow.
Капу́сты не́ было.
There was no cabbage.
Молока́ не́ было.
There was no milk.
Не́ было свобо́дных мест в купе́.
There were no free places in the compartment.
Дождя́ не бу́дет.
There will not be any rain.
Во́дки не бу́дет.
There will not be any vodka.
Рече́й не бу́дет.
There will not be any speeches.

The expressions нет, не́ было, не бу́дет may be used to indicate that a person is out or away, e.g.

Его́ здесь нет сего́дня.	*He is not here today.*
Её не́ было до́ма.	*She was not at home.*

When the verb is in the past or future the same meaning could be conveyed by using a nominative form of the noun or personal pronoun (e.g. она́ не была́ до́ма, *she was not at home*).

§6. Use of the genitive to express sufficiency or insufficiency

The following impersonal verbs are used with the genitive case to express sufficiency or insufficiency:

хвата́ть\хвати́ть	*to suffice* (usually used with у + genitive of person who has enough/not enough of sthg.)
недостава́ть\недоста́ть	*to be insufficient, not to have enough* (used with dative of person who is short of sthg.)

Examples:

Вре́мени хвата́ет.
There is enough time.
У нас не хвата́ло хра́брости.
We were not brave enough.
Ему́ недостаёт о́пыта.
He doesn't have enough experience.
Недостава́ло де́нег.
There wasn't enough money.

The genitive has a similar meaning of sufficiency after certain reflexive verbs bearing the prefix на- which mean to do something as much as one wants or in some cases to excess (see also 48.7.iii below). (These verbs will normally be perfective.) Thus:

нае́сться	*to eat one's fill of*
напи́ться	*to drink a large quantity of, get drunk*
наслу́шаться	*to listen to a lot of/more than enough of*
насмотре́ться	*to look at a lot of/more than enough of*
начита́ться	*to read a lot of*

Examples:

Они́ нае́лись хле́ба.
They ate as much bread as they wanted.
Они напи́лись воды́.
They drank as much water as they wanted.
Я насмотре́лся телеви́зора и у меня́ боля́т глаза́.
I have watched too much television and my eyes hurt.

§7. Use of the genitive for accusative of animate nouns

Masculine nouns of the animate category which end in a consonant have genitive flexions for their accusative singular, and all nouns of the animate category have genitive flexions for their accusative plural (see 16.2 above).

§8. Use of the genitive with short comparative adjectives
The genitive case may be used after a short comparative adjective to express *than* (see also 32.8 below). Examples:

Он ста́рше меня́.	*He is older than I am.*
бо́льше го́да	*more than a year*
ни́же нуля́	*below zero*

§9. Use of the genitive after cardinal numerals
The genitive case is also required after cardinal numerals (provided that the numeral itself is in the nominative or accusative case), except *one* and compound numbers in which *one* is the last component.

A noun is used in the genitive singular in the following circumstances:

i. after the numerals два\две, *two*; три, *three*; четы́ре, *four*;

ii. after any compound number in which one of these numerals is the last component;

iii. after the words о́ба\о́бе, *both* and полтора́\полторы́, *one and a half.*

Accompanying adjectives are in the genitive plural, if the noun is masculine or neuter, or in the nominative plural (or occasionally the genitive plural), if the noun is feminine. (Два, о́ба, and полтора́ are used with masculine and neuter nouns; две, о́бе, and полторы́ are used with feminine nouns.)

Examples:

два больши́х стола́	*two large tables*
три широ́ких по́ля	*three wide fields*
четы́ре но́вые кни́ги	*four new books*
о́ба авто́буса	*both buses*
полторы́ неде́ли	*one and a half weeks*
два́дцать два кра́сных пла́тья	*twenty-two red dresses*

After numerals above *four* both noun and accompanying adjective are in the genitive plural irrespective of the gender of the noun, e.g.

пять больши́х столо́в	*five large tables*
шесть широ́ких поле́й	*six wide fields*
семь но́вых книг	*seven new books*
два́дцать во́семь кра́сных пла́тьев	*twenty-eight red dresses*

The genitive plural is also used after the words ты́сяча, *thousand*; миллио́н, *million*; and миллиа́рд, *billion*, e.g. ты́сяча киломе́тров, *a thousand kilometres*; миллио́н фу́нтов, *a million pounds*; миллиа́рд до́лларов, *a billion dollars*.

Numerals are dealt with fully in later lessons (37-42).

§10. Use of the genitive in dates

The genitive case of an ordinal numeral is used without a preposition to express *on* a certain date (see also 40.3.v below). Examples:

пе́рвого ма́рта	*on the 1st of March*
тре́тьего а́вгуста	*on the 3rd of August*
два́дцать шесто́го октября́	*on the 26th of October*

Note also the expression тре́тьего дня, *the day before yesterday.*

Exercises

A. *Complete the following sentences by putting the word in brackets in the correct form, and say what function the genitive case has in each instance:* (1) Чья э́то маши́на? Э́то маши́на (Бори́с). (2) Чьи э́то кни́ги? Э́то кни́ги его́ (дя́дя). (3) Сын вы́ше (оте́ц). (4) У нас нет (биле́ты) в теа́тр. (5) Мы уезжа́ем (второ́е) ма́я. (6) Я заказа́л сто грамм (во́дка). (7) В кио́ске не́ было (ру́сские газе́ты). (8) В э́том го́роде мно́го (парк). (9) Ско́лько (европе́йские языки́) она́ зна́ет? (10) У меня́ нет (телефо́н). (11) На столе́ лежа́ло не́сколько (письмо́). (12) За́втра у меня́ не бу́дет (ле́кция) по ру́сской литерату́ре. (13) У нас ма́ло (вре́мя). (14) У меня́ два (биле́т) на конце́рт. (15) Он купи́л кило́ (са́хар). (16) У неё пять (брат) и две (сестра́). (17) (Профе́ссор) не́ было на собра́нии. (18) Ско́лько (студе́нты) в на́шей гру́ппе? (19) В Росси́и мно́го (нефть) и (у́голь). (20) В на́шем го́роде ма́ло (но́вые зда́ния). (21) Ско́лько (страни́цы) в э́той кни́ге? (22) Мадри́д — столи́ца (Испа́ния). (23) Я люблю́ стихи́ (Ле́рмонтов). (24) А́нна ста́рше (О́льга). (25) Ско́лько (ме́сяц) вы жи́ли в Росси́и? (26) Я роди́лся (пятна́дцатое) апре́ля. (27) В на́шем райо́не страны́ не хвата́ет (вода́). (28) Она́ навари́ла (варе́нье). (29) Ему недостаёт (терпе́ние). (30) (Больна́я студе́нтка) не́ было на экза́мене.

B. *Translate into Russian:* (1) My brother's room; (2) the doctor's car; (3) the student's book; (4) Turgenev's novels; (5) the price of petrol; (6) a bottle of wine; (7) the University of Oxford; (8) a lot of planes; (9) several students; (10) few towns; (11) a few trains; (12) two trams; (13) three new houses; (14) five cars; (15) seven old buses; (16) on the 3rd of May; (17) on the 21st of August; (18) so many birds; (19) a pound of potatoes; (20) a cup of tea; (21) a piece of cheese; (22) a kilogramme of sugar; (23) the price of honey; (24) the colour of his hair; (25) how many roubles? (26) There isn't any bread. (27) There are no flowers in the garden. (28) There wasn't any meat. (29) There won't be any beer. (30) I saw his brother. (31) Do you know his parents? (32) I know his sisters. (33) I know his wife. (34) We haven't got enough money. (35) They drank as much juice as they wanted.

LESSON 20

VERBS GOVERNING THE GENITIVE CASE

§1. Use of the genitive after verbs of fearing, etc.

The genitive case is used after many verbs which express fear, avoidance or apprehension, including the following:

боя́ться (no pf. as a rule)	*to fear, be afraid of*
избега́ть\избежа́ть	*to avoid*
опаса́ться (no pf.)	*to fear, shun, keep off, avoid*
пуга́ться\испуга́ться	*to be afraid of*
стесня́ться\постесня́ться	*to be shy of*
стыди́ться\постыди́ться	*to be ashamed of*

Examples:

Он бои́тся гро́ма.
He is afraid of thunder.
Бе́лый дом по-пре́жнему избега́ет како́го-либо публи́чного осужде́ния де́йствий Тель-Ави́ва.
The White House as before is avoiding any public condemnation of the actions of Tel Aviv. (Press)
Де́ти пуга́ются темноты́.
Children are afraid of the dark.
Он стыди́тся своего́ поведе́ния.
He is ashamed of his behaviour.

§2. Miscellaneous verbs governing the genitive case

Many other verbs also require a noun in the genitive, including the following:

держа́ться (no pf. in this sense)	*to keep to, hold on to, adhere to*
добива́ться* (impf.)	*to strive for*
доби́ться* (pf.)	*to get, procure*
достига́ть\дости́гнуть	*to attain, achieve*
заслу́живать (impf.)	*to deserve*
каса́ться\косну́ться	*to touch, concern*
лиша́ть\лиши́ть	*to deprive* (sb. of sthg.)

* Note that the different aspects of this verb have different meanings.

лиша́ться\лиши́ться	*to lose, be deprived of*
приде́рживаться (no pf.)	*to adhere to, stick to*
сто́ить** (no pf.)	*to be worth*

** But this verb governs the accusative when it means *to cost*.

Examples:

держа́ться пра́вой стороны́ доро́ги
to keep to the right-hand side of the road
доби́ться своего́
to get one's own way
Во вре́мя войны́ они́ дости́гли заме́тного положе́ния.
During the war they [British men spying for the Soviets] *attained notable positions.* (Press)
Уже́ тогда́ мне показа́лось, что э́ти пи́сьма заслу́живают публика́ции.
Even at that time it seemed to me that these letters deserved to be published. (Press)
Э́то бре́мя так и́ли ина́че, ра́ньше или по́зже, но всё равно́ коснётся всех катего́рий населе́ния, а не то́лько автолюби́телей.
Sooner or later, one way or another, this burden will touch all categories of the population, not just motor enthusiasts. (Press)
Молчали́вый всегда́, он, ка́жется, вообще́ лиши́лся го́лоса в тот день.
Always taciturn, he seemed to have completely lost his voice that day. (Press)

Note especially the expression что каса́ется + genitive, *as far as ... is concerned*.

The verb слу́шаться\послу́шаться, *to obey*, may be followed by the genitive case or by the accusative, e.g. он слу́шался Ве́ры or он слу́шался Ве́ру, *he obeyed Vera*. The genitive might be felt to be more correct but a little old-fashioned. However, in most cases the object of this verb will be animate and, unless it is feminine singular, the distinction between accusative and genitive will therefore be lost, e.g. он слу́шается отца́, *he obeys his father*.

§3. Verbs which may govern either the genitive or the accusative

The following verbs may govern either the genitive or the accusative case, depending on the context:

ждать\подожда́ть	*to wait for, expect*
жела́ть\пожела́ть	*to wish, want*
иска́ть (various pf.)	*to look for, seek*
ожида́ть (no pf.)	*to expect*
проси́ть\попроси́ть	*to ask for*

тре́бовать\потре́бовать	*to require, need, demand*
хоте́ть\захоте́ть	*to want*

It is not always easy to explain why one case or the other is preferred after these verbs in a given context, but as a general rule one may say that the accusative should be used if the object of the verb is particularised or concrete, whilst the genitive should be used if the object is general or abstract. Examples:

Он ждёт по́езд, кото́рый отхо́дит в по́лдень.
He is waiting for the train which leaves at midday.
Он ждёт по́езда.
He is waiting for a train.
Ефре́мов ждал отве́та.
Efremov waited for an answer. (Press)
Я ищу́ кварти́ру.
I am looking for a flat.
Он и́щет рабо́ты.
He is looking for work.
Мы ожида́ем больши́х переме́н.
We are expecting great changes.
проси́ть ви́зу на въезд в Росси́ю
to ask for a Russian entry visa
проси́ть разреше́ния
to ask for permission
Про́сим полити́ческого убе́жища.
We are seeking political asylum. (Press)
Тре́буем аре́ста Лукья́нова.
We demand the arrest of Lukyanov. (Demonstrator's placard)

When the object of the verb is a person the accusative will normally be used (providing of course that the accusative form is distinct from the genitive, in other words that the noun is feminine singular or a masculine noun ending in -а or -я), e.g.

Он ждёт дя́дю.	*He is looking for his uncle.*
Он и́щет тётю.	*He is looking for his aunt.*

The genitive is not often used after жела́ть or хоте́ть in modern Russian, except in fixed expressions in which жела́ть is understood, e.g.

Всего́ до́брого!
All the best!
Прия́тного аппети́та!
Bon appétit!
Споко́йной но́чи!
Good night!

Счастли́вого пути́!
Bon voyage!
Мы жела́ем вам всего́ наилу́чшего, сча́стья в Но́вом году́.
We wish you all the very best, happiness in the New Year. (Press)

§4. Choice of case for the direct object of a negated verb

The genitive may also be used, in preference to the accusative, to express the direct object of a negated verb, e.g. in the statement я не обраща́ю внима́ния на его́ взгля́ды, *I don't pay attention to his opinions.* This is an area of Russian grammar in which it is impossible to give hard and fast rules, as practice seems to be variable and changing. No attempt is made here to offer a comprehensive theoretical explanation of the use of the genitive in negative constructions. However, some practical guidance on usage can be given (see §5 and §6 below).

It should be noted that there is no question of a genitive object being used if the negated verb is one which, when used affirmatively, governs the dative or instrumental case. Thus in the statement *I am not interested in music* the noun *music* would be rendered by an instrumental form (я не интересу́юсь му́зыкой) just as it would if the verb интересова́ться were not negated. It is only verbs which when affirmative govern the accusative case that may govern a direct object in the genitive when they are negated.

§5. Use of genitive direct object

The genitive either must be used, or tends to be preferred, in the following circumstances.

i. When the negation is intensive, e.g. if the negative verb is strengthened by some form of никако́й, or ни одного́\одно́й, or ни...ни, then the genitive is obligatory, e.g.

   Он ни одно́й кни́ги не брал из библиоте́ки.
   He did not borrow a single book from the library.
   Никаки́х реше́ний приня́ть не смогли́.
   They could not take any decisions at all. (Press)
   Же́нщины, роди́вшие э́тих дете́й, не могли́ получи́ть ни посо́бий за рожде́ние ребёнка, ни средств на его́ погребе́ние.
   The women who gave birth to these children could obtain neither any allowance for the birth of the child nor resources for its burial. (Press)

   See also 6.C. below on the last two examples.

ii. The genitive is used as a rule when the absence of something or any part of something is indicated. (See 19.5-6 above on the use of the genitive with similar effect after нет, etc.) The English translation in such contexts may well contain the word *any*. Examples from the press:

Мото́рных ло́док здесь ещё не приобрели́.
They have not yet acquired motor boats here.
Прокуро́р не нашёл юриди́ческих основа́ний для привлече́ния его́ к суду́.
The prosecutor found no grounds for bringing him to court.
Пра́вда, в э́том хо́ре протесту́ющих голосо́в неме́цкая речь не звуча́ла: не́мцы не устра́ивали демонстра́ции, не производи́ли самово́льного захва́та земе́ль и не соверша́ли ины́х эксце́ссов.
It is true that no German speech was to be heard in this chorus of protesting voices: the Germans did not arrange any demonstration, they did not carry out any unauthorised seizure of lands or commit any other excesses.

Note that in the last example the non-existence of the objects in the genitive case is reinforced by the use of negated imperfective verbs in the past tense; see 54.1 below on this use of aspect.

A genitive object is naturally to be expected after the verb име́ть when it is negated, because не име́ть inevitably expresses the lack of something. Examples from the media:

Челове́чество не име́ло о́пыта борьбы́ с радиа́цией тако́го ти́па.
Mankind has not had experience of fighting radiation of that type. (Press)
Да́же в Кузба́ссе мно́гие электроста́нции не име́ют доста́точного запа́са то́плива.
Even in the Kuzbass many power stations do not have a sufficient supply of fuel. (TV)

iii. The genitive is normal when the negated verb and its object together form a common expression, a set phraseological combination, such as не игра́ть ро́ли, *to play no role*; не обраща́ть\ обрати́ть внима́ния на что́-нибудь, *to pay no attention to sthg.*; не составля́ть ча́сти чего́-нибудь, *to constitute no part of sthg.* Examples from the press:

Реда́кция не пожале́ет сил для того́, что́бы оправда́ть ва́ши наде́жды.
The editorial board will spare no effort to warrant your hopes.
Норве́жская рабо́чая па́ртия, находя́щаяся в оппози́ции, не сложи́ла, одна́ко, ору́жия.
The Norwegian labour party, although it was in opposition, did not lay down arms.
Францу́зское прави́тельство не несёт отве́тственности за публика́ции в пре́ссе.
The French government is not responsible for what is published in the press.

iv. A genitive object is to be expected when the negated verb is one of the verbs of perception ви́деть, *to see*, or слы́шать, *to hear*. Examples:

Я не ви́дел маши́ны, кото́рая мча́лась по у́лице на по́лной ско́рости.
I did not see the car which was tearing down the street at top speed.
Я не слы́шал звонка́.
I didn't hear the bell [ring].

v. It seems usual for a genitive to be used when the form of the verb which is negated is a gerund or active participle. Examples from the press:

Администра́ция стара́ется уче́сть пожела́ния, не обостря́я отноше́ний ни с кем.
The administration is trying to take account of [people's] wishes, without exacerbating relations with anybody.
Вско́ре по́сле выступле́ния Ри́чарда Лу́гара пресс-секрета́рь Бе́лого до́ма М. Фитсуо́тер охарактеризова́л его́ как «не представля́ющее практи́ческой по́льзы в да́нное вре́мя».
Immediately after Richard Lugar's speech the White House spokesman Marlin Fitzwater described it as 'having no practical use at the present time'.

vi. The genitive is usual when the object of the negated verb is э́то, *this, that*. Examples from the press:

Я была́ уве́рена, что он подни́мется на трибу́ну и ска́жет, что снима́ет свою́ кандидату́ру. И порази́лась, что он э́того не сде́лал.
I was sure that he would get up on the platform and say that he was withdrawing his candidature. And I was struck that he did not do this.
Я спроси́л, что̀ он ду́мает о возмо́жности вы́бора в Ю́жной А́фрике чёрного президе́нта. «Во́семьдесят проце́нтов на́шего населе́ния, включа́я чёрных, я ду́маю, не хоте́ли бы э́того».
I asked him what he thought about the possibility of a black president being elected in South Africa. 'Eighty per cent of our population, including the blacks, I think, would not want that'.

It may happen that more than one of the above considerations applies and that it is therefore difficult to define the overriding criterion for using the genitive in the given context. Examples from the press:

Причи́ны, по кото́рой лю́ди в тюрьме́, не име́ют значе́ния.
The reasons why people are in prison are of no significance.
(negated verb име́ть and set expression име́ть значе́ние)

Я не слы́шал объясне́ния того́, почему́ мы должны́ так спеши́ть.
I haven't heard any explanation as to why we should hurry so.
(negated verb слы́шать and absence of explanation)

§6. Use of the accusative after a negated verb

A. On the other hand the accusative must be used in the following circumstances:

i. when there is a double negative or when the negative occurs in a combination such as чуть не, *almost*, or едва́ не, *barely*, i.e. when the basic idea is not negative but affirmative, e.g.

Он не мог не ви́деть соба́ку.
He could not help seeing the dog.
Он чуть не разби́л ва́зу.
He almost broke the vase.
Как тут не вспо́мнить ста́рое пра́вило из фи́зики: при нагрева́нии те́ло расширя́ется, а при хо́лоде - сжима́ется.
How can one not recall [i.e. *one definitely will recall*] *the old rule of physics: a body expands when it warms up and contracts when it cools down.* (Press)

ii. when the object of the negated verb is qualified by an instrumental predicate, e.g.

Я не нахожу́ францу́зский язы́к тру́дным.
I do not find French difficult.
Он не счита́ет э́тот результа́т удовлетвори́тельным.
He does not consider this outcome satisfactory.

iii. when it is not the verb but some part of speech other than the verb that is being negated, e.g.

Не он э́то сде́лал.
It was not he who did this.
Она́ купи́ла не газе́ту а журна́л.
It was a magazine, not a paper, that she bought.
Они́ не то́лько сообщи́ли ма́ссу ва́жных све́дений...
They not only communicated a mass of important information... (Press)

B. The accusative is preferred, provided that none of the rules given in §5 above applies, in the following circumstances:

i. when the object of the negated verb is a place or specific concrete object. Examples from the press:

Э́ти де́ньги Нью-Йорк не спасу́т.
This money will not save New York.
Миллио́ны радиослу́шателей не выключа́ли радиоприёмники в тече́ние двух неде́ль.
Millions of radio listeners did not turn off their radios for a fortnight.

ii. when the object is a feminine singular noun referring to a person, e.g.

Я не зна́ю Ири́ну в лицо́
I don't know Irina by sight

C. The accusative is more common than the genitive when the negated verb is an auxiliary verb rather than the verb which governs the direct object, e.g. он не мог поня́ть план, *he could not understand the plan*, where the negated verb is the auxiliary мочь and the verb governing the object is the infinitive поня́ть. Examples from the press:

Не ста́ну приводи́ть конкре́тные аргуме́нты.
I shall not adduce any concrete arguments.
А представи́тели дина́мовских организа́ций во́время не разобрали́сь в ситуа́ции, не смогли́ защити́ть его́ интере́сы.
But representatives of Dynamo [a football team] *did not see what was going on in time, and they were not able to defend his interests.*

However, some of the criteria listed in §5 above may compel the use of a genitive even in these circumstances, e.g.

Министе́рство с бу́дущего го́да не бу́дет уже́ име́ть централизо́ванных фо́ндов.
From next year the ministry will no longer have any centralised funds. (Press; absence of sthg. indicated by negated verb име́ть)

See also the second and third examples in §5.i above, where intensive negation affects the object despite the presence of the auxiliary verb.

Exercises

A. *Put the words in brackets in the case (accusative or genitive) that is required by the context or seems preferable in it. Give a reason for your choice:* (1) Забасто́вщики тре́буют (повыше́ние) зарпла́ты, (улучше́ние) усло́вий труда́. (2) Национа́льные меньши́нства боя́тся (гражда́нская война́). (3) Делега́ция не получи́ла ни (официа́льное приглаше́ние) из США, ни (въездны́е ви́зы) для полови́ны свои́х чле́нов. (4) Вы мно́го чита́ете. Всё-таки не (всё) зна́ете. (5) Сочине́ния таки́х второстепе́нных писа́телей не произво́дят (глубо́кое впечатле́ние). (6) Три́дцать миллио́нов мужчи́н и миллио́ны же́нщин в Евро́пе умру́т в расцве́те жи́зни в ближа́йшие три́дцать лет в результа́те куре́ния, е́сли не приня́ть (сро́чные ме́ры). (7) Я не люблю́ (Татья́на). (8) (Тру́дности) мо́жно избежа́ть, е́сли име́ть перево́дчика. (9) Ме́ры, при́нятые ООН, ка́жутся поле́зными, но они не спасу́т (на́ша плане́та) от экологи́ческой катастро́фы. (10) Прави́тельство Шри-Ла́нки тре́бует (ухо́д) инди́йских во́йск. (11) Я не ви́дел (э́тот бале́т). (12) Безрабо́тица дости́гла (реко́рдный у́ровень). (13) Она́ не нахо́дит (геогра́фия) интере́сным предме́том. (14) Мно́гие не счита́ют (брита́нская систе́ма) голосова́ния справедли́вой. (15) Экономи́ческий кри́зис не игра́л (значи́тельная роль) на вы́борах. (16) Я бы (э́то) не сказа́л. (17) Совреме́нный ры́нок тре́бует (ги́бкое реаги́рование) на спрос. (18) Исчезнове́ние пятачко́в не име́ет (никако́е отноше́ние) к фина́нсовым пробле́мам моско́вского метрополите́на. (19) Мы не получи́ли (отве́т) на жа́лобу. (20) Э́то удруча́ющая кни́га, не де́лающая (честь) своему́ а́втору. (21) Она́ вошла́ в ва́нную, не сняв (шля́па). (22) На́ша систе́ма здравоохране́ния не име́ет (ана́лог) в ми́ре. (23) Ряд ви́дных америка́нских демокра́тов вы́сказался за то, что́бы администра́ция не предпринима́ла (каки́е-либо вое́нные а́кции) без согла́сия конгре́сса. (24) По́езд отхо́дит в по́лночь, а мы не зна́ли (э́то). (25) Она́ не могла́ не заме́тить его́ (гру́стное выраже́ние).

B. *Translate into Russian:* (1) He was waiting for the bus which goes to London. (2) He lost his father when he was ten.* (3) Traffic keeps to the left-hand side of the road in Britain. (4) He was afraid of his neighbour's dog. (5) I tried to avoid a meeting with him.** (6) As for your handwriting, it's illegible. (7) How is one to avoid accidents on the roads? (8) Writers do not often discuss such questions. (9) We await letters from our readers with stories about their† own idols. (10) I did not see a single car. (11) I almost dropped the plate. (12) His latest novel does not make any impression on me. (13) I have not read this. (14) We do not have the resources for this. (15) The German army did not take Leningrad. (16) We did not try to solve the problem. (17) I could not help breaking the glass. (18) Not knowing his address I cannot write to him. (19) I do not find your explanation very convincing. (20) He not only broke the window, he upset a vase as well. (21) The navy did not play an important role in the war. (22) How can one not condemn such conduct? (23) They do not sell clothes here. (24) Demonstrators were demanding the withdrawal of troops from Afghanistan. (25) Do the students reach a high standard?

* See 23.3 on expression of age.

** с ним

† об их

LESSON 21

THE PREPOSITIONS ИЗ, ОТ, С, У

A very large number of prepositions may take the genitive case. This lesson deals with four of the most common of them, из, от, с, and у. The following lesson deals with those prepositions governing the genitive which are encountered less frequently or the use of which is more straightforward.

§1. Из with the genitive case

The basic meaning of из (or before some words изо; this preposition may be used only with the genitive case) is *out of*. This preposition will often be combined with a verb bearing the prefix вы-, which carries the same meaning (see 46.7 below). Examples:

выходи́ть\вы́йти из ко́мнаты	*to go out of/leave the room*
вынима́ть\вы́нуть из карма́на	*to take out of one's pocket*

As well as indicating movement out of, из may also denote that something or someone is of a particular origin, or that an object is made of or consists of something, or is one out of a larger number. Examples:

Хрущёв был из крестья́нской семьи́.
Khrushchev was from a peasant family.
Я получи́ла письмо́ из Воро́нежа.
I received a letter from Voronezh.
пла́тье из шёлка
a silk dress
обе́д из пяти́ блюд
a five-course dinner
оди́н из са́мых тала́нтливых актёров
one of the most talented actors

It may also indicate that some action results from a certain experience or feeling, e.g.

Из пра́ктики многоле́тней рабо́ты зна́ю, что...
From the practical experience of many years of work I know that... (Press)
Она́ э́то сде́лала из любви́ к му́жу.
She did this out of love for her husband.

Note the following verbs which may be followed by из:

состоя́ть из — *to consist of*
стреля́ть из — *to fire (a weapon)*

Examples:

Одна́ из трёх произво́дственных смен на заво́де во Флори́де бу́дет целико́м состоя́ть из сове́тских колле́г.
One of the three production shifts at the Florida plant will consist entirely of Soviet colleagues. (Press)
стреля́ть из пистоле́та
to fire a pistol
стреля́ть из пу́шек по воробья́м
to take a sledgehammer to crack a walnut (lit. *to fire cannons at sparrows*)

§2. От with the genitive case
The preposition от (or before some words ото), is also used only with the genitive case. It has the basic meaning *away from*, and will often be combined with a verb bearing the prefix от-, which carries the same meaning (see 46.12 below). Examples:

По́езд отхо́дит от платфо́рмы.
The train is moving away from the platform.
Кора́бль отплыва́ет от бе́рега.
The ship is sailing away from the shore.

As well as indicating movement away from, от may also denote distance from, e.g.

на расстоя́нии пяти́ киломе́тров от це́нтра го́рода
at a distance of five kilometres from the town centre
в пяти́ мину́тах ходьбы́ от вокза́ла
five minutes' walk from the station

It may also be used to indicate the source or date of origin of something, the purpose for which something is intended, or that something may be used to counter something else. Examples:

узнава́ть/узна́ть от кого́-нибудь
to find out from someone
Год наза́д я получи́л от неё пе́рвое письмо́.
A year ago I received the first letter from her. (Press)
ва́ше письмо́ от пе́рвого ма́рта
your letter of the 1st of March
ключ от две́ри
the door key

пу́говица от руба́шки
a shirt button

страхова́ние от огня́
fire insurance
миксту́ра от ка́шля
cough mixture
таблéтки от головно́й бо́ли
headache tablets

Like из, от may also indicate that something is prompted by a certain cause. Examples from the press:

База́ры ло́пались от изоби́лия овощéй и фру́ктов.
The markets were bursting with an abundance of vegetables and fruit.
Ужé здесь я узна́л, что от э́той болéзни мо́жно умерéть.
It was here that I learnt that one might die of this disease.

It may also be used when the emotional state that causes some action is being described, e.g.

И я кипéла от негодова́ния.
And I was seething with indignation. (Press)
Он побледнéл от стра́ха.
He turned pale with fear.
Ма́льчик запры́гал от ра́дости.
The boy began jumping with joy. (Press)

Note the following expressions which incorporate от:

бли́зко от	*near to*
далеко́ от	*far from*
недалеко́ от	*not far from*
врéмя от врéмени	*from time to time*
от всей души́	*with all one's heart*
от и́мени кого́-нибудь	*on behalf of sb.*

The following verbs may be followed by от:

отка́зываться\отказа́ться от	*to refuse, decline, turn down*
отлича́ться\отличи́ться от	*to differ from*
страда́ть от	*to suffer from**

Examples:

Кутéпов отказа́лся от услу́г шофёра и пошёл пешко́м.
Kutepov refused the services of a chauffeur and set off on foot. (Press)

Их взгля́ды иногда́ отлича́лись от на́ших, коммунисти́ческих взгля́дов.
Their views sometimes differed from our communist views. (Press)
Она́ страда́ет от зубно́й бо́ли.
She is suffering from toothache.

* See also 27.4.

§3. C with the genitive case
The preposition с (or before some words со) with the genitive case has the basic meaning of *off* the surface of something, *down from*. Note especially that с will translate *away from* or *out of* when the following noun is one of those nouns that require на rather than в to translate *in* or *at* with the prepositional case (see 15.8-10 above). In the sense of *off* с will often be combined with a verb bearing the prefix с-, which carries the same meaning (see also 47.6.i below).

сходи́ть\сойти́ с горы́
to come down from the mountain
С рабо́ты придёшь ве́чером.
You'll come home from work in the evening. (Press)
снима́ть\снять со стола́
to take off the table
вид с ба́шни
the view from the tower
пря́мо со сце́ны
straight off the stage

С may also mean *since* (in a temporal sense), e.g.

с нача́ла января́ *since the beginning of January*

It may mean *from* (in the sense of *as a result of*) or *with* (in the sense of *on the basis of*), e.g.

умира́ть\умере́ть с го́лоду*
to die of hunger, starve to death
со стыда́
from shame
С разреше́ния а́втора я публику́ю не́которые из э́тих пи́сем.
With the permission of the author I publish some of these letters. (Press)

* See 22.12 on this form.

It is also synonymous with от as a preposition describing the emotional state that causes some action (see §2 above), e.g. ма́льчик запры́гал с ра́дости, *the boy began jumping for joy.* However, с is a little more colloquial than от in this sense.

Note the following expressions which incorporate с with the genitive:

с одно́й стороны́	*on the one hand*
с друго́й стороны́	*on the other hand*
с како́й ста́ти?	*to what purpose?*
с пе́рвого взгля́да	*at first sight*
с тех пор, как	*since* (conjunction)
с то́чки зре́ния кого́-нибудь	*from the point of view of sb.*

Note also the use of с with the genitive after the following verbs:

начина́ть(ся)\нача́ть(ся) с чего́-нибудь	*to begin with sthg.*
сбива́ть\сбить спесь с кого́-нибудь	*to take sb. down a peg*

§4. У with the genitive case

The preposition у may be used only with the genitive case. It means *by* in the sense of *near*, or *at* in the sense of the French *chez*.

Она́ стоя́ла у окна́.
She was standing by the window.
дом у мо́ря
a house by the sea
Мы поу́жинаем у вас.
We shall have supper at your place.
Он ещё живёт у роди́телей.
He still lives with his parents.
У нас не ку́рят.
No smoking here (lit. *people do not smoke at our place*; public notice).

It is also used with nouns and personal pronouns to indicate possession and in this sense helps to render the English verb *to have*, e.g.

У нас есть но́вая маши́на.
We've got a new car.
У них нет маши́ны.
They haven't got a car.
У моего́ бра́та была́ соба́ка.
My brother had a dog.
У меня́ к вам одна́ про́сьба.
I've got a request to make of you.

Remember that Russian also has the verb име́ть, *to have*, which is used to denote possession of abstract things rather than concrete objects, e.g. имéть возмóжность, *to have an opportunity*; имéть значéние, *to have significance*; имéть прáво, *to have a right*, etc.

Curiously, у may also have an almost opposite meaning of *from* after verbs denoting dispossession or taking away. Thus:

занимáть\занять дéньги у когó-нибудь
to borrow money from sb.
покупáть\купить цветы у бáбушки
to buy flowers from an old lady
У нас óтняли всё — вéру, надéжду, свобóду.
They have taken everything away from us, faith, hope, freedom. (Press)

Note the use of у in expressions indicating pain or discomfort:

У меня болит зуб.
I've got tooth-ache.
У негó болит головá.
He's got a headache.
У неё болит гóрло.
She's got a sore throat.
У отцá болит рукá.
[My] father's arm hurts.

The expression быть у влáсти means *to be in power*, e.g. консервативное правительство у влáсти, *a Conservative government is in power.*

Exercises

A. *Complete the following sentences by choosing the appropriate preposition (из, от, с or у) and by putting the words in brackets in the correct form:* (1) Дом был пострóен ... (крáсный кирпич). (2) Он снимáет картину ... (стенá). (3) Ромáны Толстóго во мнóгом отличáются ... (ромáны) Достоéвского. (4) ... (что) начинáется лéкция? (5) Кáждый день он выхóдит ... (общежитие) в дéсять часóв утрá. (6) Сегóдня вéчером мы ýжинаем ... (бáбушка). (7) Он зáнял дéсять фýнтов ... (сестрá). (8) Я получил открытку ... (Париж). (9) Онá это сказáла ... (зáвисть). (10) Мы не могли оторвáть егó ... (рабóта). (11) ... (кто) вы узнáли это? (12) Онá остáвила машину ... (вокзáл). (13) Онá застраховáла свой дом ... (огóнь). (14) Я отвечáю на Вáше письмó ... (вторóе) áвгуста. (15) Я знáю ... (дóлгий óпыт), что такие люди никогдá не извиняются за свои ошибки. (16) Я получил телегрáмму ... (брат). (17) Он сошёл ... (трибýна). (18) Пýговица отлетéла ... (мой пиджáк). (19) Я считáю Тютчева одним ... (сáмые лýчшие рýсские поэты). (20) Он принимáет таблéтки ... (диспепсия). (21) Миллиóны людéй умирáют ... (гóлод). (22) Я это сдéлал ... (уважéние) к вам. (23)

Музе́й нахо́дится далеко́ ... (це́нтр). (24) Я зна́ю его ... (де́тство). (25) Диктату́ра отнима́ет ... (наро́д) его челове́ческое досто́инство. (26) ... (муж) боли́т голова́. (27) Ребёнок дрожа́л ... (испу́г). (28) Солда́т стреля́л ... (пулемёт). (29) Она́ рабо́тает в столи́це ... (коне́ц) про́шлого го́да. (30) ... (ежеви́ка) ва́рят варе́нье, джёмы, компо́ты, мармела́д.

B. *Translate into Russian:* (1) Out of the box; (2) away from the centre; (3) from the market; (4) from the north; (5) at the Ivanovs' place; (6) with my agreement; (7) not far from the city; (8) on behalf of the whole group; (9) off the table; (10) by the door; (11) I haven't got any time. (12) She wanted to borrow a ladder from her neighbour. (13) I saw my brother near the station. (14) I want to thank you with all my heart. (15) At first sight it seems that you were right. (16) She was crying with joy. (17) I know from experience that this is right. (18) People are dying of hunger in Ethiopia. (19) He's got a black cat. (20) He found out from the porter that the train was leaving.

LESSON 22

OTHER PREPOSITIONS WITH THE GENITIVE CASE

All prepositions dealt with in this lesson invariably govern the genitive case.

§1. Без
The preposition без means *without*, e.g.

без оши́бок
without mistakes
Демокра́тия без поря́дка — э́то ана́рхия.
Democracy without order is anarchy. (Press)

Note the use of this preposition in expressions of time with the meaning *to* the hour, and *at* a time *to* the hour:

без пяти́ (мину́т) де́сять	*five to ten/at five to ten*
без че́тверти два (часа́)	*a quarter to two/at a quarter to two*

See also 40.2.iv below on expressions of time.

§2. Вне
The preposition вне means *outside*, e.g.

вне го́рода	*outside the town*
вне зако́на	*outside the law*

Note the expression вне о́череди, *out of turn* (lit. *outside the queue*).

Note also that the English preposition *outside* will often be translated by a Russian preposition other than вне, which has the basic function of indicating that something is outside as opposed to inside. In a statement such as *the car was outside the house*, for example, *outside* might be best translated by о́коло or пе́ред: маши́на стоя́ла о́коло до́ма, or маши́на стоя́ла пе́ред до́мом.

Outside used as an adverb in the sense of *not indoors* might be translated by на у́лице, *in the street*; на дворе́, *in the courtyard*; or на откры́том во́здухе, *in the open air*, depending on the context.

§3. Внутри́ and внутрь

The prepositions внутри́ and внутрь, both of which may be used only with the genitive case, mean *inside*, but they are not interchangeable. Внутри́ is itself a form in the prepositional case which indicates the position in which something is situated, whilst внутрь, which is itself accusative in form, indicates the direction in which movement is taking place, e.g.

> Внутри́ корабля́ — две торпе́ды с я́дерными боеголо́вками.
> *Inside the ship are two torpedoes with nuclear warheads.* (Press)
> Войска́ бы́стро продви́нулись внутрь страны́.
> *The troops quickly moved inland.*

§4 Для

The preposition для means *for the benefit of* or *for the purpose of*. Examples from the press:

> Мы создаём телеви́дение и ра́дио не для Верхо́вного Сове́та и́ли руково́дства па́ртии, а для зри́телей и слу́шателей.
> *We are creating a television and radio not for the Supreme Soviet and the leadership of the party but for viewers and listeners.*
> Для я́сности на́до заме́тить, что...
> *For clarity it must be noted that...*

A number of adjectives are commonly followed by для:

вре́дный для	*harmful for, detrimental / injurious to*
поле́зный для	*useful for, beneficial to*
типи́чный для	*typical of*
характе́рный для	*characteristic of*

Note though that для is not nearly so widely used in Russian as *for* is in English, because its meaning is relatively restricted. For translation of *for* in other contexts see the sections on за + accusative (18.1.ii and vii above), and на + accusative (17.4.iii and iv above).

§5. До

The preposition до has the basic temporal meanings of *before* and *until*, and the basic spatial meaning of *up to* or *as far as*. In the latter meaning до will often be combined with a verb bearing the prefix до-, which carries the same meaning (see also 46.8 below). Thus:

> Э́то произошло́ до войны́.
> *This happened before the war.*
> до глубо́кой о́сени
> *until well into autumn*

До оконча́ния парла́ментских кани́кул остаётся ме́сяц.
A month remains to the end of the parliamentary recess. (Press)
Он дое́хал до Владивосто́ка.
He went as far as Vladivostok.

Note the following expressions incorporating до:

до мо́зга косте́й	*to the marrow, to the core*
до на́шей э́ры	*before Christ, BC* (lit. *before our era*)
до свида́ния	*good-bye* (lit. *until the [next] meeting*)
до сих пор	*until now, hitherto*
до тех пор, как	*until* (conjunction)
до того́, как	*before* (conjunction)
до того́, что	*to such a point that*
изменя́ться\измени́ться до неузнава́емости	*to change beyond recognition*
охо́тник до чего́-нибудь	*a lover of sthg.*

See also 26.8 below on the use of пе́ред in a temporal sense.

§6. Из-за

The preposition из-за means *out from behind* or *because of* when the cause of something is looked on unfavourably, e.g.

встава́ть\встать из-за стола́
to get up from the table
В результа́те взры́ва в ша́хте о́коло ста шахтёров оказа́лись погребёнными на глубине́ пятьсо́т ме́тров под землёй. Взрыв произошёл из-за возгора́ния мета́на.
As a result of an explosion in a mine about a hundred miners were buried at a depth of 500 metres under ground. The explosion took place because methane ignited. (Press)
На бензоколо́нках огро́мные о́череди, заде́рживаются самолёты, как нам говоря́т, из-за нехва́тки горю́чего.
There are huge queues at the petrol pumps, planes are being delayed, because of lack of fuel they tell us. (Press)

§7. Из-под

The preposition из-под means *out from under* and may also indicate the purpose for which an object is designed, e.g.

Мы выбива́ем из-под себя́ стул, на кото́ром сиди́м.
We are knocking the chair on which we are sitting out from under ourselves. (Press)
торго́вля из-под прила́вка
under-the-counter trade

ба́нка из-под варе́нья
a jam-jar

§8. Около
The preposition о́коло means *near* or *by*, and also *around, about* or *approximately*, e.g.

Он сиде́л о́коло своего́ дру́га.	*He was sitting by his friend.*
о́коло полу́ночи	*around midnight*
о́коло миллио́на	*about a million*

In the last example it would have been possible to use one of the adverbs приблизи́тельно, *approximately*, or приме́рно, *roughly*, after which the nominative form of the number, миллио́н, should be used (see also 41.1 below on approximation).

§9. Про́тив
The preposition про́тив means *against*, e.g.

про́тив тече́ния
against the current
Про́тив меня́ выступа́ла да́же ме́стная це́рковь.
Even the local church came out against me. (Press)
Как свиде́тельствует после́дний опро́с обще́ственного мне́ния, про́тив неме́цкого еди́нства выступа́ют лишь четы́ре проце́нта населе́ния ГДР.
As the latest opinion poll attests, only four per cent of the population of East Germany is against German unification. (Press)

Note also the following expressions incorporating про́тив:

име́ть что́-нибудь про́тив чего́-нибудь
to have sthg. against sthg.
про́тив всех ожида́ний
contrary to all expectations
за и про́тив
for and against, pro and contra

§10. Среди́
The preposition среди́ means *among, amid*. Examples from the press:

Высо́к проце́нт neза́нятых среди́ молодёжи.
The percentage of unemployed among the young is high.
Среди́ бе́женцев — старики́, же́нщины и де́ти.
Among the refugees are old men, women and children.

Note the expression среди́ (or средь) бе́ла дня, *in broad daylight*, e.g. он исчéз в цéнтре Парйжа средь бéла дня, *he disappeared in the centre of Paris in broad daylight* (Press).

Care should be taken to distinguish between средй and мéжду (on which see 26.6 below).

§11. Miscellaneous prepositions governing the genitive case

Many other prepositions govern the genitive case, but require little comment. The following list is not exhaustive.

ввидý	*in view of*
вдоль	*along the edge of* (e.g. вдóль бéрега, *along the bank*)
взамéн	*in exchange for*
вмéсто	*instead of* (not to be confused with вмéсте, *together*)
вóзле	*by, near*
вокрýг	*round* (e.g. путешéствие вокрýг свéта, *journey round the world*)
впередй	*in front of*
вслéдствие	*owing to, because of, as a result of* (more official in tone than из-за)
крóме	*except, apart from, besides* (note крóме тогó, *furthermore*)
мймо	*past* (e.g. проходйть\пройтй мймо дóма, *to go past the house*)
напрóтив	*opposite*
насчёт	*about, regarding*
относйтельно	*concerning* (official or bookish)
по пóводу	*apropos of*
позадй	*behind*
помймо	*besides, apart from* (e.g. помймо всегó прóчего, *apart from everything else*)
пóсле	*after*
посредй	*in the middle of*
посрéдством	*by means of*
путём	*by means of, by dint of*
рáди	*for the sake of* (e.g. рáди бóга, *for God's sake*)
сверх	*over and above* (e.g. сверх плáна, *over and above the plan*)
свыше	*more than* (used with numerals, e.g. свыше ста, *more than 100*)
сзáди	*from behind*

§12. Prepositional phrases with genitive in -у

In some set phrases which incorporate one of the prepositions listed above masculine nouns have a genitive form in -у (i.e. the same as that of the obsolescent partitive forms described in 19.4 above), e.g.

говори́ть без у́молку
to talk incessantly
упуска́ть\упусти́ть что́-нибудь и́з виду
to overlook sthg.
выходи́ть\вы́йти и́з дому
to leave the house (из до́ма is also possible)
выходи́ть\вы́йти и́з лесу
to leave the wood (из ле́са is also possible)
с гла́зу на глаз
cheek-by-jowl, eyeball-to-eyeball
сбива́ть\сбить кого́-нибудь с то́лку
to confuse sb.

Exercises

A. *Complete the following sentences by choosing a preposition from the following list (без, вдоль, вме́сто, вокру́г, для, до, из-за, из-под, кро́ме, ми́мо, по́сле, про́тив, ра́ди, свы́ше, среди́) and by putting the words in brackets in the correct form. Use each preposition only once:* (1) ... (спекта́кль) все зри́тели разошли́сь по дома́м. (2) Он перевёл весь текст на ру́сский язы́к ... (оши́бка). (3) Я заболе́л, не могу́ вы́йти. Вот мой биле́т. Иди́ ... (я).* (4) Когда́ я проходи́л ... (ваш дом), я заме́тил но́вую маши́ну у подъе́зда. (5) Ко́шка вы́лезла ... (посте́ль). (6) Беспоря́дки, кото́рые вспы́хнули в дере́вне, дошли́ ... (столи́ца). (7) Я купи́л но́вые пла́тья ... (свой до́чери). (8) ... (забасто́вка) поте́ряно две́сти рабо́чих дней. (9) Он никому́ не доверя́ет ... (жена́). (10) Лейбори́стская па́ртия выступа́ет ... (приватиза́ция) желе́зных доро́г. (11) Земля́ враща́ется ... (со́лнце). (12) ... (и́згородь) растёт ряд тюльпа́нов. (13) Я э́то сде́лал ... (на́ша дру́жба). (14) ... (заключённые)† вся́кого ро́да престу́пники - во́ры, взло́мщики, уби́йцы, хулига́ны, террори́сты. (15) Населе́ние Ми́нска ... (миллио́н), мо́жет быть да́же полтора́ миллио́на.

* See 34.1 for declension of personal pronouns.
† Declined like an adjective.

B. *Translate into Russian:* (1) More than a thousand; (2) a church typical of Russian architecture; (3) after lunch; (4) for the sake of the family; (5) instead of an apology; (6) in view of the conditions; (7) a milk-bottle; (8) before the revolution; (9) without doubt; (10) as far as the station; (11) a beer-barrel; (12) He had something against my plan. (13) They have changed beyond recognition. (14) Quite apart from everything else he has lost the door key. (15) Because of the bad weather we didn't get out of the car. (16) He killed her in broad daylight. (17) I walked past the shop. (18) We decided to meet opposite the church. (19) She was standing in the middle of the square. (20) The plane did not take off on time owing to the storm.

LESSON 23

USE OF THE DATIVE CASE

§1. Use of the dative to express indirect object

The fundamental use of the dative case without a preposition is to express the indirect object of a verb, i.e. the person or thing to which something is given or done, or which is indirectly affected by an action, e.g.

> Почтальо́н даёт ему́ письмо́.
> *The postman is giving him a letter.*
> Преподава́тель обеща́л студе́нтам, что...
> *The teacher promised the students that...*
> Он заплати́л официа́нту.
> *He paid the waiter.*
> Она́ сказа́ла му́жу, что...
> *She told her husband that...*
> Оте́ц подари́л сы́ну футбо́льный мяч на рождество́.
> *The father gave his son a football for Christmas.*
> Он купи́л дру́гу па́чку сигаре́т.
> *He bought his friend a packet of cigarettes.*
> Портно́й сшил мне но́вый костю́м.
> *The tailor made me a new suit.*
> Он пожа́л е́й ру́ку.
> *He shook her hand.*

§2. Use of себе́

Note the use of this reflexive pronoun in the dative case in phrases describing injury to oneself or action on part of oneself, e.g.

лома́ть\слома́ть себе́ ру́ку	*to break one's arm*
ре́зать\поре́зать себе́ па́лец	*to cut one's finger*
потира́ть\потере́ть себе́ лоб	*to wipe one's brow*

§3. Expression of age

The dative case is also used to express a subject's age. The invariable forms бы́ло and бу́дет are used to convey past and future meaning respectively (see also 42.1 below). Examples:

> Ста́ршему её сы́ну, Ю́рию, — два́дцать семь лет. Мла́дшему, Андре́ю, — пятна́дцать лет.
> *Her eldest son, Yury, is 27. Her youngest, Andrey, is 15.* (Press)

Не зна́ю, ско́лько вам лет, а мне уже́ дово́льно мно́го, со́рок пять.
I don't know how old you are, but I am already getting on, I am forty-five. (Press)
Ему́ бы́ло пять лет.
He was five.
В а́вгусте мне бу́дет три́дцать лет.
In August I'll be thirty.

§4. Мо́жно, на́до, ну́жно, нельзя́

There are several very common impersonal expressions which combine with a noun or pronoun in the dative case, notably:

мо́жно	*it is possible to, one can*
на́до	*it is necessary to, one must*
ну́жно	*it is necessary to, one must*
нельзя́	*it is impossible to, one cannot, one must not*

There is not felt to be any difference in meaning between на́до and ну́жно.

All these expressions are followed by a verb in the infinitive (see 54.2 below on use of aspect after нельзя́). If past meaning is intended they are followed by the neuter form бы́ло, and if future meaning is intended they are followed by the third-person singular form бу́дет, e.g.

Нам мо́жно бу́дет посмотре́ть э́тот фильм сего́дня?
Shall we be able to watch this film today?
Ему́ на́до бы́ло вы́йти.
He had to go out.
Нам ну́жно сде́лать пра́вильный вы́бор.
We must make the right choice.
Вам нельзя́ кури́ть в аудито́рии.
You can't smoke in the auditorium.

Note the expression так ему́ и на́до, *it serves him right.*

All these impersonal expressions are very often used without any subject, e.g.

Здесь мо́жно кури́ть.
One can smoke here.
Нельзя́ входи́ть в пальто́.
One mustn't go in with one's coat on.

The form должно́ is not used in the sense of *one must* in the modern language. However, the masculine, feminine, neuter and plural forms до́лжен, должна́, должно́, and должны́ respectively may be used with a nominative subject to mean *must*, and if the phrase is in the past or future tense then the verb must agree in person and gender with this nominative subject, e.g.

Рабо́чий до́лжен зна́ть своё ме́сто.
The worker must know his place. (Press)
Она́ должна́ была́ вы́йти.
She had to go out.
Мы должны́ знать всё.
We must know everything.

The expression должно́ быть is used parenthetically to mean *must* in the sense *it must be the case that*, e.g.

Он, должно́ быть, уже́ ушёл.
He must have already gone away.
Она́, должно́ быть, о́чень умна́.
She must be very intelligent.

§5. Other impersonal expressions

A number of other impersonal expressions are used in the same way as мо́жно with a dative subject:

жаль	*to be sorry for, to be sorry to*
лень	*to be too lazy to*
пора́	*to be time to*
суждено́	*to be destined to*

Examples:

Мне жаль э́тих люде́й.
I am sorry for these people. (Press)
Ему́ жаль бы́ло перейти́ на другу́ю рабо́ту.
He was sorry to change to another job.
Ей лень бы́ло идти́.
She couldn't be bothered to go.
Ско́ро тебе́ пора́ бу́дет ложи́ться спать.
It will soon be time for you to go to bed.
Кому́-то бы́ло суждено́ найти́ приста́нище на гре́ческой земле́.
Some were destined to find refuge on Greek land. (Press)

As far as word order is concerned, бы́ло and бу́дет are more frequently found before жаль etc. than they are before мо́жно etc.

§6. Impersonal expressions formed with adjectives

It is also possible to form impersonal expressions using a dative subject with the neuter short form of many adjectives. The word order is more flexible. Examples:

Нам о́чень ве́село бы́ло.
We had a very good time\We enjoyed ourselves very much.
Нам гру́стно бы́ло узна́ть, что...
We were sad to hear that...
Тебе́ не ду́шно?
It's not too stuffy for you?
Вам бу́дет жа́рко там.
You'll be (too) hot there.
Мне пло́хо.
I don't feel well.
Мне всегда́ прия́тно говори́ть с ва́ми.
I always enjoy talking to you.
Де́тям ску́чно сиде́ть до́ма.
Children are bored sitting at home.
Мне бы́ло сты́дно.
I was ashamed.
Ребёнку бу́дет тепло́ в тако́й оде́жде.
The child will be (too) warm in those clothes.
Тебе́ хо́лодно?
Are you cold?

§7. Use of dative with third-person verb forms

A number of Russian verbs may be used in a third-person form together with a noun or pronoun (which in English would normally stand as the subject of the clause) in the dative case, e.g.

каза́ться\показа́ться	*to seem to*
надоеда́ть\надое́сть	*to make tired, sicken, bore*
недостава́ть\недоста́ть	*to be insufficient*
нра́виться\понра́виться	*to be pleasing to* (used in translation of *to like*)
посчастли́виться (pf.)	*to have the good fortune to*
приходи́ться\прийти́сь	*to have to*
сле́довать (no pf. in this sense)	*ought, should*
удава́ться\уда́ться	*to succeed*

Examples:

мне ка́жется, что...
I think [lit. *it seems to me*] *that...*
Лю́дям надое́ли наси́лие и неусту́пчивость.
People are tired of force and unwillingness to compromise. (Press)
Тебе́ недостаёт о́пыта.
You haven't got enough experience (see also 19.6 above).

Нáшему читáтелю И.В.Пахóмову из Краснодáрского крáя не понрáвилась публикáция А.Крушúнского о «прáжской веснé».
Our reader I.V.Pakhomov from Krasnodar Region did not like A.Krushinsky's piece about the 'Prague spring' [of 1968]. (Press)
Э́тот óпыт вам пригодúтся.
This experience will come in useful to you.
Мне пришлóсь уйтú с рабóты, так как ребёнок всё врéмя болéл.
I had to leave work, since the child was ill all the time. (Press)
Вам слéдовало бы сказáть мне э́то вчерá.
You ought to have told me that yesterday.
Мне посчастлúвилось найтú хорóшую гостúницу.
I was lucky enough to find a good hotel.
Им удалóсь побывáть и в посóльстве.
They succeeded in spending a bit of time in the embassy as well. (Press)

§8. Use of the dative after the adjective рад, рáда, рáды *(glad)*

This adjective, which may only be used predicatively and which exists only in a short form, is followed by a noun or pronoun in the dative, e.g.

Я рад слýчаю вы́ступить пéред вáми.
I am glad of the chance to address you.
Онá былá рáда моемý счáстью.
She was glad of my good fortune.

§9. Use of нéчего, нéкого, etc.

The dative case is also used with a number of negative expressions which mean *to have nothing to* or *there is nothing to*, etc. Being impersonal, these expressions are invariably used with the neuter form было, if they are in the past tense, and the third-person singular form бýдет, if they are in the future.

нéчего	*to have nothing to*
нéкого	*to have no one to*
нéкогда	*to have no time to*
нéгде	*to have nowhere to* (position indicated)
нéкуда	*to have nowhere to* (movement indicated)

Examples:

Нам нéчего дéлать.
We have nothing to do\There is nothing for us to do.
Емý нéкого бы́ло любúть.
He had no one to love.
Ей нéкогда бýдет вúдеть вас.
She will have no time to see you.

Я́блоку не́где упа́сть.
There isn't room to swing a cat [lit. *there is nowhere for an apple to fall*].
Мне не́куда бы́ло положи́ть чемода́н.
There was nowhere for me to put the case.

Note that не́чего and не́кого, which are accusative/genitive forms, also have dative, instrumental and prepositional forms as set out below, and that when these words are governed by a preposition they are generally split to enable the preposition to be inserted between the particle не and the appropriate form of кто or что:

dat.	не́чему	не́кому
instr.	не́чем	не́кем
prep.	не́ о чем	не́ о ком

Examples:

Мне не́ на кого́ полага́ться.
I have no one to rely on.
Вам не́чему удиви́ться.
There is nothing for you to be surprised at.
Ему́ не́кому дать ли́шний биле́т.
He has got no one to give the spare ticket to.
Мне не́чем есть суп.
I've got nothing to drink my soup with.
Ей не́ с кем говори́ть об э́том.
She's got no one to talk to about this.
Им не́ о чем бы́ло говори́ть.
They had nothing to talk about.

Exercises

A. *Complete the following sentences by putting the word in brackets in the correct form, and say what function the dative case has in each instance:* (1) Он дал кни́гу (свой друг). (2) Я ча́сто пишу́ пи́сьма (сын) и (дочь). (3) (Молоды́е лю́ди) не нра́вятся таки́е фи́льмы. (4) В а́вгусте (мой брат) бу́дет три́дцать лет. (5) Она́ посла́ла телегра́мму (муж). (6) (Все студе́нты) ну́жно купи́ть хоро́ший слова́рь. (7) Он купи́л (жена́) биле́т в теа́тр. (8) (Твоя́ ма́ма) понра́вился конце́рт? (9) (Моя́ сестра́) два́дцать лет. (10) (Спортсме́ны) нельзя́ кури́ть. (11) Ма́льчик пока́зывал (ро́дственники) свой альбо́м для ма́рок. (12) (Англича́не) не легко́ изуча́ть ру́сский язы́к. (13) (Де́вушка) не понра́вилась ко́мната в общежи́тии. (14) (Я) на́до купи́ть хлеб. (15) Он расска́зывал (друзья́) о свое́й пое́здке. (16) Она́ забы́ла сказа́ть (брат) о телефо́нном разгово́ре. (17) (Серге́й) на́до пойти́ на по́чту. (18) Мы подари́ли (до́чка) но́вую пласти́нку на рождество́. (19) Переда́йте (го́сти) соль и пе́рец. (20)

Учи́тель объясни́л уро́к о́чень я́сно, но (ученики́) всё бы́ло непоня́тно. (21) Официа́нт принёс (тури́сты) меню́. (22) (Больно́й) уже́ мо́жно выходи́ть на у́лицу. (23) Его́ (роди́тели) не нра́вится го́род, где они́ живу́т. (24) (Рабо́тник) всегда́ прия́тно слы́шать похвалу́ от нача́льника. (25) Её (дя́дя) шестьдеся́т лет.

B. *Translate into Russian:* (1) She gave the book to Ivan. (2) He showed the exercise to the professor. (3) They must work tomorrow. (4) One can't smoke in this carriage. (5) She often writes to her brother. (6) He sent his sister a telegram. (7) It's time for you to go home. (8) It was time to have supper. (9) You mustn't shout. (10) He had the good fortune to find the suitcase. (11) We succeeded in entering university. (12) I am very sorry for his father. (13) He could not be bothered to check his work. (14) They were destined to die in the war. (15) I am twenty-six. (16) She will be forty in August. (17) I haven't got anything to do. (18) We had nothing to eat. (19) She broke her arm. (20) She was tired of Russian cooking. (21) I paid the cashier and left the shop. (22) She bought her son a new shirt. (23) He kissed the little girl's hand. (24) My father was seventy when he died. (25) You mustn't go in in your overcoat. (26) The passengers will have to change to another train. (27) We've got no time to discuss this today. (28) You ought to take a breather. (29) I shall be sorry to return home. (30) The audience usually like this play. (31) I am ashamed. (32) The teacher is explaining the lesson to the pupils. (33) Are you cold? (34) There is nowhere for you to sit. (35) The poor girl has nowhere to go.

LESSON 24

VERBS GOVERNING THE DATIVE CASE

§1. Dative of advantage or disadvantage

A large number of verbs govern the dative case, many of which indicate advantage, assistance, permission or disadvantage, hindrance, prohibition to the object of the verb (compare the similar categories in Latin and German), e.g.

вреди́ть/повреди́ть[1]	*to injure, harm, hurt*
грози́ть (impf.)	*to threaten*
запреща́ть/запрети́ть[2]	*to forbid, prohibit*
изменя́ть/измени́ть[3]	*to betray*
меша́ть/помеша́ть	*to prevent, hinder, bother, disturb*
позволя́ть/позво́лить	*to allow, permit*
помога́ть/помо́чь	*to help*
препя́тствовать/воспрепя́тствовать	*to obstruct*
разреша́ть/разреши́ть[2]	*to allow, permit*
служи́ть/послужи́ть	*to serve*
сове́товать/посове́товать	*to advise*
соде́йствовать (impf. and pf.)	*to assist, promote, contribute to*
спосо́бствовать/поспосо́бствовать	*to assist, promote, contribute to*

1 Although вреди́ть/повреди́ть takes the dative case the pair повреждать/повредить, which also means *to damage, to injure*, or *to hurt*, takes the accusative case, e.g. он повреди́л себе́ но́гу, *he hurt his leg*.

2 Although запреща́ть/запрети́ть and разреша́ть/разреши́ть govern a noun in the dative case when reference is being made to the person to whom something is forbidden or permitted, the thing forbidden or permitted is denoted by a noun in the accusative, e.g. прави́тельство запрети́ло/разреши́ло но́вую газе́ту, *the government prohibited/permitted the new newspaper*.

3 It is only when it means *to betray* that изменя́ть/измени́ть governs the dative case. When it means *to change* or *to alter* it governs the accusative case, e.g. дире́ктор шко́лы реши́л измени́ть уче́бную програ́мму, *the headmaster decided to change the curriculum*.

Examples:

Куре́ние вреди́т здоро́вью.
Smoking damages your health.
Поку́пка нека́чественного това́ра грози́т госуда́рству огро́мным уще́рбом.
The purchase of sub-standard goods threatens the state with huge losses. (Press)
Он не́сколько лет наза́д измени́л Ро́дине и перебежа́л на сто́рону англи́йской разве́дки.
Several years ago he betrayed his country and went over to British intelligence. (Press)
Все э́ти тру́дности не меша́ют Кана́де быть одни́м из са́мых процвета́ющих в ми́ре госуда́рств.
All these difficulties do not prevent Canada from being one of the most flourishing states in the world. (Press)
Позво́льте мне предста́вить вам Алексе́я Никола́евича.
Allow me to introduce to you Aleksey Nikolaevich.
У Бо́ри была́ знако́мая, кото́рая помога́ла ему́ де́лать ксе́роксы Набо́кова и Солжени́цына.
Borya [i.e. *Boris*] *had an acquaintance who would help him to make photocopies of Nabokov and Solzhenitsyn.* (Press)
Я служи́л Оте́честву.
I have served my country. (Press)
Врач посове́товал больно́му лечь в посте́ль.
The doctor advised the patient to go to bed.
Це́рковь мо́жет соде́йствовать перестро́йке.
The Church can assist perestroika. (Press)
Но́вый фонд бу́дет спосо́бствовать разви́тию на́уки, те́хники, иску́сства, здравоохране́ния.
The new fund will assist the development of science, technology, art and health care. (Press)

§2. Miscellaneous verbs governing the dative

Many other verbs govern an object in the dative case, including the following:

веле́ть (impf. and pf.)	*to order, command*
ве́рить/пове́рить[1]	*to believe, give credence to*
зави́довать/позави́довать[2]	*to envy*
звони́ть/позвони́ть	*to ring, telephone*
изумля́ться/изуми́ться	*to be astonished at*
льстить/польсти́ть[3]	*to flatter*
повинова́ться (impf., and in past tense also pf.)	*to obey*
подража́ть (impf. only)	*to imitate*
прика́зывать/приказа́ть	*to order*

принадлежа́ть[4] (impf. only)	*to belong to*
противоре́чить (impf. only)	*to contradict*
ра́доваться/обра́доваться	*to rejoice at, be gladdened by*
сле́довать/после́довать[5]	*to follow*
соотве́тствовать (impf. only)	*to correspond to*
сопротивля́ться (impf. only)	*to resist*
сочу́вствовать (impf.)	*to sympathise with*
удивля́ться/удиви́ться	*to be surprised at*
учи́ть/научи́ть[6]	*to teach*
учи́ться/научи́ться[6]	*to learn* (a subject)

1 Ве́рить/пове́рить takes в + accusative case if it means *to believe in*, e.g. он ве́рит в коммуни́зм, *he believes in communism*, or он ве́рит в бо́га, *he believes in God* (see 17.3 above). Contrast the use of the two cases with this verb in the sentence не зна́ют, во что и кому́ ве́рить, *they don't know what to believe in and whom to believe* (Press).

2 Зави́довать/позави́довать cannot govern a direct object as can the English verb *to envy* in phrases such as *I envy you your health* (Я зави́дую твоему́ здоро́вью).

3 Although льстить/польсти́ть normally governs the dative case, note the use of the accusative form of the reflexive pronoun in the expression льстить/польсти́ть себя́ наде́ждой, *to flatter oneself with the hope*.

4 When принадлежа́ть denotes ownership it is followed by the dative case without any preposition, e.g. э́та кни́га принадлежи́т моему́ бра́ту, *this book belongs to my brother*. When on the other hand it denotes membership it must be followed by к and the dative (see 25.6 below).

5 Сле́довать/после́довать is followed by the dative case only when it means *to follow* in the sense of *to emulate*. When it means *to go after* it takes за + instrumental case (see 26.5 below).

6 After учи́ть/научи́ть, *to teach* and учи́ться/научи́ться, *to learn*, it is the subject taught or the thing learnt that is denoted by a noun in the dative case. However, after the verb изуча́ть/изучи́ть, which means *to study*, the subject is denoted by a noun in the accusative case, e.g. он изуча́ет матема́тику, *he is studying mathematics*.

Examples:

Неизве́стный челове́к позвони́л мне и попроси́л о встре́че.
An unknown man rang me and asked for a meeting. (Press)
Я изумля́юсь ва́шей на́глости.
I am astonished at your impudence.
Она́ стара́ется подража́ть ста́ршей сестре́.
She tries to imitate her elder sister.

Он счита́л, что э́то слова́ Ма́ртина Лю́тера Ки́нга, а мне каза́лось, что они́ принадлежа́т одному́ из президе́нтов США, но я забы́ла кому́.
He thought these were the words of Martin Luther King, whereas I thought they belonged to one of the presidents of the USA, but I had forgotten which one. (Press)
Фа́кты противоре́чат ва́шему заключе́нию.
The facts contradict your conclusion.
Ра́дуюсь рожде́нию вну́ка.
I rejoice at the birth of my grandson. (Press)
Он сле́дует приме́ру своего́ отца́.
He is following his father's example.
Когда́ вну́тренне он сосредото́чен на како́й-то мы́сли, иде́е, то совсе́м не сопротивля́ется вне́шним возде́йствиям.
When he is inwardly focused on some thought or idea then he does not resist external pressures at all. (Press)
Он у́чит сестру́ францу́зскому языку́.
He is teaching his sister French.

Exercise

Translate into Russian: (1) Do you often help your parents? (2) The doctor advised us to rest. (3) The radio is preventing me from working. (4) The police do not permit tourists to go there. (5) I rang my father. (6) I am learning Russian. (7) I don't believe the teacher. (8) He is imitating his elder brother. (9) He betrayed his country. (10) We rejoiced at this news. (11) You are flattering me. (12) This book belongs to a student. (13) He contradicted his sister. (14) I advise you to give up smoking. (15) Tobacco harms the lungs. (16) The doctor forbad him to swim. (17) The attack on the eastern front contributed to the victory. (18) I am surprised at your attitude. (19) I am astonished at these results. (20) She does not allow her children to play in the street. (21) I envy my sister. (22) An accident is obstructing the traffic. (23) She helped the old woman to cross the street. (24) The recession has contributed to our bankruptcy. (25) Your version of this event does not correspond to the facts. (26) Strong organisms resist diseases. (27) A drunk was threatening the old man with his fist. (28) Does the draught bother you? (29) We do not follow this old custom nowadays. (30) The dean ordered all the lecturers in the faculty to come to an urgent meeting.

LESSON 25

PREPOSITIONS WITH THE DATIVE CASE

§1. По with the dative case

The commonest preposition governing the dative case is по, which is used much more widely with the dative than with the accusative or the prepositional (on which see 18.3 and 15.16 respectively).

The basic directional meanings of по with the dative are *along, down*, and *round*. Examples:

Онá идёт по ýлице.	*She is walking along the street.*
Онá спускáется вниз по лéстнице.	*She is coming down the stairs.*
Он хóдит по кóмнате.	*He is pacing round the room.*

Other important meanings are *according to* or *in accordance with* and *by* a means of communication, e.g.

по расписáнию
according to the timetable
по подсчётам экспéртов
according to the calculations of experts
По официáльному кýрсу, однá мáрка ГДР равнéется однóй мáрке ФРГ.
According to the official rate of exchange one East German mark is equal to one West German mark. (Press)
по среднеевропéйскому врéмени
Central-European time
по телефóну
by telephone
по пóчте
by post
по желéзной дорóге
by rail
по телевúдению
by television

По may also mean *at, on* or *in* when these prepositions mean *in the field of* or *on the subject of*, e.g.

чемпио́ны по футбо́лу
football champions
Мини́стр по дела́м Се́верной Ирла́ндии
Minister for Northern-Irish Affairs
ле́кция по исто́рии
a lecture on history
перегово́ры по пробле́мам центра́льно-америка́нского регио́на
talks on the problems of the Central-American region (Press)

Note also the prepositional phrase по отноше́нию к, *with regard to, in respect of*.

§2. По понеде́льникам, etc.

По is used with the dative to mean *on* days of the week and in other expressions of time:

по понеде́льникам	*on Mondays*
по вто́рникам	*on Tuesdays*
по среда́м	*on Wednesdays*
по четверга́м	*on Thursdays*
по пя́тницам	*on Fridays*
по суббо́там	*on Saturdays*
по воскресе́ньям	*on Sundays*
по пра́здникам	*on holidays*
по утра́м	*in the mornings*
по вечера́м	*in the evenings*
по це́лым часа́м	*for hours on end/at a time*
по це́лым дням	*for days on end/at a time*
по це́лым неде́лям	*for weeks on end/at a time*

§3. Distributive expressions with по

The preposition по is also used with dative forms of the numeral один, *one*, and of ты́сяча, *a thousand*, and миллио́н, *a million*, in the distributive expression *one each*, e.g.

Мы получи́ли по одному́ рублю́.
We received a rouble each.
Мы получи́ли по ты́сяче рубле́й.
We received a thousand roubles each.

See also 41.6 below on this expression.

§4. Use of не по

Used together with the negative particle не, по may translate *for* in phrases such as *tall for his age* in which inconsistency is implied, e.g.

Он не по во́зрасту высо́к.
He is tall for his age.
Он о́пытен не по года́м.
He is experienced for his age/beyond his years.
Э́та маши́на нам не по карма́ну.
We can't afford this car [lit. *this car is not in accordance with our pocket*].
Он живёт не по сре́дствам.
He lives beyond his means.

Note also the phrase не по а́дресу, *to the wrong address.*

§5. Use of по with the dative case after certain verbs

The verb стреля́ть, *to shoot, fire*, is followed by по and the dative case if the target is a moving or mobile one, or if random shots are fired at a target, e.g.

Партиза́н стреля́ет по вертолёту.
The guerrilla is shooting at a helicopter.
Охо́тник стреля́л по куропа́тке.
The hunter was shooting at a partridge.
Мили́ция стреля́ла по толпе́.
The police fired into the crowd.

(Compare стреля́ть в + accusative; see 17.3 above.)

По is also used after verbs having the sense of *to hit* or *strike*, e.g. ударя́ть/уда́рить, to indicate the thing which is struck, e.g.

Он уда́рил меня́ по подборо́дку.
He struck me on the chin.
Он уда́рил по́ столу.
He banged the table.

The verbs скуча́ть and тоскова́ть, both of which mean *to miss, to long for*, also take по with the dative, e.g.

Он скуча́ет по свои́м де́тям.
He misses his children.
О́ба они́ си́льно тоскова́ли по далёкой свое́й ро́дине.
Both of them greatly missed their faraway native land. (Press)

The verb суди́ть is followed by по with the dative in the sense of *to judge by*, and су́дя по, *judging by*, has become a set phrase.

§6. к with the dative case

The only other preposition widely used with the dative, apart from по, is к, which may be used only with the dative. К has the directional meaning of *towards* and in this meaning will often be combined with a verb bearing the prefix под-, which carries the same meaning (see 47.2.ii below). Examples:

Он подхо́дит к мосту́.
He is going towards/approaching the bridge.
Она́ подошла́ ко мне.
She came up to me.

К also has the temporal meaning of *by* or *towards*, e.g.

Он придёт к ве́черу.
He will arrive by evening.

К is used after a large number of nouns to indicate attitude towards, e.g.

жа́лость к	*pity for*
интере́с к	*interest in*
любо́вь к	*love for*
не́нависть к	*hatred of*
отноше́ние к	*attitude towards, relation to*
презре́ние к	*contempt for*
равноду́шие к	*indifference towards*
симпа́тия к	*liking for*
скло́нность к	*inclination towards, penchant for*
сла́бость к	*weakness for*
страсть к	*passion for*
стремле́ние к	*aspiration towards, striving for*
уваже́ние к	*respect for*

К is also used after a number of verbs, especially verbs indicating approach or attachment, e.g.

относи́ться/отнести́сь к	*to look on, have a certain attitude to*
приближа́ться/прибли́зиться к	*to approach, draw near to*
привлека́ть/привле́чь к	*to attract to*
привыка́ть/привы́кнуть к	*to get used to, grow accustomed to*
прилипа́ть/прили́пнуть к	*to stick, adhere to*
принадлежа́ть к (no pf.)	*to belong to* (denoting membership)
прислоня́ться/прислони́ться к	*to lean against*
присоединя́ться/присоедини́ться к	*to join*
стреми́ться к (no pf.)	*to strive towards, aspire to*

Examples:

Как отно́сится населе́ние респу́блики к рабо́те КГБ по борьбе́ с экономи́ческим саботá́жем?
What is the attitude of the people of the republic to the work of the KGB in the fight against economic sabotage? (Press)
Мы привы́кли к тому́, что иностра́нные инвести́торы вкла́дывают капита́лы в на́ше хозя́йство.
We have got used to foreign investors putting capital into our economy. (Press)
Он принадлежи́т к футбо́льному клу́бу.
He belongs to a football club.

К also occurs in many set phrases, e.g.

к сожале́нию	*unfortunately*
к сча́стью	*fortunately*
к тому́ же	*moreover, besides*
к моему́ удивле́нию	*to my surprise*
к на́шему изумле́нию	*to our astonishment*
к ва́шим услу́гам	*at your service*
изменя́ться/измени́ться к лу́чшему	*to change for the better*
изменя́ться/измени́ться к ху́дшему	*to change for the worse*
лицо́м к лицу́	*face to face*

§7. Other prepositions governing the dative

There are a few other, less commonly used, prepositions which are followed by the dative case:

благодаря́	*thanks to*
вопреки́	*despite, contrary to*
подо́бно	*like, similar to*
согла́сно	*in accordance with* (official)

Examples:

Благодаря́ «генети́ческим отпеча́ткам» в ско́ром вре́мени престу́пникам ста́нет трудне́е скрыва́ть следы́ свои́х дея́ний.
Thanks to 'genetic finger-printing' it will soon become more difficult for criminals to conceal the traces of their actions. (Press)
Э́та исто́рия, кста́ти, пока́зывает, что вопреки́ расхо́жему мне́нию далеко́ не всегда́ я приде́рживалась бо́лее радика́льного мне́ния, чем он.
This shows, incidentally, that contrary to the opinion that goes the rounds it was by no means always the case that I adhered to a more radical opinion than he. (Press)

Деся́тки и со́тни ты́сяч сове́тских эмигра́нтов бу́дут прорыва́ться в США и в Евро́пу — подо́бно мексика́нцам, ту́ркам, югосла́вам.
Tens and hundreds of thousands of Soviet emigrants will force their way into the USA and Europe, like the Mexicans, Turks and Yugoslavs. (Press)
согла́сно гла́вной статье́ догово́ра
in accordance with the main article of the treaty

Exercise

Translate into Russian: (1) A specialist on economic questions; (2) a mathematics lesson; (3) his respect for his parents; (4) according to her calculations; (5) her attitude towards her friends; (6) contrary to the doctors' advice; (7) strong for his age; (8) his indifference towards his family; (9) judging by the latest information; (10) an interest in literature; (11) thanks to favourable conditions; (12) by Moscow time; (13) He was shouting like a madman. (14) Passengers were leaning against the door. (15) The farmer was shooting birds. (16) Unfortunately the situation has changed for the worse. (17) The glue sticks to my fingers. (18) They are earning a thousand pounds each. (19) I work in the mornings. (20) She hit him on the cheek. (21) We were travelling towards London. (22) She went to the headmaster. (23) There will be snow by Christmas. (24) There will be a lecture on Russian history. (25) She was walking down the street. (26) He is going towards the door. (27) Do you belong to the football club? (28) We have dinner in a restaurant on Fridays. (29) We belong to the Labour Party. (30) We are getting used to the Russian climate.

LESSON 26

USE OF THE INSTRUMENTAL CASE

§1. Basic use of the instrumental case

The basic use of the instrumental case is to denote the agent by whom or the instrument with which or means by which an action is carried out, e.g.

Он был уби́т солда́том.
He was killed by a soldier.
Он ест ви́лкой и ножо́м.
He is eating with a knife and fork.
«Хочу́ ви́деть черно́быльскую беду́ свои́ми глаза́ми», сказа́л Михаи́л Серге́евич.
'I want to see the Chernobyl disaster with my own eyes', said Mikhail Sergeevich [Gorbachev]. (Press)
Реши́ть афга́нскую пробле́му вое́нным путём невозмо́жно.
To solve the Afghan problem by military means is impossible. (Press)

It may also denote the thing with which something is supplied or endowed, e.g.

Его́ награди́ли о́рденом.
They awarded him a medal.
Мы здесь у себя́ на се́вере обеспе́чиваем свой ме́стный автотра́нспорт ди́зельным то́пливом, бензи́ном.
We here in the north provide our vehicles with diesel fuel and petrol. (TV)
А́томная электроста́нция снабжа́ет го́род электри́чеством.
The atomic power station supplies the town with electricity.

§2. Use of the instrumental case in impersonal expressions

The instrumental case is also used to denote the agent in impersonal expressions describing the effect of some natural force, e.g.

С мо́ря ве́тром нанесло́ тума́н.
The wind blew a mist up from the sea [lit. *it blew a mist up from the sea with a wind*].
Доро́гу занесло́ сне́гом.
The road is snowed up [lit. *it covered the road with snow*].

See also 60.5 below on the use of this sort of passive construction.

§3. Use of the instrumental in adverbial phrases

The instrumental case is used in many adverbial phrases of manner, e.g.

авто́бусом	*by bus*
автомоби́лем	*by car*
по́ездом	*by train*
самолётом	*by plane*
гро́мким го́лосом	*in a loud voice*
шёпотом	*in a whisper*
петь ба́сом	*to sing bass*
идти́ бы́стрыми шага́ми	*to walk with quick steps*

§4. Use of the instrumental in expressions of time

The instrumental case is also used in the following expressions of time:

у́тром	*in the morning*
днём	*in the afternoon*
ве́чером	*in the evening*
но́чью	*at night*
весно́й	*in spring*
ле́том	*in summer*
о́сенью	*in autumn*
зимо́й	*in winter*

Instrumental expressions of time indicate a specific point in time rather than the duration of an action (cf. the accusative case; see 16.3 above), and may therefore often be qualified by an adjective which gives even greater precision, e.g. ра́нним у́тром, *in the early morning*; по́здней весно́й, *in late spring*.

Note though that when a precise time is given, the genitive form of у́тро, etc. must be used, e.g. в во́семь часо́в утра́, *at eight o'clock in the morning*.

Note also the expression це́лыми часа́ми, *for hours on end*.

§5. За with the instrumental case

This preposition, when used with the instrumental case, may mean *behind, beyond, on the far side of*, and in certain contexts *at*, e.g.

за до́мом	*behind the house*
за спино́й	*behind one's back*
за угло́м	*round the corner*
за грани́цей	*abroad* (beyond the border)
за рубежо́м	*abroad* (beyond the border)
за бо́ртом	*overboard*

за столо́м — *at the table*
за за́втраком — *at breakfast*
за обе́дом — *at dinner*
за у́жином — *at supper*
за роя́лем — *at the piano*
за пи́вом — *over a beer*

In all the above phrases за defines the position. If on the other hand it is intended to describe movement into a position, then за must be followed by the accusative case (see 18.1.i above).

За may also be used in the sense of *after* when this preposition means *in pursuit of, in search of, supervising*, or *caring for*, and in this sense is commonly combined with certain verbs, e.g.

идти́/пойти́ за	*to go for, fetch*
наблюда́ть за (no pf.)	*to supervise*
надзира́ть за (no pf.)	*to supervise*
посыла́ть/посла́ть за	*to send for*
присма́тривать/присмотре́ть за	*to look after, keep an eye on*
следи́ть за (no pf.)	*to track, shadow, follow, keep an eye on*
сле́довать/после́довать за	*to go after, follow, succeed*
уха́живать за (no pf.)	*to court, look after*

Examples:

Он пошёл за ча́йником.
He went to fetch the kettle.
Сын заболе́л. Она́ посла́ла за врачо́м.
Her son fell ill. She sent for the doctor.
Кто бу́дет присма́тривать за ребёнком?
Who is going to look after the baby?
Я сра́зу же по́нял, что за на́ми следя́т.
I immediately realised that we were being followed. (Press)

За is used with similar meaning in the phrases вдого́нку за and вслед за, both of which mean *in pursuit of*.

Note also the expression за исключе́нием + genitive, *with the exception of*.

§6. Ме́жду with the instrumental case
Ме́жду means *between*, e.g.

ме́жду паралле́льными ли́ниями
between parallel lines

ме́жду на́ми
between ourselves
Он положи́л три́ста рубле́й ме́жду газе́тными листа́ми.
He put 300 roubles between the sheets of the newspaper. (Press)

Note the expressions ме́жду про́чим, *incidentally*, and ме́жду тем, *meanwhile*.

The conjunction ме́жду тем, как means *while*.

Ме́жду is always followed by the instrumental case except in certain fixed expressions in which it governs the genitive instead, namely: чита́ть ме́жду строк, *to read between the lines*; сиде́ть ме́жду двух сту́льев, *to fall between two stools*; and ме́жду двух огне́й, *between the devil and the deep blue sea* (lit. *between two fires*).

§7. Над with the instrumental case

Над, which may govern only the instrumental case, means *over, above, on top of*, e.g.

Над столо́м виси́т лю́стра.
A chandelier hangs over the table.

The vowel о may have to be added to над for the sake of euphony, as in the expression на́до мной, *over me*.

Note the use of над after certain verbs:

возвыша́ться/возвы́ситься над	*to tower over*
госпо́дствовать над (no pf.)	*to dominate, tower above*
издева́ться над (no pf.)	*to mock*
рабо́тать над (no pf.)	*to work at/on*
смея́ться над (no pf.)	*to laugh at*

§8. Пе́ред with the instrumental case

Пе́ред, which may govern only the instrumental case, means *in front of*, or *before* in either place or time. Examples from the press:

Я сиде́ла в Москве́ пе́ред телеви́зором.
I was sitting in Moscow in front of the television set.
Но пе́ред сме́ртью я до́лжен облегчи́ть ду́шу.
But before death I must lighten my soul.

In this temporal sense пе́ред generally means *shortly before* and may be contrasted with до (see 22.5 above) which may indicate any time before.

The vowel **о** is sometimes added to пе́ред for the sake of euphony, as in the expression пе́редо мной, *in front of me*, e.g. э́ти пи́сьма лежа́т пе́редо мной, *these letters are lying in front of me* (Press).

Note the use of пе́ред after certain verbs, e.g.

извиня́ться/извини́ться пе́ред	*to apologise to*
преклоня́ться/преклони́ться пе́ред	*to admire, worship*

Пе́ред is also used in certain expressions which define relationship, e.g.

винова́т пе́ред	*guilty towards*
отве́тственность пе́ред	*responsibility towards*
страх пе́ред	*fear of*

The conjunction пе́ред тем, как means *before.*

§9. Под with the instrumental case

The principal meaning of под is *under, below, beneath*, e.g.

под столо́м	*under the table*
под мосто́м	*under the bridge*
под пове́рхностью	*beneath the surface*
под аре́стом	*under arrest*
под влия́нием	*under the influence*

In culinary expressions под retains its literal meaning, and translates *with* a certain dressing, e.g.

ры́ба под тома́тным со́усом	*fish with tomato sauce*
яйцо́ под майоне́зом	*egg mayonnaise*

Под may also mean *in the region of* and translates *of* in the names of battles, e.g.

Аренда́торы. Нема́ло я ви́дела их под Москво́й.
Tenants [farmers]. *I have seen not a few of them in the region of Moscow.* (Press)
би́тва под Полта́вой
the battle of Poltava

Like за, под indicates location when it is used with the instrumental case, and must be followed by the accusative if movement into a position is intended (see 18.4.i above).

§10. С with the instrumental case

С means *with*, when *with* means *together with* or *in the company of*, or when it refers to some connection or attendant characteristic, e.g.

> Он пошёл в кино́ с сестро́й.
> *He went to the cinema with his sister.*
> Она́ живёт в междунаро́дном аэропорту́ Шереме́тьево-2. С сыновья́ми. С кото́м в клётке.
> *She is living at Sheremetevo-2 International Airport. With her sons. [And] with a cat in a cage.* (Press)
> в связи́ с э́тим
> *in connection with this*
> челове́к с голубы́ми глаза́ми
> *a person with light blue eyes*
> Я с ра́достью согласи́лся.
> *I gladly* [lit. *with gladness*] *agreed.* (Press)

Care should be taken not to use с in contexts where the English *with* implies only agency (see §1 above).

Note also the use of мы с in expressions such as мы с бра́том, *my brother and I*; мы с отцо́м, *my father and I*; мы с сестро́й, *my sister and I.* Examples from the press:

> Мы с му́жем собра́ли хоро́шую библиоте́ку.
> *My husband and I have collected a good library.*
> Неда́вно мы с фотоко́ром «Литерату́рной газе́ты» зае́хали в Шереме́тьево.
> *Recently 'Literaturnaya gazeta's' photographic correspondent and I called in at Sheremetevo.*

С may also mean *with* the passage of time, e.g. с ка́ждым днём стано́вится всё очеви́днее, что..., *with every [passing] day it becomes more obvious that...* (Press).

Note also the expression что с ва́ми?, *what is the matter with you?*

С is used with the instrumental case after certain verbs, e.g.

встреча́ться/встре́титься с	*to meet*[1]
здоро́ваться/поздоро́ваться с	*to greet, say hello to*
знако́миться/познако́миться с	*to meet, get acquainted with*[2]
поздравля́ть/поздра́вить с	*to congratulate on*

1 This verb should be used when the meeting is one that has been arranged. The non-reflexive forms встреча́ть/встре́тить denote a more chance encounter.

2 This verb should be used when the sense of *to meet* is *to get to know, be introduced to.*

проща́ться/попроща́ться с	*to say goodbye to*
расстава́ться/расста́ться с	*to part with*
сове́товаться/посове́товаться с	*to consult*
соглаша́ться/согласи́ться с	*to agree with*
ссо́риться/поссо́риться с	*to quarrel with*
ста́лкиваться/столкну́ться с	*to collide with, run into*

Examples:

Он по́просту не име́л прямо́го до́ступа к э́тим лю́дям, он с ни́ми не встреча́лся и не зна́ет их.
He simply did not have direct access to these people, has not met them and does not know them. (Press)
Он поздра́вил их с Но́вым го́дом.
He wished them a Happy New Year [lit. *he congratulated them with the New Year*].
Так я познако́мился с М. О., ста́рым депута́том-коммуни́стом.
That was how I met M. O., an old communist deputy. (Press)
Сего́дня, проща́ясь с ва́ми, мы жела́ем вам всего́ наилу́чшего.
Today, saying farewell to you, we wish you all the best. (Press)
Я ча́сто е́здила в Москву́ и то́же не расстава́лась с бума́гами.
I often travelled to Moscow and would not part with the papers either. (Press)
Он согласи́лся со мной.
He agreed with me.
Но здесь мы столкну́лись с упо́рным сопротивле́нием.
But at this point we came up against stubborn resistance. (Press)

§11. Adjectives governing the instrumental case

A number of adjectives are followed by the instrumental case, e.g.

бога́тый	*rich in*
дово́льный	*satisfied with*
за́нятый	*busy with*
недово́льный	*dissatisfied with*
оби́льный	*rich in*

Exercises

A. *Complete the following sentences by choosing the appropriate preposition (за, ме́жду, над, пе́ред, под, or с) and by putting the words in brackets in the correct form:* (1) Ско́лько раз вы бы́ли ... (грани́ца)? (2) Она́ рабо́тает ... (диссерта́ция) по фи́зике. (3) Шёл дождь. Все боле́льщики сиде́ли ... (зо́нтики). (4) Все го́сти сидя́т ... (стол). (5) Я соверше́нно соглаша́юсь ... (колле́ги). (6) Он ел цыпля́т табака́ ... (како́й-то пря́ный со́ус). (7) Пойма́ли престу́пника. Он сейча́с сиди́т ... (аре́ст). (8) ... (смерть) он вдруг реши́л соста́вить завеща́ние. (9) Я наме́рен встре́титься ... (дире́ктор) за́втра у́тром. (10) Миллио́ны телезри́телей следи́ли ... (олимпиа́да). (11) Я поговорю́ с ва́ми об э́том ... (ча́шка) ко́фе. (12) ... (го́ры) и (мо́ре) лежи́т небольша́я равни́на. (13) ... (кто) вы живёте? ... (роди́тели)? (14) Он пошёл в буфе́т ... (бутербро́ды). (15) Он всё ссо́рился ... (жена́). (16) Он тако́й угрю́мый! Никогда́ не здоро́вается ... (друзья́). (17) Её де́ти постоя́нно сидя́т ... (телеви́зор). (18) Мы ... (сестра́) живём в Ло́ндоне. (19) ... (я) лежи́т его́ после́днее письмо́. (20) ... (Антаркти́да) появи́лась дыра́ в озо́нном сло́е. (21) ... (како́й врач) вы бу́дете сове́товаться? (22) Они́ купи́ли да́чу ... (Москва́), в сорока́ мину́тах от го́рода. (23) ... (Рождество́) и (Но́вый год) поги́бли в автокатастро́фах со́тни люде́й. (24) Все генера́лы, кото́рые уча́ствовали в неуда́чном пу́тче, ... (исключе́ние) одного́, бы́ли смещены́ со свои́х посто́в. (25) Он что-то спря́тал ... (спина́). (26) До полу́ночи я сижу́ ... (компью́тер). (27) Все смею́тся ... (нача́льник), не уважа́ют его́. (28) ... (стекло́) окна́ во́ет си́льный ве́тер. (29) Вокза́л нахо́дится в двух мину́тах от на́шего до́ма, ... (у́гол). (30) Чита́я ... (стро́ки), он легко́ по́нял смысл кни́ги.

B. *Translate into Russian:* (1) In early summer; (2) with the exception of one student; (3) vegetables in a nice sauce; (4) under the influence of alcohol; (5) over a glass of brandy; (6) rich in forests; (7) satisfied with life; (8) in the region of Kiev; (9) while he was abroad; (10) to part with friends; (11) She was writing with a pen. (12) He was eating with a spoon. (13) They went to Novosibirsk by train. (14) She was speaking in a quiet voice. (15) I found them at the table. (16) Our parents look after the children sometimes. (17) In winter it is cold. (18) She is standing in front of our new car. (19) They are sitting under the trees. (20) He lives with his brother. (21) The town stands between a river and a mountain. (22) Your pen is under this sheet of paper. (23) He was standing behind the door. (24) I am satisfied with my meeting with you. (25) The dog is following the boy down the street. (26) I shall consult a lawyer. (27) He always says hello to me. (28) He is working on a new book. (29) I shall meet her in front of the museum at midday. (30) She was sitting at the piano. (31) He is cutting the bread with a knife. (32) My brother and I are studying history. (33) In spring and autumn it rains. (34) He sat at the table for (whole) hours. (35) She said this in a whisper. (36) The cathedral towers over the other buildings. (37) He laughed at their mistakes. (38) He went to the chemist's for the medicine. (39) A new reservoir supplies the town with water. (40) A beautiful picture hangs over the hearth.

C. Revision exercise on basic uses of cases (Lessons 16, 19, 23, 26).
Put the words in brackets into the case required by the context: (1) Он ел суп (деревя́нная ло́жка). (2) Она́ подари́ла (бра́т) но́вый зо́нтик. (3) Маши́на ве́сит (одна́ то́нна). (4) Не́ было (молоко́) в холоди́льнике. (5) (Вся весна́) он лежа́л в больни́це. (6) На про́шлой неде́ле (мать) испо́лнилось пятьдеся́т лет. (7) В саду́ мно́го (дере́вья). (8) Учени́к попроси́л (учи́тель) ещё раз объясни́ть значе́ние э́того сло́ва. (9) Представи́тель прави́тельства

сообщи́л (журнали́сты), что президе́нт отмени́л визи́т в Росси́ю. (10) Мы поéдем туда́ (пóезд). (11) Она́ посла́ла (семья́) откры́тку. (12) По вечера́м ма́ло (лю́ди) на у́лицах. (13) Я раздави́л (пау́к). (14) Из-за забасто́вки не бу́дет (поезда́). (15) Я люблю́ (насеко́мые). (16) Ско́лько (сигаре́ты) ку́рите в день? (17) Э́тот у́гольный бассе́йн снабжа́ет страну́ (то́пливо). (18) Она́ сказа́ла (муж), что ненави́дит его́ и ушла́. (19) Он говори́т (ти́хий го́лос). (20) Я люблю́ рома́ны (Гончаро́в). (21) Он купи́л два ме́тра (верёвка) и оди́н литр (кра́ска). (22) Я ви́дел вдали́ (се́рый волк). (23) Э́тот журна́л сто́ит (оди́н рубль). (24) Э́то блю́до напомина́ет мне вкус (свини́на). (25) За два дня мы прое́хали (ты́сяча) киломе́тров. (26) Маньяк уби́л его́ (серп). (27) (Пассажи́ры) на́до пересе́сть на другу́ю ли́нию. (28) Сего́дня (у́тро) я встал в семь часо́в. (29) Я провёл не́сколько (ме́сяц) в Лати́нской Аме́рике. (30) (Все жи́тели) посёлка суждено́ бы́ло поги́бнуть в результа́те землетрясе́ния. (31) Я откры́л буты́лку (апельси́новый сок). (32) (Ра́ннее ле́то) мы е́дем на морско́й куро́рт. (33) Нет (спа́льный ваго́н) в по́езде. (34) Я вы́пил ча́шку (чай). (35) Заплати́те (касси́рша), пожа́луйста. (36) (Го́сти) нельзя́ кури́ть в номера́х. (37) Мы купи́ли буты́лку (конья́к). (38) Похо́же, (снег) не бу́дет. (39) Сто́лько (ава́рия) на желе́зных доро́гах! (40) (Вся жизнь) он рабо́тал для улучше́ния своего́ о́бщества.

D. *Revision exercise on prepositions which govern only one case* (Lessons 15, 18, 21, 22, 25, 26).
Put the words in brackets into the case required by the preceding preposition: (1) по́сле (обе́д); (2) пе́ред (у́жин); (3) от (вокза́л); (4) сквозь (толпа́); (5) к (зда́ние); (6) че́рез (тропи́нка); (7) вокру́г (свет); (8) при (Горбачёв); (9) благодаря́ (хоро́шая пого́да); (10) для (оте́ц); (11) над (голова́); (12) о́коло (теа́тр); (13) у (дире́ктор); (14) из (аудито́рия); (15) пе́сня про (ро́дина); (16) без (отве́т); (17) согла́сно (пе́рвый пункт) догово́ра; (18) буты́лка из-под (у́ксус); (19) про́тив (тече́ние); (20) ме́жду (Евро́па и А́зия); (21) ми́мо (зоопа́рк); (22) из-за (боле́знь); (23) до (за́втрак); (24) че́рез (мину́та); (25) среди́ (молодёжь); (26) к (зима́); (27) ра́ди (охра́на) окружа́ющей среды́; (28) вне (зако́н); (29) при (музе́й); (30) кро́ме (столи́ца); (31) внутри́ (я́щик); (32) вме́сто (карто́шка); (33) до (коне́ц); (34) при (туше́ние) огня́; (35) одно́ из (са́мые интере́сные произведе́ния) Достое́вского; (36) пе́ред (телеви́зор); (37) далеко́ от (мо́ре); (38) вопреки́ (сове́т) экспе́ртов; (39) вдоль (побере́жье); (40) относи́тельно (са́мые о́стрые социа́льные пробле́мы); (41) для (ве́жливость); (42) свы́ше (ты́сяча) жи́телей; (43) для (здоро́вье); (44) из-под (куст); (45) че́рез (столи́ца); (46) путём (многочасова́я рабо́та); (47) над (вход); (48) ввиду́ (но́вые фа́кты); (49) вследствие (сло́жная полити́ческая ситуа́ция); (50) у (тётя).

E. Revision exercise on prepositions which may govern two or three cases (Lessons 15, 17, 18, 21, 25, 26).
Put the words in brackets in the following sentences in the case required by the context: (1) Он пошёл в (ку́хня). (2) Мы шли по (коридо́р). (3) Она́ стои́т на (платфо́рма). (4) Мы сиде́ли под (берёза). (5) За (одна́ неде́ля) все чле́ны ро́ты бы́ли ра́нены. (6) Она́ говори́ла о (но́вый фильм).

(7) Он лежа́л в (больни́ца). (8) Крестья́не стоя́ли по (по́яс) в пшени́це. (9) Он на (одна́ неде́ля) ста́рше меня́. (10) Он заплати́л за (кни́га). (11) Вы бы́ли за (грани́ца)? (12) Мы е́ли ры́бу под (сы́рный со́ус). (13) Ко́шка сошла́ с (кры́ша). (14) Мы с (сестра́) пошли́ в кино́. (15) В темноте́ она́ споткну́лась о (кни́га), кото́рая валя́лась на полу́. (16) Он слу́жит атташе́ по (вое́нные дела́). (17) Он лю́бит рабо́тать под (пя́тая симфо́ния) Бетхо́вена. (18) Пое́здка продолжа́ется с (неде́ля). (19) Я проголосу́ю за (зелёная па́ртия) на вы́борах. (20) Он положи́л свой портфе́ль на (по́лка). (21) За́втра он е́дет за (грани́ца). (22) В (среда́) они́ прихо́дят к нам в го́сти. (23) По (понеде́льники) мы посеща́ем ба́бушку. (24) На ней бы́ло пла́тье в (кра́пинка). (25) Он специали́ст по (пробле́мы) национа́льных меньши́нств. (26) Все пассажи́ры за (исключе́ние) одного́ поги́бли в катастро́фе. (27) Она́ чита́ет ле́кцию по (эконо́мика). (28) Он уезжа́ет на (одна́ неде́ля). (29) Шахтёры рабо́тают под (земля́). (30) Змея́ ползла́ под (куст). (31) Я люблю́ соси́ски с (капу́ста). (32) Она́ вы́шла за́муж за (инжене́р). (33) Го́сти сиде́ли за (стол). (34) Война́ ста́вит под (угро́за) на́ши торго́вые отноше́ния с Да́льним восто́ком. (35) Он уезжа́ет с (разреше́ние) дире́ктора. (36) Он живёт с (роди́тели). (37) Он там живёт с (коне́ц) войны́. (38) Она́ но́сит ожере́лье под (серебро́). (39) Мы ме́дленно спуска́лись вниз по (ле́стница). (40) Тот го́род нахо́дится на (юг) страны́. (41) Она́ рабо́тает в (универма́г). (42) Он уда́рил меня́ по (щека́). (43) Она́ пла́вала в (бассе́йн). (44) Он отдыха́ет по (вечера́). (45) Он был в (бе́лая руба́шка) и (голубы́е джи́нсы). (46) Ба́за закры́та на (зима́). (47) Он схвати́л меня́ за (рука́). (48) Они́ прие́дут в (по́лдень). (49) Мно́го таки́х посёлков под (гла́вные сиби́рские города́). (50) Они́ бо́рются за (свобо́да).

LESSON 27

VERBS GOVERNING THE INSTRUMENTAL CASE

§1. Verbs denoting control

Some of the verbs which govern the instrumental case denote control, command, government, direction, etc. A large proportion of these verbs are by their nature not capable of having perfective forms, e.g.

владе́ть	*to command, master, own*
дирижи́ровать	*to conduct* (orchestra)
заве́довать	*to be in charge of*
кома́ндовать	*to command* (armed forces)
облада́ть	*to possess*
пра́вить	*to govern, rule, drive* (vehicle)
располага́ть	*to have at one's disposal*
руководи́ть	*to manage, direct*
управля́ть	*to govern, rule, drive* (vehicle)

Examples:

Кто бу́дет владе́ть землёй — го́род и́ли райо́ны?
Who is going to own the land – the towns or the rural settlements? (Press)
заве́дующий лаборато́рией
the person in charge of the laboratory
кома́ндовать полко́м
to command a regiment
Де́вушка облада́ла необходи́мым хладнокро́вием.
The girl possessed the necessary presence of mind. (Press)
Ни «Э́ксон» ни порто́вое хозя́йство не располага́ли обору́дованием, спосо́бным сдержа́ть нефтяно́е пятно́.
Neither the 'Exxon' nor the port authority had at their disposal equipment [that was] capable of keeping the oil slick in check. (Press)
Михаи́л Нена́шев управля́л телеви́дением ме́ньше двух лет.
Mikhail Nenashev was in charge of television for less than two years. (Press)

§2. Verbs denoting movement of parts of the body

Other verbs which govern the instrumental case denote movement of something, especially of part of the subject's body, as in the following phrases:

виля́ть/вильну́ть хвосто́м	*to wag (its) tail*
дви́гать/дви́нуть ного́й	*to move (one's) foot*
кача́ть/покача́ть голово́й	*to shake (one's) head*
кива́ть/кивну́ть голово́й	*to nod (one's) head*
маха́ть/махну́ть руко́й	*to wave (one's) hand*
мига́ть/мигну́ть гла́зом	*to wink, blink (one's) eye*
морга́ть/моргну́ть гла́зом	*to wink, blink (one's) eye*
пожима́ть/пожа́ть плеча́ми	*to shrug (one's) shoulders*
разма́хивать мечо́м (no pf.)	*to brandish a sword*
то́пать/то́пнуть ного́й	*to stamp (one's) foot*
ша́ркать/ша́ркнуть ного́й	*to shuffle (one's) foot*

Examples from the press:

> Все лётчики пожима́ли плеча́ми и недоумева́ли, что̀ заставля́ет его́ забира́ться в таку́ю глушь.
> *All the airmen shrugged their shoulders and wondered what made him go to such an out-of-the-way place.*
> Андре́й ничего́ не написа́л в отве́т, а то́лько покача́л голово́й.
> *Andrey did not write anything in reply but just shook his head.*

Note though that when the part of the body belongs to someone other than the subject the accusative is used, e.g. пожима́ть/пожа́ть кому́-нибудь ру́ку, *to shake someone's* [i.e. somebody else's] *hand* (see 23.1 above).

§3. Similarly a few verbs which govern the instrumental case denote noise made with something, as in the following phrases:

бряца́ть це́пью (no pf.)	*to rattle, clank a chain*
звене́ть деньга́ми (no pf.)	*to jingle money*
звя́кать/звя́кнуть моне́тами	*to jingle coins*
скрежета́ть зуба́ми (no pf.)	*to gnash (one's) teeth*
хло́пать/хло́пнуть две́рью	*to slam a door*

§4. Miscellaneous other verbs governing the instrumental case

Miscellaneous other verbs (several of which exist only in an imperfective form) also govern the instrumental case, e.g.

восхища́ться/восхити́ться	*to admire* (i.e. *to be very impressed by*)
горди́ться (no pf.)	*to be proud of*
дорожи́ть (no pf.)	*to value, prize*
дыша́ть (no pf.)	*to breathe*
же́ртвовать/поже́ртвовать	*to sacrifice*
занима́ться/заня́ться	*to be engaged in, be occupied with, study*

злоупотребля́ть/злоупотреби́ть	*to abuse*
интересова́ться/заинтересова́ться	*to be interested in*
любова́ться/полюбова́ться	*to admire* (i.e. *to enjoy looking at*)
наслажда́ться/наслади́ться	*to enjoy*
обзаводи́ться/обзавести́сь	*to provide oneself with*
па́хнуть (impf. only)	*to smell of* (used impersonally)
по́льзоваться/воспо́льзоваться[1]	*to use, make use of, to enjoy* (in sense of *to have*)
пренебрега́ть/пренебре́чь	*to ignore, neglect, scorn*
рискова́ть (no pf.)	*to risk, hazard*
страда́ть[2] (no pf.)	*to suffer from*
торгова́ть (no pf.)	*to trade in*
увлека́ться/увле́чься	*to be fond of, be carried away by*
хва́статься/похва́статься	*to boast of*

1 But the verb испо́льзовать (impf. and pf.), *to utilise*, governs the accusative case.

2 Used with the instrumental case страда́ть implies chronic or permanent predicament, e.g. страда́ть диабе́том, *to suffer from diabetes*. Страда́ть от implies more temporary suffering, e.g. страда́ть от зубно́й бо́ли, *to suffer from toothache*.

Examples:

горди́ться свои́ми достиже́ниями
to be proud of one's achievements
дыша́ть све́жим во́здухом
to breathe fresh air
же́ртвовать свое́й жи́знью
to sacrifice one's life
Разве́дывательной де́ятельностью всегда́ занима́лись все госуда́рства, занима́ются и сейча́с.
All states have always engaged in intelligence gathering activity, [and] they are engaged in it now too. (Press)
Афана́сьева, злоупотребля́я свои́м служе́бным положе́нием, неоднокра́тно получа́ла взя́тки.
Afanaseva, abusing her official position, repeatedly accepted bribes. (Press)
Он интересова́лся литерату́рой, э́то нас и сбли́зило.
He was interested in literature, this drew us close together. (Press)
Э́то ава́нс! — ворку́ет Руза́нна на у́шко Ма́йе Анто́новне. Та любу́ется золоты́м коле́чком с ро́зовым ка́мнем.
'This is some money in advance!' coos Ruzanna in Maya Antonovna's ear. The latter is admiring a little gold ring with a pink stone. (Press)

обзавести́сь семьёй
to settle down with a family
Здесь па́хнет табако́м.
It smells of tobacco here.
Я по́льзовалась любо́й возмо́жностью, что́бы каки́е-то куски́ перепра́вить де́тям в США.
I made use of any opportunity to convey any bits [of a manuscript] to my children in the USA. (Press)
Капита́н М.Гали́мов пренебрёг запре́том на пла́вание во льда́х.
Captain M. Galimov ignored the ban on sailing in ice. (Press)
рискова́ть свое́й голово́й
to risk one's life (lit. *head*)
По́льская поли́ция арестова́ла сове́тского граждани́на, кото́рый на база́ре откры́то торгова́л огнестре́льным ору́жием.
Polish police arrested a Soviet citizen who was openly trading in firearms in the market place. (Press)
Не торопи́тесь напра́во и налёво хва́статься свои́ми пла́нами и уда́чами.
Don't rush right and left to boast about your plans and successes. (Press)

§5. Use of instrumental and nominative cases after быть

When the verb *to be* is in the present tense, and is therefore understood but not actually stated in the Russian, a nominative complement must be used, e.g.

Он профе́ссор.	*He is a professor.*
Мой брат — инжене́р.	*My brother is an engineer.*
Моя́ мать — учи́тельница.	*My mother is a teacher.*

Departures from this rule are rare, unless the complement is вина́, *fault, blame*, or причи́на, *cause*, e.g.

Тут, коне́чно, не одно́ телеви́дение вино́й.
Here, of course, television alone is not to blame. (Press)

On the other hand whenever any part of the verb быть is actually stated in the Russian (i.e. when the past and future tenses, infinitive, imperative, present gerund, past active participle are used) the following noun is nowadays normally in the instrumental case, e.g.

Все его́ дя́ди и бра́тья бы́ли людьми́ вое́нными.
All his uncles and brothers were military men. (Press)
Был я секретарём комсомо́льской организа́ции Ива́новской сре́дней шко́лы.
I was secretary of the Komsomol organisation of Ivanovo secondary school. (Press)

Он бу́дет диплома́том.
He will be a diplomat.
Мне показа́лось, что э́то мо́жет быть подгото́вкой обще́ственного мне́ния к бу́дущим репре́ссиям.
It seemed to me that this might be a preparation of public opinion for future repression. (Press)
Бу́дьте врачо́м.
Be a doctor.
Бу́дучи дурако́м, он не по́нял.
Being a fool, he didn't understand.

Formerly the complement of быть was often put in the nominative case, particularly when the verb was in the past tense and when the complement indicated that the subject possessed some ability or permanent quality, e.g. Пу́шкин был вели́кий поэ́т, *Pushkin was a great poet.* Instances of the use of a nominative complement may still be found. However, the use of a nominative complement is now widely felt to be obsolete even in this sort of context, and the student is on safe ground if he or she always uses the instrumental instead.

Note though the construction это был/была́/бы́ло/бы́ли + noun in nominative case:

Это был Ива́н.	*It was Ivan.*
Это была́ Татья́на.	*It was Tatyana.*
Это бы́ло францу́зское сло́во.	*It was a French word.*
Это бы́ли дере́вья.	*They were trees.*

§6. Verbs requiring a complement in the instrumental case

A number of other verbs, apart from быть, require an instrumental complement, at least in some contexts:

вы́глядеть (impf.)	*to look (like)*
де́латься/сде́латься	*to become*
каза́ться/показа́ться	*to seem*
называ́ть/назва́ть	*to call, name*
находи́ть/найти́	*to find*
ока́зываться/оказа́ться	*to turn out to be, prove to be*
остава́ться/оста́ться	*to remain*
притворя́ться/притвори́ться	*to pretend to be*
рабо́тать (no pf.)	*to work as*
служи́ть/послужи́ть	*to serve as*
слыть/прослы́ть	*to be reputed to be*
станови́ться/стать	*to become*
счита́ть/счесть	*to consider*
счита́ться (no pf.)	*to be considered*
явля́ться/яви́ться	*to be*

Examples from the press:

Он каза́лся мне больны́м физи́чески от утра́ты.
He seemed to me physically ill from the loss.
Пире́й называ́ют морски́ми воро́тами Гре́ции.
People call Piraeus the marine gates of Greece.
Са́мым сло́жным мо́жет оказа́ться психологи́ческий фа́ктор.
The psychological factor may prove the most complicated thing.
Бы́ли и до конца́ оста́немся друзья́ми.
We have been and shall to the end remain friends.
Он рабо́тал официа́нтом в рестора́не в Новокузне́цке.
He worked as a waiter in a restaurant in Novokuznetsk.
Три́дцать два го́да служи́л свяще́нником в подмоско́вных церква́х.
For thirty-two years [he] served as a priest in churches around Moscow.
Как стать владе́льцем кварти́ры?
How does one become the owner of a flat?
Он счита́ется одни́м из крупне́йших богосло́вов ми́ра.
He is considered one of the greatest theologians in the world.

For further discussion of the translation of the verb *to be* into Russian, and particularly for examples of the use of явля́ться/яви́ться, see Lesson 61.3 below.

Exercises

A. *Translate into Russian:* (1) They are trading in arms. (2) I admire their talent. (3) You ought to make use of this service. (4) At last we could breathe fresh air. (5) The team is proud of its achievements. (6) The dog was wagging its tail. (7) This dictionary will prove useful. (8) He mastered Russian. (9) They boasted of their success. (10) They are interested in the theatre. (11) Driving a car is easy. (12) A scientist is directing the programme. (13) You are neglecting your health. (14) He abuses his position. (15) He shook his head sadly. (16) She slammed the door. (17) The passengers waved their hats as the train moved off. (18) The plan seems impracticable. (19) He became an engineer. (20) Spanish is sometimes considered an easy language. (21) People publicly called him a coward. (22) My father is a chemist. (23) He'll be a novelist. (24) He was a footballer. (25) It smells of fish in the kitchen.

B. Revision exercise on government of cases by verbs (Lessons 16, 20, 24, 27). *Put the words in brackets in the case required by the preceding verb:* (1) Он лю́бит (му́зыка). (2) Она́ интересу́ется (теа́тр). (3) Ребёнок бои́тся (эскала́торы). (4) Чай помога́ет (расстро́енные не́рвы). (5) Я пишу́ (кни́га). (6) Она́ занима́ется (хи́мия). (7) Кто кома́ндует (а́рмия)? (8) Стресс вреди́т (здоро́вье). (9) Она́ заве́дует (ка́федра) англи́йского языка́. (10)

Преподава́тель посове́товал (студе́нт) чита́ть побо́льше. (11) Он пуга́ется (возмо́жные после́дствия) свои́х посту́пков. (12) Когда́ он не понима́ет, он пожима́ет (пле́чи). (13) Забасто́вщики тре́буют (повыше́ние) зарпла́ты. (14) Е́сли соглаша́етесь, кива́йте (голова́). (15) Она́ лиши́лась (мать), когда́ ей бы́ло четы́ре го́да. (16) Ка́жется, я оби́дел (де́вушка). (17) Она́ разозли́лась на меня́ и хло́пнула (дверь). (18) Она́ избега́ет (встре́ча) со мной. (19) Я предви́жу (затрудне́ние). (20) Я сочу́вствую (сосе́д), но не могу́ помо́чь (он).* (21) Он слу́шал (пласти́нка). (22) Гул движе́ния на у́лице меша́ет (чита́тели) в библиоте́ке. (23) Бы́вшие солда́ты торгу́ют (ружья́) и (боеприпа́сы). (24) Он не уме́ет держа́ться (те́ма) в свои́х ле́кциях. (25) Он хва́стается (своя́ си́ла). (26) Инфля́ция дости́гла (реко́рдный у́ровень). (27) Води́тели пренебрега́ли (зна́ки) предупрежде́ния. (28) Поли́тика прави́тельства не спосо́бствует (улучше́ние) экономи́ческого положе́ния. (29) В индустриа́льных города́х жи́тели ды́шат (загрязнённый во́здух). (30) Ма́льчик вёл себя́ подозри́тельно, ша́ркал (но́ги). (31) Он ре́жет (хлеб). (32) (Програ́мма) руководи́т изве́стный ру́сский учёный. (33) Не позволя́ют (зри́тели) кури́ть в кино́. (34) Он стыди́тся (своё неве́жество). (35) В три́дцать лет он обзавёлся (семья́). (36) Они́ про́сто не ве́рят (свои́ полити́ческие ли́деры). (37) Они́ горд́ятся (свои́ де́ти). (38) Я удиви́лся их (сме́лость). (39) Прави́тельство разреши́ло (но́вая газе́та). (40) Она́ владе́ет (кита́йский язы́к). (41) Мы дорожи́м (сотру́дничество) со свои́ми ру́сскими партнёрами. (42) Мы пи́ли (во́дка). (43) Мы напи́лись (пи́во). (44) Я учу́сь (ара́бский язы́к). (45) Я изуча́ю (япо́нский язы́к). (46) Здесь па́хнет (ро́зы). (47) Де́вочка нае́лась (конфе́ты). (48) Она́ облада́ет (огро́мный тала́нт). (49) Уезжа́я, она́ махну́ла (рука́). (50) Президе́нт приказа́л (все рабо́тники) в госуда́рственном се́кторе эконо́мики повы́сить производи́тельность.

* See 34.1 for declension of personal pronouns.

LESSON 28

THE MAIN TYPES OF LONG ADJECTIVE, THEIR DECLENSION AND USE

§1. Long and short forms of adjectives

The majority of Russian adjectives have both long forms and short forms.

The long forms agree with the noun they qualify in gender, case and number and may be used either attributively (i.e. they are placed either immediately before or immediately after the noun they qualify, as in the phrase *a new house*) or predicatively (i.e. as the complement of the verb *to be*, as for example in the statement *the house is new*).

The short forms agree with the noun they qualify in gender and number only and in the modern language do not decline (except in certain fixed phrases). As a general rule they should only be used predicatively. Short adjectives will be dealt with separately in Lesson 30 below.

§2. Declension and stress of long forms of adjectives

There is basically one system of declension for adjectives, with hard and soft variants and other variations which are explained by the familiar rules relating to spelling and stress (see Lesson 1).

Adjectives with stressed endings differ from those with unstressed endings in that they invariably have -óй in their masculine nominative singular form and have endings in **о** as opposed to **е** after sibilants. Like all other adjectives, however, they are subject to the spelling rule that **ы** must always be replaced by **и** after velars and sibilants.

Note that in all types of adjective the masculine accusative singular form and the accusative plural form will coincide with the genitive when the adjective qualifies an animate noun in the accusative/genitive case (see 16.2 above).

In addition to the feminine instrumental singular endings in -ой and -ей, endings in -ою and -ею will also be found. These are bookish and may be used by writers for stylistic or rhythmic purposes, or, in poetry, for metrical purposes. They are found more frequently in classical Russian literature than in the modern language.

The stress on the long forms of adjectives remains fixed throughout their declension.

§3. Standard adjectival declension

Most Russian adjectives decline like но́вый, *new*:

	sing.			pl.
	masc.	neut.	fem.	all genders
nom.	но́вый	но́вое	но́вая	но́вые
acc.	но́вый	но́вое	но́вую	но́вые
gen.	но́вого		но́вой	но́вых
dat.	но́вому		но́вой	но́вым
instr.	но́вым		но́вой	но́выми
prep.	но́вом		но́вой	но́вых

Adjectives of this type with stressed endings decline like молодо́й, *young*:

	sing.			pl.
	masc.	neut.	fem.	all genders
nom.	молодо́й	молодо́е	молода́я	молоды́е
acc.	молодо́й	молодо́е	молоду́ю	молоды́е
gen.	молодо́го		молодо́й	молоды́х
dat.	молодо́му		молодо́й	молоды́м
instr.	молоды́м		молодо́й	молоды́ми
prep.	молодо́м		молодо́й	молоды́х

§4. Adjectives with a stem in one of the velars (г, к, х)

These adjectives decline in the same way as adjectives like но́вый, except that the spelling rule dictates the use of **и** where adjectives like но́вый have **ы** Thus ру́сский, *Russian*, declines as follows:

	sing.			pl.
	masc.	neut.	fem.	all genders
nom.	ру́сский	ру́сское	ру́сская	ру́сские
acc.	ру́сский	ру́сское	ру́сскую	ру́сские
gen.	ру́сского		ру́сской	ру́сских
dat.	ру́сскому		ру́сской	ру́сским
instr.	ру́сским		ру́сской	ру́сскими
prep.	ру́сском		ру́сской	ру́сских

Adjectives such as стро́гий, *strict* (stem in **г**) and ти́хий, *quiet* (stem in **х**) follow this pattern.

Adjectives of this type with stressed endings decline like дорого́й, *dear, expensive*:

	sing.			pl.
	masc.	neut.	fem.	all genders
nom.	дорого́й	дорого́е	дорога́я	дороги́е
acc.	дорого́й	дорого́е	дорогу́ю	дороги́е

gen.	дорого́го		дорого́й	дороги́х
dat.	дорого́му		дорого́й	дороги́м
instr.	дороги́м		дорого́й	дороги́ми
prep.	дорого́м		дорого́й	дороги́х

§5. Adjectives with a stem in one of the sibilants ж, ч, ш, щ (but not ц)
In these adjectives, as in those with a stem in a velar, **и** is required in all those endings in which но́вый has **ы** Adjectives with a stem in a sibilant differ from those with a stem in a velar, however, in that they also have **е** in all those endings in which adjectives like но́вый have **о**.

	sing.			pl.
	masc.	neut.	fem.	all genders
nom.	хоро́ший	хоро́шее	хоро́шая	хоро́шие
acc.	хоро́ший	хоро́шее	хоро́шую	хоро́шие
gen.	хоро́шего		хоро́шей	хоро́ших
dat.	хоро́шему		хоро́шей	хоро́шим
instr.	хоро́шим		хоро́шей	хоро́шими
prep.	хоро́шем		хоро́шей	хоро́ших

Adjectives such as све́жий, *fresh* (stem in **ж**); горя́чий, *hot* (stem in **ч**); and о́бщий, *common, general* (stem in **щ**) follow this pattern.

Adjectives of this type with stressed endings decline like большо́й, *big*. Note that большо́й has **о** in all endings where хоро́ший has **е**.

	sing.			pl.
	masc.	neut.	fem.	all genders
nom.	большо́й	большо́е	больша́я	больши́е
acc.	большо́й	большо́е	большу́ю	больши́е
gen.	большо́го		большо́й	больши́х
dat.	большо́му		большо́й	больши́м
instr.	больши́м		большо́й	больши́ми
prep.	большо́м		большо́й	больши́х

§6. Adjectives with a stem in soft н
The vowels found in the endings of adjectives like но́вый are replaced in the endings of adjectives of this type according to the following pattern: ы — и; о — е; а — я; у — ю. Thus си́ний, *(dark) blue*, declines as follows:

	sing.			pl.
	masc.	neut.	fem.	all genders
nom.	си́ний	си́нее	си́няя	си́ние
acc.	си́ний	си́нее	си́нюю	си́ние
gen.	си́него		си́ней	си́них
dat.	си́нему		си́ней	си́ним
instr.	си́ним		си́ней	си́ними
prep.	си́нем		си́ней	си́них

It will be noted that every ending which in но́вый is hard is soft in this paradigm.

§7. Common adjectives which decline like си́ний

Since the endings in this type of adjective are not dictated by any spelling rule (as they are in the case of adjectives with a stem in a velar or in a sibilant other than ц), and since the consonant **н** is in most adjectival endings hard (e.g. интере́сный, *interesting*; кра́сный, *red*), it is as well to list some of the more common adjectives which have the ending -ний and which decline like си́ний. Note that many of these adjectives define time or location.

по́здний	*late*
ра́нний	*early*
весе́нний	*spring*
ле́тний	*summer*
осе́нний	*autumn*
зи́мний	*winter*
у́тренний	*morning*
вече́рний	*evening*
вчера́шний	*yesterday's*
сего́дняшний	*today's*
за́втрашний	*tomorrow's*
ны́нешний	*present-day*
тепе́решний (coll.)	*of the present time*
да́вний	*ancient, of long standing*
дре́вний	*ancient*
пре́жний	*former*
тогда́шний (coll.)	*of that time*
после́дний	*last* (in series; cf. про́шлый, *last* in sense of *past*)
предпосле́дний	*penultimate* (i.e. *one before last*)
бли́жний	*near, neighbouring*
да́льний	*far, distant*
ве́рхний	*upper*
ни́жний	*lower*
пере́дний	*front*
за́дний	*back, rear*
вне́шний	*outer, external*
вну́тренний	*inner, internal*
сре́дний	*middle, medium, average*
кра́йний	*extreme*
посторо́нний	*extraneous, outside* (see also 29.5 below)
сосе́дний	*neighbouring* (cf. сосе́дский, *of/belonging to one's neighbour*)
дома́шний	*home, domestic*
зде́шний (coll.)	*local, of this place*
та́мошний (coll.)	*of that place*
ли́шний	*superfluous, spare*

изли́шний	*excessive, unnecessary, superfluous*
и́скренний	*sincere*

Adjectives in this list occur in many common phrases, e.g.

ле́тние кани́кулы	*summer holidays*
дре́вние языки́	*classical languages*
бли́жний восто́к	*the Near East*
да́льний восто́к	*the Far East*
вне́шняя торго́вля	*foreign trade*
Министе́рство вну́тренних дел	*Ministry of Home Affairs*
сре́днего ро́ста	*of medium height*
в кра́йнем слу́чае	*in an emergency*
дома́шнее зада́ние	*homework*
ли́шний челове́к	*superfluous man* (Russian literary type)

§8. Use of adjectives in the long form

The long form of the adjective must agree with the noun it qualifies in gender, case and number, e.g.

Пе́ред до́мом стоя́л но́вый автомоби́ль.
A new car was standing in front of the house.
На тропи́нке сиде́ла чёрная ко́шка.
A black cat was sitting on the path.
Учи́тель за́дал ученика́м тру́дное упражне́ние.
The teacher set the pupils a difficult exercise.
Она́ купи́ла дешёвую кни́гу.
She bought a cheap book.
Зоопа́рк приобрёл африка́нского слона́.
The zoo has acquired an African elephant.
Она́ подошла́ к молодо́му милиционе́ру.
She went up to the young policeman.
пе́ред высо́ким зда́нием
in front of a tall building
на ле́вом берегу́ реки́
on the left bank of the river
Мы заказа́ли горя́чие блю́да.
We ordered hot dishes.
студе́нты из ра́зных университе́тов
students from various universities
по широ́ким у́лицам
down broad streets
ме́жду круты́ми гора́ми
between steep hills
в да́льних места́х
in distant places

The adjective is generally placed before the noun, as in all the above examples, but it may also be placed after the noun and may be used predicatively as well as attributively, e.g.

> язы́к тру́дный
> *a difficult language*
> Река́ — дли́нная.
> *The river is a long one.*

With nouns which belong to the predominantly feminine declension in -а or -я but which denote a male person and are therefore masculine, the qualifying adjective is also masculine, e.g.

у́мный мужчи́на	*an intelligent man*
прия́тный ю́ноша	*a pleasant youth*
ста́рый дя́дя	*old uncle*

When such nouns are used in the accusative singular qualifying adjectives have a masculine genitive singular form, e.g. он заста́л ста́рого дя́дю до́ма, *he found his old uncle at home.*

Rules relating to the use of adjectives after numerals will be given in 37. 2-4 below.

Exercises

A.1. *Give the neuter nominative singular forms of:* горя́чий, дре́вний, жёлтый, кре́пкий, тёплый, ти́хий.

2. *Give the feminine accusative singular forms of:* вече́рний, ма́ленький, о́бщий, по́льский, про́шлый, холо́дный.

3. *Give the masculine/neuter genitive singular forms of:* бы́стрый, вели́кий, испа́нский, кра́сный, после́дний, све́жий.

4. *Give the masculine/neuter dative singular forms of:* армя́нский, лени́вый, ме́дленный, настоя́щий, угрю́мый, у́тренний.

5. *Give the masculine/neuter instrumental singular forms of:* зи́мний, похо́жий, прия́тный, ры́жий, стро́гий, у́мный.

6. *Give the masculine/neuter prepositional singular forms of:* гру́стный, моско́вский, подходя́щий, плохо́й, сре́дний, ста́рый.

7. *Give the feminine genitive/dative/instrumental/prepositional singular forms of:* бе́лый, вне́шний, жа́ркий, и́скренний, кра́ткий, могу́чий.

8. *Give the nominative plural forms of:* внýтренний, высóкий, дорогóй, нúщий, ýзкий, чúстый.

9. *Give the genitive/prepositional plural forms of:* блестя́щий, домáшний, красúвый, лéтний, ширóкий, шýмный.

10. *Give the dative plural forms of:* азербайджáнский, богáтый, грóмкий, куря́щий, пóздний, свéтлый.

B. *Translate into Russian:* (1) They live in the white house. (2) They are talking about an interesting book. (3) They are sitting in the big room. (4) He is writing with a new pen. (5) The peasants live in small villages. (6) She bought a blue exercise-book. (7) They went past the front entrance. (8) They saw a red bird. (9) They were walking towards the old square. (10) He closed the back door. (11) He comes home on the last bus. (12) She is reading a good book. (13) The town is situated between broad rivers. (14) I consider him a talented young actor. (15) I drank a cup of strong tea.

LESSON 29

SOFT ADJECTIVES, POSSESSIVE ADJECTIVES, AND ADJECTIVES USED AS NOUNS

§1. Adjectives with a stem ending in a soft sign

In addition to the types of adjective examined in Lesson 28 above there is a relatively small group of adjectives which have a stem in -ь in all forms except the masculine nominative/accusative singular. In all the oblique cases these adjectives have the same endings as adjectives of the type си́ний, but nominative and accusative endings in the neuter, feminine, and plural are unusual in that they consist of only one vowel (е, я, и respectively) instead of the two vowels found in these forms in all the other types of adjective.

The commonest adjective of this type is тре́тий, *third*, which declines as follows:

	sing.			pl.
	masc.	neut.	fem.	all genders
nom.	тре́тий	тре́тье	тре́тья	тре́тьи
acc.	тре́тий	тре́тье	тре́тью	тре́тьи
gen.	тре́тьего		тре́тьей	тре́тьих
dat.	тре́тьему		тре́тьей	тре́тьим
instr.	тре́тьим		тре́тьей	тре́тьими
prep.	тре́тьем		тре́тьей	тре́тьих

All the other adjectives of this type are possessive adjectives, and most of them are derived from the names of animals, e.g.

во́лчий	*wolf's*
коро́вий	*cow's*
коша́чий	*cat's*
медве́жий	*bear's*
ове́чий	*sheep's*
пти́чий	*bird's*
ры́бий	*fish's*
соба́чий	*dog's*

These adjectives may denote possession, origin, or characteristic quality, and they also occur in certain fixed phrases, e.g.

во́лчий аппети́т	*voracious appetite*
коро́вье молоко́	*cow's milk*

ли́сий мех	*fox fur*
медве́жий у́гол	*god-forsaken place*
волк в ове́чьей шку́ре	*wolf in sheep's clothing*
пти́чье гнездо́	*bird's nest*
вид с пти́чьего полёта	*bird's-eye view*
ры́бий жир	*codliver oil*
соба́чья жизнь	*a dog's life*

§2. Possessive adjectives in -ин

Adjectives with this ending may be formed from Christian names, especially from their diminutive forms (e.g. Пе́тин, *Peter's*, from Пе́тя, diminutive of Пётр; На́дин, *Nadya's*, from На́дя, diminutive of Наде́жда), and from a number of words denoting relationships within the family (e.g. ма́мин, *mother's, mum's*, from ма́ма).

Both noun and adjectival endings are to be found in the declension of these adjectives, though different textbooks give different endings for certain cases. The fact that native speakers are unsure as to which forms are correct further testifies to the instability of these adjectives in the language.

Only a few adjectives of this sort will ever be encountered in the modern language, e.g. ма́мин зо́нтик, *mum's umbrella*; тётино пла́тье, *auntie's dress*; дя́дина шля́па, *uncle's hat*. A phrase with a noun in the genitive case to denote the possessor (e.g. зо́нтик ма́мы; пла́тье тёти; шля́па дя́ди respectively) can always be used – and is now more likely to be heard – instead.

It is however these possessive adjectives that have given rise in the language to the very numerous surnames in -ин (e.g. Пу́шкин) and to place names in -ино (e.g. Пу́шкино) after which the neuter noun село́, *village*, is understood. In practice the locative form of such place names is now likely to be the same as the nominative, e.g. в Пу́шкино.

§3. Possessive adjectives in -ов

Like the possessive adjectives in -ин, possessive adjectives in -ов may be formed from Christian names (e.g. Ива́нов, *Ivan's*, from Ива́н) and from words denoting relationships within the family (e.g. отцо́в, *father's*, from оте́ц). The possessives in -ов also have given rise to many surnames, e.g. Ива́но́в, i.e. *Ivan's* (*son* understood).

Like the possessive adjectives in -ин (see §2 above), these adjectives are no longer widely used and can always be replaced by the genitive form of the noun from which they are derived, except when they occur in certain set expressions (many of them biblical or classical allusions) such as ахилле́сова пята́, *Achilles' heel*; но́ев ковче́г, *Noah's Ark*; пи́ррова побе́да, *Pyrrhic victory*. (Note that the possessive adjectives in these expressions begin with a small letter.)

Like the possessive adjectives in -ин again, possessive adjectives in -ов give rise to place names in -о, e.g. Ю́зово, after which the neuter noun село́ is understood.

§4. Possessive adjectives in -инский and -овский

The suffix -ский is commonly added to the possessive adjectives in -ин and -ов dealt with in §§2 and 3 above, and also to surnames ending in -ин or -ов which are derived from them, e.g. матери́нский, отцо́вский, пу́шкинский, че́ховский.

These adjectives in -инский and -овский decline in exactly the same way as adjectives like ру́сский (see 28.4 above).

Some possessive adjectives in -инский and -овский may denote possession by a specific individual, as do the possessives in -ин and -ов (e.g. отцо́вский дом, *father's house*). More often though they have a broader meaning, denoting a quality characteristic of a type rather than an individual (e.g. матери́нская любо́вь, *maternal love*), or suggesting some association with a particular individual (e.g. никола́евская эпо́ха, *the age of Nicholas*).

§5. Adjectives used as nouns (substantivised adjectives)

There are many adjectives, of all three genders, which are used as nouns. Of these some no longer have an adjectival use, only an adjectival form (e.g. вселе́нная, *universe*), while others may be used as either adjectives or nouns (though the noun generally has a much more specific, limited meaning than the adjective). Many of these adjectives denote professions or occupations, or rooms or places.

больно́й	*sick person, patient, invalid*
ва́нная	*bathroom*
вое́нный	*person in the armed forces, serviceman*
вселе́нная	*universe*
гости́ная	*lounge, living-room*
де́тская	*nursery* (room)
диспе́тчерская	*control room, control tower* (at airport)
дозо́рный	*scout* (military)
живо́тное	*animal*
заключённый	*prisoner, convict*
заку́сочная	*snack-bar*
запята́я	*comma*
знако́мый/знако́мая	*acquaintance*
лёгкое	*lung*
моро́женое	*ice-cream*
мостова́я	*roadway*
на́бережная	*embankment*
насеко́мое	*insect*

нищий	*destitute person, beggar*
обвиня́емый	*defendant* (i.e. person being accused)
операцио́нная	*operating theatre*
пивна́я	*pub, bar*
плéнный	*captive, prisoner*
портно́й	*tailor*
посторо́нний	*outsider, unauthorised person*
пра́чечная	*laundry* (place)
приёмная	*waiting-room, reception-room*
прохо́жий	*passer-by*
рабо́чий	*worker*
рядово́й	*private* (soldier in the ranks)
столо́вая	*dining-room, canteen, refectory*
убо́рная	*toilet*
уполномо́ченный	*person authorised* (to do sthg.)
уча́щийся	*student, pupil*
учёный	*scientist, scholar*
учи́тельская	*common-room* (for school-teachers)
шта́тский	*civilian*

Some of these words (e.g. моро́женое, обвиня́емый) are of participial origin.

The gender of these words is explained by the original or understood presence after them of a specific noun (e.g. the word ко́мната after столо́вая [lit. *the table room*], etc.).

Exercise

Translate into Russian: (1) In the bathroom; (2) out of the living-room; (3) an expensive ice-cream; (4) a fish's tail; (5) a cat's paw; (6) the third book; (7) in the third row; (8) out of the third exit; (9) a lot of insects; (10) before the comma; (11) with my new acquaintances; (12) American scientists; (13) the taste of cow's milk; (14) groups of workers; (15) harmful to the lungs; (16) among the passers-by; (17) many civilians; (18) into the dining-room; (19) at the laundry; (20) two tailors; (21) with a sick man; (22) mum's hat; (23) the mewing of cats; (24) the Stalin period; (25) to eat with a wolfish appetite.

LESSON 30

FORMATION AND USE OF SHORT ADJECTIVES

§1. Formation of short adjectives

Many adjectives have a short form as well as a long form conforming to one of the patterns set out in Lesson 28 above.

Short adjectives, like the past tense of verbs, have only four forms: separate masculine, feminine, and neuter forms in the singular, and one plural form for all three genders.

The masculine short form of the adjective is found by removing the masculine nominative singular ending -ый, -ий, or -ой. Thus но́вый has masculine short form нов. (Note though that in many adjectives one of the vowels **о**, **е**, or **ё** has to be inserted between the final consonant and a preceding consonant in the short masculine form, e.g. ло́вок from ло́вкий; see §2 below.)

The feminine short form consists of the masculine short form (less any mobile vowel) and the ending -а (e.g. нова́).

The neuter short form consists of the masculine short form (less any mobile vowel) and the ending -о (e.g. но́во) or -е (the latter occurs after the sibilants **ж**, **ч**, **ш**, **щ**, when the neuter ending is unstressed).

The plural short form consists of the masculine short form (less any mobile vowel) and the ending -ы (e.g. но́вы) or -и (the latter occurs instead of -ы, in accordance with the normal spelling rule [see 1.3 above], after the velars **г**, **к**, **х**, and the sibilants **ж**, **ч**, **ш**, **щ**).

Theoretically soft adjectives like си́ний have soft endings in their masculine and feminine short forms as well as -е in the neuter and -и in the plural. Thus си́ний has short forms синь, синя́, си́не, си́ни. However, hardly any adjectives in -ний have short forms at all, and the short forms of those that do, such as си́ний, are so rarely used that they need not be learned by the foreign student.

Further examples:

long forms (masc. nom. sing.)	short forms masc.	fem.	neut.	pl.
бога́тый *rich*	бога́т	бога́та	бога́то	бога́ты

краси́вый	краси́в	краси́ва	краси́во	краси́вы
beautiful				
блестя́щий	блестя́щ	блестя́ща	блестя́ще	блестя́щи
brilliant				
све́жий	свеж	свежа́	свежо́	свежи́
fresh				

§2. Adjectives requiring insertion of a vowel in the masculine short form

The following common adjectives require the insertion of **о**, **е**, or **ё** between the final two consonants of the stem in the masculine short form:

long forms			short forms	
(masc. nom. sing.)	masc.	fem.	neut.	pl.
бли́зкий	бли́зок	близка́	бли́зко	бли́зки
near				
ги́бкий	ги́бок	гибка́	ги́бко	ги́бки
flexible				
гла́дкий	гла́док	гладка́	гла́дко	гла́дки
smooth				
де́рзкий	де́рзок	дерзка́	де́рзко	де́рзки
cheeky				
до́лгий	до́лог	долга́	до́лго	до́лги
long (of time)				
кре́пкий	кре́пок	крепка́	кре́пко	кре́пки
strong				
лёгкий	лёгок	легка́	легко́	легки́
easy, light				
ло́вкий	ло́вок	ловка́	ло́вко	ло́вки
adroit, agile				
мя́гкий	мя́гок	мягка́	мя́гко	мя́гки
soft				
ни́зкий	ни́зок	низка́	ни́зко	ни́зки
low				
по́лный	по́лон	полна́	полно́	полны́
full				
ре́дкий	ре́док	редка́	ре́дко	ре́дки
rare				
ре́зкий	ре́зок	резка́	ре́зко	ре́зки
sharp, harsh				
сла́дкий	сла́док	сладка́	сла́дко	сла́дки
sweet				
то́нкий	то́нок	тонка́	то́нко	то́нки
thin				
у́зкий	у́зок	узка́	у́зко	у́зки
narrow				
бе́дный	бе́ден	бедна́	бе́дно	бе́дны
poor				

бле́дный *pale*	бле́ден	бледна́	бле́дно	бле́дны
ве́рный *true, loyal*	ве́рен	верна́	ве́рно	ве́рны
вре́дный *harmful*	вре́ден	вредна́	вре́дно	вре́дны
гру́стный *sad*	гру́стен	грустна́	гру́стно	гру́стны
интере́сный *interesting*	интере́сен	интере́сна	интере́сно	интере́сны
кра́сный *red*	кра́сен	красна́	кра́сно	кра́сны
прия́тный *pleasant*	прия́тен	прия́тна	прия́тно	прия́тны
све́тлый *bright*	све́тел	светла́	све́тло	све́тлы
ску́чный *boring*	ску́чен	скучна́	ску́чно	ску́чны
то́чный *exact, precise*	то́чен	точна́	то́чно	то́чны
тру́дный *difficult*	тру́ден	трудна́	тру́дно	тру́дны
че́стный *honest*	че́стен	честна́	че́стно	че́стны
я́сный *clear*	я́сен	ясна́	я́сно	я́сны
смешно́й *funny*	смешо́н	смешна́	смешно́	смешны́
у́мный *intelligent*	умён	умна́	у́мно	у́мны

The adjective си́льный, *strong*, may have either си́лен or силён as its masculine short form.

Note that whereas in the long forms of adjectives the stress is always on the same syllable throughout, in the short forms it is mobile and several patterns are found. A particularly common feature is stress on the feminine ending in adjectives which have monosyllabic stems (see the numerous examples in the list above).

§3. Adjectives which have no short form

Many adjectives have no short form. These include:

i. all adjectives ending in the suffixes -ский and its stressed variant -ско́й (e.g. англи́йский, *English*; ру́сский, *Russian*; морско́й, *naval, marine*).

Note however that some adjectives, e.g. ве́ский, *weighty*, do have short forms (ве́сок, ве́ска, ве́ско, ве́ски) because their suffix is not -ский but -кий, the -с- being part of the stem.

Note also that many adjectives in -ический have synonyms in -ичный which do have short forms, e.g. траги́чный (= траги́ческий), *tragic*; short forms траги́чен, траги́чна, траги́чно, траги́чны. Similarly геро́йчный (= геро́йческий), *heroic*; драмати́чный (= драмати́ческий), *dramatic*; коми́чный (= коми́ческий), *comic*; крити́чный (= крити́ческий), *critical*; лакони́чный (= лакони́ческий), *laconic*; логи́чный (= логи́ческий), *logical*; типи́чный (= типи́ческий), *typical*, etc.;

ii. almost all adjectives with certain other suffixes, viz. -ний, e.g. весе́нний, *spring*; после́дний, *last* (see the list of adjectives with this suffix in 28.7 above); -шний, e.g. дома́шний, *domestic* (see also 28.7 above); -о́вый and -ово́й, e.g. фиоле́товый, *violet*; adjectives in -лый which are formed from the past tense of verbs, e.g. уста́лый, *tired*;

iii. all adjectives denoting material, many of which end in -а́н(н)ый or -я́н(н)ый, e.g. деревя́нный, *wooden*; желе́зный, *iron*; ко́жаный, *leather*; сере́бряный, *silver*; стально́й, *steel*; стекля́нный, *made of glass*; шерстяно́й, *woollen*.

The adjectives большо́й, *big*, and ма́ленький, *small*, have as their short forms вели́к, велика́, велико́, велики́ and мал, мала́, мало́, малы́ respectively.

It should be noted too that some adjectives have short forms whose meaning is limited and which may not be used in the whole range of meanings of which the long form is capable. For example, the short forms of живо́й (жив, жива́, жи́во, жи́вы) may mean *alive* but not *lively*. Similarly, the short forms of ста́рый (стар, стара́, ста́ро, ста́ры) may mean *old* in the sense *not young* and *not new*, but not in the sense *of long standing* as does ста́рый in, for example, the phrase ста́рый друг.

Note finally that the adjective рад, ра́да, ра́до, ра́ды, *glad*, is only ever found in the short form. (The long-form adjective with equivalent meaning is ра́достный.)

§4. General remarks on the use of short adjectives

The short forms of the adjective may only be used when the adjective is predicative, that is to say when in the English translation of the Russian some form of the verb *to be* stands between the subject and the adjective, as in the statements де́вушка была́ грустна́, *the girl was sad*; студе́нт умён, *the student is intelligent*. (It may be that in the Russian no part of the verb *to be* is actually stated; see the second example.) If the adjective is not separated from the noun in this way, then only a long form of the adjective may be used, irrespective of the word order employed, e.g. она́ была́ грýстной дéвушкой, *she was a sad girl*; он ýмный студéнт/он студéнт ýмный/ýмный он студéнт, *he is an intelligent student*.

The short form is very often obligatory when the adjective is used predicatively (see §5 below), but it is not always so. In many instances the long form and the short form are interchangeable without the meaning being affected. In yet other instances only a long form may be used even when the adjective is predicative (see also §6 below).

The question as to which form of the adjective, long or short, is appropriate when the adjective is used predicatively is a complicated one, of comparable difficulty to the question of the choice of the accusative or genitive case in the direct object of negated verbs (see 20.4-6 above). What follows here is not a theoretical explanation of the distinction between long and short forms but practical guidance which should hold good in the majority of cases in which an adjective is used predicatively and in which long and short forms are not interchangeable.

§5. Use of short adjectives

In the following circumstances a short form should be used, provided that the adjective is predicative.

i. When the adjective is followed by some sort of complement. (The complement is that which completes the meaning, e.g. the phrase *to leave* in the statement *you are free to leave* [вы свобóдны уйти́].)

A complement may consist of:

(a) a verb in the infinitive, e.g. он готóв приня́ть нас, *he is ready to receive us*;
(b) a phrase consisting of preposition + noun or pronoun, e.g. я равнодýшен к мýзыке, *I am indifferent to music*;
(c) a noun or pronoun in some oblique case, e.g. онá — недовóльна своéй зарплáтой, *she is dissatisfied with her pay*;
(d) some other qualifying phrase, e.g. этот райóн извéстен как рóдина Шекспи́ра, *this region is famous as Shakespeare's birthplace*.

The examples given below are arranged in groups according to the definition of the nature of the adjective's complement given in the previous paragraph. Several common adjectives included in these examples will be found only in the short form when used predicatively, e.g. виновáт, *guilty*; готóв, *ready*; далёк, *far, distant*; довóлен, *satisfied with*; недовóлен, *dissatisfied with*; дóлжен, *bound to* (i.e. *must*); достóин (fem. достóйна, etc.), *worthy of*; недостóин (fem. недостóйна, etc.), *unworthy of*; намéрен, *intending to*; нýжен, *necessary*; похóж, *like, similar*; непохóж, *unlike, dissimilar*; прав, *right*; свобóден, *free*; склóнен, *inclined to*; соглáсен, *agreeable to*; спосóбен, *capable of*.

(a) Она́ наме́рена е́здить в И́ндию.
She intends to travel to India.
Он спосо́бен уби́ть свои́х враго́в.
He is capable of killing his enemies.

(b) Ва́ше откры́тие ва́жно для нау́ки.
Your discovery is important for science.
Таба́к вре́ден для лёгких.
Tobacco is harmful to the lungs.
Мы гото́вы на всё.
We are prepared for everything.
Она́ непохо́жа на бра́та.
She is unlike her brother.
Полити́ческие де́ятели скло́нны к преувеличе́нию.
Politicians are inclined to exaggeration.
Для Росси́и типи́чны берёзовые леса́.
Birch forests are typical of Russia.

(c) Сау́довская Ара́вия бога́та не́фтью.
Saudi Arabia is rich in oil.
Го́ры изве́стны чистото́й своего́ во́здуха.
The mountains are well known for the purity of their air.
Са́дик был по́лон роз.
The little garden was full of roses.

(d) Ки́ев интере́сен как столи́ца древнеру́сского госуда́рства.
Kiev is interesting as the capital of the ancient Russian state.
Их рабо́та поле́зна с экономи́ческой то́чки зре́ния.
Their work is useful from the economic point of view.

ii. When the subject of the statement is one of the words то, *that*; э́то, *this, it*; что, in the sense of *which* or *what*; всё, *everything*; друго́е, *another thing*; одно́, *one thing*; остально́е, *what remains*; пе́рвое, *the first thing*. Examples:

Он гру́стен; э́то поня́тно по́сле сме́рти отца́.
He is sad; that is understandable after his father's death. (Press)
Одно́ я́сно: все пассажи́ры, должно́ быть, поги́бли.
One thing is clear: all the passengers must have been killed.

iii. When the subject is qualified by some word or phrase which has the effect of generalising an idea, such as вся́кий, *any*; ка́ждый, *every*; любо́й, *any*; подо́бный, *such*; тако́й, *such*; тако́го ро́да, *of such a sort, that sort of*; тако́го ти́па, *of such a kind*. Examples:

«Отцы́ и де́ти» замеча́тельный рома́н: ка́ждое сло́во в нём уме́стно.
'Fathers and Children' is a wonderful novel: every word in it is apt.

Как пра́вило, подо́бные зада́чи просты́.
As a rule such tasks are simple.
Таки́е до́воды неубеди́тельны.
Such arguments are unconvincing.

iv. When the adjective is derived from a present active participle (ending in -щий, e.g. блестя́щий, *brilliant*; све́дущий, *knowledgeable*; see 58.1 below); a present passive participle (ending in -мый, e.g. уважа́емый, *respected*, необъясни́мый, *inexplicable*; see 59.1-2 below); or a past passive participle (ending in -тый or -нный, e.g. жена́тый, *married*; неожи́данный, *unexpected*; see 59.3-6 below). Examples:

В Росси́и урака́н вездесу́щ.
The cockroach is ubiquitous in Russia.
Ва́ше поведе́ние неприе́млемо.
Your conduct is unacceptable.
Он был жена́т.
He was married.

v. When the adjective denotes excessive possession of a quality, e.g. э́ти ту́фли мне малы́, *these shoes are too small for me*. The following adjectives denoting size or price are commonly used in this way when they occur predicatively:

большо́й:	вели́к	велика́	велико́	велики́	*too big*
ма́ленький:	мал	мала́	мало́	малы́	*too small*
дорого́й:	до́рог	дорога́	до́рого	до́роги	*too dear*
дешёвый:	дёшев	дешева́	дёшево	дёшевы	*too cheap*
широ́кий:	широ́к	широка́	широко́	широки́	*too wide*
у́зкий:	у́зок	узка́	у́зко	у́зки	*too narrow*

vi. In general statements of a philosophical nature, e.g.

Душа́ челове́ка бессме́ртна.
Man's soul is immortal.
Судьба́ Росси́и зага́дочна.
Russia's fate is enigmatic.
Достиже́ния челове́ка мимолётны.
Man's achievements are transient.

Preference for the short form of the adjective in such statements reflects the sense that, in contexts where both forms are possible, the short form is more bookish and the long form more colloquial.

§6. Use of the long form when the adjective is predicative
The main function of the long form when the adjective is used predicatively is to particularise, to draw attention to the fact that a particular subject possesses the quality denoted by the adjective.

It is useful in this connection to bear in mind the point made by Borras and Christian (see page ix) that the long form predominates in contexts where in English the pronoun *one* is included or understood after the predicative adjective, e.g. кни́га ужа́сная, *the book is a terrible one*. The inclusion of the pronoun *one* indicates the singling out of one object from among several or many. Contrast the opposite tendency at work in statements whose subject is qualified by words such as тако́й, and in which the short form is preferred (see §5.iii above). In such statements the tendency is to generalise, to broaden the range of a statement from a single example to many examples of a type.

It is because the long form indicates possession of a quality by a particular subject that it is preferred in statements incorporating a phrase with у + genitive, e.g.

> Глаза́ у неё краси́вые.
> *She has beautiful eyes* [i.e. *her eyes are beautiful ones*].
> Во́лосы у него́ дли́нные.
> *He has long hair.*

It follows from what has been said about the particularising tendency of the long form that the short form is preferred if the object described is unique, for in such cases there can be no question of singling the object out for individual attention. Thus *Russia is enormous* could only be rendered thus, with the aid of the short form: Росси́я огро́мна.

With some adjectives the long form may also indicate that a quality is permanent, e.g.

	Он — больно́й	*He is an invalid.*
Contrast:	Он бо́лен	*He is ill.*

Exercises

A. *Translate the following sentences into English and explain on what grounds long or short forms of the adjective are used in each of them:* (1) Вре́мя рассу́дит, кто был прав. (2) Жизнь полна́ парадо́ксов. (3) Ка́ждый из тех заво́дов экологи́чески безвре́ден для окружа́ющей среды́ и населе́ния. (4) Ны́нешнее вре́мя уника́льно те́ми переме́нами, кото́рые происхо́дят во всех сфе́рах о́бщества. (5) Байка́л знамени́т не то́лько свое́й красото́й, но бога́тством и разнообра́зием живо́тного и расти́тельного ми́ра. (6) Ле́том в ка́ждом кру́пном селе́ Алта́я устра́ивают пра́здники. Тради́ция э́та дре́вняя и му́драя. (7) Бесспо́рно одно́: пробле́му эмигра́ции на́до осозна́ть как глоба́льную стратеги́ческую пробле́му. (8) Необходи́м комите́т по дела́м эмигра́ции, иммигра́ции и бе́женцев. (9) Ру́сский сарафа́н прекра́сен. (10) Ста́рая актри́са полна́ пла́нов, хо́чет и мо́жет рабо́тать. (11) Вероя́тно, что по́сле 17 ию́ля вы смо́жете почу́вствовать себя́ легко́ и свобо́дно; осо́бенно необы́чен в э́том смы́сле пери́од с 17 по 24 ию́ля, когда́ вы бу́дете спосо́бны прояви́ть свои́ са́мые лу́чшие ка́чества. (12) Э́тот пери́од благоприя́тен для встреч с бу́дущими спо́нсорами. (13) Э́тот пери́од кра́йне ва́жен для ва́шей карье́ры. (14) Нача́ло ию́ля для мно́гих Стрельцо́в — пери́од динами́чный. (15) Це́ны в Росси́и фантасти́ческие по сравне́нию с зарпла́той. (16) Она́ была́ полна́ впечатле́ний от пое́здки. (17) Ско́лько я чита́ю ва́шу газе́ту, и везде́ есть заме́тки люде́й, кото́рые недово́льны музыка́льными програ́ммами. (18) Те́ма любви́, одино́чества, сме́рти — класси́ческая для теа́тра всех времён и наро́дов. (19) Курс разрабо́тан Брита́нским лингафо́нным институ́том в Ло́ндоне. Заня́тия возмо́жны без предвари́тельного зна́ния языка́. (20) Он продемонстри́ровал спорти́вную фо́рму на́ших зи́мних олимпи́йцев. Фо́рма э́та удо́бная и краси́вая.

B. *Translate into Russian:* (1) The play was tragic. (2) His shirt was too small for him. (3) The hat was too big for me. (4) She intends to see you tomorrow. (5) We are ready to go out. (6) The manager was satisfied with my work. (7) People are mean. (8) The roses which I bought are red. (9) Lions are brave. (10) The earth is round. (11) I am inclined to think that you are right. (12) She agreed with me. (13) The Volga is a long river, the Thames is a short one. (14) He is well known for his sense of humour. (15) She has a pale face. (16) One thing is obvious: you will be late. (17) This is useful. (18) Every chapter is interesting. (19) Such ideas are dangerous. (20) I think he is invincible. (21) The penguin is ungainly on land. (22) You are free to go home. (23) That sort of tea is very strong. (24) Paris is a beautiful city. (25) His hair is black. (26) He is married to a Frenchwoman. (27) Meat is too expensive in that shop. (28) Flowers are beautiful. (29) His conduct was inexplicable. (30) They are like their father.

LESSON 31

COMPARATIVE ADJECTIVES: LONG FORMS

§1. Long and short comparative forms

Like adjectives in the positive degree (e.g. long form но́вый, etc.; short form нов, etc.), adjectives in the comparative degree have both long forms (бо́лее но́вый) and short forms (нове́е).

When the comparative adjective is attributive (e.g. in the Russian equivalent of phrases such as *a newer house*, in which the adjective is placed immediately before or after the noun it qualifies), then only the long form of the comparative (бо́лее но́вый) may be used. The short form (нове́е) may be used only when the comparative adjective is predicative, i.e. when it is separated from the noun it qualifies by some part of the verb *to be* (e.g. in phrases such as *the house is newer*).

This lesson deals with long comparative forms. The formation and use of short comparative adjectives are dealt with in the following lesson.

§2. Long comparative forms with бо́лее and ме́нее

The long form of the comparative is obtained simply by placing one of the indeclinable words бо́лее, *more*, or ме́нее, *less*, before the long form of the adjective in its positive degree. The adjective continues to agree in number, gender and case with the noun it qualifies, e.g.

бо́лее но́вый дом	*a newer house*
бо́лее интере́сная кни́га	*a more interesting book*
бо́лее тру́дное упражне́ние	*a more difficult exercise*
ме́нее поле́зный уро́к	*a less useful lesson*
Я чита́ю бо́лее интере́сную кни́гу.	*I am reading a more interesting book.*
на бо́лее кру́пных заво́дах	*in larger factories*

Than after long comparatives is rendered by чем + whichever case is appropriate in the context, including nominative, e.g.

Он живёт в бо́лее но́вом до́ме, чем я.
He lives in a newer house than I do.

§3. Adjectives with special long comparative forms

There are six adjectives which have a long comparative which is formed without the use of бо́лее:

positive degree		long comp. form	
большо́й	*big, great*	бо́льший	*bigger, greater*
ма́ленький	*small*	ме́ньший	*smaller, lesser*
хоро́ший	*good*	лу́чший	*better*
плохо́й	*bad*	ху́дший	*worse*
ста́рый	*old*	ста́рший	*elder, senior*
молодо́й	*young*	мла́дший	*younger, junior*

The forms ста́рший and мла́дший are used with reference to age differences and seniority. In other circumstances бо́лее ста́рый and бо́лее молодо́й are used, e.g. бо́лее ста́рый дом, *an older house*. (The difference between ста́рший and бо́лее ста́рый may be compared to that between the English comparative forms *elder* and *older* respectively.)

These comparative forms do not always correspond to an English comparative adjective, since with the exception of бо́льший and ме́ньший, they may also have superlative meaning, i.e. *best*, *worst* as well as *better*, *worse* (see 33.2 below).

The forms вы́сший, *higher*, and ни́зший, *lower*, now tend to be used only as superlatives of высо́кий, *high*, and ни́зкий, *low*, as in the following expressions (though the equivalent English expressions do not all contain the superlative *highest*):

вы́сшее кома́ндование	*high command* (military)
вы́сшее образова́ние	*higher education*
в вы́сшей сте́пени	*in the highest degree*
перегово́ры на вы́сшем у́ровне	*summit* (political talks)
вы́сшее учё́бное заведе́ние	*higher educational institution*

Exercises

A. *Put the adjectives in the following phrases into the comparative degree:* (1) молодо́й брат; (2) поле́зное упражне́ние; (3) но́вая кни́га; (4) ста́рое поколе́ние; (5) хоро́ший слова́рь; (6) больша́я часть; (7) плоха́я пого́да; (8) лени́вый челове́к; (9) высо́кая гора́; (10) ста́рое зда́ние.

B. *Translate into Russian:* (1) This is a more interesting theme. (2) He is wearing a warmer suit than I am. (3) She writes in a more modern style. (4) We live in a taller building. (5) He always buys less expensive meat. (6) I have an elder brother. (7) My younger sister lives in London. (8) I am reading a better book. (9) It is difficult to imagine a worse film. (10) How much does the government spend on higher education?

LESSON 32

FORMATION AND USE OF SHORT COMPARATIVE ADJECTIVES

§1. Short comparative forms

Most – but not all – adjectives also have short comparative forms, which are used predicatively (see §8 below). The invariable ending for the short comparative form of most adjectives is -ee, which is added to the adjectival stem (i.e. what remains when the suffix -ый/-ий/-ой is removed from the long masculine nominative singular form), e.g.

long form (positive degree)		short comp. form	
до́брый	*good, kind*	добре́е	*kinder*
интере́сный	*interesting*	интере́снее	*more interesting*
но́вый	*new*	нове́е	*newer*
о́стрый	*sharp*	остре́е	*sharper*
полёзный	*useful*	полёзнее	*more useful*
сла́бый	*weak*	слабе́е	*weaker*
счастли́вый	*happy*	счастли́вее	*happier*
тупо́й	*blunt*	тупе́е	*blunter*
у́мный	*intelligent*	умне́е	*more intelligent*
хи́трый	*cunning*	хитре́е	*more cunning*

The ending -ей (e.g. нове́й), which is also invariable, will be found as an alternative to -ee; it is a more colloquial form, and is also used frequently in poetry if the metre requires it.

Short comparative forms in -ee (and in -ей) are indeclinable (as are the short forms of adjectives in the positive degree) and do not change according to the gender of the noun to which they relate.

§2. Stress on regular short comparative forms

The stress in the short comparative form is almost always on the same syllable as in the long positive form, provided that the long positive form in the masculine nominative singular has more than two syllables. Thus the three-syllable adjective полёзный has полёзнее, and the four-syllable adjective интере́сный has интере́снее. Exceptions to this rule are здорове́е, *healthier* (from здоро́вый) and холодне́е, *colder* (from холо́дный).

If however the long positive form has only two syllables in the masculine nominative singular, then the stress in the short comparative form is on the ending. Thus но́вый has нове́е. (See also the other examples in §1 above.)

This stress shift may dictate the change **ё > е** in the stem of the adjective, e.g. темне́е, *darker* (cf. тёмный); тепле́е, *warmer* (cf. тёплый); and желте́е, *yellower* (cf. жёлтый).

§3. Short comparative forms with a consonant change

In a large number of adjectives the final consonant of the stem undergoes a change in the short comparative form, and in these circumstances the ending is contracted to -е. This ending is never stressed, the stress always falling on the penultimate syllable in such forms. The consonants which undergo change, and the consonants which replace them in the short comparatives, are as follows:

г	>	ж
д	>	ж
ст	>	щ
т	>	ч
х	>	ш

(The consonant **к**, like the other velars **г** and **х**, also undergoes change, but as the change is not uniform stems with this consonant are dealt with separately in §§4 and 5 below.)

Thus:

long form (positive degree)		short comp. form	
дорого́й	*dear, expensive*	доро́же	*dearer, more expensive*
стро́гий	*strict*	стро́же	*stricter*
твёрдый	*hard, firm*	твёрже	*harder, firmer*
густо́й	*dense*	гу́ще	*denser*
просто́й	*simple*	про́ще	*simpler*
то́лстый	*thick, fat*	то́лще	*thicker, fatter*
ча́стый	*frequent*	ча́ще	*more frequent*
чи́стый	*clean, pure*	чи́ще	*cleaner, purer*
бога́тый	*rich*	бога́че	*richer*
глухо́й	*deaf*	глу́ше	*deafer*
сухо́й	*dry*	су́ше	*drier*
ти́хий	*quiet*	ти́ше	*quieter*

Note though that in the adjectives жёлтый, *yellow*; лю́тый, *ferocious*; свято́й, *holy, sacred, saintly*; and сы́тый, *satisfied, replete*, the final **т** does not change to **ч** in the short comparative; these adjectives have the forms желте́е, люте́е, святе́е, and сыте́е respectively. Similarly худо́й, *thin*, has short comparative худе́е, *thinner*.

§4. Short comparative form of adjectives with a stem in к

The formation of the short comparative of adjectives with stems ending in **к** gives more difficulty.

In many of these adjectives the к does simply change to ч, to which the ending -е is added, e.g.

long form (positive degree)		short comp. form	
гро́мкий	*loud*	гро́мче	*louder*
жа́ркий	*hot*	жа́рче	*hotter*
жёсткий	*hard, harsh*	жёстче	*harder, harsher*
кре́пкий	*strong*	кре́пче	*stronger*
лёгкий	*light, easy*	ле́гче*	*lighter, easier*
мя́гкий	*soft, mild*	мя́гче	*softer, milder*
ре́зкий	*sharp*	ре́зче	*sharper*
я́ркий	*bright*	я́рче	*brighter*

* Note that ё changes to е.

In the adjective ме́лкий, *small, shallow*, the л becomes soft in the short comparative form: ме́льче.

In many other adjectives with a stem ending in к, however, the к disappears and the preceding consonant undergoes a change in accordance with the pattern given in §3 above, or, in the case of з, changes to ж. Thus:

long form (positive degree)		short comp. form	
бли́зкий	*near*	бли́же	*nearer*
гла́дкий	*smooth*	гла́же	*smoother*
коро́ткий	*short*	короче	*shorter*
ре́дкий	*rare*	ре́же	*rarer*
у́зкий	*narrow*	у́же	*narrower*

§5. Irregular short comparative forms

Other adjectives with stems ending in к have yet other short comparative endings, and these are best learnt, together with the short comparatives of a few other adjectives, as exceptions to all the rules given above:

long form (positive degree)		short comp. form	
глубо́кий	*deep*	глу́бже	*deeper*
далёкий	*distant, far*	да́льше	*further*
дешёвый	*cheap*	деше́вле	*cheaper*
до́лгий	*long* (of time)	до́льше	*longer*
пло́ский	*flat*	пло́ще	*flatter*
по́здний	*late*	по́зже	*later*
ра́нний	*early*	ра́ньше	*earlier*
сла́дкий	*sweet*	сла́ще	*sweeter*
то́нкий	*slim, delicate*	то́ньше	*slimmer, more delicate*
широ́кий	*wide*	ши́ре	*wider*

§6. Short comparative forms of бо́льший, etc.

The six adjectives which are capable of forming a long comparative without бо́лее (and which were given in 31.3 above) have the following short comparative forms:

long comp. form		short comp. form
бо́льший	*bigger*	бо́льше
ме́ньший	*smaller*	ме́ньше
лу́чший	*better*	лу́чше
ху́дший	*worse*	ху́же
ста́рший	*older, senior*	ста́рше
мла́дший	*younger, junior*	моло́же or мла́дше

Note particularly the spelling of ху́же.

Note also that молодо́й, *young*, does have short comparative моло́же. The form мла́дше may only mean *junior*.

The forms старе́е and худе́е do exist, but they mean *older* (of things) and *thinner* respectively.

Note also the forms вы́ше, *higher*, and ни́же, *lower*, from высо́кий and ни́зкий respectively.

§7. Adjectives with no short comparative form

There are some adjectives which are not capable of forming a short comparative. These include:

i. adjectives ending in the suffix -ский, (e.g. ру́сский, *Russian*) and in the stressed form of this suffix, -ско́й (e.g. мастерско́й, *masterly*);

ii. adjectives ending in the suffixes -овый and -евый (e.g. ма́ссовый, *mass*), and in the stressed forms of these suffixes -ово́й and -ево́й (e.g. передово́й, *leading*);

iii. many adjectives of verbal origin ending in -лый (e.g. уста́лый, *tired*);

iv. a number of adjectives with stems in к (e.g. де́рзкий, *audacious, daring*; ли́пкий, *sticky*; ро́бкий, *shy, timid*; ско́льзкий, *slippery*; тя́жкий, *severe, grave*);

v. a number of miscellaneous adjectives (e.g. больно́й, *ill*; ве́тхий, *ancient, decrepit*; го́рдый, *proud*; ли́шний, *superfluous*).

Some adjectives in -ский, though, have synonymous forms in -и́чный from which short comparatives can be formed in the usual way (e.g. траги́ческий/траги́чный, *tragic*, and the latter has траги́чнее).

§8. Use of short comparative forms

Short comparative forms are very widely used. They tend to be preferred to the long comparative forms with бóлее (see 31.2 above), since they are less cumbersome. However, they may only be used when the comparative adjective is predicative, i.e. when it is separated from the noun it qualifies by some form of the verb *to be*, e.g.

> Э́та кни́га интерéснее.
> *This book is more interesting.*
> Э́то здáние новée.
> *This building is newer.*
> Легкó вы́лечить тéло, труднée — дýшу.
> *It is easy to cure the body, it is more difficult [to cure] the soul.* (Press)

Than is rendered after short comparative adjectives by either чем + whichever case is appropriate in the context, or – more commonly, especially if the object of comparison is a pronoun – by the genitive case of the object of comparison. Note that чем must be preceded by a comma. Examples:

> Наш дом новée, чем ваш.
> *Our house is newer than yours.*
> Э́та лéкция былá интерéснее, чем вчерáшняя.
> *This lecture was more interesting than yesterday's.*
> Ры́ба дешéвле, чем мя́со.
> *Fish is cheaper than meat.*
> Её плáтье я́рче твоегó.
> *Her dress is brighter than yours.*
> Мой брат стáрше меня́.
> *My brother is older than I am.*
> Он богáче их.
> *He is richer than them.*

Note, though, that чем must be used when the objects compared are not in the nominative case, and when the object of comparison is *his, hers* or *theirs*, i.e. when the object of comparison is a word which is in any case genitive in form, e.g.

> Кли́мат в А́нглии мя́гче, чем в Росси́и.
> *The climate in England is milder than in Russia.*
> Мой чемодáн лéгче, чем егó.
> *My suitcase is lighter than his.* (The statement мой чемодáн лéгче егó would mean *my suitcase is lighter than him.*)

§9. Use of the prefix по-

The meaning of the short comparative may be modified by the addition of the prefix по-, which conveys the sense of *a little, a bit*, e.g. побóльше, *a little bigger*; подорóже, *a little more expensive*; пошире, *a bit wider*; поумнée, *a bit more intelligent*.

§10. Гора́здо, куда́ and намно́го

The adverbial phrases *much, considerably, a lot*, may be rendered before short comparatives by гора́здо, e.g. гора́здо бога́че, *much richer*; гора́здо вы́ше, *much taller*; гора́здо интере́снее, *a lot more interesting*; гора́здо нове́е, *a lot newer*.

The same meaning of *much* may be conveyed by намно́го or, more colloquially and expressively, by куда́. Examples from the press:

> Жа́нна Биче́вская стои́т намно́го бли́же к исто́кам ру́сского пе́сенного тво́рчества, чем госпожа́ Зы́кина.
> *Zhanna Bichevskaya* [a popular singer] *is much closer to the sources of Russian folk song than Ms Zykina.*
> Они́ несу́т не то́лько физи́ческие лише́ния. Куда́ тяжеле́е потрясе́ния нра́вственные.
> *They do not just bear physical privations. Considerably more severe are the moral shocks.*

§11. Comparison of adverbs

The short comparative forms may also be used as comparative adverbs. Thus краси́вее may mean *more beautifully* as well as *more beautiful*. For translation of *than* see §8 above. Examples from the press:

> Э́ти вещества́ разруша́ют защи́тный слой Земли́ быстре́е, чем образу́ется озо́н.
> *These substances destroy the Earth's protective layer more quickly than the ozone is formed.*
> В часы́ на́ших встреч майо́р глу́бже и ши́ре открыва́л зада́чи, кото́рые ста́вила пе́редо мной госбезопа́сность.
> *During our meetings the major revealed more deeply and widely the tasks which state security was setting me.*

§12. Set phrases

Short comparative adjectives or adverbs occur in a number of set phrases or constructions, e.g.

бо́льше всего́	*most of all*
как мо́жно быстре́е	*as quickly as possible*
скоре́е чем	*rather/sooner than*
чем бо́льше..., тем бо́льше...	*the more..., the more...*

Exercises

A. *Give the short comparative form of the following adjectives:* бе́дный, бле́дный, бли́зкий, бы́стрый, вре́дный, глубо́кий, глу́пый, гру́бый, гру́стный, дешёвый, до́брый, до́лгий, кре́пкий, лёгкий, логи́чный, по́лный, прия́тный, свéжий, симпати́чный, ску́чный, смéлый, смешнóй, сухóй, тёмный, типи́чный, ти́хий, тóчный, холóдный, чáстый, чéстный.

B. *Translate into Russian:* (1) It's colder in Moscow than in England. (2) He is happier than he was last year. (3) She is far more intelligent than he is. (4) She is wealthier than her sister. (5) This train is more comfortable. (6) Meat is a bit more expensive in this shop. (7) Fish is much cheaper. (8) It's much quieter in the country than in the town. (9) They are a bit more generous than my parents. (10) The Volga is wider than the Don. (11) This book is better. (12) That hotel is worse. (13) She is younger than me. (14) Your car is bigger. (15) My house is smaller. (16) The standard of living is higher. (17) Prices are lower in the country. (18) He is walking more quickly than she is. (19) He works more slowly. (20) He speaks more clearly. (21) Russian is more difficult than French. (22) Pears are sweeter than oranges. (23) She plays tennis better than I do. (24) Is this car better than yours? (25) Are cigarettes cheaper in England than they are in Russia?

LESSON 33

FORMATION AND USE OF SUPERLATIVE ADJECTIVES

§1. Superlatives formed with са́мый

Superlatives may be formed in a number of ways. The commonest form of the superlative in modern Russian is that in which са́мый is placed before an adjective in the positive degree. Са́мый agrees in number, gender and case with the adjective it precedes, and itself declines in exactly the same way as an adjective in -ый, e.g.

са́мый я́сный отве́т
the clearest answer
са́мая дешёвая маши́на
the cheapest car
са́мое тру́дное упражне́ние
the most difficult exercise
в са́мый холо́дный день
on the coldest day
из са́мого бога́того райо́на
from the richest region
по са́мой у́зкой у́лице
down the narrowest street
пе́ред са́мым краси́вым зда́нием
in front of the most beautiful building
в са́мой интере́сной статье́
in the most interesting article
Ве́чер и ночь до трёх-четырёх у меня́ са́мое све́тлое вре́мя су́ток.
The evening and the night up to three or four o'clock is the lightest part of the day for me. (Press)

§2. Superlative of лу́чший, etc.

The adjectives лу́чший, ху́дший, ста́рший, мла́дший, вы́сший, and ни́зший (but not бо́льший and ме́ньший) may have superlative as well as comparative meaning (i.e. *best, worst, oldest, youngest, highest, lowest* respectively).

All six of these adjectives may be combined with са́мый in a strong superlative sense, e.g. са́мый лу́чший студе́нт, *the very best student*. It is also possible to render *best*, etc. by са́мый + the appropriate adjective in the positive degree, e.g. са́мый хоро́ший, etc.

The superlatives са́мый большо́й, *biggest* and са́мый ма́ленький, *smallest* are much commoner than the superlatives са́мый бо́льший and са́мый ме́ньший. Examples from the press:

> Са́мый большо́й абсолю́тный приро́ст населе́ния име́ли все те же Москва́, Ленингра́д и Ки́ев.
> *Those same* [cities], *Moscow, Leningrad and Kiev, had the largest absolute population growth.*
> Воспита́ние де́ятельных гра́ждан — ещё оди́н, мо́жет быть, са́мый большо́й по ва́жности результа́т полити́ческой рефо́рмы.
> *The cultivation of active citizens is yet another result, perhaps the greatest in importance, of the political reform.*

§3. Superlatives in -ейший and -айший

As well as superlatives consisting of са́мый + adjective in the positive degree, Russian has superlative forms in -ейший or (in the case of certain adjectives) -айший.

The normal ending is -ейший, which is added to the adjectival stem, e.g.

positive degree (stem + ending)		sup. form	
бога́т-ый	*rich*	богате́йший	*richest*
до́бр-ый	*kind*	добре́йший	*kindest*
но́в-ый	*new*	нове́йший	*newest*
прост-о́й	*simple*	просте́йший	*simplest*
у́мн-ый	*intelligent*	умне́йший	*most intelligent*

In adjectives which have a stem ending in one of the velars **г**, **к**, **х**, however, the velar changes (to **ж**, **ч**, **ш**, respectively) and the ending -айший is added to the resultant stem, e.g.

positive degree (stem + ending)		sup. form	
стро́г-ий	*strict*	строжа́йший	*strictest*
глубо́к-ий	*deep*	глубоча́йший	*deepest*
сла́дк-ий	*sweet*	сладча́йший	*sweetest*
ти́х-ий	*quiet*	тиша́йший	*quietest*

A few forms do not conform to the rules given above, e.g.

positive degree (stem + ending)		sup. form	
бли́зк-ий	*near*	ближа́йший	*nearest*
ни́зк-ий	*low*	нижа́йший	*lowest*
тя́жк-ий	*grave*	тягча́йший	*gravest*

In the case of коро́ткий, *short*, the superlative from кра́ткий (кратча́йший) is used instead.

Those adjectives which do not have a short comparative form (see 32.7 above) do not as a rule have a superlative in -ейший or -айший either.

§4. Use of superlatives in -ейший and -айший

These forms have two uses. Firstly, they are an alternative to the superlative forms which consist of са́мый + adjective in the positive degree. This usage is generally literary but widespread in the modern written language. Example from the press:

> В результа́те сильне́йших лесны́х пожа́ров за после́дние два́дцать лет...
> *As a result of the fiercest forest fires of the last twenty years...*

Secondly, the superlatives in -ейший and -айший indicate in an expressive way that a quality is possessed to the utmost degree. In this meaning they will often correspond to an English superlative with the indefinite article *a* rather than the definite article *the*, e.g. интере́снейший факт, *a most interesting fact*, or зле́йший враг, *a most malevolent enemy* (i.e. not literally the most malevolent one, but one who is extremely ill-disposed). Examples from the media:

> Все райо́ны свя́заны друг с дру́гом тесне́йшим о́бразом.
> *All the regions are linked to one another in the closest way.* (Press)
> Э́то чисте́йшая пра́вда.
> *This is the purest truth.* (Press)
> Горбачёв подписа́л ряд важне́йших ука́зов.
> *Gorbachev signed a series of most important edicts.* (TV)
> при мале́йшем подозре́нии
> *on the slightest suspicion* (Press)

Superlatives in -ейший and -айший occur in many set phrases, e.g.

ближа́йший ро́дственник	*next of kin*
в ближа́йшем бу́дущем	*in the very near future*
глубоча́йшее уваже́ние	*the greatest respect*
до мельча́йших подро́бностей	*down to the smallest details*
кратча́йший срок	*the shortest possible time*
нет ни мале́йшего сомне́ния	*there is not the slightest doubt*
чисте́йший вздор	*utter nonsense*

§5. The prefix наи-

It is possible to intensify even the superlative forms in -ейший and -айший by the addition of the prefix наи-, e.g. наитала́нтливейший актёр, *the most (incredibly) talented actor*; наистрожа́йший запре́т, *the strictest (possible) ban.* The forms наибо́льший, наиме́ньший, and наилу́чший are commonly used for *biggest, smallest,* and *best* respectively, but other forms with наи- are rare.

§6. Наибо́лее and наиме́нее

A further way of forming a superlative is by the use of one of the adverbs наибо́лее, *most*, or наиме́нее, *least*, with the positive form of the adjective, e.g. наибо́лее сло́жный вопро́с, *the most complex question*; при наибо́лее благоприя́тных пого́дных усло́виях, *when the most favourable weather conditions obtain* (Press). This usage is particularly common in scientific or technical parlance.

Exercises

A. *Give a superlative form in -ейший or -айший for the following adjectives:* бе́дный, бы́стрый, вели́кий, вре́дный, глу́пый, гру́бый, гря́зный, кре́пкий, по́лный, прия́тный, си́льный, сла́бый, тёмный, то́нкий, тяжёлый.

B. *Translate into Russian:* (1) The newest house in town; (2) in the smallest room; (3) the youngest brother; (4) the eldest sister; (5) the best essay; (6) the worst plan; (7) the most intelligent candidate; (8) the most expensive refrigerator; (9) a most intelligent thought; (10) the strictest discipline; (11) the weakest student; (12) the easiest language; (13) the kindest of men; (14) a most interesting book; (15) an extremely complex question; (16) the most unfavourable weather; (17) a most serious social problem; (18) the most useful dictionaries; (19) the highest ranks; (20) given the slightest doubt.

C. Revision exercise on adjectives (Lessons 28-33).
Put the adjectives in brackets (including any adjectives used as nouns) in the correct form, using a comparative or superlative form of the adjective where the context requires it: (1) в (се́льскохозя́йственный) райо́не; (2) по (ста́рый) сти́лю; (3) е́хать на (ско́рый) по́езде; (4) гру́ппы (неме́цкий) тури́стов; (5) ба́нка (сла́дкий) мёда; (6) купи́ть (но́вый) кни́гу; (7) в (си́ний) руба́шке; (8) рю́мка (белору́сский) во́дки; (9) (дли́нный жёлтый) ю́бка; (10) (дорого́й) пла́тье; (11) в (стари́нный) собо́ре; (12) по (гла́вный) у́лице; (13) стака́н (грузи́нский) ча́я; (14) в (спа́льный) ваго́не; (15) на (тре́тий) ме́сте; (16) по (после́дний) подсчётам; (17) писа́ть (кра́сный) карандашо́м; (18) (краси́вый) цветы́; (19) кило́ (спе́лый) ви́шен; (20) по (пеки́нский) вре́мени; (21) в (небольшо́й) масшта́бе; (22) в (кра́йний) слу́чае; (23) с (ры́жий) волоса́ми; (24) меша́ть ка́шу (деревя́нный) ло́жкой; (25) (по́здний) ле́том; (26) (ра́нний) о́сенью; (27) по (круто́й) тропи́нке; (28) под (тени́стый) дере́вьями; (29) (хоро́ший) сочине́ние; (30) по (техни́ческий) причи́нам; (31) с (глубо́кий) уваже́нием; (32) (крокоди́лов) слёзы; (33) вид с (пти́чий) полёта; (34) хара́ктер (бре́жневский) пери́ода; (35) цена́ шокола́дного (моро́женое); (36) вы́йти

из (столóвая); (37) стать (воéнный); (38) рабóтать в (диспéтчерская); (39) Мешóк (пóлный) зернá. (40) Óзеро Байкáл (прозрáчный) до огрóмной глубины́. (41) Матч бу́дет (интерéсный) для любителей футбóла. (42) Вáше áлиби (фантастический). (43) Лицó у неё (кру́глый). (44) Её судьбá (трагичный). (45) Такие фильмы (неинтерéсный). (46) Э́та блу́зка ей (мáлый). (47) Э́тот свитер мне (великий). (48) Елéна Петрóвна — хрáбрая жéнщина. Онá (достóйный) наградáы. (49) Однó (непоня́тный): почему́ он э́того не сказáл. (50) Прирóда (равноду́шный) к судьбé человéка. (51) Промы́шленные отхóды (врéдный) для здорóвья. (52) Гóрод был (разру́шенный) и (пострóенный) зáново. (53) Есть у вас какие-нибудь вопрóсы? Нет, всё (я́сный). (54) Э́тот сюжéт (незабывáемый). (55) Василёк голубóй цветóк, а лю́тик (жёлтый). (56) Лисица — (хитрый) живóтное. (57) Глазá у тигра (зелёный). (58) Онá (ру́сский). (59) Отéц (стáрый) мáтери. (60) Он (высóкий) брáта. (61) Лéтом (жáркий) в Испáнии, чем в Áнглии. (62) Зимóй (холóдный) в Сибири, чем в Зáпадной Еврóпе. (63) В пусты́нях Áфрики (сухóй), чем в савáннах. (64) Э́то (полéзный) учéбник, чем мой. (65) Температу́ра у негó (низкий) сегóдня, чем вчерá. (66) Горáздо (тёплый) лéтом, чем óсенью. (67) Сигáры кудá (дорогóй), чем сигарéты. (68) Вóздух в дерéвне намнóго (чистый), чем в гóроде. (69) Рекá (глубóкий) и (ширóкий), чем ручéй. (70) Пруд (мéлкий), чем óзеро. (71) Э́то (у́мный) в клáссе студéнтка. (72) Тигр (опáсный) в джу́нглях зверь. (73) Совéтский Сою́з был (большóй) в мире странóй. (74) Из всех больны́х в палáте э́тот человéк (слáбый). (75) Домá бы́ли разру́шены в результáте (сильный) урагáнов за послéдние пять лет.

LESSON 34

PERSONAL PRONOUNS

§1. Personal pronouns

Like nouns, the personal pronouns take different forms according to their function in the sentence. (Compare the English *I, he, she, we* [nominative forms] with *me, him, her, us* [accusative forms].) The personal pronouns decline as follows:

	1st pers. sing.	2nd pers. sing.	1st pers. pl.	2nd pers. pl.
nom.	я	ты	мы	вы
acc./gen.	меня́	тебя́	нас	вас
dat.	мне	тебе́	нам	вам
instr.	мной (мно́ю)	тобо́й (тобо́ю)	на́ми	ва́ми
prep.	(обо) мне	(о) тебе́	(о) нас	(о) вас

	3rd pers. sing.			3rd pers. pl.
	masc.	neut.	fem.	all genders
nom.	он	оно́	она́	они́
acc./gen.	его́		её	их
dat.	ему́		ей	им
instr.	им		ей (е́ю)	и́ми
prep.	(о) нём		(о) ней	(о) них

The instrumental forms мно́ю, тобо́ю, е́ю are alternatives to the forms мно́й, тобо́й, ей, respectively. They are used mainly in the written language and for stylistic or rhythmical reasons. They seem to dominate after past passive participles, e.g. подпи́санный мно́ю докуме́нт, *the document signed by me.*

The prepositional forms of the personal pronouns can only be used with prepositions, and never occur independently of them. Note that о is lengthened to обо before мне.

§2. Use of prosthetic н- with third-person personal pronouns

The letter н must be added to the third-person pronouns when they occur after the great majority of prepositions, e.g. от него́, *away from him*; к нему́, *towards him*; с ним, *with him*; без неё, *without her*; по ней, *according to her*; пе́ред ней, *in front of her*; из них, *out of them*; к ним, *towards them*; ме́жду ни́ми, *between them*; and all prepositions governing the prepositional case (о нём, *about him*, etc.).

Only after a very small number of prepositions is the prosthetic **н** not added to third-person personal pronouns, namely благодаря́, вопреки́, подо́бно, согла́сно (all of which govern the dative case; see 25.7 above), and вне and внутри́ (which govern the genitive case; see 22.2 and 3 above).

The prosthetic **н** is not required with personal pronouns used in the genitive case after the short comparative adjectives (see 19.8 and 32.8 above), e.g. я ста́рше его́, *I am older than him.*

Note especially that его́, её, их, do not take the prosthetic **н** when they are possessive pronouns (i.e. when they mean *his/its* rather than *him; belonging to her/it* rather than *her/it*; and *their* rather than *them* respectively), e.g. от его́ бра́та, *from his brother*; из её ко́мнаты, *out of her room*; на их оде́жде, *on their clothes.*

§3. The reflexive personal pronoun себя́

Given its function as direct or indirect object of a verb, the reflexive pronoun can never be the subject of a clause, and it therefore has no nominative form. In the remaining cases it has the following forms:

acc./gen.	себя́
dat.	себе́
instr.	собо́й (собо́ю)
prep.	себе́

The instrumental form собо́ю is a less common and generally more bookish alternative to собо́й.

Examples:

Он был вне себя́ от гне́ва.
He was beside himself with anger.
Они́ мо́гут позво́лить себе́ списа́ть убы́тки.
They can allow themselves to write off the losses. (Press)
Джон Ме́йджор, стра́стный люби́тель чте́ния, берёт с собо́й после́дний рома́н Дже́ффри А́рчера.
John Major, a great lover of reading, is taking Jeffrey Archer's latest novel with him. (Press)
Расскажи́те о себе́.
Tell us about yourself.

Note in particular the following expressions in which the reflexive pronoun occurs:

вести́ себя́	*to behave* (i.e. *to conduct oneself*)
чу́вствовать себя́ пло́хо/хорошо́	*to feel ill/well*

читáть про себя́	*to read to oneself*
от себя́	*push* (lit. *away from oneself*; notice on door)
к себé	*pull* (lit. *to oneself*; notice on door)
ломáть/сломáть себé рýку/нóгу	*to break one's arm/leg*
так себé	*so-so*
хорóш/хорошá собóй	*handsome, good-looking*
влечь/повлéчь за собóй	*to entail, involve*
имéть при себé	*to have on one* (lit. *in one's possession*)

§4. Сам *(myself, yourself, himself, herself, itself, ourselves, yourselves, themselves)*

This pronoun declines as follows:

	masc.		neut.	fem.	pl.
nom.	сам		самó	самá	сáми
acc.	сам/	самогó	самó	самý	сáми/сами́х
gen.		самогó		самóй	сами́х
dat.		самомý		самóй	сами́м
instr.		сами́м		самóй (самóю)	сами́ми
prep.		самóм		самóй	сами́х

Сам must agree with the noun or pronoun to which it refers in number, gender and case. It is used to give emphasis to a noun or pronoun. Examples:

> Спрáшивали тáкже, чем занимáлся сам Алексáндр Бессмéртных в э́ти дни.
> *They also asked what Alexander Bessmertnykh himself had been doing during those days.* (TV)
> Суди́те сáми.
> *Judge for yourselves.* (Press)
> Я говори́л с сами́м дирéктором.
> *I spoke to the manager himself.*

§5. Сáмый

This pronoun declines in exactly the same way as an adjective of the type нóвый (see 28.3 above). Сáмый has three functions:

i. it may be used with an adjective to form a superlative, e.g. сáмый ýмный студéнт, *the most intelligent student* (see 33.1 above);

ii. it may combine with the phrases тот же, та же, etc., *the same*, to reinforce their meaning, e.g. тот же сáмый человéк, *the very same person*;

iii. it may be used with many inanimate nouns, particularly nouns indicating time or place, in the meaning of *the very*, e.g. с са́мого нача́ла, *from the very beginning*; в са́мом углу́, *right in the corner.* Example from the press:

Он опусти́лся, пьёт. Но си́льный хара́ктер помога́ет ему́ не упа́сть на са́мое дно.
He went to pieces, started drinking. But a strong character helped him not to fall to the very bottom.

Note in particular the phrases в са́мом де́ле, *really, indeed*, and на са́мом де́ле, *really, in actual fact*. The first of these two phrases affirms a preceding statement whereas the second refutes what has gone before. Examples:

Па́рень каза́лся у́мным и в са́мом де́ле оказа́лся отли́чным студе́нтом.
The lad seemed intelligent and indeed proved an excellent student.

При пе́рвом знако́мстве его́ ча́сто принима́ли за легкомы́сленного па́рня, а Ко́ллинз был на са́мом де́ле челове́ком у́мным и серьёзным.
On first acquaintance he was often taken for a frivolous lad, but in fact Collins was an intelligent and serious person. (Press)

§6. The compound pronoun друг дру́га *(each other, one another)*
Like the reflexive pronoun, this compound pronoun cannot be the subject of a clause. The first component of this pronoun (corresponding to *each* in the English expression) remains constant, while the second component declines in the same way as a masculine noun with a hard ending. Note that any preposition is placed between the two forms.

acc./gen.	друг дру́га
dat.	друг дру́гу
instr.	друг дру́гом
prep.	друг (о) дру́ге

Examples:

Они́ ненави́дят друг дру́га.
They hate one another.
Мы помога́ем друг дру́гу.
We help one another.
Друзья́ проща́ются друг с дру́гом.
The friends are saying goodbye to one another.
Сосе́ди говоря́т друг о дру́ге.
The neighbours are talking about one another.

Exercises

A. *Put the pronouns in brackets in their correct form in the following contexts, adding the prosthetic н- where necessary:* (1) прóтив (я); (2) к (он); (3) вмéсте с (онá); (4) мúмо (мы); (5) чéрез (онá); (6) сквозь (он); (7) говорúть о (онú); (8) помогáть (вы); (9) слýшать (онú); (10) дýмать о (ты); (11) мéжду (онú); (12) при (я); (13) пóсле (онó); (14) благодаря́ (онú); (15) средú (мы); (16) смотрéть на (я); (17) вопрекú (вы); (18) идтú за (ты); (19) над (онó); (20) на (онá) чёрное плáтье.

B. *Complete the following sentences by supplying the appropriate pronoun (себя́, сам, сáмый, друг дрýга) in the form required by the context:* (1) Я ... пойдý. (2) Он взял с ... бутербрóды. (3) Развóд караýлов у Букингéмского дворцá úли в Тáуэре привлекáет к ... ты́сячи и ты́сячи турúстов. (4) Онá купúла ... нóвый компью́тер. (5) Друзья́ бесéдовали друг с ... (6) Как онú относятся друг к ... ? (7) Он потёр ... лицó. (8) Вáше здорóвье во мнóгом завúсит от вас ... (9) Информациóнные прогрáммы Центрáльного телевúдения и Телевúдения Россúи не конкурúруют, а скорéе, дополня́ют друг ... (10) Водолéи бýдут спосóбны в ию́ле к крáйне неожúданным постýпкам, чтò впослéдствии бýдет вызывáть удивлéние дáже у них ... (11) Другóе дéло, éсли мы помóжем друг ... (12) Рáньше онú не знáли друг ... (13) Ваш корреспондéнт и ... бы хотéл получúть отвéт на э́тот вопрóс. (14) Сýдя по документáм, товáры бы́ли напрáвлены на реализáцию в Самаркáнд, а на ... дéле продавáли их в Ташкéнте чéрез спекуля́нтов. (15) Мы друг ... óчень лю́бим. (16) Американские избирáтели считáют, что их президéнт рабóтает так ... úли дáже плóхо. (17) Почемý нáши рýсские лю́ди так ненавúдят друг ...? (18) Онá чýвствует ... прекрáсно. (19) В ... начáле мáтча он забúл гол. (20) Беларýсь и Пóльша договорúлись, что онú не имéют территориáльных претéнзий друг к ...

C. *Translate into Russian:* (1) I myself am not interested in music. (2) She did this herself. (3) I received this copy of the book from the author himself. (4) I spoke to the prime minister himself. (5) She said this at the very beginning of the lesson. (6) The hero dies at the very end of the play. (7) They respect each other. (8) I have broken a finger. (9) They all know one another. (10) He loves himself more than her. (11) He looks ill, and indeed he is. (12) She chose a magazine for herself and a toy for her daughter. (13) They are always arguing with one another. (14) At first sight he seems a quiet person, but in fact he is very talkative. (15) This entails a lot of work. (16) He considers himself an expert. (17) She was standing right at the top of the ladder. (18) What did they say to one another? (19) Why do people kill one another? (20) This happened at the very end of the performance. (21) I saw them. (22) They saw me. (23) She telephoned him. (24) They are afraid of us. (25) We are helping her. (26) They were talking about you. (27) I love her. (28) I'll go with you, mum. (29) Are you listening to me? (30) I shall meet them.

LESSON 35

POSSESSIVE AND DEMONSTRATIVE PRONOUNS (MY, YOUR, THIS, ETC.)

§1. The possessive pronouns мой *(my)*, твой *(your)*, наш *(our)*, ваш *(your)*

These words decline as follows:

	masc.	neut.	fem.	pl.
nom.	мой	моё	моя́	мои́
acc.	мой	моё	мою́	мои́
gen.	моего́		мое́й	мои́х
dat.	моему́		мое́й	мои́м
instr.	мои́м		мое́й	мои́ми
prep.	моём		мое́й	мои́х
nom.	наш	на́ше	на́ша	на́ши
acc.	наш	на́ше	на́шу	на́ши
gen.	на́шего		на́шей	на́ших
dat.	на́шему		на́шей	на́шим
instr.	на́шим		на́шей	на́шими
prep.	на́шем		на́шей	на́ших

Твой, which is singular and informal, declines like мой; ваш, which is plural or formal, declines like наш.

These possessive pronouns are frequently omitted if the meaning is clear without them. One is likely to say, for example, я ви́дел сестру́ *(I saw my sister)*, rather than я ви́дел мою́ сестру́, although the latter sentence is also theoretically possible. The personal possessive pronouns may also give way to свой (see §3 below) if they refer to the person who is the subject of the sentence.

§2. Third-person possessive pronouns его́ *(his, its)*, её *(her, its)*, их *(their)*

These words are already genitive in form (*of him*, the genitive of он and оно́; *of her*, the genitive of она́; and *of them*, the genitive of они́, respectively). Therefore they cannot decline when used as possessive pronouns and are in this function invariable, irrespective of the gender, number and case of the noun they qualify, e.g. его́ шля́па, *his hat*; её пла́тье, *her dress*; цена́ его́ часо́в, *the price of his watch*; цвет её воло́с, *the colour of her hair*; в их саду́, *in their garden*.

Note that an initial н- is never added to его́, её, их, when they are used with this possessive function (cf. their use as personal pronouns; see 34.1-2 above).

§3. The reflexive possessive pronoun свой

Свой declines like мой and agrees in number, gender and case with the noun it qualifies.

Свой may mean *my, your, his, her, its, our, their,* or *one's*. It is used to denote possession by the person or thing which is the subject of the clause in which the possessive pronoun occurs. Consider the following examples:

i.	Я потеря́л свои́ де́ньги.	*I have lost my money.*
ii.	Ты потеря́л свои́ де́ньги.	*You have lost your money.*
iii.	Он потеря́л свои́ де́ньги.	*He has lost his money.*
iv.	Она́ потеря́ла свои́ де́ньги.	*She has lost her money.*
v.	Мы потеря́ли свои́ де́ньги.	*We have lost our money.*
vi.	Вы потеря́ли свои́ де́ньги.	*You have lost your money.*
vii.	Они́ потеря́ли свои́ де́ньги.	*They have lost their money.*

In all of these sentences свои makes it clear that it is money belonging to the subject of the sentence that has been lost. In the first, second, fifth, and sixth examples, the possessive pronouns мои́, твои́, на́ши, and ва́ши respectively might have been used instead without infringing any grammatical rule. It is particularly important to note, though, that if *his*, *her*, and *their* in the third, fourth, and seventh examples had been rendered by его́, её, and их respectively, then the meaning of these sentences would have been different: он потеря́л его́ де́ньги, for instance, would mean that he had lost his (somebody else's) money.

Examples from the press:

> Водохрани́лищем «Дру́жба» ста́ли по́льзоваться то́лько кирги́зы. Для свои́х нужд узбе́ки постро́или своё.
> *The 'Friendship' Reservoir has started to be used by the Kirghizians alone. The Uzbeks have built their own [reservoir] for their needs.*
> Я защища́ю свою́ корпора́цию. То́чно так же, как защища́ет свою́ фи́рму любо́й настоя́щий рабо́тник.
> *I defend my corporation. Just as any genuine worker defends his firm.*
> Он сообщи́л мне, что наме́рен созда́ть свой теа́тр.
> *He informed me that he intended to create his own theatre.*

In the last example above свой is used because it refers to the same person as the subject of the clause in which it occurs. *He* is the subject of the verb *intended* as well as of the verb *informed* in the main clause. However, свой may not be used when the possessive pronoun indicates possession by a subject which stands in another clause. In the sentence *He knows that I have lost his money*, for example, *his* indicates possession by the person who is the subject of the sentence as a whole, but *I*, not *he*, is the subject of the subordinate clause in which *his* occurs. This sentence must therefore be translated: Он зна́ет, что я потеря́л его́ де́ньги.

Note also that as a rule свой should not itself qualify the subject of a clause. In the statement *his money has been lost*, in which *money* is the subject, *his* must be translated by его́, and it would be wrong to use свой. However, this rule is waived in:

i. certain fixed expressions, such as своя́ руба́шка бли́же к те́лу, *charity begins at home*;

ii. certain impersonal constructions in which the subject appears in the dative or is not stated, e.g. на́до служи́ть свое́й ро́дине, *one must serve one's country*;

iii. constructions with the preposition у, which have the meaning of the English verb *to have*, e.g.

   У нас есть свой дом в дере́вне.
   We have a house of our own in the country.
   У ка́ждого но́мера своя́ ва́нная.
   Every room has its own bathroom.
   У ка́ждого из вас нашли́сь свои́ причи́ны отказа́ться от газе́ты.
   Each of you had your reasons for rejecting the paper. (Press)

Note also the use of свой in the following idiomatic expressions:

в своё вре́мя	*in one's time*
доби́ться своего́	*to get one's own way*
наста́ивать/настоя́ть на своём	*to insist on having things one's own way*

It should be added that in some sentences there are really two subjects and predicates within one clause. In the sentence *The teacher asked the pupil to pass his book*, for example, *teacher* is the main subject, and the predicate is *asked*, but we also have the verb *to pass*, and the subject of this verb is *the pupil*. The possessive pronoun *his* might mean here *the teacher's* or *the pupil's*. It is sometimes said that the use of свой in a context such as this would signify possession by the subject of the nearest verb, i.e. *the pupil* in this instance. However, in practice the Russian sentence Учи́тель попроси́л ученика́ переда́ть свою́ кни́гу would probably be no more free of ambiguity than the English sentence which it translates. In a given context, of course, ambiguity is as unlikely to arise in Russian as it is in English.

§4. The demonstrative pronouns э́тот *(this)* and тот *(that)*
These pronouns agree in number, gender and case with the noun which they precede, and they decline as follows:

	masc.	neut.	fem.	pl.
nom.	э́тот	э́то	э́та	э́ти
acc.	э́тот	э́то	э́ту	э́ти
gen.	э́того		э́той	э́тих
dat.	э́тому		э́той	э́тим
instr.	э́тим		э́той	э́тими
prep.	э́том		э́той	э́тих

	masc.	neut.	fem.	pl.
nom.	тот	то	та	те
acc.	тот	то	ту	те
gen.	того́		той	тех
dat.	тому́		той	тем
instr.	тем		той	те́ми
prep.	том		той	тех

Note the use of the neuter nominative singular form э́то in phrases such as:

Э́то был Ива́н.	*It was Ivan.*
Э́то была́ Татья́на.	*It was Tatyana.*
Э́то бы́ли Петро́вы.	*It was the Petrovs.*

Note also that (i) тот же, (ii) тот са́мый, and (iii) тот же са́мый may all translate *the same*, e.g.

в то же вре́мя	*at the same time*
та же са́мая оши́бка	*the very same mistake*

A number of adverbs have been formed by the combination of a preposition with то, in an appropriate case, e.g. пото́м, *then*; зате́м, *next*.

The words сейча́с, *now* (lit. *this hour*) and сего́дня, *today* (lit. *of this day*) contain forms of a further demonstrative pronoun сей, *this*, which survives independently in the modern language only in certain fixed expressions such as до сих пор, *hitherto* (lit. *up until these times*).

§5. The pronoun весь *(all)*
Like an adjective, весь agrees in gender, case and number with the noun it qualifies. It declines as follows:

	masc.	neut.	fem.	pl.
nom.	весь	всё	вся	все
acc.	весь	всё	всю	все

gen.	всего́	всей	всех
dat.	всему́	всей	всем
instr.	всем	всей	всéми
prep.	всём	всей	всех

The neuter form всё and the plural form все (and their oblique cases) may stand on their own in the meanings *everything* and *everyone* respectively. The form всё may also be used as an adverb to mean *constantly, all the time,* and in this sense may be combined with an imperfective verb to translate the English verb *to keep* when it denotes constant action, e.g.

> Жена́ фе́рмера пла́кала, всё повторя́ла, ука́зывая на меня́: «Мой ру́сский сын».
> *The farmer's wife wept and kept repeating, pointing at me, 'my Russian son'.* (Press)

Exercises

A. *Put the words in brackets in the correct form:* (1) с (мой) бра́том; (2) к (наш) отцу́; (3) о (твой) кни́ге; (4) во (весь) дома́х; (5) над (мой) голово́й; (6) в (тот) ме́сте; (7) на (твой) голове́; (8) о́коло (наш) до́ма; (9) (весь) неде́лю; (10) за (э́тот) исключе́нием; (11) по́сле (э́то); (12) со (свой) ма́терью; (13) с (ваш) роди́телями; (14) по (мой) мне́нию; (15) при (тот) усло́виях; (16) в результа́те (мой) рабо́ты; (17) с (тот) людьми́; (18) (ваш) друзья́; (19) по (весь) ми́ру; (20) собра́ние (весь) сочине́ний (э́тот) а́второв.

B. *Choose the appropriate Russian possessive pronoun with which to translate the English word in brackets in each of the following sentences and put it in the form required by the context:* (1) У э́той междунаро́дной организа́ции нет пока́ (its) ги́мна. (2) В статье́ вы узна́ете о (his) куми́рах в спо́рте. (3) До́лгие го́ды его́ относи́ли к кру́гу диссиде́нтов, а (his) статьи́ появля́лись лишь в «самизда́те». (4) Вы должны́ рассказа́ть о (your) успе́хах и достиже́ниях в рабо́те и учёбе. (5) Он встаёт во главе́ движе́ния за улучше́ние усло́вий труда́ и жи́зни (his) согра́ждан. (6) Про́сим вас изложи́ть (your) взгляд на собы́тия в стране́. (7) Э́то — челове́к, кото́рый чрезвыча́йно це́нит (his) вре́мя. (8) Речь пойдёт о ме́сте арти́ста в жи́зни, о (his) пози́ции в о́бществе. (9) Он влюби́лся в неё, когда́ она́ рабо́тала (his) секрета́ршей. (10) В ско́ром вре́мени у нас был со́здан (our) моско́вский филиа́л фи́рмы. (11) Есть у них (their) деви́зы. Наприме́р «спаса́ясь сам, спаса́ешь други́х». (12) Жизнь (his) была́ сли́шком коротка́. (13) Бори́су Пастерна́ку пришло́сь прожи́ть (his) зре́лые го́ды в траги́чески тру́дное вре́мя. (14) Как испо́льзуют (their) свобо́дное вре́мя жи́тели Москвы́? (15) Ира́к начнёт возвраще́ние Куве́йту (its) зо́лота, укра́денного в хо́де оккупа́ции эмира́та. (16) Президе́нт отли́чно справля́ется со (his) обя́занностями. (17) Ло́ндонцы не лю́бят (their) метро́, но лю́бят (their) зоопа́рк. (18) У люде́й ра́зных поколе́ний (their) вку́сы, (their) люби́мые кинофи́льмы. (19) Для ка́ждого во́зраста мо́жно найти́ (its) люби́мую переда́чу по телеви́дению. (20) Короле́ва-мать соверши́ла небольшу́ю прогу́лку вокру́г (her) ло́ндонского до́ма.

C. *Translate into Russian:* (1) She is talking about her brother. (2) He is talking to his (own) father. (3) They are waiting for his parents. (4) He says that his sister is at home. (5) They said their father had died. (6) He is talking about her brother. (7) They are helping their (own) parents. (8) Each year he would leave his (own) family. (9) She knows her mother does not like her job. (10) The pupil showed the teacher his first essay. (11) Every student has his own room in the hostel. (12) This theory has its advantages and disadvantages. (13) He bought his suit in London. (14) Have you received a letter from your brother? (15) She has got her own car. (16) She keeps reading the same book. (17) He took my newspaper. (18) They stole our television. (19) I talked to your mother. (20) She kept shouting at her husband.

LESSON 36

INTERROGATIVE AND RELATIVE PRONOUNS

§1. The interrogative and relative pronoun кто ***(who)***
This pronoun declines as follows:

nom.	кто
acc./gen.	когó
dat.	комý
instr.	кем
prep.	(о) ком

The main function of кто is interrogative (i.e. to ask the question *who?*). Note though the way in which its forms change depending on the function of the pronoun in the sentence. Examples:

Кто он?	*Who is he?*
Когó спрáшиваете?	*Who are you asking?*
Комý дадите подáрок?	*Who will you give the present to?*
С кем онá говорила?	*Who was she talking to?*
О ком вы говорите?	*Who are you talking about?*

In its interrogative function кто is invariably treated as a masculine singular word, even if it plainly refers to a female or to more than one person, as is clear from the following example:

> Дéвушки, кто из вас сказáл э́то?
> *Who among you / Which of you said that, girls?*

The most frequently used relative pronoun (i.e. pronoun linking a subordinate clause to an antecedent in the main clause) is котóрый (see §3.i below). However, кто may be used when the antecedent is itself a pronoun and commonly occurs with this function after various forms of тот, *that, the one, the person*, and after plural forms of весь, *all*. In its relative function too кто is generally followed by a masculine singular verb, even when it clearly refers to more than one person. Examples from the press:

> Те, кто читáл э́ту скáзку брáтьев Гримм, навернякá пóмнят истóрию милой принцéссы...
> *Those who have read this Grimms' fairy-tale no doubt remember the story of the sweet princess...*

Тем, кто де́лал револю́цию в Росси́и и тем, кто пове́рил в неё по́зже, пока́ не удало́сь осуществи́ть свою́ мечту́.
Those who made the revolution in Russia and those who later on believed in it have not yet succeeded in bringing their dream to fulfilment.
Мы привы́кли говори́ть начистоту́ со все́ми, кто обраща́ется в журна́л.
We have formed the habit of speaking without equivocation with all those who approach the journal.

§2. The interrogative and relative pronoun что *(what)*

This pronoun declines as follows:

nom./acc.	что
gen.	чего́
dat.	чему́
instr.	чем
prep.	(о) чём

Что asks the question *what?* and is invariably treated as a neuter singular word. Note the way in which its forms change depending on the function of the word in the sentence. Examples:

Что случи́лось?	*What has happened?*
Что э́то тако́е?	*What is this?*
Что вы купи́ли?	*What have you bought?*
Из чего́ э́то сде́лано?	*What's this made of?*
К чему́ стреми́тесь?	*What are you striving for?*
Чем занима́етесь?	*What are you working on/What are you studying?*
О чём ду́маете?	*What are you thinking about?*

Что frequently occurs in conjunction with some form of то, e.g. я не соглаша́юсь с тем, что он говори́т, *I do not agree with what he says.*

§3. The relative and interrogative pronouns кото́рый and како́й *(which)*

i. Кото́рый as a relative pronoun

The most frequently used relative pronoun is кото́рый, which may refer to both animate and inanimate antecedents (i.e. it may render either *who* or *which*). Кото́рый declines in the same way as an adjective of the type но́вый (see 28.3 above).

Like an adjective, кото́рый must agree in both gender and number with its antecedent, but its case is determined by the role it plays within the subordinate clause which it introduces. In the sentence

The car which is standing in front of the station has broken down, for example, the pronoun *which* is the subject of the subordinate clause *which is standing in front of the station* and must therefore be rendered in Russian by a nominative form of кото́рый (маши́на, кото́рая стои́т пе́ред вокза́лом, слома́лась). In the sentence *The car which I bought yesterday has broken down*, on the other hand, *which* is the direct object of the verb *bought* and must therefore be rendered in Russian by an accusative form of кото́рый (маши́на, кото́рую я купи́л вчера́, слома́лась). Further examples:

Маши́на, из кото́рой вы́шла ва́ша жена́, слома́лась.
The car which your wife got out of has broken down.
Маши́на, в кото́рой е́хал президе́нт, слома́лась.
The car which the president was travelling in broke down.
Маши́на, за кото́рой стои́т милиционе́р, слома́лась.
The car which the policeman is standing behind has broken down.
Маши́ны, к кото́рым шёл авто́бус, слома́лись.
The cars which the bus was travelling towards have broken down.

Note that whereas the relative pronoun may often be omitted in English (it would be possible to say for example *The car I bought yesterday has broken down*), in Russian it may never be omitted.

ii. Како́й as a relative pronoun

Како́й, which declines like an adjective with a stem in a velar and with stressed endings (e.g. дорого́й; see 28.4 above), is much less common than кото́рый as a relative pronoun. It implies that the antecedent is a certain type of thing, of a certain sort, and is most frequently encountered when тако́й, *such*, is included, or at least understood, in the antecedent. Examples:

Она́ вы́брала таки́е пла́тья, каки́е каза́лись подходя́щими для рабо́ты.
She chose dresses which seemed suitable for work [i.e. *such dresses as seemed suitable*].
Есть утвержде́ние, что смерть совсе́м не така́я, како́й мы обы́чно её представля́ем.
Some people assert that death is not at all the sort of thing which we usually present it as. (Press)

iii. Како́й and кото́рый as interrogative pronouns (*what? which?*)

Both како́й and кото́рый may be used interrogatively, in questions asking *what?* or *which?*

A clear distinction used to be made between какóй and котóрый as interrogative pronouns, namely:

(a) какóй should be used if the answer is expected to describe the quality or type of something, to say what sort of thing it is, e.g. Какáя сегóдня погóда? *What is the weather like today?*

whereas

(b) котóрый should be used if the answer is expected to select an item out of a limited number or give the position of something in a numerical series, e.g. Котóрую из э́тих книг вы предпочитáете? *Which of these books do you prefer?* (given as an example by Borras and Christian)

However, nowadays almost all questions requiring the use of one of these pronouns may be put by using какóй, e.g.

Какóй у вас нóмер? — Двáдцать шестóй.
'Which is your room?' 'Twenty-six'.
Какáя из двух книг тебé нрáвится бóльше?
Which of the two books do you prefer?
Дай мне кни́гу. — Какýю?
'Give me a book'. 'Which one?'
Каки́е ви́на вы лю́бите?
What wines do you like?
Каки́х рýсских áвторов вы читáли?
Which Russian authors have you read?

Котóрый, as an interrogative pronoun, can only really be considered obligatory in expressions of time such as Котóрый час? *What time is it?* and В котóром часý вы уезжáете? *At what time are you leaving?*

iv. Какóв

Какóй has a predicative form (masc. какóв; fem. каковá; neut. каковó; pl. каковы́) which may be used when some part of the verb *to be* intervenes between the interrogative pronoun and the noun to which it refers. Examples from the media:

Какóв ýровень профессионали́зма госудáрственных коммерсáнтов?
What is the level of professionalism of state businessmen? (Press)
Каковó вáше отношéние к сою́зному договóру?
What is your attitude to the union treaty? (TV)
Каковы́ пéрвые результáты рабóты?
What are the first results of the work? (Press)

Какóв may also mean *what...like?*, e.g. Какóв он?, *What's he like?*

§4. Exclamatory pronouns (какóй, такóй, какóв, такóв)

Какóй may also be used in an exclamatory sense, e.g. Какóй чудéсный вид!, *What a marvellous view!*; Какáя нáглость! *What impertinence!*

The predicative forms of какóй (какóв, etc., see §3.iv above) may also be used in an exclamatory sense, e.g. Каковá погóда! *What weather!*

Такóй, *such, so, as*, should be used in its long form if the adjective that follows it is also in the long form, but if the adjective is in the short form then the invariable adverbial form так should be used, e.g. такúе дешёвые билéты, *such cheap tickets*, but билéты так дёшевы, *the tickets are so cheap*.

Like какóй, такóй has predicative forms (masc. такóв; fem. таковá; neut. таковó; pl. таковы́). Example:

> Ситуáция для них таковá, что и присни́ться лу́чше не мóжет.
> *The situation for them is such that he cannot dream of [anything] better.* (Press)

Такóв may also mean *like that*, e.g. Он такóв, *He's like that.*

The predicative form also occurs in the expression и был такóв, *and that was the last we saw of him.*

§5. The interrogative pronoun чей *(whose)*

This pronoun declines as follows:

	masc.	neut.	fem.	pl.
nom.	чей	чьё	чья	чьи
acc.	чей	чьё	чью	чьи
gen.	чьегó		чьей	чьих
dat.	чьему́		чьей	чьим
instr.	чьим		чьей (чьéю)	чьи́ми
prep.	(о) чьём		(о) чьей	(о) чьих

Чей, like an adjective, must agree in gender, case and number with the noun to which it refers, e.g.

> Чей э́то словáрь?
> *Whose dictionary is this?*
> Чья э́то кни́га?
> *Whose is this book?*
> Чью кни́гу читáешь?
> *Whose book are you reading?*
> Из чьегó дóма выходи́ла?
> *Whose house was she coming out of?*

В чьей квартúре вы остáвили зóнтик?
In whose flat did you leave your umbrella?
О чьих взглядах вы говорúте?
Whose views are you talking about?

Note the use of the neuter form э́то in questions framed with чей irrespective of the gender of the noun that follows (see the first and second examples above).

Чей may also be used as a relative pronoun, e.g. áвтор, чья кнúга извéстна, *the author whose book is well-known.* However, this example could equally well be recast using котóрый (áвтор, кнúга котóрого извéстна), and котóрый is generally preferred to чей as a relative pronoun.

§6. The suffixes -то, -нибудь, and -либо

These suffixes may be added to кто, что, когдá, где, кудá, какóй, как, to render *someone, something, some time, somewhere, (to) somewhere, some, somehow,* etc.

Of the two suffixes -то and -нибудь, the former indicates someone or something more definite than the latter. Consequently -то will translate into English as *some-*, whereas -нибудь may translate as either *some-* or *any-* depending on the context. Examples:

Он сказáл чтó-то, но я не расслы́шал.
He said something, but I did not catch it [i.e. something definitely was said, but what exactly it was is not known].
Ваш друг приходúл и остáвил вам чтó-то.
Your friend came and left something for you [i.e. something was definitely left, but what precisely is not known by the speaker, or the speaker will not say].
Ктó-то разбúл стеклó машúны и сýнул емý в лицó спрей.
Someone [a particular person, although his identity is not known] *broke the car window and shoved a spray in his face.* (Press)
Он ищет когó-то.
He is looking for someone [i.e. someone in particular, but the speaker does not know whom].
Почтú кáждый день ктó-нибудь мне звонúт и пúшет.
Almost every day someone [or other, different people on different days] *rings me and writes.* (Press)
Éсли ктó-нибудь позвонúт, скажúте им, что я придý в вóсемь часóв.
If anyone rings, tell them I'll come at eight o'clock.

Being vaguer, -нибудь tends to occur more than -то with the future, about which there is less certainty, and with the interrogative.

An indication of the uncertainty often associated with -нибудь is the frequent presence in the context of some such expression as вероя́тно, *probably*;

должно́ быть, *must* (i.e. *it must be the case*); наве́рно, *probably, most likely, I expect.* Example:

> Наве́рно он пойдёт в магази́н и ку́пит что́-нибудь.
> *I expect he'll go to the shop and buy something* [what exactly is not yet known].

In the past tense -нибудь will be used if there is a choice or range of possibilities. Compare the following examples:

> Он всё вре́мя свиста́л каку́ю-то мело́дию.
> *He was always whistling some tune* [but the speaker cannot remember which one].
> Он всё вре́мя свиста́л каку́ю-нибудь мело́дию.
> *He was always whistling some tune or other.*
> Ка́ждое у́тро он уходи́л куда́-то.
> *Every morning he went somewhere* [always the same place].
> Ка́ждое у́тро он уходи́л куда́-нибудь.
> *Every morning he went somewhere* [different places on different mornings].

This sense of choice or range of possibilities is what lies behind the exclusive use of -нибудь with the imperative, e.g.

> Поговори́те с ке́м-нибудь об э́том.
> *Have a talk with somebody about it.*

The suffix -либо has two functions: (i) it is a less common alternative to -нибудь, and (ii) it may indicate even greater vagueness than -нибудь, and in this function is often equivalent to an English expression including *at all*, e.g.

> Спроси́те кого́-либо.
> *Ask anyone at all.*

§7. Negative pronouns

The forms никто́, *nobody*; ничто́, *nothing*; никогда́, *never*; нигде́, *nowhere*; никуда́, *(to) nowhere*; никако́й, *no, not a single*; ника́к, *in no way*, must be combined with the negative particle не to complete the meaning. The first two of these pronouns decline like кто and что respectively:

nom.	никто́	ничто́
acc./gen.	никого́	ничего́
gen.	никому́	ничему́
instr.	нике́м	ниче́м
prep.	ни (о) ком	ни (о) чём

If a preposition is combined with either of these words or with никакóй, then it is placed between the particle ни and the appropriate form of кто, что or какóй (e.g. ни от когó, *from nobody*; ни к чемý, *to nothing*; ни с кем, *with nobody*; ни в какúх, *not in any*), as is invariably the case in the prepositional. Examples:

Никтó не вúдел егó.	*Nobody saw him.*
Онá ничегó не вúдела.	*She saw nothing.*
Мы никомý не помогáем.	*We are not helping anybody.*
Он ни с кéм не говорúл.	*He was not speaking to anybody.*
Я ни о чём не дýмаю.	*I'm not thinking about anything.*
Мы никогдá не говорúм об э́том.	*We never speak about this.*
Я никудá не ходúл.	*I didn't go anywhere.*

Note though that when ничтó is split by prepositions governing the accusative then its second component is что, not чегó, e.g. ни за что, *not for anything*.

These negative pronouns should not be confused with нéкто, нéчто, нéкогда, нéгде, нéкуда (see 23.9 above).

Exercises

A. *Put the interrogative pronouns in brackets in the correct form in the following contexts:* (1) О (кто) вы говорúли? (2) С (кто) вы идёте в кинó? (3) (Что) бойтесь? (4) (Кто) вы вúдели? (5) (Что) удивля́етесь? (6) На (что) положúли кнúгу? На стол úли на пóлку? (7) (Кто) бýдете помогáть, мне úли емý? (8) Что вы лю́бите дéлать в свобóдное врéмя, (что) интересýетесь? (9) За (кто) бýдете голосовáть на вы́борах? (10) О (что) дýмаете?

B. *Insert the correct form of the relative pronoun* котóрый *in the space provided in each of the following sentences:* (1) Мой брат ýчится в шкóле, ... нахóдится в цéнтре гóрода. (2) Мы бы́ли в кинó, ... нахóдится на сосéдней ýлице. (3) Вы вúдели пúсьма, ... лежáли на столé? (4) Я получúл письмó, в ... отéц пúшет о болéзни мáмы. (5) Вы читáли кнúгу, в ... Толстóй пúшет о своём дéтстве? (6) В том дóме живёт человéк, ... я знáю с дéтства. (7) Пьéса «Три сестры́», ... я в пéрвый раз вúдел в прóшлом годý, мне кáжется сáмым удáчным произведéнием Чéхова. (8) Я не знáю студéнтов, о ... вы говорúли. (9) Дéвушка, с ... я встрéтился вчерá, рабóтает в библиотéке. (10) Дéвушка, ... стоúт у останóвки, рабóтает в университéте. (11) Гóрод, к ... мы приближáемся, столúца Грýзии. (12) Ýлица, по ... мы идём, Нéвский проспéкт. (13) Лю́ди, с ... я говорúл, эстóнцы. (14) Жéнщина, от ... вы узнáли э́то, моя́ бáбушка. (15) Лýчше не доверя́ть лю́дям, ... не знáете.

C. *Replace the English words in brackets in the following sentences with the appropriate Russian pronoun in the form required by the context:* (1) (Which) газе́ту вы чита́ете? (2) Биле́ты (so) до́роги, что они́ мне не по карма́ну. (3) В (what) часу́ вы встаёте по утра́м? (4) Он не зна́ет таки́х люде́й, с (whom) он хоте́л бы говори́ть об э́том. (5) Вам ску́чно? Чита́йте (something). (6) Детекти́вы подозрева́ли (someone), но не арестова́ли его́. (7) (Whose) э́то кольцо́? (8) Мо́жет быть я (sometime) пое́ду туда́. (9) (Such) судьба́ мое́й ро́дины. (10) В (which) ряду́ сиде́ли в теа́тре? (11) Есть у вас (any) вопро́сы? (12) Она́ (never) не звони́т мне. (13) (What) перспекти́вы вы́сшего образова́ния в Брита́нии? (14) (What) краси́вые цветы́! (15) Пу́шкин, запи́сывая ру́сские наро́дные пе́сни, отмеча́л и при (what) обстоя́тельствах они́ пою́тся.

D. *Translate into Russian:* (1) What sort of weather do you like, hot or cold? (2) Which dish did you choose, the meat or the fish? (3) Which shirt did you buy? (4) At what time do you go to work? (5) What a fool! (6) He is such a braggart! (7) The oranges were so nice. (8) Whose car were you travelling in? (9) Whose house is that? (10) Whose words do you believe, mine or his? (11) He saw someone at the station. (12) He took something with him. (13) Someone will come. (14) He'll probably go away somewhere. (15) The children were playing somewhere. (16) Someone came into the shop. (17) You must take something for yourself. (18) You should talk to someone about it. (19) He'll ring me sometime. (20) He met some girl in Cyprus. (21) She never reads. (22) She is not afraid of anyone. (23) He knows nothing. (24) I'm not going anywhere. (25) They never help anyone.

E. Revision exercise on pronouns (Lessons 34-36).
Complete the following phrases and sentences by putting the words in brackets in the form required by the context or (in nos. 63-69) by choosing the correct particle, or (in nos. 70-75) by providing the correct translation: (1) во (весь) магази́нах; (2) смотре́ть на (я); (3) купи́ть (себя́) но́вое пла́тье; (4) к (ты); (5) по (весь) ми́ру; (6) встре́титься с (они́); (7) боро́ться друг с (друг); (8) говори́ть обо (всё); (9) носи́ть при (себя́); (10) сказа́ть э́то при (он); (11) говори́ть про (себя́); (12) со (весь) сторо́н; (13) по (мой) мне́нию; (14) из-за (тот) фа́кта; (15) расста́ться с (они́); (16) до (э́то); (17) ре́зать (себя́) губу́; (18) ви́деть пе́ред (себя́); (19) благодаря́ (она́); (20) в связи́ с (э́то); (21) из-за (вы); (22) ме́жду (мы); (23) про́тив (ты); (24) вы́йти за́муж за (он); (25) пе́ред (наш) визи́том; (26) люби́ть друг (друг); (27) по (э́тот) причи́не; (28) в отве́т на (ваш) письмо́; (29) ря́дом с (он); (30) пе́ред (твой) глаза́ми; (31) в (тот) числе́; (32) без (э́то); (33) помога́ть друг (друг); (34) Она́ (сам) не хоте́ла э́того. (35) У (он) была́ гре́ческая жена́. (36) У (мы) есть но́вая кварти́ра. (37) (Что) вы бои́тесь? (38) (Кто) звони́те? (39) (Что) они́ интересу́ются? (40) (Кто) вы спра́шивали? (41) О (что) говори́те? (42) Они́ (сам) по́няли э́то. (43) Он жени́лся на (она́). (44) Он соста́рился. Ско́лько (он) лет? (45) Э́то удиви́ло их (сам). (46) С (како́й) результа́том? (47) На (что) сиде́ли? (48) В (како́й) смы́сле? (49) На (како́й) уро́ках? (50) В (кото́рый) часу́ придёшь? (51) (Како́й) замеча́тельные глаза́! (52) (Чей) э́то маши́на? (53) (Чей) э́то пальто́? (54) (Чей) э́то

чемода́ны? (55) (Чей) э́то пиджа́к? (56) На́до уче́сть, в (како́й) тру́дных усло́виях они́ рабо́тают. (57) Я не чита́л кни́гу, о (кото́рый) вы говори́те. (58) По́езд, на (кото́рый) он е́дет, опа́здывает на два часа́. (59) Вы уже́ зна́ете люде́й, с (кото́рый) вы бу́дете рабо́тать? (60) В э́том регио́не нахо́дятся за́лежи мно́гих ви́дов поле́зных ископа́емых, среди́ (кото́рый) у́голь, нефть, газ. (61) Це́рковь публи́чно выска́зывается о пробле́мах свое́й вну́тренней жи́зни, в числе́ (кото́рый) и пробле́мы религио́зного образова́ния и воспита́ния. (62) Я познако́мился с челове́ком, (кото́рый) дли́тельное вре́мя рабо́тал в Кита́е. (63) Она́ была́ когда́-(...) на Кавка́зе. (64) Приходи́те ко мне, е́сли когда́-(...) бу́дете в Москве́. (65) Спроси́те кого́-(...). (66) Он кого́-(...) ви́дел, но не узна́л его́. (67) Он куда́-(...) ушёл. (68) Вы́берите что-(...) для до́чки. (69) Он как-(...) дошёл до вокза́ла. (70) Аспира́нт защити́л (his) диссерта́цию. (71) Аспира́нт говори́т, что профе́ссор хва́лит (his) диссерта́цию. (72) Она́ не лю́бит (her) ро́дину. (73) Они́ сиде́ли в (their) саду́. (74) (Their) сад был по́лон цвето́в. (75) Она́ слы́шала, как пла́кал (her) ребёнок.

LESSON 37

CARDINAL NUMERALS

This lesson will deal with the nominative/accusative forms of cardinal numerals (оди́н, два, три, etc.) and their usage. The following lesson (38) will deal with the declension of the cardinal numerals and their use in the oblique cases. Subsequent lessons will deal with other words expressing quantity, collective numerals (дво́е, тро́е, че́тверо, etc.), and nouns which express number (дво́йка, тро́йка, четвёрка, etc.; see 39); ordinal numbers (пе́рвый, второ́й, тре́тий, etc.), time and dates (40); miscellaneous points relating to the use of numerals (41); and the use of numerals in expression of age, distance, measurement and computation (42).

§1. The cardinal numbers

These are as follows:

1	оди́н/одна́/одно́	30	три́дцать
2	два/две	40	со́рок
3	три	50	пятьдеся́т
4	четы́ре	60	шестьдеся́т
5	пять	70	се́мьдесят
6	шесть	80	во́семьдесят
7	семь	90	девяно́сто
8	во́семь	100	сто
9	де́вять	200	две́сти
10	де́сять	300	три́ста
11	оди́ннадцать	400	четы́реста
12	двена́дцать	500	пятьсо́т
13	трина́дцать	600	шестьсо́т
14	четы́рнадцать	700	семьсо́т
15	пятна́дцать	800	восемьсо́т
16	шестна́дцать	900	девятьсо́т
17	семна́дцать	1000	ты́сяча
18	восемна́дцать	*a million*	миллио́н
19	девятна́дцать	*a billion*	миллиа́рд
20	два́дцать		

Note in particular the distribution of soft signs in these numerals: in all the numbers 5 to 30 there is a soft sign at the end of the word but never in any other position, while in the numbers 50, 60, 70, 80, 500, 600, 700, 800, and 900 there is a soft sign in the middle, between the two components, but never at the end.

Note also the numerals óба/óбе, *both*, and полторá/полторы́, *one and a half*. The word полторáста, *one hundred and fifty*, may also be encountered, but it is less widely used than the synonymous сто пятьдеся́т.

§2. Оди́н

This word declines like the adjective э́тот (see 35.4 above):

	masc.	neut.	fem.	pl.
nom.	оди́н	однó	однá	одни́
acc.	оди́н	однó	однý	одни́
gen.	одногó		однóй	одни́х
dat.	одномý		однóй	одни́м
instr.	одни́м		однóй	одни́ми
prep.	однóм		однóй	одни́х

The plural forms are for use with nouns which exist in the plural form only (see 3.2 above), e.g. одни́ часы́, *one clock*; одни́ нóжницы, *one pair of scissors*. They may also be used when the word has the meaning of *only* or *alone* rather than *one*, e.g. онá читáет одни́ рýсские ромáны, *she reads only/nothing but Russian novels.*

Оди́н/однá/однó not only declines but is also used in the same way as an adjective, in that it agrees in gender and case with the following noun, e.g.

оди́н стол	*one table*
однá кни́га	*one book*
однó окнó	*one window*
одногó столá	*of one table*
под одни́м столóм	*under one table*
в однóй кни́ге	*in one book*

Even when оди́н/однá/однó is the final component of a compound number the following noun and any predicate remain singular, e.g.

двáдцать оди́н стол
21 tables
сто двáдцать однá кни́га
121 books
Тóлько три́дцать оди́н избирáтель проголосовáл за коммуни-сти́ческую пáртию.
Only 31 electors voted for the Communist Party.

An adjective qualifying the noun has the same gender, case and number as the numeral and the noun, e.g.

оди́н деревя́нный стол *one wooden table*

однá интерéсная кни́га	*one interesting book*
однó гря́зное окнó	*one dirty window*

§3. Два/две, три, четы́ре, óба/óбе, полторá/полторы́

The forms два, *two*; óба, *both*; and полторá, *one and a half*, are used with masculine and neuter nouns, while две, óбе, and полторы́ are used with feminine nouns. Три and четы́ре may be used with nouns of all three genders.

When два/две, óба/óбе, полторá/полторы́, три, and четы́ре are themselves used in the nominative or accusative case the noun that follows them is in the genitive singular case, e.g.

два столá	*two tables*
два окнá	*two windows*
две кни́ги	*two books*
óба телефóна	*both telephones*
óба пóля	*both fields*
óбе газéты	*both newspapers*
полторá часá	*one and a half hours*
полторы́ недéли	*one and a half weeks*
три мéсяца	*three months*
четы́ре журнáла	*four journals*

Even when два/две, три, четы́ре is the final component of a compound number the following noun remains in the genitive singular, e.g.

двáдцать два столá	*22 tables*
сто двáдцать два окнá	*122 windows*
ты́сяча сто двáдцать две кни́ги	*1122 books*
сóрок три корабля́	*43 ships*
пятьдеся́т четы́ре дóма	*54 houses*

If an adjective is used with a noun after any of these numerals then it will be in the genitive plural if the noun is masculine or neuter, and in the nominative/accusative plural (or possibly genitive plural) if the noun is feminine, e.g.

два больши́х столá	*two large tables*
три зелёных пóля	*three green fields*
четы́ре чёрные (or чёрных) кóшки	*four black cats*

This rule holds good even with nouns which are substantivised adjectives (i.e. adjectives in form that are used as nouns), e.g.

четы́ре портны́х	*four tailors*
три морóженых	*three ice-creams*
две столóвые	*two dining-rooms*

Adjectives qualifying feminine nouns were more often used in the genitive plural after the numerals две, три and четыре in the nineteenth century than they are nowadays.

§4. Пять, etc.

After all other numerals (i.e. пять, шесть, etc. and all compound numbers in which a numeral other than 1, 2, 3, or 4 is the last component) the genitive plural must be used for both the noun and any adjective which qualifies it (assuming the numeral itself is in the nominative or accusative case), e.g.

пять больши́х столо́в	*five large tables*
шесть интере́сных книг	*six interesting books*
семь высо́ких зда́ний	*seven tall buildings*
пятьдеся́т я́сных приме́ров	*fifty clear examples*
Компа́ния купи́ла сто де́сять но́вых маши́н.	*The company bought 110 new cars.*
полтора́ста киломе́тров	*150 kilometres*
две́сти фа́брик	*200 factories*
пятьсо́т часо́в	*500 hours*

Ты́сяча, when used in the nominative or accusative, is also always followed by a genitive plural of the noun and any accompanying adjectives, e.g.

ты́сяча цветны́х телеви́зоров
1000 colour television sets
Я ви́дел ты́сячу жёлтых цвето́в.
I saw a thousand yellow flowers.

Exercises

A. *Write out the numerals in the following sentences and put the nouns and adjectives in brackets in the correct case and number:* (1) На нефтедобыва́ющей платфо́рме на моме́нт ава́рии находи́лся 121 (рабо́чий). (2) В тот день в столи́це Хорва́тии прогреме́ли ещё 4 (мо́щный взрыв). (3) Годово́й оборо́т фе́рмы 200 (ты́сяча) до́лларов. (4) Не исключено́, что сове́тские телезри́тели смо́гут уви́деть все 52 (матч) чемпиона́та ми́ра в Ита́лии. (5) По прогно́зам Моско́вской би́ржи труда́, по́сле пе́рвого ию́ля в Москве́ зарегистри́руются 57000 (безрабо́тный). (6) 28 (проце́нт) анке́т запо́лнены уча́щейся молодёжью, 21 (проце́нт) — пенсионе́рами. (7) Число́ иностра́нных гра́ждан, изуча́ющих ру́сский язы́к, превыша́ет 25 (миллио́н) челове́к. (8) Расчёты пока́зывают, что произво́дтсво автомоби́льного бензи́на сни́зится на 5 (проце́нт). Произво́дство то́почного мазу́та уме́ньшится на 2-3 (проце́нт). (9) Сове́тские спортсме́ны завоева́ли 188 (меда́ль). Из них 66 (золото́й), 68 (серебряный) и 54 (бро́нзовый). Кома́нда Соединённых Шта́тов получи́ла соотве́тственно 60, 53 и 48 — то есть 161 (награ́да). На тре́тьем ме́сте сбо́рная кома́нда ГДР — 11 (золото́й), 8 (сере́бряный) и 24 (бро́нзовая награ́да) — всего́ 43. (10) В Эсто́нии насчи́тывается 23843 (предприя́тие). Из них госуда́рственных — 8264, кооперати́вных — 7530, акционе́рных — 3692, ча́стных — 1450, совме́стных с зарубе́жными партнёрами — 266. Во второ́м кварта́ле теку́щего го́да ликвиди́ровано 78 (предприя́тие), из них 21 (кооперати́вный) и 47 (госуда́рственный).

B. *Translate into Russian:* (1) One house; one flat; one exercise; twenty-one houses; twenty-one flats; twenty-one exercises; (2) two houses; two flats; two exercises; twenty-two houses; twenty-two flats; twenty-two exercises; (3) three houses; three flats; three exercises; thirty-three houses; thirty-three flats; thirty-three exercises; (4) four houses; twenty-four houses; forty-four houses; a hundred and four houses; a hundred and fifty-four houses; (5) five houses; six houses; seven houses; eight houses; nine houses; ten houses; (6) five rooms; six rooms; seven rooms; eight rooms; nine rooms; ten rooms; (7) five fields; six fields; seven fields; eight fields; nine fields; ten fields; (8) twenty rooms; twenty-five fields; forty houses; ninety houses; a hundred houses; (9) a hundred and forty houses; two hundred and twenty-five houses; three hundred and fifty houses; four hundred and sixty houses; five hundred and thirty-two women; five hundred and thirty-three women; seven hundred and sixty-eight women; (10) a thousand houses; a million houses; two million houses; five million houses.

LESSON 38

DECLENSION OF CARDINAL NUMERALS

With the exception of оди́н all numerals dealt with in the previous lesson were used only in their nominative or accusative forms. Obviously, though, numerals are used in many contexts where they are not the subject of a verb or its direct object, and where they themselves will therefore have to be used in an oblique case.

The full declension of the cardinal numerals is set out below.

§1. Declension of два/две, три, четы́ре

	masc./neut.	fem.	all genders	all genders
nom.	два	две	три	четы́ре
acc.	два/двух	две/двух	три/трёх	четы́ре/четырёх
gen.	двух		трёх	четырёх
dat.	двум		трём	четырём
instr.	двумя́		тремя́	четырьмя́
prep.	двух		трёх	четырёх

It will be noted that два, три, and четы́ре have two accusative forms, one identical with the nominative, the other identical with the genitive. On the use of these forms see 41.2 below.

§2. Declension of о́ба/о́бе

	masc./neut.	fem.
nom.	о́ба	о́бе
acc.	о́ба/обо́их	о́бе/обе́их
gen.	обо́их	обе́их
dat.	обо́им	обе́им
instr.	обо́ими	обе́ими
prep.	обо́их	обе́их

A genitive singular form of the masculine о́ба survives in the phrase обо́его по́ла, *of both sexes*, e.g. совме́стное обуче́ние ученико́в обо́его по́ла, *co-education* (lit. *joint education of pupils of both sexes*).

Strictly speaking the masculine/neuter form полторá and the feminine form полторы́, *one and a half*, have полу́тора in all oblique cases, e.g. объéкт, имéющий в длину́ óколо полу́тора мéтров, *an object about one and a half metres long* (Press). However, this form is likely to be avoided in the modern spoken language.

§3. Declension of пять, etc. up to двáдцать and три́дцать

nom./acc.	пять
gen./dat./prep.	пяти́
instr.	пятью́

All the numerals above пять and up to двáдцать, and also три́дцать, decline like пять (i.e. like a feminine noun ending in a soft sign). Note that the stress of the numerals up to and including дéсять, and also of двáдцать and три́дцать, is on the ending in all the oblique cases. In the numerals from оди́ннадцать to девятнáдцать inclusive, on the other hand, the stress remains on the stem in all cases.

Note also that вóсемь has a mobile vowel, with the result that the genitive/dative/prepositional form is восьми́ and the instrumental form is восьмью́. (The form восемью́ may also be found.)

§4. Declension of сóрок, девянóсто, сто, полторáста

The first three of these numerals have the ending -а in all oblique cases. Thus the forms сорокá, девянóста, and ста may serve as the genitive, dative, instrumental or prepositional case of сóрок, девянóсто and сто respectively.

Полторáста, *one hundred and fifty*, theoretically has полу́тораста in all oblique cases, but this form is likely to be avoided in the modern spoken language.

§5. Declension of пятьдеся́т, шестьдеся́т, сéмьдесят, вóсемьдесят

The declension of these numerals is more complicated, because both their components decline, albeit in the same way as пять, шесть, семь, вóсемь, and дéсять.

nom./acc.	пятьдеся́т	шестьдеся́т
gen./dat./prep.	пяти́десяти	шести́десяти
instr.	пятью́десятью	шестью́десятью
nom./acc.	сéмьдесят	вóсемьдесят
gen./dat./prep.	семи́десяти	восьми́десяти
instr.	семью́десятью	восьмью́десятью

§6. Declension of двéсти, трúста, четы́реста

These words decline as follows:

nom./acc.	двéсти	трúста	четы́реста
gen.	двухсóт	трёхсóт	четырёхсóт
dat.	двумстáм	тремстáм	четырёмстáм
instr.	двумястáми	тремястáми	четырьмястáми
prep.	двухстáх	трёхстáх	четырёхстáх

§7. Declension of пятьсóт, шестьсóт, семьсóт, восемьсóт, девятьсóт

These words decline according to the following pattern:

nom./acc.	пятьсóт	восемьсóт
gen.	пятисóт	восьмисóт
dat.	пятистáм	восьмистáм
instr.	пятьюстáми	восьмьюстáми
prep.	пятистáх	восьмистáх

§8. Declension of ты́сяча, миллиóн, миллиáрд

Ты́сяча may be treated either as a noun (in which case it is followed, irrespective of its own case, by a noun in the genitive plural, e.g. в ты́сяче деревéнь, *in a thousand villages*) or a numeral (in which case it is followed by a noun in the same case as itself, and in the plural, e.g. в ты́сяче деревня́х, also meaning *in a thousand villages*). It has accusative ты́сячу, genitive ты́сячи, and dative/prepositional ты́сяче. The instrumental form is ты́сячей when the word is treated as a noun, but ты́сячью when it is treated as a numeral.

Both миллиóн and миллиáрд are nouns. They are declined like автóбус.

§9. Use of numerals in oblique cases

Whenever any numeral other than одúн (or a compound number ending in одúн) is used in an oblique case, then the noun that follows it, and also any adjectives which qualify the noun, must be in the same case as the numeral and in the plural. In other words the rules given in 37.3 and 4 above (on the use of genitive singular nouns after два, etc., and genitive plural nouns after пять, etc.) cease to apply once the number itself is put into the genitive, dative, instrumental, or prepositional case. Thus:

Провелú мы в милúции бóлее двух часóв.
We spent more than two hours at the police station. (Press)
прóтив пятú сúльных оппонéнтов
against five strong opponents
по обéим сторонáм
down both sides

по шести́ ли́ниям
along six lines
Соглаше́ние, подпи́санное сандини́стским прави́тельством и двадцатью́ оппозицио́нными па́ртиями...
An agreement signed by the Sandinista government and by twenty opposition parties... (Press)
ме́жду двумя́ широ́кими река́ми
between two broad rivers
в семи́ кни́гах
in seven books
о двадцати́ неприя́тных инциде́нтах
concerning twenty unpleasant incidents

If the number is a compound one, then all its components, as well as the noun and any qualifying adjectives, must be in the same case, e.g.

из пяти́десяти восьми́ сиби́рских райо́нов
from 58 Siberian regions
по тридцати́ четырём америка́нским специали́стам
according to 34 American specialists
законопрое́кт, при́нятый девяно́ста пятью́ голоса́ми про́тив четырёх
a bill accepted by 95 votes to 4 (Press)
на ста сорока́ двух кру́пных фа́бриках
in 142 large factories
в ты́сяче шестиста́х девяно́ста пяти́ деревня́х
in 1,695 villages

If the last component of the compound number is оди́н, then the noun must be singular, though it will still be in the same case as all the elements of the number, including оди́н, e.g.

в семи́десяти одно́м го́роде
in 71 towns
за ста пятью́десятью одни́м исключе́нием
with 151 exceptions

If the number is a very high one a speaker might, in informal speech, put only key components of the number in the appropriate oblique case, e.g.

с се́мьдесят одно́й ты́сячью пятьсо́т шестьдеся́т девятью́ солда́тами
with 71,569 soldiers

However, strictly speaking this variant is not correct; one should say instead с семью́десятью одно́й ты́сячью пятьюста́ми шестью́десятью девятью́ солда́тами.

It should be emphasised though that such complex use of numerals as that illustrated in the last example is unlikely ever to be encountered in ordinary speech. The question of putting as many as six or more components in an oblique case therefore does not arise. A speaker would most probably use an approximation if the number was a very high one, or – if a precise number had to be given – would use a construction in which the numerals did not have to be put into an oblique case.

Exercises

A. *Write out the numerals in the following sentences in the form correct in the context and put the nouns and adjectives in brackets in the appropriate case and number:* (1) В США хоро́ший инжене́р получа́ет о́коло 5000 (до́ллар) в ме́сяц. (2) Из 101 (у́гольное предприя́тие) по́лностью и́ли части́чно не рабо́тали 15 шахт. (3) Плани́руется, что в бу́дущем году́ обме́н полётами ме́жду Москво́й, Санкт-Петербу́ргом, Нью-Йо́рком и Вашингто́ном дости́гнет 37 (рейс) в неде́лю. (4) За пе́рвые шесть ме́сяцев э́того го́да ма́ссовые невы́ходы на рабо́ту продолжи́тельностью бо́лее одного́ дня отмеча́лись на 642 (предприя́тие) Росси́и. (5) Сейча́с в э́том междунаро́дном де́тском движе́нии уча́ствуют бо́лее 6 (миллио́н) челове́к из 152 (страна́) ми́ра. (6) Вы́ставка поло́тен Я́ковлева проходи́ла в 30 (го́род) ми́ра. (7) В це́лом с середи́ны пятидеся́тых годо́в сре́дняя за́работная пла́та колхо́зников возросла́ с 68 до 300 (рубль). (8) Э́та переда́ча помо́жет телезри́телям узна́ть информа́цию о торга́х на 10 (сове́тская би́ржа). (9) Собы́тия, кото́рые отно́сятся к я́дерной и́ли радиацио́нной безопа́сности, классифици́руются по 7 (у́ровень). (10) В 107 (ты́сяча) дереве́нь Сове́тского Сою́за отсу́тствовала телефо́нная связь.

B. *Translate into Russian:* (1) I have lived in five cities. (2) I was talking to six teachers. (3) In front of seven houses there are cars, in front of three there are bicycles. (4) By eight o'clock he will be home. (5) I want to talk about four films. (6) She is learning two languages. (7) In twenty-five of the rooms in the hotel there is a shower. (8) In ninety-nine cases out of a hundred he is right. (9) He was walking towards fifty soldiers. (10) Out of three hundred pounds I have spent a hundred and fifty.

LESSON 39

OTHER QUANTITATIVE WORDS; COLLECTIVE NUMERALS; NOUNS EXPRESSING NUMBER

§1. Other quantitative words

The indefinite numerals мно́го, *many, a lot of*; немно́го, *a few, some*; не́сколько, *several*; ско́лько, *how many? how much?* and сто́лько, *so many, so much*, are all followed by a noun in the genitive. Any adjectives qualifying the noun must also be in the genitive. Thus:

мно́го просто́рных па́рков	*a lot of spacious parks*
немно́го пробле́м	*a few problems*
не́сколько небольши́х городо́в	*several small towns*
ско́лько рубле́й?	*how many roubles?*
сто́лько све́тлых воспомина́ний!	*so many joyful recollections!*

All these quantitative words have adjectival endings in their oblique cases, but only plural forms exist:

nom.	мно́го	немно́го	не́сколько	ско́лько	сто́лько
acc.	мно́го/ мно́гих	немно́го/ немно́гих	не́сколько/ не́скольких	ско́лько/ ско́льких	сто́лько/ сто́льких
gen.	мно́гих	немно́гих	не́скольких	ско́льких	сто́льких
dat.	мно́гим	немно́гим	не́скольким	ско́льким	сто́льким
instr.	мно́гими	немно́гими	не́сколькими	ско́лькими	сто́лькими
prep.	мно́гих	немно́гих	не́скольких	ско́льких	сто́льких

These quantitative words are used in the same way as numerals in the oblique cases, that is to say the following noun and any adjectives qualifying it must be in the same case as the indefinite numeral, and must be in the plural. Examples:

Мно́гих ру́сских беспоко́ит дезинтегра́ция Сою́за, его́ распа́д.
The disintegration of the [Soviet] Union, its break-up, worries many Russians. (Press)
Предста́вьте, ско́льких люде́й спасла́ на́ша сестра́ от зараже́ния.
Imagine how many people our sister [i.e. nurse] *saved from infection.* (Press)
согла́сно немно́гим экспе́ртам
according to some experts
Она́ говори́т с не́сколькими друзья́ми.
She is talking to several friends.

When these indefinite numerals are combined with an animate direct object then the accusative may coincide with the genitive (as in the first two examples above) or it may coincide with the nominative, e.g.

> Я встре́тил не́сколько делега́тов [but не́скольких делега́тов is also possible].
> *I met several delegates.*

§2. Collective numerals
There are a number of other numerals that may be used in certain contexts, viz.

дво́е	*two*
тро́е	*three*
че́тверо	*four*
пя́теро	*five*
ше́стеро	*six*
се́меро	*seven*

Higher numerals of this type are no longer used at all. Nor are пя́теро, ше́стеро and се́меро used in all the contexts in which дво́е, тро́е and че́тверо are possible.

Any noun following these numerals must be in the genitive plural, and any adjectives qualifying the noun must also be in the genitive plural.

The collective numerals have three main functions:

i. to indicate the number of people in a group. Examples from the press:

   Из семи́ челове́к тро́е поги́бли на ме́сте и тро́е госпитализи́рованы.
   Out of seven people three were killed on the spot and three were hospitalised.
   За него́ проголосова́ли 198 [сто девяно́сто во́семь] чле́нов парла́мента, дво́е бы́ли про́тив и ше́стеро воздержа́лись.
   One hundred and ninety-eight Members of Parliament voted for him, two were against and six abstained.
   В 30х-40х [тридца́тых-сороковы́х] и в нача́ле 50х [пятидеся́тых] годо́в в Великобрита́нии де́йствовали пя́теро о́чень кру́пных, хорошо́ информи́рованных аге́нтов КГБ.
   In the 30s and 40s and at the beginning of the 50s five very major well-informed agents of the KGB were operating in Great Britain.

ii. to indicate a number of male persons, particularly with the noun мужчи́на, *man*, and also with де́ти, *children*, to indicate the number of children in a family, e.g.

чéтверо рабóчих
four workers
У нас двóе детéй.
We have two children.
Помогáют и дéти. Их у Фёдора и Валентúны трóе, да чéтверо внучáт.
The children help too. Fyodor and Valentina have three of them, and four little grandchildren as well. (Press)

iii. двóе, трóе, and чéтверо, but not пя́теро, etc., are used with a noun which in Russian exists only in the plural, e.g.

двóе сýток	*two days* (i.e. whole 24-hour periods)
двóе нóвых джúнсов	*two new pairs of jeans*
двóе часóв	*two clocks*
трóе санéй	*three sledges*
чéтверо нóжниц	*four pairs of scissors*

The collective numerals decline like adjectives in the plural:

nom.	двóе	трóе	чéтверо	пя́теро
acc.	двóе/ двоúх	трóе/ троúх	чéтверо/ четверы́х	пя́теро/ пятеры́х
gen.	двоúх	троúх	четверы́х	пятеры́х
dat.	двоúм	троúм	четверы́м	пятеры́м
instr.	двоúми	троúми	четверы́ми	пятеры́ми
prep.	двоúх	троúх	четверы́х	пятеры́х

In the oblique cases the collective numerals are used in the same way as the cardinal numerals, that is to say the noun and any adjectives which qualify it must be in the same case as the numeral. For example the dative form of the Russian for *two clocks*, would be двоúм часáм, although a speaker would very probably revert to the use of a phrase with the cardinal numeral, двум часáм, if an oblique case were needed.

§3. The collective noun сóтня *(a hundred)*

This collective word declines like a normal noun in -ня, i.e.

	sing.	pl.
nom.	сóтня	сóтни
acc.	сóтню	сóтни
gen.	сóтни	сóтен
dat.	сóтне	сóтням
instr.	сóтней	сóтнями
prep.	сóтне	сóтнях

It is followed by a noun in the genitive plural, and is used in the following way:

Сóтни турúстов ждáли в аэропортý.
Hundreds of tourists were waiting at the airport.
Кнúга э́та интерéсна тем, что онá объединя́ет всё, что бы́ло напечáтано в сóтнях издáний о рабóте КГБ в инострáнных госудáрствах.
This book is interesting in that it brings together everything that has been published in hundreds of books about the work of the KGB in foreign countries. (Press)

§4. Nouns expressing number

There are a number of feminine nouns ending in -ка which express number, viz.

двóйка	*two*
трóйка	*three*
четвёрка	*four*
пятёрка	*five*
шестёрка	*six*
семёрка	*seven*
восьмёрка	*eight*
девя́тка	*nine*
деся́тка	*ten*

These nouns all decline like a feminine noun in -а with a stem in a velar, e.g. рукá. They have a number of uses:

i. they indicate the numbers of playing cards, e.g.

бубнóвая двóйка	*the two of diamonds*
пиковая семёрка	*the seven of spades*
трéфовая восьмёрка	*the eight of clubs*
червóнная деся́тка	*the ten of hearts*

(The other cards are валéт, *jack*; дáма, *queen*; корóль (masc.), *king*; and туз, *ace*.)

ii. двóйка, трóйка, четвёрка, and пятёрка, in ascending order, are marks throughout the Russian school system, e.g. студéнт получúл пятёрку, *the student got a five* (i.e. the top mark);

iii. they may denote the numbers of e.g. buses, or the shape of the digit, or they may have other special uses, e.g.

Сейчáс подхóдит шестёрка.	*A no. 6 is coming.*
Ученúк нарисовáл пятёрку.	*The pupil drew a figure 5.*
трóйка	*à three-horse carriage; man's three-piece suit*

пятёрка	*five-rouble note*
восьмёрка	*an eight* (i.e. at rowing)
деся́тка	*ten-rouble note; ten-year sentence*

Exercises

A. *Put the word in brackets in the following sentences in the form correct in the context:* (1) Веду́тся перегово́ры с (не́сколько) австри́йскими фи́рмами о приёме тури́стских групп в э́том регио́не. (2) В тече́ние (не́сколько) дней специали́сты вели́ по́иски метеори́та. (3) В числе́ (немно́го) нерешённых пробле́м — вы́боры президе́нта кинофестива́ля. (4) И́мя знамени́того цирково́го силача́ В. И. Ди́куля изве́стно (мно́го) из вас. (5) По мне́нию За́пада, утаена́ информа́ция о (со́тни) баллисти́ческих раке́т. (6) Дете́й, пострада́вших от Черно́быльской ава́рии, беспла́тно ле́чат во (мно́го) стра́нах ми́ра. (7) Ру́сский язы́к стал официа́льным рабо́чим языко́м (мно́го) междунаро́дных организа́ций. (8) Речь идёт о (не́сколько) населённых пу́нктах вблизи́ грани́цы. (9) Его́ ве́щи бы́ли укра́дены на глаза́х у (сто́лько) люде́й. (10) В ию́ле (мно́го) Близнеца́м придётся порабо́тать бо́льше обы́чного.

B. *Translate into Russian:* (1) In a lot of dictionaries; (2) from many sources; (3) with a few exceptions; (4) two clocks; (5) three twenty-four-hour periods; (6) the two of spades; (7) the seven of hearts; (8) the nine of clubs; (9) the three of diamonds; (10) the ten of diamonds; (11) the six of clubs; (12) hundreds of questions; (13) in hundreds of instances; (14) three pairs of jeans; (15) in how many examples? (16) The pupil got a three in his examination. (17) Which stop does the No. 3 go from? (18) There were four of us. (19) He has got three children. (20) How many Russians do you know?

LESSON 40

ORDINAL NUMBERS; TIME AND DATES

§1. Ordinal numbers

The ordinal numerals, which are adjectival in form, are as follows:

пéрвый	*first*	тридцáтый	*thirtieth*
вторóй	*second*	сороковóй	*fortieth*
трéтий	*third*	пятидесятый	*fiftieth*
четвёртый	*fourth*	шестидесятый	*sixtieth*
пятый	*fifth*	семидесятый	*seventieth*
шестóй	*sixth*	восьмидесятый	*eightieth*
седьмóй	*seventh*	девянóстый	*ninetieth*
восьмóй	*eighth*	сóтый	*hundredth*
девятый	*ninth*	двухсóтый	*two-hundredth*
десятый	*tenth*	трёхсóтый	*three-hundredth*
одúннадцатый	*eleventh*	четырёхсóтый	*four-hundredth*
двенáдцатый	*twelfth*	пятисóтый	*five-hundredth*
тринáдцатый	*thirteenth*	шестисóтый	*six-hundredth*
четы́рнадцатый	*fourteenth*	семисóтый	*seven-hundredth*
пятнáдцатый	*fifteenth*	восьмисóтый	*eight-hundredth*
шестнáдцатый	*sixteenth*	девятисóтый	*nine-hundredth*
семнáдцатый	*seventeenth*	ты́сячный	*thousandth*
восемнáдцатый	*eighteenth*	двухты́сячный	*two-thousandth*
девятнáдцатый	*nineteenth*	трёхты́сячный	*three-thousandth*
двадцáтый	*twentieth*		

All the ordinal numerals decline precisely like adjectives, and must agree in number, gender and case with the noun they qualify. Вторóй, шестóй, седьмóй, восьмóй, and сороковóй, having stressed endings, decline like молодóй (see 28.3 above). Трéтий is a soft adjective (see 29.1 above). All the others decline like нóвый (see 28.3 above), e.g.

Пéрвый гость пришёл рáно.
The first guest arrived early.
Он сегóдня читáет вторýю лéкцию.
He is delivering the second lecture today.
конéц трéтьего кóрпуса
the end of the third block
соглáсно четвёртому делегáту
according to the fourth delegate

под пя́тым окно́м
under the fifth window
в шесто́м авто́бусе
in the sixth bus

In compound numbers only the last component is ever an ordinal, and in such numbers only the ordinal ever declines, e.g.

два́дцать пе́рвый ряд	*the twenty-first row*
сто три́дцать второ́й раз	*the hundred-and-thirty-second time*
в со́рок четвёртом ряду́	*in the forty-fourth row*
по́сле пятьдеся́т девя́той поéздки	*after the fifty-ninth journey*
к се́мьдесят восьмо́му до́му	*towards the seventy-eighth house*

§2. Time

i. *O'clock*: numeral + appropriate case (though оди́н is generally omitted), e.g.

час	*one o'clock*
два часа́	*two o'clock*
пять часо́в	*five o'clock*

At with time on the hour is в + accusative, e.g.

в четы́ре часа́	*at four o'clock*
в де́сять часо́в	*at ten o'clock*

ii. Time past the hour: numeral + мину́та in the appropriate case + genitive singular of the ordinal indicating the hour (first hour, second hour, etc.), e.g.

две мину́ты второ́го	*two minutes past one* (lit. *two minutes of the second hour*)
семь мину́т тре́тьего	*seven minutes past two*
два́дцать пять мину́т восьмо́го	*twenty-five past seven*

A quarter past the hour is че́тверть (fem.) + genitive singular of the ordinal indicating the hour, e.g.

че́тверть седьмо́го	*a quarter past six*

At with a time past the hour is в + accusative case, e.g.

в два́дцать две мину́ты девя́того	*at twenty-two minutes past eight*
в че́тверть оди́ннадцатого	*at a quarter past ten*

iii. *Half past* the hour: полови́на + genitive singular of the ordinal indicating the hour, e.g.

полови́на двена́дцатого	*half past eleven*

At with half past the hour is в + prepositional case, e.g.

в полови́не пе́рвого	*at half past twelve*

In colloquial speech such phrases are abbreviated, e.g. в полпе́рвого.

iv. Time to the hour: без + genitive case of cardinal numeral (all components of it), or of че́тверть, + the hour itself, e.g.

без десяти́ оди́ннадцать	*ten to eleven* (lit. *without ten minutes eleven o'clock*)
без двадцати́ пяти́ два	*twenty-five to two*
без че́тверти шесть	*a quarter to six*

At with time to the hour is not expressed. The above examples could also mean *at 10.50, at 1.35,* and *at 5.45* respectively.

v. If a time is followed by one of the phrases *in the morning, in the afternoon, in the evening, at night,* then the genitive case of the word for *morning*, etc. must be used, e.g.

в де́вять часо́в утра́	*at nine o'clock in the morning*
в семь часо́в ве́чера	*at seven o'clock in the evening*

Contrast у́тром, ве́чером, etc., when the phrases *in the morning, in the evening,* etc. stand on their own (see 26.4 above).

vi. Note also the following expressions:

Кото́рый час?	*What time is it?*
В кото́ром часу́?	*At what time?*
Ско́лько вре́мени? (coll.)	*What time is it?*
Во ско́лько? (coll.)	*At what time?*

§3. Dates

i. *On* a day of the week: в + accusative case (see also 17.2.iv above), e.g.

в понеде́льник	*on Monday*
в суббо́ту	*on Saturday*

ii. *On* days of the week: по + dative case (see 25.2 above), e.g.

по вто́рникам *on Tuesdays*
по среда́м *on Wednesdays*

iii. *In* a month: в + prepositional case (see 15.3 above), e.g.

в январе́ *in January*
в феврале́ *in February*
в ма́рте *in March*
в апре́ле *in April*
в ма́е *in May*
в ию́не *in June*
в ию́ле *in July*
в а́вгусте *in August*
в сентябре́ *in September*
в октябре́ *in October*
в ноябре́ *in November*
в декабре́ *in December*

Note also:

в про́шлом ме́сяце *last month*
в э́том ме́сяце *this month*
в бу́дущем ме́сяце *next month*
в сле́дующем ме́сяце *the following month*

iv. A date in a month: an ordinal numeral in the neuter nominative singular form (i.e. число́, *number, date*, is understood), followed by the genitive of the month, e.g.

пе́рвое ма́я *the 1st of May*
второ́е а́вгуста *the 2nd of June*
тре́тье сентября́ *the 3rd of September*
два́дцать восьмо́е декабря́ *the 28th of December*

v. To translate *on* a date, put the ordinal numeral in the genitive singular, e.g.

пе́рвого ма́я *on the 1st of May*
второ́го а́вгуста *on the 2nd of August*
тре́тьего сентября́ *on the 3rd of September*
два́дцать восьмо́го декабря́ *on the 28th of December*

vi. A year is expressed by using an ordinal as the last component of the compound number, e.g.

ты́сяча девятьсо́т шестьдеся́т второ́й год *1962*
ты́сяча восемьсо́т двена́дцатый год *1812*

vii. *In* a year: в + prepositional case of the ordinal and of год (i.e. году́), e.g.

в ты́сяча девятьсо́т во́семьдесят восьмо́м году́	*in 1988*
в ты́сяча шестьдеся́т шесто́м году́	*in 1066*

Note also:

в про́шлом году́	*last year*
в э́том году́	*this year*
в бу́дущем году́	*next year*
в сле́дующем году́	*the following year*

viii. If mention of the year is preceded by a more precise date, then the ordinal in the number indicating the year must be in the genitive case and must be followed by го́да (compare use of утра́, ве́чера in §2.v above), e.g.

пе́рвое ма́рта ты́сяча девятьсо́т восьмидеся́того го́да
the 1st of March 1980
второ́го апре́ля ты́сяча девятьсо́т три́дцать седьмо́го го́да
on the 2nd of April 1937

ix. *In* a century: в + prepositional case, e.g.

в двадца́том ве́ке	*in the 20th century*
в девятна́дцатом ве́ке	*in the 19th century*

x. *A.D.* is на́шей э́ры (lit. *of our era*), and *B.C.* is до на́шей э́ры (lit. *before our era*), e.g.

в сто пятидеся́том году́ на́шей э́ры	*in 150 A.D.*
в две́сти пя́том году́ до на́шей э́ры	*in 205 B.C.*

These phrases may be abbreviated to н.э. and до н.э. respectively.

Exercises

A. *Translate into Russian:* (1) The tenth house; (2) in the fourth carriage; (3) the third book; (4) in the fifth example; (5) behind the second bus; (6) after the sixth lesson; (7) the twenty-first name; (8) the ninth time; (9) in the seventh class; (10) the eighth chapter.

B. *Write out the following times in Russian:* 1.05, 5.20, 9.10, 11.25, 3.17, 12.10, 12.30, 2.15, 2.45, 4.30, 4.40, 4.45, 9.40, 9.35, 9.50, 8.55, 10.15, 10.30, 10.45, 10.55.

C. *Write out 'at 1.05' etc. as above.*

D. *Translate into Russian:* The 1st of January; the 2nd of February; the 3rd of March; the 4th of April; the 5th of May; the 6th of June; the 7th of July; the 8th of August; the 9th of September; the 10th of October; the 11th of November; the 12th of December; the 21st of January; the 22nd of February; the 23rd of March.

E. *Translate into Russian 'on the 1st of January', etc. as above.*

F. *Write out the following dates in Russian:* 1976; 1960; 1959; 1815; 1861; 1431; 989; 1372; 1613; 1905; 1917; 1984; 2000; 24 A.D.; 481 B.C.

G. *Translate into Russian 'in 1976', etc. as above.*

H. *Write out in Russian:* 1.II.1976; 4.III.1945; 6.VIII.1922; 5.IX.1930; 7.VII.1938; 8.V.1802; 21.X.1981; 17.XII.1984; 13.IV.1970; 23.VI.1992.

LESSON 41

MISCELLANEOUS POINTS CONCERNING NUMERALS

§1. Approximation

There are several ways of expressing approximation.

i. One of the adverbs приблизи́тельно, *approximately,* or приме́рно, *roughly* may be placed before the number, e.g.

   приблизи́тельно сто рубле́й
   approximately 100 roubles
   приме́рно три́дцать студе́нтов
   roughly 30 students

ii. The order of the numeral and the noun may be reversed, with the noun being moved to the beginning of the phrase, e.g.

   часа́ два
   about two hours (cf. два часа́, *two hours*)
   неде́ли че́рез две по́сле моего́ возвраще́ния
   about two weeks after my return (Press)
   В посы́лке бы́ли: килогра́мма три сыро́й карто́шки, чёрные сухари́, две па́ры тёплых носко́в и мешо́чек с са́харом. Са́хара бы́ло гра́ммов три́ста пятьдеся́т-четы́реста.
   In the parcel were about three kilogrammes of uncooked potato, some black rusks, two pairs of warm socks and a bag of sugar. There were about 350-400 grammes of sugar. (Press)

iii. The preposition о́коло, *about,* may be placed before the numeral, which will then have to be used in the genitive case, e.g.

   о́коло пяти́десяти киломе́тров от Москвы́
   about 50 kilometres from Moscow

§2. Use of numerals with animate direct object

When the numerals два, три, четы́ре are the direct object of a verb and are used with an animate noun denoting a person, then their genitive form should, strictly speaking, be used as the accusative. The following noun must be in the genitive plural. Any adjectives qualifying the noun must also be in the genitive plural. Examples from the press:

> Он ви́дел недалеко́ от перекрёстка двух мужчи́н [rather than два мужчи́ны] кре́пкого телосложе́ния.
> *He saw not far from the crossroad two men of strong build.*
> За э́то вре́мя англи́йская слу́жба безопа́сности откры́ла четырёх аге́нтов [rather than четы́ре аге́нта].
> *In this period of time the English security service discovered four agents.*

Although the use of the genitive of the numeral is felt to be obligatory in these circumstances, and prevails in the written language, one may also hear accusative forms which coincide with the nominative.

When the animate object is a female the accusative is even more widespread. Thus although it might be considered correct to say я ви́жу трёх де́вушек (*I can see three girls*), one may also hear я ви́жу три де́вушки.

When the animate object is an animal denoted by a masculine noun, then the genitive form of the numeral is less likely to be used. Thus я ви́жу два слона́ (*I can see two elephants*) might be preferred to я ви́жу двух слоно́в, particularly in conversation, although the latter sentence is also possible and may seem more correct.

If the animate object is an animal denoted by a feminine noun, then the accusative form of the numeral is definitely preferred. Thus я ви́жу две коро́вы [not двух коро́в], *I can see two cows*.

If the numerals два/две, три, четы́ре occur as the last component of a compound number, then the genitive forms are not likely to be encountered. Thus one would say я ви́жу два́дцать два ма́льчика [not два́дцать двух ма́льчиков], *I can see twenty-two boys*.

Два/две, три, and четы́ре are the only numerals in which the animate category finds expression. With the numerals пять and above the accusative case of the numeral itself always coincides with the nominative, even when the noun in the direct object is animate, e.g. я ви́жу пять [not пяти́] студе́нтов, *I can see five students*.

§3. Agreement of predicate with a subject containing a cardinal numeral

When the numeral is the subject of the clause, or when it is combined with a noun to form the subject, then the predicate may be in the third person plural (or plural form if it is in the past tense) or it may be in the third person singular (or neuter form if it is in the past tense).

This is an area in which it is difficult to lay down hard and fast rules. However, reading of the press suggests that plural verbs seem to be preferred if the subject is animate, whilst singular verbs tend to predominate if the subject is inanimate, particularly if the subject denotes a period of time. Examples from the press:

i. plural verb with a subject that is animate, or with a numeral which refers to an animate subject:

За него́ проголосова́ли 198 [сто девяно́сто во́семь] чле́нов парла́мента.
One hundred and ninety-eight Members of Parliament voted for him.
В феврале́ э́того го́да 30 [три́дцать] механиза́торов собрали́сь и единогла́сно при́няли реше́ние.
In February this year 30 [farm] machine operators gathered and unanimously took a decision.
Свы́ше 30 [тридцати́] проце́нтов ира́кских солда́т дезерти́ровали и о́коло 100 [ста] ты́сяч — угоди́ли в плен.
Over 30 per cent of Iraqi soldiers deserted and about 100,000 landed up in captivity.

ii. singular verb (and neuter if it is in the past tense) with a subject that is inanimate, and especially if the subject is a phrase defining a period of time:

Прошло́ пять ме́сяцев.
Five months passed.
Переселено́ пока́ два́дцать во́семь дереве́нь.
So far 28 villages have been resettled.
Из 4200 [четырёх ты́сяч двухсо́т] та́нков, кото́рыми располага́ли ира́кцы, к настоя́щему вре́мени уничто́жено свы́ше 3700 [трёх ты́сяч семисо́т].
Out of the 4,200 tanks which the Iraqis had at their disposal over 3,700 have been destroyed up to now.

It should be added though that the factors determining choice of plural or singular verb may often be more complex than those described above. The choice may depend on where the speaker or writer wishes to place emphasis, a singular verb being preferred if attention is drawn to the number, perhaps on account of its large or small size or because the context is a statistical one, e.g.

То́лько за после́дние семь ме́сяцев заде́ржано 2960 [две ты́сячи девятьсо́т шестьдеся́т] бе́женцев из По́льши и 5422 [пять ты́сяч четы́реста два́дцать два] из Чехослова́кии.
Over the last seven months alone 2,960 refugees from Poland and 5,422 from Czechoslovakia have been detained. (Press)
Всего́ пришло́ пять госте́й.
Five guests came in all.

On the other hand a plural verb is usual if the numeral is qualified by a plural adjective, e.g.

Поги́бли все де́сять чле́нов экипа́жа.
All ten members of the crew were killed. (Press)

§4. Translation of *years* and *people* after numerals

Two words which frequently occur after numerals, *year* and *people*, give some difficulty as they may be translated in different ways depending on the numeral which precedes them.

i. After оди́н (and any numeral in which оди́н is the last component) *year* is translated as год. After два, три, четы́ре (and any numeral in which one of these words is the last component), о́ба and полтора́, i.e. after all numerals requiring a genitive singular noun, it is translated as го́да. Thus:

оди́н год	*one year*
два го́да	*two years*
три го́да	*three years*
два́дцать оди́н год	*21 years*
три́дцать четы́ре го́да	*34 years*

After пять and all other numerals requiring a genitive plural noun, and after the quantitative words given in 39.1 above (мно́го, etc.), on the other hand, *years* is translated as лет, i.e. the genitive plural form of the word ле́то, *summer.* Thus:

пять лет	*five years*
два́дцать лет	*20 years*
со́рок лет	*40 years*
сто лет	*100 years*
мно́го лет	*many years*
не́сколько лет	*several years*
ско́лько лет?	*how many years?*

Note though that the genitive plural of год itself is used in reference to decades, e.g. рефо́рмы шестидеся́тых годо́в, *the reforms of the sixties*; писа́тели двадца́тых годо́в, *the writers of the twenties.*

ii. After оди́н (and any numeral in which оди́н is the last component) *person* or *people* is translated as челове́к. After два, три, четы́ре (and any numeral in which one of these words is the last component), о́ба, and полтора́ (should the context demand it), *people* is translated by челове́ка. Thus:

оди́н челове́к	*one person*
два челове́ка	*two people*
три челове́ка	*three people*
два́дцать оди́н челове́к	*21 people*
три́дцать четы́ре челове́ка	*34 people*

After пять and all other numerals requiring a genitive plural noun *people* is translated as челове́к, i.e. the genitive plural form of the word челове́к, e.g.

пять челове́к	*five people*
два́дцать челове́к	*20 people*
со́рок челове́к	*40 people*
сто челове́к	*100 people*

There is also a tendency now to use челове́к after the words ты́сяча and миллио́н, although люде́й may also be found. Examples from the press:

десятки ты́сяч челове́к
tens of thousands of people
В э́тот день осироте́ли ты́сячи люде́й.
On that day thousands of people were orphaned.
почти́ 2,5 [два с полови́ной] миллио́на челове́к
almost 2.5 million people

After мно́го and немно́го *people* should be rendered by люде́й. Thus мно́го люде́й, *a lot of people*. (*A lot of people* may also be translated as мно́го наро́ду when the speaker means a place is crowded; similarly *a few people* may be rendered as немно́го наро́ду.)

After не́сколько, *people* should be rendered by челове́к.

After ско́лько and сто́лько, *people* should be rendered by челове́к unless the meaning is exclamatory, in which case it should be rendered by люде́й. Compare the following examples:

Ско́лько челове́к бы́ло в аудито́рии?
How many people were there in the lecture theatre?
Ско́лько люде́й поги́бли [or поги́бло] на войне́!
How many people died in the war!
Вот сто́лько челове́к поедет: А́ня, Та́ня, На́дя, Са́ша...
This is how many people will go: Anya, Tanya, Nadya, Sasha...
Сто́лько люде́й там бы́ло!
There were so many people there!

Remember too that раз, *time, occasion*, which will also occur frequently after numerals, has genitive plural раз. Thus:

оди́н раз	*once*
два ра́за	*twice*
пять раз	*five times*
сто раз	*100 times*
мно́го раз	*many times*

не́сколько раз	*several times*
Ско́лько раз?	*How many times?*

§5. Translation of *first*

Note the way Russian renders the following expressions incorporating the word *first*:

at first	снача́ла
for the first time	впервы́е
in the first instance	на пе́рвых пора́х
first of all	пре́жде всего́
at first sight	на пе́рвый взгляд or с пе́рвого взгля́да
in the first place, firstly	во-пе́рвых
at the first opportunity	при пе́рвой возмо́жности

The construction *to be the first to do sthg.* is rendered thus with пе́рвый in a nominative or instrumental form:

Он пе́рвый пришёл.
He was the first to arrive.
Мы пе́рвыми по́няли значе́ние э́того собы́тия.
We were the first to understand the significance of this event.

The nominative form is more colloquial. The instrumental is preferred if the expression conveys a sense of achievement.

Note also the expressions во-вторы́х, *in the second place, secondly*; в-тре́тьих, *in the third place, thirdly*; в-четвёртых, *in the fourth place, fourthly*.

§6. Distributive expressions with по

The current use of numerals in this expression is as follows.

i. The numeral оди́н is put in the dative case after по, and the noun and any adjectives which qualify it are also put in the dative case, e.g.

   Учи́тель дал ученика́м по одному́ но́вому уче́бнику.
   The teacher gave the pupils a new textbook each.

   If there is no accompanying adjective then оди́н is often omitted, e.g.

   О́бе кома́нды име́ют по ма́тчу в запа́се.
   Both teams have a game in hand. (Press)

   The nouns ты́сяча and миллио́н will also be put in the dative case after по in such expressions, e.g.

Он дал им по ты́сяче рубле́й.
He gave them a thousand roubles each.

ii. All other numerals (два/две, три, четы́ре, пять, etc.; пятьдеся́т, etc.; две́сти, три́ста, четы́реста, пятьсо́т, etc.), on the other hand, are nowadays put in the accusative case, and the following noun and any adjectives qualifying the noun conform to the normal rules applicable after these numerals. Examples from the press:

По описа́ниям, «прише́льцы» бы́ли трёхметро́вого ро́ста, име́ли по три гла́за, бы́ли облачены́ в серебри́стые комбинезо́ны.
According to descriptions, the arrivals [from another planet] *were three metres tall, had three eyes each and were clothed in silvery overalls.*
Килогра́мм ри́са идёт по шесть рубле́й, ма́сло — по во́семь.
A kilogramme of rice goes for six roubles, butter for eight.
С ка́ждого квадра́тного ме́тра тепли́цы — по два́дцать пять килогра́ммов овоще́й.
From each square metre of greenhouse [you get] 25 kilogrammes of vegetables.

The use of the numerals пять and above in the dative case after по with the noun in the genitive plural is old-fashioned. Thus a sentence of the sort Он дал им по пяти́ рубле́й, although it may be found in textbooks and dictionaries, would no longer seem natural to a native speaker.

Exercises

A. *Choose the appropriate word or phrase from the pair given in brackets to complete each of the following sentences. Give reasons for your choice and indicate in which instances the other word or phrase might also be possible:* (1) Три челове́ка (отпра́влено/отпра́влены) с тра́вмами в больни́цу. (2) (Израсхо́довано/Израсхо́дованы) 744 миллио́на рубле́й. (3) (Про́дано/Про́даны) о́коло ты́сячи компью́теров. (4) (Проанализи́ровано/Проанализи́рованы) бо́лее двух ты́сяч пи́сем. (5) (Поги́бло/Поги́бли) 23 челове́ка, о́коло 20 (ра́нено/ра́нены). (6) На э́тот вопро́с он (во-пе́рвых/снача́ла) отве́тил отрица́тельно. (7) (Впервы́е/снача́ла) за до́лгие десятиле́тия о́бщество начина́ет слу́шать го́лос це́ркви. (8) Он уби́л (два милиционе́ра/двух милиционе́ров). (9) Прошло́ де́сять (годо́в/лет). (10) Она́ родила́сь в нача́ле семидеся́тых (годо́в/лет). (11) Поли́ция конфискова́ла у него́ во́семь караби́нов и не́сколько револьве́ров, кото́рые он продава́л по (семьсо́т/семисо́т) ты́сяч зло́тых. (12) Кирги́зы постро́или свой аэропо́рт, кото́рый испо́льзуют по (три часа́/трём часа́м) в су́тки. (13) Он отдыха́ет по (одну́ неде́лю/одно́й неде́ле) в ме́сяц. (14) Деше́вле купи́ть, ска́жем, оди́н раз пять килогра́ммов помидо́ров и храни́ть их в тече́ние неде́ли, чем бе́гать на база́р по (два ра́за/двум ра́зам) в неде́лю. (15) Бо́лее трёхсот домовладе́льцев зарабо́тали хоро́шие де́ньги, сдава́я ко́мнаты по (два́дцать до́лларов/двадцати́ до́лларов) в день.

B. *Translate into Russian:* (1) About fifty kopecks; (2) approximately thirty roubles; (3) about six hours; (4) roughly twenty kilometres; (5) five years; (6) twenty-one years; (7) forty-two people; (8) once; (9) six times; (10) one rouble each; (11) two roubles each; (12) five roubles each; (13) three hundred roubles each; (14) one kopeck each; (15) fifty kopecks each; (16) the philosophers of the forties; (17) the pop music of the sixties; (18) the revolutionaries of the 1870s; (19) thirty-two years; (20) six people; (21) We saw two tourists at the station. (22) We saw ten tourists at the station. (23) He saw four students. (24) We counted twenty-two students. (25) The hunter killed two tigers. (26) They picked five new players. (27) Five hundred cars were produced. (28) Six years passed. (29) Only five people attended the lecture. (30) About five hundred members of parliament voted. (31) All ten students arrived early. (32) I am visiting this theatre for the first time. (33) Gagarin was the first man to fly in space. (34) Three chairs were standing in the corner. (35) At first I did not believe him.

LESSON 42

AGE, DISTANCE, MEASUREMENT AND COMPUTATION

§1. Age

The noun or pronoun indicating the person whose age is being described must be in the dative case, and is followed by the cardinal numeral and the appropriate form of the word for *year*, e.g.

Мне два́дцать оди́н год.
I am 21.
Ему́ два́дцать два го́да.
He is 22.
Ей два́дцать пять лет.
She is 25.
Тогда́ мне бы́ло пятна́дцать лет.
I was 15 then.
На про́шлой неде́ле ей испо́лнилось два го́да.
She was two last week.
На бу́дущей неде́ле им испо́лнится де́сять лет.
They will be ten next week.

Note also the following expressions:

Ему́ уже́ за со́рок.
He is already over 40.
Ему́ под шестьдеся́т.
He is getting on for 60.

See also 23.3 above.

§2. Distance

This may be expressed in three ways.

i. With the prepositions от and до and a cardinal numeral in the nominative case, e.g.

   От Санкт-Петербу́рга до Москвы́ киломе́тров шестьсо́т.
   It is about 600 kilometres from St. Petersburg to Moscow.

ii. With в + prepositional case of the cardinal numeral (see also 15.4 above), e.g.

Э́тот го́род нахо́дится в двухста́х киломе́трах от Москвы́.
This town is situated 200 kilometres from Moscow.
Электроста́нция нахо́дится киломе́трах в десяти́ от це́нтра го́рода.
The power station is about 10 kilometres from the town centre.

Note the use of the nouns ходьба́, *walking*, and езда́, *travelling, driving*, to express the idea that a place takes a certain time to reach on foot or by transport, e.g.

Вокза́л нахо́дится в двадцати́ пяти́ мину́тах ходьбы́ от университе́та.
The station is a 25-minute walk from the university.
Собо́р нахо́дится в пяти́ мину́тах езды́ от музе́я.
The cathedral is a five-minute drive from the museum.

iii. With the phrase на расстоя́нии + genitive case of the cardinal numeral, e.g.

Они́ живу́т на расстоя́нии двух киломе́тров от нас.
They live two kilometres away from us [lit. *at a distance of two kilometres from us*].

Note the analogous expressions на высоте́, *at a height of* and на глубине́, *at a depth of*, e.g.

Самолёт лети́т на высоте́ де́сять ты́сяч ме́тров.
The plane is flying at a height of 10,000 metres.
Ныря́льщики рабо́тают на глубине́ пятьдеся́т ме́тров.
The divers are working at a depth of 50 metres.

Note that in ordinary speech the numerals tend not to be used in an oblique case in these contexts. (One might have expected десяти́ and пяти́десяти in the above examples.)

§3. Measurement

The main nouns indicating dimension are:

высота́	*height*
глубина́	*depth*
длина́	*length*
рост	*stature, height* (of people)
толщина́	*thickness*
ширина́	*width*

The dimensions of an object may be described in two ways, viz.

i. by using the appropriate noun from the list above, in the instrumental case, + в + cardinal numeral in the accusative case, e.g.

ба́шня высото́й в сто ме́тров
a tower 100 metres high
река́ глубино́й в три ме́тра
a river three metres deep
сук длино́й в два ме́тра
a branch two metres long
мужчи́на ро́стом в оди́н метр се́мьдесят сантиме́тров
a man one metre 70 centimetres tall
стена́ толщино́й в де́сять сантиме́тров
a wall ten centimetres thick
у́лица ширино́й в со́рок ме́тров
a street 40 metres wide

Nouns such as вмести́мость, *capacity*; ёмкость, *volume, capacity*; сто́имость, *cost, value*; and чи́сленность, *numerical quantity, strength in numbers*, may be used in the same way as the above dimensions, e.g.

бензоба́к ёмкостью в два́дцать пять ли́тров
a 25-litre petrol tank
сто́имостью почти́ в пятна́дцать ты́сяч рубле́й
almost 15 thousand roubles in value (Press)
а́рмия чи́сленностью в не́сколько ты́сяч
an army several thousand strong
Э́то зо́на о́тдыха пло́щадью в ты́сячу пятьсо́т гекта́ров с иску́сственными пруда́ми.
It is a recreation zone with an area of 1500 hectares and artificial ponds. (Press)

ii. by using в + the noun indicating dimension in the accusative case, e.g.

сук два ме́тра в длину́ *a branch two metres long*

and so on, as in i. above.

Note the form of questions concerning dimensions:

Какова́ [or кака́я] длина́ футбо́льной площа́дки?
How long is a football pitch? (lit. *What is the length of a football pitch?*)
Какова́ [or кака́я] глубина́ той реки́?
How deep is that river?
Какова́ [or кака́я] высота́ того́ де́рева?
How tall is that tree?

The Russian words for the English measurements, which will not be universally understood in Russia where the metric system is used, are:

дюйм	*inch*
фут	*foot*
ярд	*yard*
ми́ля	*mile*

§4. Computation

The basic forms of calculation are expressed in the following way.

i. Addition (сложе́ние): the verb *to add* is скла́дывать/сложи́ть. To translate *to add* a number to another number the verb прибавля́ть/ приба́вить should be used, e.g. к двум приба́вить два, *to add 2 and 2*. One may also say два плюс два, *2 + 2*.

ii. Subtraction (вычита́ние): the verb *to subtract* is вычита́ть/вы́честь, and *from* is rendered by из, e.g. вы́честь пять из десяти́, *to subtract 5 from 10*.

iii. Multiplication (умноже́ние): the verb *to multiply* is умножа́ть/ умно́жить, and *by* is rendered by на + accusative, e.g. умно́жить пять на два, *to multiply 5 by 2*.

Note also:

два́жды два	*twice two, 2 x 2*
три́жды два	*3 x 2*
четы́режды два	*4 x 2*
пятью́ два	*5 x 2*
шестью́ два	*6 x 2*
семью́ два	*7 x 2*
восьмью́ два	*8 x 2*

The stress on the instrumental forms of the cardinal numerals may be shifted to the stem (пя́тью, etc.) when these numerals are used in multiplication tables, e.g. in the classroom.

With numerals above 10 a formula with на is preferred, e.g. оди́ннадцать на два, *11 x 2*.

iv. Division (деле́ние): the verb *to divide* is дели́ть/раздели́ть, and *by* is rendered by на + accusative, e.g. раздели́ть две́сти на четы́ре, *to divide 200 by 4*.

v. Fractions (дро́би): the first component of the fraction is expressed by a cardinal numeral, as in English. The second component is expressed by полови́на, *half*; треть, *third*; че́тверть, *quarter*; or, for higher numbers, the feminine form of the ordinal, e.g. пя́тая, *fifth*; шеста́я, *sixth*, etc., the word часть, *part*, being understood. The second component of the fraction must decline in accordance with the normal rules governing words which follow cardinal numerals. (Note, though, that genitive plural forms of the ordinals, not nominative plural forms, are used even when the feminine noun часть is understood after them.) Examples:

однá треть	*one third*
две трéти	*two thirds*
однá чéтверть	*one quarter*
три чéтверти	*three quarters*
однá пя́тая	*one fifth*
две пя́тых	*two fifths*
семь восьмы́х	*seven eighths*
однá деся́тая	*one tenth*
оди́ннадцать двенáдцатых	*eleven twelfths*
семь сóтых	*seven hundredths*

В ны́нешнем годý в Казахстáне поги́бли в автокатастрóфах 1267 [ты́сяча двéсти шестьдеся́т семь] человéк, почти́ на пя́тую часть бóльше, чем в прóшлом.
In the current year 1,267 people have died in car crashes in Kazakhstan, almost one fifth more than last year. (Press)

In oblique cases both parts of the fraction decline according to the normal rules governing declension of numerals, e.g.

вы́честь однý восьмýю из семи́ восьмы́х
to subtract one eighth from seven eighths
вы́честь две пя́тых из трёх пя́тых
to subtract two fifths from three fifths

The expression for *decimal* is десяти́чная дробь. A decimal point is rendered in a Russian text by a comma, e.g. 5,6. This fraction would be read as пять цéлых (и) шесть деся́тых, i.e. *five whole [numbers] and six tenths.* A noun after such expressions will be in the genitive singular, e.g. инфля́ция сейчáс поднялáсь до 5,9 [пяти́ цéлых (и) девяти́ деся́тых] процéнта, *inflation has now risen to 5.9 per cent* (Press).

Further examples:

3.2	три цéлых (и) две деся́тых
4.7	четы́ре цéлых (и) семь деся́тых
6.8	шесть цéлых (и) вóсемь деся́тых
7.9	семь цéлых (и) дéвять деся́тых

A decimal number with .5 in it may be rendered with the phrase с полови́ной, e.g.

5.5 пять цéлых (и) пять деся́тых or пять с полови́ной

If there is more than one number after the decimal point then деся́тых should be replaced by со́тых, *hundredths*; ты́сячных, *thousandths*; etc., as appropriate, e.g.

3.22 три це́лых (и) два́дцать две со́тых
4.777 четы́ре це́лых (и) семьсо́т се́мьдесят семь ты́сячных

However, it is unlikely that such complex numbers will be used in normal speech.

vi. Counting (счёт): the verb *to count* is счита́ть/счесть or сосчита́ть or посчита́ть (alternative perfectives). The verb подсчи́тывать/ подсчита́ть means *to count up* or *to reckon up*.

считать до десяти́
to count up to 10
Он сейча́с посчита́ет до ста.
He will now count up to 100.
Она́ подсчита́ла свои́ расхо́ды.
She reckoned up her expenses.
Вам подсчита́ть?
Would you like your bill? (lit. *Shall I calculate [your bill]?*)

Note that when counting *one, two, three,* etc. раз should be used instead of оди́н (i.e. раз, два, три).

Exercises

A. *Write out the numerals in the following sentences and put any words and numerals in brackets in the form required by the context:* (1) Семья́ молода́я: (оте́ц) 35 лет, (мать) 30 лет, (сын) 10 лет, (дочь) 8 лет. (2) (Э́то уче́бное заведе́ние) исполня́ется 70 лет. (3) В (68 киломе́тр) к восто́ку от Москвы́ на берегу́ реки́ Кля́зьмы нахо́дится стари́нный го́род Па́вловский Поса́д. (4) Второ́й взрыв прогреме́л не́которое вре́мя спустя́ в (500 метр) от ме́ста пе́рвого взры́ва. (5) Жил я недалеко́ от Балтимо́ра, в (30 мину́та). (6) В США 2,2 миллио́на фе́рмеров. (7) Результа́ты голосова́ния бы́ли о́чень смешны́ми: 99,09 проце́нта. (8) В госуда́рственные закрома́ на 12 а́вгуста поступи́ло лишь 7,5 миллио́на тонн зерна́ — что̀ на 5,5 миллио́на тонн ме́ньше, чем в про́шлом году. (9) Годово́й объём произво́дства холоди́льников и морози́льников — 8,8 миллио́на штук. (10) Увели́чиваются масшта́бы недопоста́вок проду́кции потреби́телям. То́лько за май по промы́шленности они́ увели́чились на 3,4 миллиа́рда рубле́й, за ию́нь — на 4,6 миллиа́рда рубле́й.

B. *Translate into Russian:* (1) A room ten feet high; (2) a room twelve metres wide; (3) a room five metres long; (4) a room two metres long; (5) walls ten inches thick; (6) a river a hundred kilometres long; (7) a river twenty feet deep; (8) a man six feet tall; (9) a woman five feet six inches tall; (10) a plank two inches thick; (11) ice four feet thick; (12) at a depth of two hundred metres; (13) armed forces a million strong; (14) How long is this garden? (15) How high is the mountain? (16) How wide is the road? (17) How deep is the river? (18) He is twenty-eight. (19) She was thirty-three. (20) I shall be forty-one. (21) This town is forty-four kilometres from Moscow. (22) The airport is twenty-seven kilometres from the centre. (23) The lake is fifty-six kilometres from your house. (24) The Urals are nine hundred kilometres from Moscow. (25) The village is about five miles from the border. (26) Nine times four is thirty-six. (27) If you multiply six by three you get eighteen. (28) Their mother divided the meat into three portions. (29) The teacher told the pupils to subtract four from twenty. (30) The little girl can count up to thirty.

C. *Revision exercise on numerals (Lessons 37-39 and 41-42). Write out the numerals in the following phrases and put the words in brackets in the form required by the context:* (1) 1 (кни́га); (2) 2 (дом); (3) 5 (телефо́н); (4) 6 (ста́рый друг); (5) 10 (кра́сная маши́на); (6) 20 (но́вый учё́бник); (7) 24 (студе́нт); (8) о́коло (60 трамва́й); (9) в (84 дере́вня); (10) на (109 фа́брика); (11) из (121 страна́) ми́ра; (12) в (со́тни) больни́ц; (13) бубно́вая 7; (14) пи́ковая 4; (15) тре́фовая 10; (16) черво́нная 8; (17) получи́ть 5 на экза́мене; (18) в (2 киломе́тр) от го́рода; (19) в (5 мину́та) ходьбы́ от вокза́ла; (20) в (3 час) езды́ от столи́цы; (21) на расстоя́нии (5 ми́ля) от Ло́ндона; (22) 10 (челове́к); (23) 82 (челове́к); (24) 61 (челове́к); (25) ты́сячи (челове́к); (26) К концу́ го́да с большо́й вероя́тностью мо́жно прогнози́ровать сниже́ние добы́чи не́фти до 505 (миллио́н) тонн, угля́ до 620 (миллио́н) тонн. (27) В Ме́ксике зарегистри́ровано о́коло 400 (слу́чай) холе́ры, в США — бо́лее 40, в Кана́де — о́коло 10. (28) У них (2 де́ти). (29) Нас бы́ло 3. (30) Я ви́дел (3 студе́нт). (31) Ему́ 12 (год). (32) За́втра ей испо́лнится 80 (год). (33) Мне бы́ло 22 (год). (34) Он дал до́чкам по (1 конфе́та). (35) Они́ несли́ по (2 чемода́н). (36) Все 90 пассажи́ров на борту́ (past tense of поги́бнуть). (37) (Past tense of прису́тствовать) лишь 30 чле́нов парла́мента. (38) В (500 метр) от истори́ческого анса́мбля размещена́ машинотра́кторная ста́нция с желе́зными и кирпи́чными анга́рами. (39) В 1989 году́, по официа́льным да́нным, эмигри́ровали 235,6 ты́сячи челове́к. (40) В 1990 году́ те́мпы инфля́ции составля́ли 27,3 проце́нта, а эконо́мика возросла́ лишь на 2,1 проце́нта.

D. *Revision exercise on numerals (Lessons 40 and 42). Write out in Russian the following times, dates, calculations and fractions:* 6.00, at 7.00, 8.15, 9.25, 10.30, at 11.30, 10.40, 11.45, at 12.50, 6.30 am, 8.00 pm, at 12.00 noon; 1 March, 3 June, 26 August, on 8 September, on 29 November; 20 BC, 988, 1970, 1991, in 1946, in 1992, 12.III.1986, on 15.VI.1993; 6.9, 7.95, 3.2%, 4.5%, 10.8%.

LESSON 43

FORMATION AND USE OF THE IMPERATIVE

§1. Formation of the imperative

The imperative may be formed from either aspect of the Russian verb.

In the case of the vast majority of Russian verbs the stem to which the imperative endings are added is formed by taking away the last two letters of the 3rd person plural of the indicative (i.e. the present tense in the case of imperfective verbs, and the future tense in the case of perfective verbs). Thus:

infin.		3rd pers. pl.	stem of imp.
конча́ть (impf.)	*to finish*	конча́ют	конча-
объясня́ть (impf.)	*to explain*	объясня́ют	объясня-
уме́ть (impf.)	*to know how to*	уме́ют	уме-
организова́ть (impf.)	*to organise*	организу́ют	организу-
мыть (impf.)	*to wash*	мо́ют	мо-
петь (impf.)	*to sing*	пою́т	по-
писа́ть (impf.)	*to write*	пи́шут	пиш-
ре́зать (impf.)	*to cut*	ре́жут	реж-
вести́ (impf.)	*to lead*	веду́т	вед-
нести́ (impf.)	*to carry*	несу́т	нес-
везти́ (impf.)	*to take* (by transport)	везу́т	вез-
ждать (impf.)	*to wait for*	ждут	жд-
говори́ть (impf.)	*to speak*	говоря́т	говор-
ко́нчить (pf.)	*to finish*	ко́нчат	конч-
объясни́ть (pf.)	*to explain*	объясня́т	объясн-
отве́тить (pf.)	*to reply*	отве́тят	ответ-
купи́ть (pf.)	*to buy*	ку́пят	куп-

To these stems are added various endings to form the imperative.

i. If the stem ends in a vowel (any vowel), then -й is added, e.g.

infin.	imp.
конча́ть	конча́й
объясня́ть	объясня́й
уме́ть	уме́й
организова́ть	организу́й
мыть	мой
петь	пой

The only exceptions to this rule are a few second-conjugation verbs with vowel stems and stressed endings in -ить in the infinitive, e.g. доúть (impf., *to milk*), which has 3rd person plural доя́т, imperative stem до-, but imperative дой, and кроúть (impf.; *to cut out* [a pattern]), 3rd person plural кроя́т, imperative stem кро-, but imperative крой.

ii. If the stem ends in a single consonant and the stress in the 1st person singular of the indicative is on the ending, then the imperative ending is stressed -и, e.g.

infin.	1st pers. sing.	imp.
писа́ть	пишу́	пиши́
вести́	веду́	веди́
нести́	несу́	неси́
везти́	везу́	вези́
говори́ть	говорю́	говори́
купи́ть	куплю́	купи́

iii. If the stem ends in a single consonant, but the stress in the 1st person singular is on the stem, then the imperative ends in -ь, e.g.

infin.	1st pers. sing.	imp.
ре́зать	ре́жу	режь
отве́тить	отве́чу	отве́ть

Note though that the perfective verb лечь, *to lie down*, has imperative ляг without a soft sign.

Note also that perfective verbs which are derived from basic verbs with end stress but which have the stressed prefix вы́- depart from this pattern and have imperatives in -и, e.g. вы́беги (from вы́бежать, *to run out*); вы́йди (from вы́йти, *to go out*); вы́неси (from вы́нести, *to carry/take out*); вы́плыви (from вы́плыть, *to swim/sail out*).

iv. If the stem ends in two or more consonants, then the imperative ending is again -и, irrespective of the position of the stress, e.g.

infin.	imp.
ждать	жди
ко́нчить	ко́нчи
объясни́ть	объясни́

§2. Verbs with irregular imperative forms

There are a few common verbs whose imperative is not formed according to the above rules.

i. The five monosyllabic verbs in -ить with a stem in a soft consonant (see 9.5 above), and all their compounds, have an imperative in -ей, e.g.

infin.		imp.
бить	*to beat*	бей
вить	*to wind*	вей
пить	*to drink*	пей
налúть	*to pour*	налéй
шить	*to sew*	шей

ii. Verbs in -ава́ть and all their compound forms have an imperative in -й, but this ending is added to the stem of the infinitive rather than to the stem of the present/future tense, e.g.

infin.		imp.
дава́ть	*to give*	дава́й
передава́ть	*to pass, transfer*	передава́й
продава́ть	*to sell*	продава́й
встава́ть	*to get up*	встава́й

iii. Both the imperfective éхать, *to go by transport*, and its perfective поéхать have imperative поезжа́й.

iv. All compounds of éхать, and of the imperfective forms in prefix + -езжа́ть, have an imperative ending in -езжа́й, e.g.

infin. (impf./pf.)		imp. for both aspects
приезжа́ть/приéхать	*to arrive*	приезжа́й
уезжа́ть/уéхать	*to go away*	уезжа́й

v. Дать, *to give*, has the imperative дай, and дай also occurs in all compound forms of this verb, e.g. переда́ть has переда́й; прода́ть has прода́й; разда́ть has разда́й.

vi. Есть, *to eat*, has the imperative form ешь.

§3. Forms of address in the imperative

All the forms of the imperative given above may be used if the form of address ты is appropriate to the person to whom the order is being given or the request being made. If, on the other hand, the appropriate form of address is вы, then the suffix -те is added to the imperative forms already given, e.g. конча́йте, объясня́йте, умéйте, организу́йте, мóйте, etc.

§4. Imperative of reflexive verbs

Reflexive verbs retain the full particle -ся after the endings -й and -ь, but after the vowel ending -и and after the particle -те the reflexive particle is shortened to -сь, e.g.

infin.		2nd sing. imp.	2nd pl. imp.
интересова́ться	*to be interested in*	интересу́йся	интересу́йтесь
встре́титься	*to meet*	встре́ться	встре́тьтесь
бере́чься	*to be careful, beware*	береги́сь	береги́тесь

§5. Use of aspects in the imperative

Choice of aspect in the imperative may pose problems, but broadly speaking the following points may be made and the following distinctions drawn.

i. In commands which refer to actions that are to be repeated the imperfective should be used, e.g.

Чита́йте газе́ту ка́ждый день.
Read the newspaper every day.
По воскресе́ньям отдыха́йте, посеща́йте музе́и.
On Sundays relax, visit museums.

ii. When the speaker is inviting someone to do something (and the tone of such commands tends to be polite), the imperfective should be used, e.g.

Сади́тесь, пожа́луйста.
Sit down please.
По доро́ге домо́й заходи́ ко мне.
Call in to see me on the way home.
Раздева́йтесь и проходи́те в ко́мнату.
Take your coat off and go on into the room.

If on the other hand the command is an instruction to do something on a single occasion, then the perfective would normally be used, as in the following examples which may be contrasted with those above:

Ся́дьте побли́же к све́ту.
Sit nearer the light.
По доро́ге домо́й зайди́ в апте́ку.
Call in at the chemist's on the way home.
— Разде́ньтесь, пожа́луйста, сказа́л врач больно́му.
'Get undressed, please', the doctor said to the patient.

iii. Even an instruction may though be couched in the imperfective if it is expressed by a transitive verb used without a direct object, as in the following examples:

Чита́йте ме́дленнее.
Read more slowly.
Пиши́те аккура́тнее.
Write more neatly.

Contrast the use of the perfective in instructions involving the use of the same verbs with a direct object. Examples:

Прочита́йте э́то предложе́ние ме́дленнее.
Read this sentence more slowly.
Напиши́те э́то сло́во на доске́.
Write this word on the board.

iv. If the speaker is asking someone to begin to do something or to carry on doing something, or if the command is given because it is time to be getting on with something, then the imperfective imperative should be used. Examples:

Ко́нчили чита́ть? Тепе́рь задава́йте вопро́сы.
Have you finished reading? Now ask questions.
Почему́ вы останови́лись? Продолжа́йте.
Why have you stopped? Carry on.
Встава́й, уже́ по́здно.
Get up, it's already late.

v. Requests that someone do something are often couched in the perfective, though they may be softened either by placing after the imperative the word пожа́луйста, *please*, or by introducing the request with some such phrase as бу́дь(те) добры́ or бу́дь(те) любе́зны, both of which mean *be so good/kind as to,* e.g.

Скажи́те пожа́луйста, где по́чта.
Could you tell me where the post office is?
Бу́дьте добры́, покажи́те мне ту кни́гу.
Would you be good enough to show me that book?
Бу́дьте любе́зны, закро́йте дверь.
Would you be so kind as to close the door?

A further means of softening a request or instruction is to attach the particle -ка to the imperative, e.g. иди́-ка сюда́, *come over here would you*; подви́ньтесь-ка побли́же, *move up a little bit closer.* This particle is colloquial.

§6. Use of aspect in negative imperatives

If the imperative is negative, then the imperfective should be used in prohibitions, while the perfective should be used in warnings. Contrast, for example, an order not to do something:

Бóльше, пожáлуйста, ко мне не приходи́те.
Please don't come to me any more. (Press)

with the following warning (which also contains apprehension lest something happen):

Осторóжно, не упади́те, здесь скóльзко.
Be careful, don't fall over, it's slippery here.

The imperative смотри́/смотри́те, *look out, be careful* often precedes a negative imperative, especially a warning, e.g.

Смотри́те, не урони́те вáзу.
Be careful, don't drop the vase.

Note that the perfective imperative is used in the phrase не забýдьте, *don't forget.*

§7. Imperatives expressed with an infinitive

A prohibition may also be expressed by the negated imperfective infinitive of the verb. This usage is particularly common in public notices, e.g.

Не выходи́ть до пóлной останóвки трамвáя.
Don't get off until the tram has completely stopped.
Не ходи́ть по травé.
Keep off the grass.
Не кури́ть.
No smoking.
Не бéгать по эскалáторам.
No running up and down the escalators.
Не прислоня́ться.
Do not lean. (Notice on doors of underground train)

Formal instructions may also be couched in the infinitive, but these will be expressed by a perfective verb, provided that they relate to single actions, because the verb is not negated, e.g.

При авáрии разби́ть стеклó молоткóм.
In the event of an accident break the window with a hammer. (Notice on bus)

§8. Third-person imperatives

As well as the second-person imperative forms dealt with so far Russian also has third-person imperative forms with the meaning *let him / her / them do something*. The third-person imperative is made up of the invariable particle пусть (or the more colloquial alternative пускáй) and the 3rd person singular or plural of the imperfective or perfective verb, the number and aspect of the verb depending on the context, e.g.

Пусть он чита́ет.
Let him read.
Пусть они́ приду́т.
Let them come.
Пусть она́ сама́ реши́т.
Let her decide herself.
Пусть бу́дет так.
Let it be thus/So be it.
Прихо́дит на рабо́ту, а ему́ хала́т не выдаю́т. «Пусть тебе́ Горбачёв даст.»
He arrives for work, but they won't issue him with overalls. 'Let Gorbachev give them to you.' (Press)

§9. Use of да

In solemn wishes or appeals the particle да may be used instead of пусть to express a third-person imperative with the meaning of *may* something happen. In the modern language да is used mainly with the third-person singular forms of быть, *to be*, and здра́вствовать, *to prosper, be healthy,* e.g.

Да бу́дет мир!
May there be peace!
Да здра́вствует на́ша ро́дина!
Long live our country!
Да здра́вствует коро́ль!
Long live the king!

§10. First-person plural imperatives

There is also a first-person plural imperative form with the meaning of *let us* do something which is identical with the 1st person plural of the future tense. Either a perfective future or an imperfective future may be used according to the context, e.g.

Посиди́м.
Let's sit for a while.
Пойдём в кино́.
Let's go to the cinema.
Бу́дем чита́ть газе́ты по воскресе́ньям.
Let's read the newspapers on Sundays.

If the first-person plural imperative is negative, then an imperfective future should be used, e.g.

Не бу́дем чита́ть.
Let's not read.
Не бу́дем толка́ться.
Let's not push one another.
Дава́йте об э́том не бу́дем забыва́ть.
Let's not forget this. (TV)

§11. Use of дава́й/дава́йте

The first-person plural imperative may also be expressed, with no change of meaning, by means of дава́й/дава́йте and the 1st person plural of the perfective verb, e.g.

Дава́йте передохнём.
Let's take a breather.
Дава́йте напи́шем письмо́.
Let's write a letter.
Как э́то сде́лать — дава́йте обсу́дим, попро́буем реши́ть вме́сте.
As to how to do this – let's discuss it, let's try to solve it together.
(Press)

§12. Use of past tense of пойти́ as imperative

The past tense of пойти́ may be used with imperative meaning, e.g. Пошёл! *Be off!*; Пошли́! *Let's go!*; also Пое́хали! *Let's go!*.

Exercises

A. *Give the second-person singular imperative form of the following verbs:* боя́ться, брать, бро́сить, взять, вста́вить, встать, входи́ть, ду́мать, за́втракать, лома́ть, налива́ть, открыва́ть, откры́ть, познако́миться, понима́ть, поня́ть, принести́, приноси́ть, про́бовать, продолжа́ть, рабо́тать, рекомендова́ть, рыть, сади́ться, сесть, слу́шать, сове́товать, создава́ть, спра́шивать, стара́ться, съесть, уе́хать, узнава́ть, управля́ть, чи́стить.

B. *Translate into Russian:* (1) Write me a letter every day. (2) Would you tell me how much that book costs? (3) Get dressed, you are holding us up. (4) Buy me some bread on the way home. (5) 'Open your mouth, please', said the dentist. (6) Come in and sit down. (7) Take a sweet. (8) Could you tell me what the time is? (9) Let's read the paper. (10) Let's not argue. (11) Be careful, don't touch the saucepan: it's hot. (12) No smoking in the classroom. (13) No eating in the library. (14) Don't forget, I am going out tonight. (15) Don't watch that programme. (16) Would you buy me a newspaper? (17) Let him go to the zoo. (18) Let her do it. (19) Long live the queen! (20) Let's go!

LESSON 44

VERBS OF MOTION

§1. Verbs with indeterminate and determinate forms

There are fourteen verbs, all of them expressing motion, which have two quite distinct imperfective forms. One form is generally termed indeterminate, the other determinate. This lesson sets out the conjugation of the fourteen pairs of verbs in question. The following lesson deals with their use.

§2. Conjugation of verbs of motion

The fourteen pairs conjugate as follows, arranged with the pairs including determinate verbs of conjugation 1b first. The past tense is given in brackets below the present tense of each verb.

	indeterminate impf.		determinate impf.		
i.	ходи́ть:	хожу́	идти́:	иду́	*to go* (on foot),
		хо́дишь		идёшь	*to walk*
		хо́дит		идёт	
		хо́дим		идём	
		хо́дите		идёте	
		хо́дят		иду́т	
		(ходи́л, ходи́ла,		(шёл, шла,	
		ходи́ло, ходи́ли)		шло, шли)	
ii.	е́здить:	е́зжу	е́хать:	е́ду	*to go* (by
		е́здишь		е́дешь	transport),
		е́здит		е́дет	*to travel*
		е́здим		е́дем	
		е́здите		е́дете	
		е́здят		е́дут	
		(е́здил, е́здила,		(е́хал, е́хала,	
		е́здило, е́здили)		е́хало, е́хали)	
iii.	води́ть:	вожу́	вести́:	веду́	*to lead, to*
		во́дишь		ведёшь	*take* (on
		во́дит		ведёт	foot)
		во́дим		ведём	
		во́дите		ведёте	
		во́дят		веду́т	

		(води́л, води́ла,		(вёл, вела́,	
		води́ло, води́ли)		вело́, вели́	
iv.	вози́ть:	вожу́	везти́:	везу́	*to transport,*
		во́зишь		везёшь	*to take* (by
		во́зит		везёт	transport)
		во́зим		везём	
		во́зите		везёте	
		во́зят		везу́т	
		(вози́л, вози́ла,		(вёз, везла́,	
		вози́ло, вози́ли)		везло́, везли́)	
v.	носи́ть:	ношу́	нести́:	несу́	*to carry, to*
		но́сишь		несёшь	*take* (by hand)
		но́сит		несёт	
		но́сим		несём	
		но́сите		несёте	
		но́сят		несу́т	
		(носи́л, носи́ла,		(нёс, несла́,	
		носи́ло, носи́ли)		несло́, несли́)	
vi.	броди́ть:	брожу́	брести́:	бреду́	indeterminate
		бро́дишь		бредёшь	form means *to*
		бро́дит		бредёт	*wander, to*
		бро́дим		бредём	*roam*; deter-
		бро́дите		бредёте	minate form
		бро́дят		бреду́т	*to amble*
		(броди́л, броди́ла,		(брёл, брела́,	
		броди́ло, броди́ли)		брело́, брели́)	
vii.	ла́зить:	ла́жу	лезть:	ле́зу	*to climb*
		ла́зишь		ле́зешь	
		ла́зит		ле́зет	
		ла́зим		ле́зем	
		ла́зите		ле́зете	
		ла́зят		ле́зут	
		(ла́зил, ла́зила,		(лез, ле́зла,	
		ла́зило, ла́зили)		ле́зло, ле́зли)	
viii.	пла́вать:	пла́ваю	плыть:	плыву́	*to swim, to*
		пла́ваешь		плывёшь	*sail, to*
		пла́вает		плывёт	*float*
		пла́ваем		плывём	
		пла́ваете		плывёте	
		пла́вают		плыву́т	

		(пла́вал, пла́вала,		(плыл, плыла́,	
		пла́вало, пла́вали)		плы́ло, плы́ли)	
ix.	по́лзать:	по́лзаю	ползти́:	ползу́	*to crawl*
		по́лзаешь		ползёшь	
		по́лзает		ползёт	
		по́лзаем		ползём	
		по́лзаете		ползёте	
		по́лзают		ползу́т	
		(по́лзал, по́лзала,		(полз, ползла́,	
		по́лзало, по́лзали)		ползло́, ползли́)	
x.	бе́гать:	бе́гаю	бежа́ть:	бегу́	*to run*
		бе́гаешь		бежи́шь	
		бе́гает		бежи́т	
		бе́гаем		бежи́м	
		бе́гаете		бежи́те	
		бе́гают		бегу́т	
		(бе́гал, бе́гала,		(бежа́л, бежа́ла,	
		бе́гало, бе́гали)		бежа́ло, бежа́ли)	
xi.	гоня́ть:	гоня́ю	гнать:	гоню́	*to chase, to*
		гоня́ешь		го́нишь	*drive, to*
		гоня́ет		го́нит	*pursue*
		гоня́ем		го́ним	
		гоня́ете		го́ните	
		гоня́ют		го́нят	
		(гоня́л, гоня́ла,		(гнал, гнала́,	
		гоня́ло, гоня́ли)		гна́ло, гна́ли)	
xii.	ката́ть:	ката́ю	кати́ть:	качу́	*to roll, to*
		ката́ешь		ка́тишь	*push* (sthg.
		ката́ет		ка́тит	on wheels)
		ката́ем		ка́тим	
		ката́ете		ка́тите	
		ката́ют		ка́тят	
		(ката́л, ката́ла,		(кати́л, кати́ла,	
		ката́ло, ката́ли)		кати́ло, кати́ли)	
xiii.	лета́ть:	лета́ю	лете́ть:	лечу́	*to fly*
		лета́ешь		лети́шь	
		лета́ет		лети́т	

		лета́ем		лети́м	
		лета́ете		лети́те	
		лета́ют		летя́т	
		(лета́л, лета́ла, лета́ло, лета́ли)		(лете́л, лете́ла, лете́ло, лете́ли)	
xiv.	таска́ть:	таска́ю	тащи́ть:	тащу́	*to drag, to pull*
		таска́ешь		та́щишь	
		таска́ет		та́щит	
		таска́ем		та́щим	
		таска́ете		та́щите	
		таска́ют		та́щат	
		(таска́л, таска́ла, таска́ло, таска́ли)		(тащи́л, тащи́ла, тащи́ло, тащи́ли)	

All the determinate verbs have perfectives in по- (пойти́, пое́хать, etc.). On perfective forms of the indeterminate verbs see 45.3.ii and iii.

§3. Note on the use of е́здить/е́хать and ходи́ть/идти́

The appropriate form of е́здить or е́хать should be used to describe movement by passengers on any form of transport (unless flying or sailing is implied), e.g. bus, car, train, bicycle, even lift or horseback. Thus:

Мы е́здим/е́дем в Москву́ на ско́ром по́езде.
We go/are going to Moscow on the fast train.

However, if it is the vehicle itself whose motion is being described and if the vehicle is a large form of public transport such as a train, bus, tram, etc., then an appropriate form of ходи́ть or идти́ is generally used, e.g. по́езд идёт бы́стро, *the train is going fast.*

If on the other hand one is talking about a smaller vehicle then an appropriate form of е́хать seems to predominate. One says, for example, такси е́дет, маши́на е́дет.

An appropriate form of ходи́ть or идти́ must also be used to describe the movement of things (e.g. letters, parcels, goods) as opposed to people, even though it is clear that they are going by transport, e.g.

Письмо́ идёт авиапо́чтой.
The letter is going by airmail.

LESSON 45

USE OF VERBS OF MOTION

§1. Use of determinate and indeterminate forms
It is not easy for the foreign student fully to understand the distinction between these two types of verb of motion.

The best way of approaching the problem is perhaps to define the function of the determinate type of verb of motion, which is basically quite straightforward, and then to treat the indeterminate type as having various uses whose only common denominator is that they fall outside the scope of the determinate type.

It is worth saying in this connection that Russians themselves may not think of the indeterminate forms as positively having all the meanings which are attributed to them in §3 below (particularly in §3.iii). It is rather that we may infer these meanings on the grounds that the verb means something other than what a determinate form would mean in the same context.

(Similar considerations may operate in choice of aspect. There are circumstances in which an imperfective may be used not so much because it does have a specific meaning as because it lacks a meaning which is inherent in the perfective and which the speaker does not intend in a particular context [see Lesson 53].)

It should be added that even the simple rule given for the use of the determinate forms in §2 below may appear in certain circumstances to be broken (see §4 below).

§2. Use of the determinate forms
The basic function of the determinate forms (идти́, etc.) is to describe movement in one general direction. The movement is not necessarily in a straight line, but it does involve a sense of progress from A towards B. The movement is also usually on one occasion, though this is not necessarily the case (see §4 below). Examples:

> Ма́льчик идёт в шко́лу.
> *The boy is going to school.*
> Мы подыма́лись по ле́стнице. Андре́й шёл впереди́.
> *We were going up the staircase. Andrey was walking in front.* (Press)

В э́том году́ мы е́дем на Кавка́з.
This year we are going to the Caucasus.
Она́ несла́ чемода́н по коридо́ру.
She was carrying a suitcase down the corridor.
Пти́ца лети́т на юг.
The bird is flying south.

Note that in these examples the Russian verb is in each instance translated by the English present or past continuous tense *(is going, was walking, are going, was carrying, is flying)*. Those verbs which are in the present tense (идёт, е́дем, лети́т) could not be translated in these sentences by the other type of English present tense (*goes, go, flies*) because the sense of movement on one occasion characteristic of the determinate type of verb would thereby be lost.

Note also that determinate verbs of motion may be used in the present tense to describe an action that will take place in the near future, e.g.

За́втра мы е́дем в Москву́.
We are going to Moscow tomorrow.

This usage again parallels the use of the English present continuous tense.

§3. Use of the indeterminate forms
The function of the indeterminate type of verb (ходи́ть, etc.) is to describe movement which is not from A towards B and on one occasion. The indeterminate verbs are therefore used in the following circumstances.

i. To describe movement which is repeated or habitual. This frequentative function is perhaps the one which Russians most readily associate with the indeterminate verb, the function in which the verb has a positive meaning that springs to mind. In contrasting this use of ходи́ть, etc. with the use of идти́ one may argue that ходи́ть focuses not on a particular journey in a particular direction and on a particular occasion but on the fact that some movement of a particular kind takes place. Examples:

   Я ча́сто хожу́ туда́.
   I often go there.
   Ка́ждый день рабо́чие е́здят на фа́брику на трамва́е.
   Every day the workers travel to the factory on the tram.
   Четы́ре го́да я води́ла его́ туда́ за ру́чку.
   For four years I led him there [to a special school for backward children] *by the hand.* (Press)
   Про́шлой зимо́й из на́шей страны́ лета́ло в США во́семь самолётов в неде́лю. Тепе́рь двена́дцать. Причём в Нью-Йорк по понеде́льникам, среда́м и пя́тницам лета́ет Ил-86.

Last winter eight planes a week flew from our country to the USA. Now it is twelve. And on Mondays, Wednesdays and Fridays an Ilyushin 86 flies to New York. (Press)

It is helpful again to remember in this connection that English makes a distinction in the present tense between an action which takes place regularly and one which is taking place when the speaker is reporting it, e.g. *he reads the newspaper every day* and *he is reading the newspaper*. As a rule the same Russian imperfective may express both types of present tense (see also 52.5 below), but in the case of the fourteen verbs which have both an indeterminate and a determinate form Russian too observes the distinction which is made clear in English by the use of the two different types of present tense.

ii. A further function which the determinate verb does not fulfil, and which is therefore taken on by the indeterminate form instead, is to describe movement which has no specific direction or is multidirectional, e.g. он хо́дит по ко́мнате, *he is walking round the room [pacing about]*. In this sense the indeterminate verb is often followed by по and the dative case to convey the meaning of *round, about*. Examples from the press:

Сейча́с по Куве́йтской пусты́не бро́дят гру́ппы голо́дных и изму́ченных ира́кских солда́т.
Groups of hungry and worn-out Iraqi soldiers are roaming round the Kuwaiti desert.
По ковро́вой доро́жке по́лзали малыши́, от го́дика до трёх-четырёх.
Little children aged from one to three or four were crawling round a strip of carpet.
Повсю́ду таска́ла су́мку с ру́кописью.
I dragged the bag with the manuscript round everywhere.

When an indeterminate verb of motion is used with this meaning it may take the prefix по-, which makes the verb perfective and indicates that the movement was carried out, or will be carried out, *for a while*, e.g.

Мы поёздили по го́роду.
We drove round the town for a while [and that action was completed].

iii. Because the determinate verb describes movement in one direction, from A to B, it follows that the indeterminate verb should be used if the speaker has in mind not a particular journey but a whole trip, perhaps for a particular purpose, i.e. a journey to a place and a journey back again. (It should be emphasised though that there is no strong sense of two-way movement in the indeterminate verb. It is also possible that this sense will in many cases be difficult to separate from the frequentative sense described in Section i above.) Examples:

В про́шлом году́ мы е́здили на Кавка́з.
Last year we went/made a trip to the Caucasus.
Я ча́сто е́здила в Москву́.
I often travelled/made trips to Moscow. (Press)

When an indeterminate verb of motion is used with this meaning it may take the prefix с-, which makes the verb perfective and emphasises the fact that the action has been completed or is expected to be completed (possibly, but not necessarily, quite quickly), e.g.

В мой день рожде́ния ра́но у́тром он съе́здил на ры́нок за цвета́ми.
On my birthday, early in the morning, he went to the market for some flowers. (Press)

Indeterminate perfectives with the prefix с- are also commonly used:

(a) when the reference is to a future action (and a perfective verb is therefore needed), e.g. он схо́дит в магази́н за хле́бом, *he'll pop down to the shop for some bread*;

(b) when a sequence of actions in the past is being listed (and a perfective verb is again needed to denote that one action was completed before the next action began), e.g. в суббо́ту мы съе́здили в Заго́рск, в воскресе́нье верну́лись в Брита́нию, *on Saturday we made a trip to Zagorsk and on Sunday we returned to Britain*;

(c) in imperatives where the demand is for some trip to be made or some errand carried out, e.g. сбе́гай на по́чту, *pop down to the post office*.

Note that if the prefix с- is added to the verb е́здить, then a hard sign must be inserted after the с to indicate that it remains hard in spite of the presence of the following vowel е.

The use of the prefix с- in this sense with indeterminate verbs should not be confused with its use with many verbs (including verbs of motion) in the sense of *together* or *off*. (This subject will be dealt with in 47.6.i and ii below.)

iv. A fourth function of the indeterminate verb, which the determinate verb cannot fulfil, is to describe so-called non-contextual movement. That is to say the speaker or writer names a particular type of movement (e.g. walking, travelling, flying), but does not have in mind any particular instance of it. Examples from the press:

Есть ку́рсы, где они́ мо́гут повыша́ть квалифика́цию и специализи́роваться — рабо́тать с соба́ками, стреля́ть, е́здить верхо́м.
There are courses on which they [prison-workers] *can better their qualifications and specialise: in dog-handling, shooting, horse-riding.*
Вме́сто компью́теров мо́жно вози́ть видеоте́хнику, радиоаппарату́ру, же́мчуг — сло́вом всё то, что там дёшево, а у нас до́рого.
Instead of computers one can transport video equipment, radio apparatus, pearls, in a word everything that is cheap there [in the West] *but expensive in our country.*

It is this function that the verb of motion is fulfilling when a speaker indicates whether a subject has the physical capacity or ability to perform a type of movement, e.g.

Ребёнок уже́ хо́дит.
The child can already walk.
Больно́й уже́ мо́жет ходи́ть.
The invalid is already up and about.
Я не уме́ю пла́вать.
I can't swim.

It is also with this non-contextual function that the participial forms of indeterminate verbs are used in such phrases as неопо́знанные лета́ющие объе́кты, *unidentified flying objects.*

§4. Use of determinate verbs where an indeterminate verb might be expected

It is important to emphasise that the choice of determinate or indeterminate form may depend not on the intrinsic nature of the movement but on the speaker's perspective or on how he or she wishes to present it.

For example, if the sense of making progress from A to B is dominant, then the determinate form may be used even if the action is repeated or habitual, e.g.

Ка́ждое у́тро он выхо́дит из до́ма, идёт на остано́вку авто́буса, сади́тся на авто́бус и е́дет в го́род.
Every morning he leaves home, goes to the bus stop, gets on a bus and goes into town.

Again, if it is wished to give a graphic account of some movement, to actualise a particular instance of it, then a determinate form may be used even if the action is a habitual one which might seem to require the use of an indeterminate verb. Examples from the press:

> Чтóбы отпрáвить письмó нýжно идти́ дéсять киломéтров.
> *In order to send a letter one has to walk ten kilometres.*
> Чёрные стрáусы бегýт легкó, вы́прямив шéю, как балери́ны на пуáнтах.
> *The black ostrich runs easily, straightening its neck, like a ballerina on the tips of her toes.*

In the first example attention is being focused on the difficulty of each journey to post a letter and the determinate form is therefore used, even though such journeys are always the same. In the second example the writer is inviting his readers to visualise an instance of the ostrich running along and therefore uses a determinate verb even though ostriches always do run in this way.

§5. Use of indeterminate or determinate forms in set expressions

There are certain set expressions in which the determinate verb (especially идти, вести́, нести́) is used even when the meaning is frequentative, e.g.

идти́ + dat. (or + к + dat.)	*to suit*
идёт дождь	*it is raining, it rains*
идёт снег	*it is snowing, it snows*
идёт пьéса	*a play is on*
речь идёт о + prep.	*it is a question of* (compare French *il s'agit de*)
вести́ дневни́к	*to keep a diary*
вести́ кампáнию	*to conduct a campaign*
вести́ переговóры	*to hold talks*
нести́ отвéтственность	*to bear responsibility*
мне/тебé/емý везёт	*I am/you are/he is lucky*
врéмя лети́т	*time flies*

In certain other expressions only the indeterminate verb may be used:

катáться на конькáх	*to skate*
катáться на лы́жах	*to ski*
ходи́ть за + instr.	*to look after*
ходи́ть с + gen.	*to lead* (a playing card)

The indeterminate form носи́ть, unlike нести́, may also mean *to wear* (clothes, habitually), e.g. обы́чно онá нóсит чёрное, но сегóдня онá одéта в я́рко-крáсное, *she usually wears black, but today she is dressed in bright red.*

Exercises

A. *Translate the following sentences into English and explain the reason for the use of the indeterminate verb or the determinate verb in them:* (1) С весны́ прóшлого гóда росси́йские лáйнеры мóгут летáть поми́мо Нью-Йо́рка и Вашингто́на та́кже в Сан-Франци́ско, Чика́го и Майа́ми. (2) Подсуди́мый ведёт себя́ ти́хо. (3) Чем ста́рше становлю́сь, тем бо́льше тя́нет к земле́. Уезжа́ю на да́чу, про́сто брожу́ по ле́су. (4) Ча́сто ходи́л в Третьяко́вскую галере́ю, при́стально рассма́тривал карти́ны, на кото́рых бы́ли изображены́ ру́сские де́ти. (5) Пусть хоть на неде́лю в году́ к нам опя́ть присоединя́т Финля́ндию, мы съе́здим туда́ и оде́немся на всю оста́вшуюся жизнь. (6) Речь идёт об агре́ссии Се́рбии. (7) Тако́е же чу́вство бы́ло в я́сный ма́йский день про́шлого го́да. Мы шли на день рожде́ния к мое́й тёте. (8) Ко́шки не уме́ют пла́вать. (9) К бе́регу одна́ за друго́й полете́ли ча́йки. (10) Сын стал проси́ть у отца́ маши́ну. Он хоте́л съе́здить в сосе́днюю дере́вню, навести́ть подру́гу. (11) По не́бу, ряд за ря́дом, шли тяжёлые ту́чи. (12) В любо́й диску́ссии об экономи́ческом разви́тии стран Восто́чной Евро́пы упомина́ется «план Ма́ршалла». А ведь о нём хо́дит нема́ло леге́нд. (13) Иду́ по у́лице. Грязь, сля́коть. Спуска́юсь в подзе́мный перехо́д и вдруг слы́шу му́зыку. (14) Ми́ссис Э́шдаун уча́ствует в избира́тельной камп́ании, но на лока́льном у́ровне. Е́здит по сосе́дним деревня́м в избира́тельном о́круге Пэ́дди. (15) Журавли́ всегда́ летя́т с се́вера на юго-за́пад, гу́си — то́чно на юг. Как они́ ориенти́руются в пути́? (16) Ре́дкие её конце́рты прохо́дят без рекла́мы, в ма́леньких за́лах, и хо́дят на них лишь знатоки́ её тво́рчества. (17) Чле́ны белару́сской делега́ции пое́хали в По́льшу с чёткой це́лью — договори́ться о поста́вке в Белару́сь хле́ба. (18) Пе́рвые две неде́ли фе́рмер вози́л меня́ к свои́м знако́мым, родны́м, с го́рдостью говори́л, что в их семье́ ру́сский студе́нт. (19) Всю зи́му идёт та же са́мая пье́са. (20) Ребёнку уже́ полтора́ го́да, но он ещё не хо́дит.

B. *Translate into Russian:* (1) I used to walk to the museum every day. (2) On Saturday he went to London by train and bought some presents. (3) I walked round the town in the morning and then went home by bus. (4) Fish swim and snakes crawl. (5) The bird was flying round the garden. (6) Swallows fly south in autumn. (7) The plane is flying to Paris. (8) We flew to London on Monday and spent two days there. (9) She is walking down the street. (10) She was walking down the street when she met her friend. (11) The ship is sailing to St. Petersburg tomorrow. (12) All summer the ship sailed between London and St. Petersburg. (13) He is taking us to the airport in his car. (14) I shall lead you to them. (15) He is taking his children to the park (on foot). (16) She is taking her children round the park. (17) He dragged the sack round the garden. (18) She dragged her case down the corridor. (19) This colour doesn't suit you. (20) His mother has been looking after him all winter. (21) It was raining when she arrived. (22) In Russia it always snows in winter. (23) She swam for a while in the lake. (24) We used to fly a lot. (25) She was carrying a book. (26) All dogs can swim. (27) The children were running towards the lake. (28) He is pushing a pram down the street. (29) Every day they go to work by bus. (30) The boy ran down to the shop for some bread.

LESSON 46

VERBAL PREFIXES (в- TO от-): DIRECTIONAL MEANINGS

§1. Introductory remarks

There are some two dozen prefixes which may be added to a simple verb in order to modify its meaning or to create a verb with a related but different meaning. A few of these prefixes are to be found in only a small number of verbs, but the majority occur in very many verbs.

Most of the widely used prefixes may themselves be used in various senses. They may have a directional meaning (that is to say they make clear the direction of the movement indicated by the basic verb), or they may in some other way define the precise nature of the action indicated by the verb.

In this and the following lesson the directional meanings of the prefixes will be given, and in Lessons 48-49 other, non-directional meanings will be listed.

§2. Prefix and aspect

Normally the addition of a prefix to a simple imperfective verb makes the verb perfective, e.g. писáть (impf.), написáть (pf.); вязáть (impf.), связáть (pf.). In some instances (e.g. in the verb написáть) the prefix has no function other than to make the verb perfective (that is to say it adds only the sense of completeness of the action to the sense already conveyed by the imperfective). However, in other instances (e.g. in the verb связáть) the prefix provides a further modification of the meaning (вязáть means *to tie*, but связáть means *to tie together*, i.e. *to unite, to join, to link*).

When a prefix conveys some meaning which needs to be retained in an imperfective verb, then the new imperfective with prefix is usually formed by the lengthening of the basic verb. This lengthening is achieved by the insertion of some infix such as -ыв- or -ив-, and results in the formation of a verb ending in -ать and belonging to the conjugation 1a, e.g. imperfective свя́зывать.

Note, however, that with the verbs of motion which have both an indeterminate and a determinate imperfective (ходи́ть and идти́, носи́ть and нести́, etc.), very numerous pairs of verbs exist in which the imperfective is invariably made up of prefix + indeterminate form and the perfective of prefix + determinate form, e.g. приноси́ть (impf.)/принести́ (pf.). (On the various modifications to the simple verbs that may be required, see §3 below.)

It should be added that many verbs with prefixes are derived not from simple verbs but from other parts of speech, e.g. обрамля́ть/обра́мить, *to frame*, from the noun ра́ма, *frame*, and ускоря́ть/уско́рить, *to quicken, speed up*, from the adjective ско́рый, *fast*.

§3. Modification of simple verbs of motion when a prefix is added

Before examining the very numerous compounds which consist of prefix + verb of motion it is as well to note the small modification which several of the simple verbs of motion undergo when a prefix with directional meaning is attached to them:

i. the determinate form идти́ is contracted to -йти, e.g. войти́, *to go in*; прийти́, *to arrive*; пройти́, *to go past*; уйти́, *to go away*;

ii. the indeterminate form е́здить (which belongs to the 2nd conjugation) becomes -езжа́ть, and the new verb belongs to conjugation 1a. Note also that if the prefix consists of a single consonant (e.g. в-) or if it ends in a consonant (e.g. раз-), then a hard sign **ъ** must precede the **е**, e.g. въезжа́ть, *to drive in*; разъезжа́ться, *to disperse*. (It is necessary to insert a hard sign in similar circumstances before the **е** of е́хать, e.g. въе́хать, разъе́хаться);

iii. whereas the stress is on the stem of the indeterminate forms бе́гать and по́лзать, it is on the ending of the imperfectives which consist of directional prefix + these indeterminate forms, e.g. вбега́ть, *to run in*; вполза́ть, *to crawl in*;

iv. the imperfective forms of compounds of плыть are derived by means of the infix -ва-, e.g. вплыва́ть, *to sail in*;

v. the imperfective forms of compounds of лезть are derived by means of the infix -а-, e.g. влеза́ть, *to climb in*;

vi. the imperfective forms of compounds of кати́ть and тащи́ть are derived by means of the infixes -ыва- and -ива- respectively, e.g. ска́тывать, *to roll down*, and вта́скивать, *to drag in*.

§4. Basic prefixes

There follows a list of the basic prefixes which have directional meanings, and examples of their application in (a) verbs of motion and (b) other verbs. Many of the verbs of both types may have figurative as well as literal meanings. It should be noted that not only is the list highly selective (necessarily, in view of the vast number of verbs in which the prefixes are found), but also that many of the verbs given, particularly the verbs of motion among them, have more meanings than it is possible to list here.

Note also that prefixes consisting of a single consonant or ending in a consonant may have to add -о- for the sake of euphony, and that the **з** in вз- (воз-) and раз- is changed to **с** before unvoiced consonants (**к, п, с, т, ф, х, ч, ш, щ**).

§5. В-/во-

The prefix в- (во-) implies movement *into*, e.g.

вбега́ть/вбежа́ть	*to run into*
ввози́ть/ввезти́	*to bring in* (by transport), *import*
вводи́ть/ввести́	*to bring in, introduce* (law, custom, etc.)
влеза́ть/влезть	*to climb into, get into*
входи́ть/войти́	*to go into, enter*
вкла́дывать/вложи́ть	*to put in, insert, invest*
включа́ть/включи́ть	*to include*
вовлека́ть/вовле́чь	*to drag in, involve*
вска́кивать/вскочи́ть	*to leap up into/on to*
вступа́ть/вступи́ть	*to enter, step in*

The verb to which the prefix в- is added will generally be followed by the preposition в, or sometimes на, and the accusative case. Examples from the press:

> Мы вошли́ в де́тскую ко́мнату.
> *We went into the nursery.*
> То́лько в о́бщей сло́жности со́рок америка́нских компа́ний согласи́лись вкла́дывать де́ньги в СССР.
> *In total only 40 American companies agreed to invest money in the USSR.*
> Но́вый день вовлека́ет в валю́тный би́знес но́вых люде́й.
> *Each new day involves new people in the foreign currency business.*
> Но едва́ маши́на тро́нулась, э́тот са́мый полице́йский вскочи́л в неё!
> *But no sooner had the car set off than this same policeman leapt into it!*
> Реше́ние мэ́ра вступи́ло в си́лу неме́дленно.
> *The mayor's decision came into effect without delay.*

§6. Вз-/взо-/вс-

The prefix вз- (взо-; вс- before unvoiced consonants) implies movement *up*. This prefix also has the variants воз- and вос-. Examples:

взлета́ть/взлете́ть	*to fly up, take off*
в(о)сходи́ть/взойти́	*to go up, mount, ascend, rise*
взва́ливать/взвали́ть	*to lift, load up on to*
взвива́ться/взви́ться	*to go up* (of curtain, flag), *to soar* (of birds)

There is no particular preposition with which the prefix вз- is associated. Various prepositions may be appropriate depending on the context, though in many instances no preposition at all will be necessary. Examples:

> Самолёт взлете́л.
> *The plane took off.*
> Со́лнце взошло́ в шесть часо́в.
> *The sun rose at six o'clock.*
> Всю вину́ взвали́ли на мини́стра.
> *All the blame was heaped on the minister.*

§7. Вы-

The prefix вы- implies movement *out of*, e.g.

выбега́ть/вы́бежать	*to run out*
выводи́ть/вы́вести	*to lead out, withdraw*
вывози́ть/вы́везти	*to take out* (by transport), *export*
вылеза́ть/вы́лезть	*to climb out*
вылета́ть/вы́лететь	*to fly out*
выноси́ть/вы́нести	*to carry out*
выходи́ть/вы́йти	*to go out, leave*
выбива́ть/вы́бить	*to beat out, dislodge*
вызыва́ть/вы́звать	*to call out, summon, evoke, cause*
вынима́ть/вы́нуть	*to take out*

Note that the prefix вы- always bears the stress if the verb is perfective. It follows that perfective verbs with the prefix вы- cannot have endings in -ёшь, -ёт, -ём, -ёте in the future tense but must have the endings -ешь, -ет, -ем, -ете instead if they belong to conjugation 1b, e.g. вы́йдешь, вы́йдет, вы́йдем, вы́йдете. The same vowel change affects the masculine past tense forms вы́шел, вы́вез, вы́вел and вы́нес.

Verbs with the prefix вы- are generally followed by the preposition из, *out of*, and the genitive case, if any preposition is necessary. Examples from the press:

> Мы наде́емся, что таки́м о́бразом смо́жем убеди́ть Са́дда́ма Хуссе́йна в необходи́мости вы́вести ира́кские войска́ из Куве́йта.
> *We hope that in this way we shall be able to convince Saddam Hussein of the necessity of withdrawing Iraqi troops from Kuwait.*
> Невозмо́жно подсчита́ть ско́лько това́ров и проду́ктов они́ вы́везли из ГДР за э́ти го́ды.
> *It is impossible to calculate how many goods and products they exported from East Germany over these years.*

Два представи́теля президе́нта СССР вы́летели на Бли́жний восто́к.
Two representatives of the President of the USSR flew out to the Middle East.
Бе́лые шахтёры, кото́рых не обы́скивают, как чёрных, при вы́ходе из рудника́, выно́сят взрывча́тку.
White miners, who are not searched as black miners are when they come out of the pit, carry out explosives.
Он до́лжен вы́йти отсю́да лу́чшим челове́ком, чем был.
He should leave here [a prison] *a better person than he was...*
Сосе́ди вы́звали «Ско́рую». Пото́м — мили́цию.
The neighbours called an ambulance. Then the police.
Вы́нула из су́мочки пистоле́т, дала́ мне подержа́ть.
She took a pistol out of her handbag and gave it to me to hold for a bit.

§8. До-

The prefix до- implies movement *as far as* or *up to* a certain point, e.g.

доплыва́ть/доплы́ть *to reach* (by swimming)
доходи́ть/дойти́ *to reach* (on foot)

добира́ться/добра́ться *to reach, get as far as*

Verbs with the prefix до- will be followed by the preposition до and the genitive case, if any preposition is required. Examples from the press:

Они́ доплы́ли до стоя́вшего на ре́йде ру́сского вое́нного фрега́та. На его́ борту́ они́ добрали́сь до Росси́и.
They swam to a Russian frigate that was standing in the shipping lane. On board the frigate they reached Russia.
В 1954 году́ на чемпиона́те ми́ра ве́нгры легко́ дошли́ до фина́ла.
In the 1954 World Cup the Hungarians easily got through to the final.

§9. За-

The prefix за- implies movement *behind* or *beyond*, or indeed *a long way*, e.g.

забега́ть/забежа́ть (вперёд) *to run (ahead)*
заезжа́ть/зае́хать *to drive beyond*
заноси́ть/занести́ *to carry off, bear away*
заходи́ть/зайти́ *to go behind, set* (of sun)

закла́дывать/заложи́ть *to put behind*

Examples from the press:

Потóм судьбá занеслá меня́ в Беларýсь.
Then fate bore me out to Belorussia.
Не сли́шком ли бы́стро и далекó зашли́ США в э́тих дéйствиях?
Has the USA not gone too far too quickly in these actions?

§10. На-

The prefix на- implies movement *onto* or *into* (in the sense of collision), e.g.

наезжáть/наéхать	*to run into, run over*
налетáть/налетéть	*to swoop on, run into* (of vehicles)
находи́ть/найти́	*to come upon, find*
набрáсываться/нabрóситься	*to throw oneself on, fall upon*
наклéивать/наклéить	*to stick on*
наступáть/наступи́ть	*to come on, set in* (of time, seasons)

Verbs with the prefix на- used in this sense will generally be followed by the preposition на and the accusative case, if any preposition is required. Examples:

Автóбус налетéл на грузови́к.
The bus ran into a lorry.
Мнóгие набрáсываются на ковры́, дороги́е мехá.
Many [shoppers] fall upon the carpets, the expensive furs. (Press)
Я наклéиваю мáрку на конвéрт.
I am sticking a stamp on the envelope.
Шло лéто, наступи́ла óсень.
Summer was passing, autumn came on. (Press)

§11. О-/об-/обо-

The prefix о- (об-, обо-) implies movement *round* in a number of senses: comprehensive coverage (e.g. *to go round* in the sense of *to do the rounds of*); bypassing or overtaking (e.g. *to go round* a town, as opposed to *through* it); and encircling, encompassing or surrounding, e.g.

обгоня́ть/обогнáть	*to overtake*
обходи́ть/обойти́	*to go all round, get round*
объезжáть/объéхать	*to travel all over, bypass, overtake*
обклáдывать/обложи́ть	*to surround*
обрамля́ть/обрáмить	*to frame*
обсáживать/обсади́ть	*to plant round*

Examples:

Éсли не обгóним грузови́к, опоздáем.
If we don't overtake the lorry we shall be late.
Онá обошлá лýжу.
She went round the puddle.
Слух обошёл гóрод.
A rumour went round the town.
Тогдá обложи́ли войскáми дом, где я был на óтдыхе.
Then they surrounded the house where I was holidaying with troops. (TV)
Он обсáживает сад цветáми.
He is planting flowers round the garden.

Note that the word which would be the direct object of the basic verb must in some contexts after a verb with the prefix о- be rendered by a noun in the instrumental case, and is replaced by a different direct object. The last example above illustrates this point. In the sentence он обсáживает сад цветáми (*he is planting flowers round [the edge of] the garden*), for instance, the noun denoting the things planted is in the instrumental case and сад is the direct object, whereas the verb сажáть/посади́ть, *to plant,* used without the prefix о-, would have as its direct object the word denoting the things planted, e.g. он сажáет цветы́ в садý, *he is planting flowers in the garden*.

§12. От-/ото-
The prefix от- (ото-) implies movement *away from*, or *off*, e.g.

отлетáть/отлетéть	*to fly away, fly off, rebound*
отплывáть/отплы́ть	*to swim away, sail off*
отходи́ть/отойти́	*to go away, go off, depart* (of transport)
отбирáть/отобрáть	*to take away*
откáлывать/отколóть	*to chop off, hack off*
отнимáть/отня́ть	*to take away*
отрезáть/отрéзать	*to cut off*
отрывáть/оторвáть	*to tear off*

See also 47.7 below on the difference in meaning of от- and у-.

If they require a preposition, verbs with the prefix от- are generally followed by the preposition от and the genitive case, or, in some contexts where they indicate removal or deprivation, by the preposition у and the genitive case. Examples from the press:

На ми́тинге я отошлá от негó, замéтив, что телевизиóнщики готóвятся егó снимáть.
At the rally I moved away from him, having noticed that the television people were getting ready to film him.

У ле́вых сил ото́брано уже́ всё, что мо́жно бы́ло отобра́ть. Иму́щество, па́мятники, назва́ния у́лиц... Нельзя́, одна́ко, отня́ть у люде́й их взгля́ды.
Everything has already been taken away from left-wing forces [in Poland] *that it has been possible to take away. Property, memorials, street names... It is impossible, however, to take away from people their views.*
Со́тни люде́й, вооружи́вшись зуби́лами и молотка́ми, на́чали отка́лывать от неё куски́ в ка́честве сувени́ра на па́мять.
Hundreds of people, having armed themselves with chisels and hammers, started to hack bits off it [the Berlin Wall] *to keep as a souvenir.*

Exercises

A. *Translate into English and indicate the meaning of the prefix in the verbs in bold print:* (1) Он **отре́зал** кусо́к хле́ба. (2) Мы **зале́зли** в боло́то и ника́к не могли́ **вы́лезть.** (3) Они́ **вы́шли** из шко́лы. Уже́ **наступи́ла** ночь. (4) Из ло́дки **вы́скочил** рыба́к. (5) Она́ **отошла́** к столу́, но че́рез мину́ту он сно́ва её позва́л. (6) О́ба президе́нта согласи́лись, что необходи́мо **вы́вести** всё тяжёлое вооруже́ние с террито́рии Бо́снии и Герцегови́ны. (7) Води́тель взя́лся за ключ зажига́ния, но в э́то вре́мя в авто́бус **вошли́** дво́е кре́пких молоды́х люде́й. (8) Гул движе́ния иногда́ **доно́сится** до на́шей кварти́ры. (9) Куве́йт **отозва́л** свои́х посло́в в шести́ ара́бских стра́нах, кото́рых он обвиня́ет в подде́ржке Ира́ка во вре́мя кри́зиса в Перси́дском зали́ве. (10) На́ши поли́тики **завели́** нас в тупи́к. (11) Ра́зве на́ши шко́льные уче́бники не **отвраща́ли** нас от Пу́шкина? (12) Где мо́жно в моско́вском кинотеа́тре посмотре́ть таки́е интере́сные рабо́ты, как «И **взошёл** он на́ гору»? (13) Звоно́к в дверь. На поро́ге незнако́мый челове́к. Наконе́ц, вы **впуска́ете** его́ в дом. (14) — Иде́я **довести́** никому́ не изве́стную кома́нду до вы́сшей ли́ги — мне по душе́, сказа́л но́вый гла́вный тре́нер футбо́льного клу́ба «Дина́мо». (15) В феврале́ име́ли ме́сто слу́чаи нападе́ния на води́телей людьми́, кото́рые попроси́ли их подвезти́. Владе́льца маши́ны при э́том про́сто **выбра́сывали** на доро́гу.

B. *Translate into Russian:* (1) He is going into the restaurant. (2) They are going into the building. (3) He came into the room. (4) The company exports television sets. (5) We shall not go in. (6) He is coming out of the library. (7) Are you going out today? (8) She will go out at nine o'clock. (9) He went out. (10) My parents don't often go out. (11) The boy ran out of the house. (12) They ran into the room. (13) Parliament introduces new laws. (14) The plane is taking off. (15) He has got as far as Novosibirsk. (16) The car ran into a bus. (17) I shall bypass the stadium. (18) The train is moving away from the station. (19) The pilot climbed out of his cabin. (20) He ran on ahead. (21) She tore a page out of the book. (22) We must call a doctor. (23) Russia imports a lot of grain. (24) He cut off a slice of bread. (25) I took a five-rouble note out of my pocket.

LESSON 47

VERBAL PREFIXES (пере- TO у-): DIRECTIONAL MEANINGS

§1. Пере-

The prefix пере- implies movement *across* or transference from one place to another. Verbs which incorporate this prefix often correspond to an English verb with the synonymous Latin prefix *trans-*.

переводи́ть/перевести́	*to take across/over, transfer, translate*
переноси́ть/перенести́	*to transfer, move, carry across/over*
переходи́ть/перейти́	*to cross* (on foot)
передава́ть/переда́ть	*to pass across, transfer, transmit, convey*
переса́живаться/пересе́сть	*to change* (transport)

Of the prepositions that may be required after verbs bearing this prefix че́рез, *across*, в, *into*, and на, *on to*, all governing the accusative case, are the commonest. Examples:

> Он перево́дит э́ту кни́гу с англи́йского языка́ на ру́сский.
> *He is translating this book from English into Russian.*
> Она́ перешла́ (че́рез) у́лицу.
> *She crossed the street.*
> Мы переся́дем на кольцеву́ю ли́нию.
> *We shall change to the circle line.*

§2. Под-/подо-

The prefix под- (подо-) implies (i) action *from below* or (ii) movement *towards* (this is the commonest directional meaning of this prefix when it is used with the verbs of motion) or (iii) movement *upwards*, e.g.

i.	подде́рживать/поддержа́ть	*to support* (lit. *to hold up*)
	подпи́сывать/подписа́ть	*to sign* (lit. *to write underneath*)
	подчёркивать/подчеркну́ть	*to stress, emphasise* (lit. *to underline*)

Verbs incorporating the prefix под- used in this sense may require the preposition под and the accusative case, but more commonly they will simply be followed by a direct object without a preposition. Examples from the press:

Контра́кт с э́той кома́ндой И́горь действи́тельно подписа́л.
Igor [Dobrovolsky: a footballer] *has indeed signed a contract with this team.*
Тэ́тчер подчеркну́ла, что брита́нское прави́тельство ни в ко́ем слу́чае не стреми́тся к ухудше́нию ситуа́ции в СССР, но в то же вре́мя бу́дет подде́рживать прибалти́йские респу́блики в их стремле́нии к незави́симости.
Mrs Thatcher emphasised that the British government would in no eventuality seek to worsen the situation in the USSR, but at the same time would support the Baltic republics in their quest for independence.

ii. подбега́ть/подбежа́ть — *to run up to*
подводи́ть/подвести́ — *to lead up to*
подходи́ть/подойти́ — *to approach, go towards/up to*
подъезжа́ть/подъе́хать — *to drive up to*

подзыва́ть/подозва́ть — *to call up, beckon*

The preposition generally required after verbs bearing the prefix под- used in this sense is к, *towards/up to*, which is invariably followed by the dative case. Examples from the press:

Лицо́ его́ бы́ло соверше́нно бе́лым. Я подбежа́ла и схвати́ла его́ ру́ки.
His face was completely white. I ran up and seized his hands.
Крис подвёл меня́ к гнезду́.
Chris took/led me up to a nest.
К нам подхо́дит крепы́ш в ма́йке и шо́ртах.
A strongly-built man in a T-shirt and shorts comes up to us.
Подъезжа́ют маши́ны, сную́т лю́ди, перета́скивая огро́мные коро́бки.
Cars drive up, people scurry about, shifting huge boxes.
Необы́чный велосипеди́ст останови́лся и подозва́л меня́ к себе́.
The unusual cyclist stopped and beckoned to me.

iii. подбра́сывать/подбро́сить — *to throw/toss up*
поднима́ть/подня́ть — *to lift, raise*

Example:

Ма́льчик подбро́сил моне́ту и спроси́л: «Орёл и́ли ре́шка?»
The boy tossed a coin and asked 'heads or tails?'.

§3. При-

The prefix при- implies (i) movement to a destination, or (ii) the attachment or fastening of an object to something else, e.g.

i. приводи́ть/привести́ — *to bring* (on foot), *lead to*
привози́ть/привезти́ — *to bring* (by transport)
приезжа́ть/прие́хать — *to come, arrive* (by transport)
приноси́ть/принести́ — *to bring* (by hand)
приходи́ть/прийти́ — *to come, arrive* (on foot)

Verbs of motion bearing the prefix при- will generally be followed by в or на and the accusative case if a preposition is required. Examples from the press:

Реформа́торские иде́и прави́тельства, переда́ча вла́сти чёрному большинству́, мо́гут привести́ к геноци́ду африка́неров.
The reformist ideas of the [South-African] *government, the transfer of power to the black majority, may lead to genocide of the Afrikaners.*
Сейча́с рабо́таю в филиа́ле, куда́ приво́зят на прове́рку бомже́й, бродя́г...
Now I am working in a branch where they bring homeless people and vagrants in for check-ups [for sexually transmitted diseases]...
Компью́теры прино́сят басносло́вную при́быль.
Computers bring fabulous profit [to black-marketeers].
Прихо́дят больши́ми гру́ппами, ча́сто приезжа́ют це́лыми авто́бусами.
They come in large groups, often they arrive in whole busloads.

ii. привя́зывать/привяза́ть — *to tie/attach/fasten to*
прика́лывать/приколо́ть — *to pin to*
прикрепля́ть/прикрепи́ть — *to fasten/attach/fix to*

After verbs bearing the prefix при- used in this sense the preposition к will generally be used to translate *to*. Examples:

Он привя́зывает соба́ку к воро́там.
He is tying the dog to the gate.
Секрета́рша приколо́ла запи́ску к две́ри.
The secretary pinned a note to the door.

§4. Про-

The prefix про- implies (i) movement *by* or *past*, or (ii) movement *through*.

i. пробега́ть/пробежа́ть — *to run past*
проезжа́ть/прое́хать — *to go past* (by transport)
проходи́ть/пройти́ — *to go past* (on foot)

After verbs bearing the prefix про- used in this sense the prepositions *by* and *past* will generally be translated by ми́мо, which is invariably followed by the genitive case, though they may not need to be translated at all. Examples:

Я пробежа́л ми́мо всех люде́й, кото́рые стоя́ли в о́череди.
I ran past all the people standing in the queue.
Она́ прое́хала свою́ остано́вку.
She went past her stop.
Мы прохо́дим ми́мо но́вого магази́на.
We are going past the new shop.

ii.

проеда́ть/прое́сть	*to eat through, corrode*
прока́лывать/проколо́ть	*to perforate, puncture*
пропуска́ть/пропусти́ть	*to let through, admit, omit*
протека́ть/проте́чь	*to seep, ooze*

After verbs bearing the prefix про- in this sense the preposition *through* will generally be translated by че́рез or сквозь followed by the accusative case. Examples:

Ржа́вчина проеда́ет желе́зо.
Rust corrodes iron.
Гвоздь проколо́л ши́ну.
A nail punctured the tyre.
Вахтёр не пропу́стит нас.
The janitor won't let us in.

§5. Раз-/разо-/рас-

The prefix раз- (разо-; рас- before unvoiced consonants) implies movement in various directions or distribution. Verbs which incorporate this prefix will often correspond to English verbs bearing the synonymous prefix of Latin origin *dis-*. Note that when verbs of motion take this prefix they become reflexive.

разбега́ться/разбежа́ться	*to run off* (in various directions)
разъезжа́ться/разъе́хаться	*to drive off* (to different destinations)
разлета́ться/разлете́ться	*to fly off, scatter, be shattered*
расходи́ться/разойти́сь	*to go off* (in various directions, on foot), *disperse*
размеща́ть/размести́ть	*to accommodate, place* (in various places)
расставля́ть/расста́вить	*to set out, arrange* (in various places)

The preposition that will occur most commonly after verbs in which the prefix раз- is used in this sense is по, *round,* followed by the dative. Examples:

После спектакля все зрители разъехались.
After the performance all the audience drove off [in various directions].
По сторонам от них разместились остальные члены собора.
To the side of them were placed the other members of the [ecclesiastical] council. (Press)
Полиция расставляет специальные дорожные знаки предупреждения.
The police set out special road warning signs. (Press)

§6. С-/со-

The prefix с- (со-) implies (i) movement *off* or *down from* or (ii) convergence. Note that in this second meaning the prefix с- may correspond to the English prefix of Latin origin *con-*, and that the verb to which it is attached, if it is intransitive, becomes reflexive.

i. сбегать/сбежать — *to run down*
слезать/слезть — *to climb down/off*
сходить/сойти — *to come down*

сбивать/сбить — *to knock off, dislodge, shoot down* (plane)
снимать/снять — *to take off*

After verbs bearing the prefix с- used in this sense the prepositions *off* and *from* will be translated by с + genitive case. Examples:

Пошёл дождь и мы быстро сбежали с горы.
It started to rain and we quickly ran down from the hill.
Меня сбили с ног. Лицо в крови.
They knocked me off my feet. My face [was all covered] in blood. (Press)
За это я снимаю перед ним шляпу.
I take my hat off to him for that. (Press)

ii. сбегаться/сбежаться — *to run and come together*
сводить/свести — *to bring together*
сходиться/сойтись — *to come together, meet, gather, tally* (of figures)
съезжаться/съехаться — *to come together, meet, gather* (after journey)

стекаться/стечься — *to flow together, blend, mingle*

Examples from the press:

По́мню, как мои́ колле́ги сбега́лись посмотре́ть на восемнадцатиле́тнюю больну́ю.
I remember how my colleagues [other medical students] *would come running to look at a sick eighteen-year-old girl.*
Слу́чай свёл меня́ с людьми́, кото́рых у нас называ́ют валю́тчиками.
Chance brought me together with people who in our country are called currency speculators.
Большинство́ полити́ческих обозрева́телей схо́дятся во мне́нии, что...
The majority of political commentators share the opinion that...
Из всех моско́вских церкве́й кре́стные хо́ды стека́лись к Кра́сной пло́щади.
Religious processions flowed towards Red Square from all the churches of Moscow.

§7. У-

The prefix у- implies movement *away from*. This prefix differs from от- in that it suggests that the subject moves *right off*, whereas от- describes the progressive separation of the subject from the point of departure.

уезжа́ть/уе́хать	*to go away* (by transport)
уноси́ть/унести́	*to take away*
уходи́ть/уйти́	*to go away*
убира́ть/убра́ть	*to remove, take away, clear away*

Examples from the press:

Пе́рвыми из райо́на уезжа́ют те, кто до́лжен бы уе́хать после́дними, — медици́нские рабо́тники.
The first to leave the region are those who ought to be the last to leave, the medical workers.
Траге́дия унесла́ оди́ннадцать жи́зней.
The tragedy took away eleven lives.
Кака́я-то часть «зарабо́танной» валю́ты ухо́дит на жите́йские ра́дости — вы́пивку, сигаре́ты, пода́рки люби́мым же́нщинам.
A certain part of the currency that has been 'earned' goes on worldly pleasures – a drinking bout, cigarettes, presents for the women one loves.
Убира́ю наво́з, хотя́ я сама́ коренна́я ленингра́дка с дипло́мом хи́мика.
I clear away the dung, although I am a native of Leningrad with a diploma in chemistry.

Exercises

A. *Translate into English and indicate the meaning of the prefix in the verbs in bold print:* (1) Семья́ покида́ет Украи́ну, **уезжа́ет** в США. (2) Вре́мя от вре́мени мы **проезжа́ли** че́рез дере́вни. (3) Все делега́ты вошли́ в зал и **разошли́сь** по свои́м места́м. (4) В Москву́ **съе́дется** весь цвет оте́чественной гимна́стики. Э́то гимна́сты двена́дцати сою́зных респу́блик, Москвы́ и Ленингра́да. (5) Он **подверну́л** штаны́ и поле́з в руче́й. (6) Пти́цы **перелете́ли** с одного́ де́рева на друго́е. (7) Е́сли да́льше бу́дет продолжа́ться экономи́ческая война́ ме́жду респу́бликами, то мо́гут вы́йти на у́лицы то́лпы, кото́рые **смету́т** всё. (8) К моему́ сто́лику **подошёл** друг, кото́рого я мно́го лет не ви́дел. (9) По Москве́ **разбро́саны** магази́ны, куда́ **приво́зят** э́тот това́р. (10) Сквозь тишину́ **прорва́лся** крик. (11) Как-то она́ **пришла́** домо́й поздне́е, чем обы́чно. (12) В ваго́не появи́лись носи́льщики, кото́рых никто́ не вызыва́л. Не **уходи́ли**. (13) Вода́ **протека́ет** сквозь щель. (14) Пчёлы вы́летели из у́льев, **смеша́лись** в еди́ную ма́ссу. (15) Де́вушка **принесла́** буты́лку во́дки. (16) С берёзы **слете́ла** се́рая пти́чка. (17) Де́вочка **прижа́лась** к ма́тери. (18) Мы **перета́скиваем** всю ме́бель в коридо́р. (19) Ма́льчик **подбежа́л** к ма́тери. (20) Лет де́сять уже́ **прошло́**, как он у́мер.

B. *Translate into Russian:* (1) She is coming home today. (2) He is flying in from Moscow this morning. (3) You will arrive in London at eight o'clock. (4) She will come to the shop this afternoon. (5) She said hello and then went away. (6) Go away, I don't want to talk to you. (7) The bird flew away. (8) Every day he brings her to school. (9) He brought her to school. (10) He is bringing the coffee. (11) I am translating a French book. (12) We shall sail across the Channel. (13) She is crossing the road. (14) He went up to the captain. (15) We are going through customs. (16) The play finished and everybody walked home. (17) He came down off the stage. (18) They ran down from the tower. (19) Members of the party come together each year at the conference. (20) The child climbed down from the sofa. (21) He took off the child's shoes. (22) We walked past the house. (23) Let the doctor through please. (24) We must change to another line at the Kiev Station. (25) They ask people who eat in the canteen to clear away their own dishes.

LESSON 48

VERBAL PREFIXES (в- TO от-): NON-DIRECTIONAL MEANINGS

§1. Non-directional meaning of prefixes

All the prefixes which have directional meanings, and which have been dealt with in the preceding lessons, have other, non-directional meanings as well. A prefix may indicate, for example, that the action has begun (as may за-), or that it has a certain duration (as may про-), or is intermittent (as may по- if used together with the infix -ыва- or -ива-), or that the subject is engrossed in the action (as may за- if used together with the reflexive particle -ся). In many instances the prefix bears a very subtle meaning which in English must be rendered by some adverbial modification of the verb or even by the use of a different verb from the one which translates the Russian root verb, e.g. застрелить, *to shoot dead*; набе́гаться, *to have had enough of running about*; посвистывать, *to whistle from time to time*; приоткры́ть, *to open slightly.*

In addition to the prefixes dealt with in the preceding lesson there are a number of others which have non-directional meanings only, or whose original directional meaning has been lost sight of in the modern language.

It should be noted that many prefixes (e.g. на-, по-, с-) may also be used with neutral meaning merely to render an imperfective verb perfective (see 50.3 below).

The majority of prefixes with non-directional meanings are listed in this and the following lesson, though some of the meanings which may be borne by some of the prefixes are uncommon and are omitted.

§2. в-

The prefix в-, used together with the reflexive particle -ся, implies that the action described by the verb was carried out with care, concentration or absorption, e.g.

вгля́дываться/вгляде́ться	*to look carefully/peer at*
вду́мываться/вду́маться	*to meditate on, ponder*
вслу́шиваться/вслу́шаться	*to listen attentively to*
всма́триваться/всмотре́ться	*to peer at, scrutinise*
вчи́тываться/вчита́ться	*to read carefully*

These verbs are followed by в + accusative. Examples from the press:

Вглядитесь в фотографию Холодной с одной из дочерей.
Have a good look at the photograph of Kholodnaya with one of her daughters.

Меня публично называли предателем, не вдумываясь в смысл того, что или кого я предал.
They publicly called me a traitor without pondering [the question] of what or whom I had betrayed.

§3. Вы-

The prefix вы- has a number of functions besides its directional function, though these secondary functions are much less common, viz. (i) to indicate that an action has been carried out to the fullest possible extent, e.g. вываривать/выварить, *to boil thoroughly*; (ii) to indicate that an action has been carried out to an extent sufficient to obtain the desired result, e.g. выпрашивать/выпросить, *to obtain through asking* (the imperfective here will carry a sense of trying to obtain through asking); (iii) combined with the reflexive particle -ся, вы- may be used to form a number of perfective verbs which indicate that an action has been carried out to a sufficient degree, e.g. выплакаться, *to have a good cry*; выспаться, *to have a good sleep*.

§4. До-

The prefix до- also has functions besides its directional function, though again the secondary functions are relatively uncommon, viz. (i) to indicate that an action is supplementary to some action already carried out, e.g. доплачивать/доплатить, *to make an additional payment*; (ii) combined with the reflexive particle -ся, до- may indicate that the action has been carried through to its intended outcome, e.g. дозвониться, *to get through* (on the telephone), or to such an extent that adverse consequences ensue, e.g. он до того дочитался, что глаза заболели, *he read so much that his eyes hurt*.

§5. За-

The prefix за- has several important meanings as well as its directional meaning.

i. Used as a prefix to render basic verbs (including indeterminate verbs of motion such as ходить) perfective it may indicate the beginning of an action. This usage is particularly common in verbs describing some sound. Examples from the press:

Однажды, с одним своим приятелем я заговорил о Боре.
One day I got talking about Borya [i.e.Boris] *with one of my friends.*

Вновь зазвенéли колоколá на дрéвней козéльской землé.
Once again the bells have begun to ring out on the ancient Kozelsk land [where there is an old Russian monastery].
И вдруг захохотáла жéнщина.
And suddenly a woman began to laugh loudly.

ii. This prefix is also used with a number of verbs to indicate that a call or visit is/was/will be made, e.g.

забегáть/забежáть	*to call in/on, drop in on*
заглядывать/заглянýть	*to look in on*
заезжáть/заéхать	*to call in, visit* (during journey)
заходи́ть/зайти́	*to call in/on, drop in on*

These verbs will be followed by the preposition к + dative case, if it is a person who is visited, or by в + accusative if it is a place. Example from the press:

Éсли вам позарéз нужнá какáя-то кни́га и вы регуля́рно загля́дываете к букини́стам — кни́га у вас бýдет.
If you badly need some book and you regularly drop into second-hand bookshops, the book will be yours.

iii. The prefix за- may also indicate that a space is filled or that something is covered or closed by the action in question, e.g.

завáливать/завали́ть	*to block up, obstruct, pile up with*
задёргивать/задёрнуть	*to pull, draw* (curtains)
заклéивать/заклéить	*to glue up* (envelope), *seal up* (windows)
закрывáть/закры́ть	*to close, cover*
заполня́ть/запóлнить	*to fill in* (form, questionnaire)

Examples from the press:

Прилáвки магази́нов завáлены овощáми.
The counters of the shops are piled up with vegetables.
Но всех вéрующих, пришéдших на торжествó, не вмести́л ни Кремль, ни дáже Крáсная плóщадь, а они́ запóлнили близлежáщие ýлицы.
Neither the Kremlin nor even Red Square could accommodate all the [religious] believers who had come to the celebration, and they filled the adjacent streets.

iv. The prefix за- may also be used as a perfective prefix to indicate that an action, particularly a harmful one, has been carried out to an extreme degree, e.g. запорóть, *to flog to death*; застрели́ть, *to shoot* (and kill). The following example from the press also illustrates the point:

Тогда́ его́ брат заколо́л генера́ла ножо́м.
Then his brother stabbed the general to death.

v. Finally, the prefix за-, combined with the reflexive particle -ся, may indicate that the action has gone on for longer than one might expect or that the agent has been more than normally engrossed in it, e.g.

заба́лтываться/заболта́ться	*to get carried away talking*
загова́риваться/заговори́ться	*to be/get engrossed in conversation*
заси́живаться/засиде́ться	*to sit for a very long time*
зачи́тываться/зачита́ться	*to be/get engrossed in reading*

Examples:

Мы заболта́лись и я забы́л позвони́ть жене́.
We got carried away by our conversation and I forgot to telephone my wife.
По суббо́там мы обы́чно заси́живаемся в гостя́х.
On Saturdays we usually sit up late at friends' places.
Я зачита́лся э́тим рома́ном.
I got carried away reading this novel.

§6. Из-/изо-/ис-

The prefix из- (изо-; ис- before unvoiced consonants) has a number of functions, including the following.

i. In many verbs it does have the original directional meaning *out of*, (though this meaning has now largely been lost sight of); it may in this sense correspond to the English prefix of Latin origin *ex-* (in some circumstances abridged to *e-*), e.g.

избира́ть/избра́ть	*to elect*
извлека́ть/извле́чь	*to extract, derive*
изгоня́ть/изгна́ть	*to banish, exile*
издава́ть/изда́ть	*to edit, publish*
исключа́ть/исключи́ть	*to exclude, rule out*

Examples:

Она́ извлекла́ по́льзу из э́того уро́ка.
She derived benefit from this lesson.
Он не исключа́ет и возмо́жности «альтернати́вного вариа́нта».
He does not rule out the possibility of an 'alternative variant'. (Press)

ii. With a number of verbs the prefix из- may also indicate that the action in question has affected the entire surface of something, e.g.

изгрыза́ть/изгры́зть	*to gnaw to shreds*
издира́ть/изодра́ть	*to tear to pieces*
изра́нить (pf. only)	*to cover in wounds*
изре́зывать/изре́зать	*to cut to pieces/in many places*
изрыва́ть/изорва́ть	*to tear up*

Мы́ши изгры́зли мешо́к.
The mice have gnawed the sack to bits.
В изра́ненный Кремль с разреше́ния власте́й откры́ли воро́та.
With the permission of the authorities they opened the gates into the scarred Kremlin. (Press)
пейза́ж, изре́занный кана́лами
a landscape cut up by canals

iii. This prefix may also indicate exhaustion of a supply of something, as in the verb испи́сывать/исписа́ть, *to use up* (all of some writing material, e.g. paper or ink in a pen). Example from the press:

Он опя́ть говори́л о том, что с кни́гой ничего́ не вы́йдет, а на тре́тий день так пло́тно засе́л за рабо́ту, что испи́сывал иногда́ до тридцати́ страни́ц в день.
He again spoke about nothing coming of the book, but on the third day he got down to work in such earnest that he would sometimes cover up to thirty pages a day.

This prefix may also indicate that an action has been carried out to the fullest possible extent, e.g. иссыха́ть/иссо́хнуть, *to dry up altogether* (intrans.); and combined with the reflexive particle -ся, and in perfective forms only, to do or suffer something unpleasant to the extent that it becomes habitual, e.g. изолга́ться, *to become an inveterate liar.*

§7. На-

The prefix на- has several functions other than those given in 46.10 above, including the following.

i. In a number of verbs, predominantly perfectives, it may be used if the action in question affects a certain quantity of an object, e.g.

навари́ть	*to boil a certain quantity of*
накупи́ть	*to buy up a certain quantity of*
напе́чь	*to bake a certain quantity of*
нарва́ть	*to pick, tear a certain quantity of*

Verbs which incorporate the prefix на- in this meaning often govern an object in the genitive case (the genitive here conveying partitive meaning), e.g.

Он накупи́л книг.
He bought up a number of books.
Мы нарвём цвето́в
We shall pick some flowers.

ii. When attached to some indeterminate verbs of motion the prefix на- has the meaning of clocking up, e.g. мы нае́здили сто киломе́тров за два́ часа́, *we covered a hundred kilometres in two hours*; он налета́л ты́сячи часо́в, *he has flown thousands of hours*.

iii. The prefix на- may be combined with the reflexive particle -ся to form verbs (predominantly perfectives) which indicate that enough or even more than enough of an action has taken place, e.g. нае́сться, *to eat one's fill*; напи́ться, *to drink as much as one wants, to get drunk* (see 19.6).

§8. Недо-
The prefix недо-, which may only be attached to a few verbs, indicates insufficiency, e.g. недодава́ть/недода́ть, *to give short*; недостава́ть/недоста́ть, *to be insufficient*; недооце́нивать/недооцени́ть, *to underestimate*. Example from the press:

С нача́ла го́да предприя́тия ассоциа́ции недода́ли потреби́телям уже́ бо́лее шести́ миллио́нов тонн не́фти.
Since the beginning of the year the enterprises of the association have already sold the consumers short by more than six million tonnes of oil.

§9. О-/об-/обо-
The prefix о- (об-, обо-) has various functions other than those given in 46.11 above, including the following.

i. In a very large number of verbs the function of this prefix is to help to create a verb out of a different part of speech, especially an adjective, e.g.

обогаща́ть/обогати́ть	*to enrich* (from бога́тый)
объясня́ть/объясни́ть	*to explain* (from я́сный)
оглуша́ть/оглуши́ть	*to deafen* (from глухо́й)
освобожда́ть/освободи́ть	*to liberate, free* (from свобо́дный)
ослабля́ть/осла́бить	*to weaken* (from сла́бый)
ослепля́ть/ослепи́ть	*to blind, dazzle* (from слепо́й)
осложня́ть/осложни́ть	*to complicate* (from сло́жный)

Example from the press:

Цель э́той встре́чи — успоко́ить нестаби́льный ры́нок нефтепроду́ктов, ситуа́ция на кото́ром ре́зко осложни́лась из-за кри́зиса в Перси́дском зали́ве.
The aim of this meeting is to calm the unstable market for oil products in which the situation has become very complicated as a result of the Gulf crisis. (Press)

ii. This prefix may also indicate that an action was thorough or covered the whole surface of something, e.g.

окле́ивать/окле́ить	*to paste over*
осма́тривать/осмотре́ть	*to look over, inspect*

Examples from the press:

Она́ ста́ла обзва́нивать фо́ндовые би́ржи.
She started ringing round the stock-exchanges.
Мы в состоя́нии осмотре́ть лишь деся́тую часть пересека́ющего грани́цу багажа́.
We are able to inspect only a tenth of the baggage that crosses the frontier.

iii. This prefix may also be combined with the reflexive particle -ся to form some verbs which indicate that an action is mistaken, e.g.

обсчи́тываться/обсчита́ться	*to make a mistake* (in counting)
огова́риваться/оговори́ться	*to make a slip* (in speaking)
ослы́шаться (pf. only)	*to mishear*
оступа́ться/оступи́ться	*to stumble* (lit. *to take a false step*)

§10. Обез-/обес-

The prefix обез- (обес- before unvoiced consonants), which is a combination of the verbal prefix о- and the adjectival prefix без-, *without*, is used with only a few verbs. It indicates loss or deprivation of the thing denoted by the root of the word, e.g.

обезбо́ливать/обезбо́лить	*to anaesthetise* (lit. *to take away pain*)
обезво́живать/обезво́дить	*to dehydrate* (lit. *to take away water*)
обезвре́живать/обезвре́дить	*to render harmless, neutralise*
обезгла́вливать/обезгла́вить	*to decapitate, deprive of a head/leader*
обезжи́ривать/обезжи́рить	*to skim* (lit. *to take away fat*)
обезору́живать/обезору́жить	*to disarm*
обесси́ливать/обесси́лить	*to weaken* (lit. *to take away strength*)

обесцéнивать/обесцéнить — *to depreciate, cheapen* (lit. *to take away value*)

Examples from the press:

Обезглáвлена Беклеми́шевская бáшня.
The top had come off the Beklemishev Tower [of the Kremlin].
Агéнтам спецслу́жб удалóсь обезврéдить бóмбу.
Agents of the special services succeeded in defusing the bomb.

§11. От-/ото-
The prefix от- (ото-) is used mainly in a directional sense, or in a sense closely related to the directional one, and there is therefore little to add here to what has been said in Lesson 46. Note though that (i) it may in verbs with figurative meaning have the sense of *back* and may thus correspond to the English prefix *re-*, e.g. отбивáть/отби́ть, *to beat back, repel;* отвергáть/отвéргнуть, *to reject*; отражáть/отрази́ть, *to reflect;* and (ii) as a prefix on perfective verbs it may emphasise that an action is at an end, that it has been carried out to its required limit, e.g. отдежу́рить, *to come off duty*; отрабóтать, *to finish one's work*; оту́жинать, *to have had supper*.

Exercises

A. *Translate into English and indicate the meaning or function of the prefix in the verbs in bold print:* (1) Ты **вы́спался**? (2) Николáй I **изгнáл** Лéрмонтова на Кавкáз. (3) **Загляни́те** в аптéку по дорóге домóй. (4) К нам прихóдят гóсти. Женá **напеклá** пирожкóв. (5) Приятно э́то нам и́ли неприя́тно, хóчется и́ли не хóчется, но придётся мнóгим из нас до пéрвого апрéля **заполня́ть** налóговые декларáции. (6) Спускáюсь в метрó — Брамс, «Венгéрский тáнец». Лю́ди останáвливаются, **вслу́шиваются**, улыбáются, бросáют монéтки. (7) Все **заговори́ли** рáзом, перебивáя друг дру́га. (8) Боевики́ «Исля́мской пáртии Афганистáна» **обстрéливают** ракéтами президéнтский дворéц. (9) Он стал **вгля́дываться** в толпу́ и отыскáл свои́х роди́телей. (10) Онá лю́бит самá **обклéивать** стéны своегó дóма обóями. (11) Вдруг **загремéл** звонóк, все с тревóгой **замолчáли**. (12) Забастовáл мéстный автозавóд. Чтóбы потуши́ть «пожáр», вы́ехал на мéсто сам Президéнт Туркменистáна. Тут все и **забéгали**. (13) **Обостря́ется** ситуáция в Прибáлтике. (14) Кто лу́чше Алексéева **запóлнит** вакáнтное мéсто? (15) Сою́зники по коали́ции не **ослáбят** давлéние на ирáкский режи́м. (16) Москóвская мили́ция **обезврéдила** бáнду угóнщиков автомоби́лей. (17) Милиционéр **застрели́л** террори́ста на мéсте преступлéния. (18) Чéхов был мои́м люби́мым писáтелем. Я **зачи́тывался** егó расскáзами и пьéсами. (19) Я не могу́ **наслу́шаться** э́того оркéстра. (20) Во врéмя послéдних вы́боров оди́н из депутáтов пообещáл мéстным жи́телям, что обеспéчит их прирóдным гáзом. Вы́рыли траншéю, проложи́ли не́сколько сот ме́тров трубы́. Вы́боры прошли́ с успе́хом. Обеща́ния бы́ли забы́ты. Трубу́ увезли́, транше́ю **закопа́ли**.

B. *Translate into Russian:* (1) She was listening carefully to the radio. (2) I started to walk around the room. (3) They burst out laughing. (4) He fell ill at the beginning of the winter. (5) They called in to see me on their return journey. (6) The tourists blocked up the entrance with their suitcases. (7) She is filling in a visa application form. (8) I got carried away reading this novel. (9) We are electing a new chairman today. (10) They excluded him from the list of candidates. (11) The children ate as many sweets as they wanted. (12) Travel enriches a person. (13) The sun dazzled him. (14) We underestimated his abilities. (15) They beat back the attack of the enemy. (16) I started to cry. (17) He drank too much and woke up with a hangover. (18) Read the book carefully and you will understand it. (19) The illness weakened her heart. (20) I didn't mean it; it was a slip of the tongue.

LESSON 49

VERBAL PREFIXES (пере- TO у-): NON-DIRECTIONAL MEANINGS

§1. Пере-

The prefix пере- has three important non-directional uses.

i. To do something *again*, in which sense it often corresponds to an English verb with the prefix *re-*, e.g.

перезаряжа́ть/перезаряди́ть	*to reload, recharge*
переизбира́ть/переизбра́ть	*to re-elect*
перепроверя́ть/перепрове́рить	*to re-check*
пересма́тривать/пересмотре́ть	*to look at again, review*
перестра́ивать/перестро́ить	*to rebuild, reconstruct*

Examples from the press:

Коне́ц ию́ля — са́мое подходя́щее вре́мя, что́бы пойти́ в о́тпуск и перезаряди́ть органи́зм эне́ргией.
The end of July is the most suitable time to go on holiday and recharge the organism.
Республика́нская фра́кция переизбрала́ на пост ли́дера меньшинства́ Ро́берта До́ула.
The Republican faction [in the US Senate] *has re-elected Robert Doyle to the post of leader of the minority.*
Все лека́рства, да́же са́мых изве́стных зарубе́жных фирм, у нас перепроверя́ются, е́сли мы приобрета́ем их проду́кцию.
All medicines, even [those] of the best-known foreign firms, are rechecked if we acquire [the right] to produce them.

ii. To do something *too much*, in which sense it often corresponds to an English verb with the prefix *over-*, e.g.

перегрева́ть/перегре́ть	*to overheat*
перегружа́ть/перегрузи́ть	*to overload*
переоце́нивать/переоцени́ть	*to overestimate*

Examples:

Е́сли не сба́вите ско́рость, вы перегре́ете мото́р.
If you don't slow down you'll overheat the engine.

Он переоце́нивает свои́ си́лы.
He overestimates his strength.

iii. When combined with the reflexive particle -ся the prefix пере- often denotes reciprocal action, e.g.

перегля́дываться/перегляну́ться	*to exchange glances*
перепи́сываться (impf. only)	*to correspond* (lit. *exchange letters*)

Examples:

Она́ мо́лча перегляну́лась с му́жем.
She silently exchanged glances with her husband.
Я перепи́сываюсь с ру́сским дру́гом.
I correspond with a Russian friend.

§2. По-

The prefix по- has many uses, including the following.

i. In many perfective verbs the prefix по- indicates that the action is of short duration or limited extent, e.g.

поговори́ть	*to have a talk, talk for a bit*
погуля́ть	*to take a stroll*
пое́сть	*to have a bite to eat*
поигра́ть	*to play for a bit*
поиска́ть	*to have a look for*
помолча́ть	*to be silent for a while*
порабо́тать	*to do a bit of work*
посиде́ть	*to sit down for a while*
посмотре́ть	*to have a look at*
постоя́ть	*to stand for a bit*
почита́ть	*to have a read*

Examples from the press:

Мне хоте́лось ещё поговори́ть с рижа́нкой.
I wanted to talk a bit longer to the woman from Riga.
Он придёт в ваш дом, что́бы развле́чь взро́слых и дете́й, поигра́ть на миниатю́рном орга́не.
He'll come to your house to entertain the adults and the children, to play for a bit on a miniature organ.
Пришёл не́кто по фами́лии Гло́ссен и попроси́л посмотре́ть па́спорт Андре́я. Андре́й поиска́л в бума́гах, нашёл и о́тдал.
Someone by the name of Glossen came and asked to have a look at Andrey's passport. Andrey had a look [for it] among his papers, found it and handed it over.

The prefix по- may be attached to the indeterminate verbs of motion (ходи́ть, etc.) to form perfectives with this meaning (see 45.3.ii above).

Since по-, when used in this sense, renders a simple verb perfective, all the verbs given above could only be used in the past or future tense; they could not be used to form a present tense.

ii. The prefix по- is also combined in many verbs with the infix -ыва- or -ива- to form an imperfective verb with iterative meaning (i.e. the action in question is repeated off and on for some time), e.g.

погля́дывать *to look at from time to time*
погова́ривать *to talk about every so often*
пока́шливать *to cough from time to time*
поку́ривать *to have a smoke every now and then*
посви́стывать *to whistle off and on*
посма́тривать *to look at every now and again*

Example:

Она́ погля́дывала на телеви́зор, пока́ ши́ла пла́тье.
She looked at the television every now and then as she was making the dress.

§3. Под-/подо-

The prefix под- (подо-) may signify:

i. that the action in question is not far-reaching, e.g.

подкра́шивать/подкра́сить *to tint, touch up*
подреза́ть/подре́зать *to clip, trim*
подта́ивать/подта́ять *to thaw a little*

Examples:

Дво́е рабо́чих и́зо всех сил де́ржат стра́уса, тре́тий, подня́в крыло́, подреза́ет но́жницами чёрные пе́рья.
Two workmen hold the ostrich with all their might and a third, lifting the wing, clips the black plumage with scissors. (Press)
Ста́ло потепле́е и снег подта́ял.
It got a bit warmer and the snow thawed a little.

ii. that the action augments something, e.g.

подбавля́ть/подба́вить *to add*
подбра́сывать/подбро́сить *to throw in/on* (sthg. more)

подлива́ть/подли́ть	*to add* (by pouring liquid)
подраба́тывать/подрабо́тать	*to earn some additional money*

Example from the press:

Са́ми подраба́тывали — ухо́дом за больны́ми, прода́жей газе́т.
They themselves would earn some additional money, by looking after the sick or selling newspapers.

iii. that the action is underhand, e.g.

поджига́ть/подже́чь	*to set fire to* (criminally), *commit arson*
подкупа́ть/подкупи́ть	*to bribe, suborn*
подслу́шивать (no pf. in this sense)	*to eavesdrop*

Examples from the press:

Ира́кцы подожгли́ нефтяны́е сква́жины.
The Iraqis set fire to the oil wells.
Она́ объясни́ла, что я до́лжен был подслу́шивать вра́жеские разгово́ры.
She explained that I should have eavesdropped on the enemy's conversations.

§4. Пред-/предо-

The prefix пред- (предо-), which is rather bookish, often indicates that the action in question precedes or anticipates something, and may correspond to the English prefix *fore-*, e.g.

предви́деть (no pf.)	*to foresee*
предотвраща́ть/предотврати́ть	*to avert, prevent, stave off*
предска́зывать/предсказа́ть	*to foretell, prophesy*
предстоя́ть (no pf.)	*to await, lie in store*
предупрежда́ть/предупреди́ть	*to forewarn*
предусма́тривать/предусмотре́ть	*to envisage, make provision for*
предчу́вствовать (no pf.)	*to anticipate, have a presentiment*

Examples from the press:

Законопрое́кт предусма́тривает предоставле́ние наибо́льшей экономи́ческой свобо́ды сами́м желе́зным доро́гам.
The bill provides for the granting of the greatest [possible] economic freedom to the railways themselves.

Он ведь уже̇ предчу́вствовал, что̀ ему́ предстои́т.
For he already had a presentiment of what was in store for him.

§5. При-

The prefix при- is used with many verbs, including some which already have a prefix, to indicate that an action is not fully carried out, e.g.

привстава́ть/привста́ть	*to half-rise, get up for a moment*
приостана́вливать/приостанови́ть	*to halt*
приоткрыва́ть/приоткры́ть	*to half-open*
приподнима́ть(ся)/приподня́ть(ся)	*to half-raise, half-get up*
приспуска́ть/приспусти́ть	*to lower a little*

Examples:

Забасто́вка в Воркуте́ была́ приостано́влена на во́семь дней.
The strike in Vorkuta was halted for eight days. (Press)
приоткры́тая дверь
a door which is ajar
Он приподня́лся на ло́кте.
He propped himself up on his elbow [from a lying position].
приспу́щенный флаг
a flag at half-mast

§6. Про-

The prefix про- has a number of non-directional functions, including the following.

i. It may be attached as a perfective prefix to many basic verbs when the duration of the action or the distance covered by it is defined. Examples from the press:

Просиде́л за колю́чей про́волокой до конца́ войны́.
He was behind barbed wire [in a labour camp] *until the end of the war.*
Невозмо́жно подсчита́ть ско́лько просиде́ли в рестора́нах и кафе́.
It is impossible to calculate how much [time] they spent sitting in restaurants and cafés.
Вале́рий пробежа́л на дю́жину киломе́тров бо́льше Ната́льи.
Valery ran a dozen kilometres more than Natalya.
Граждани́н ГДР, что́бы купи́ть шесть бока́лов из боге́мского стекла́, до́лжен прорабо́тать це́лую неде́лю.
A citizen of East Germany would have to work for a whole week in order to buy six wine-glasses of Bohemian crystal.

This prefix may be attached to some indeterminate verbs of motion to form a perfective verb, e.g. проéздить, *to travel* (for a defined period), проходи́ть, *to walk* (for a defined period).

ii. It may also indicate that an action is thorough, e.g.

проду́мывать/проду́мать	*to think over*
прожа́ривать/прожа́рить	*to roast thoroughly*
проку́ривать/прокури́ть	*to fill with tobacco smoke*
промока́ть/промо́кнуть	*to get drenched*
промыва́ть/промы́ть	*to wash well, bathe* (a wound)

Examples:

проду́манный план
a considered plan
В за́ле бы́ло проку́рено по́сле приёма.
The hall smelt of smoking [lit. *smoking had filled the hall*] *after the reception.*

iii. Among the other meanings that the prefix про- occasionally carries are oversight (e.g. прогля́дывать/проглядéть, *to overlook*); loss (e.g. прои́грывать/проигра́ть, *to lose* [game, at cards]); and, with the reflexive particle -ся, unintentional revelation (e.g. прогова́риваться/проговори́ться, *to let the cat out of the bag*).

§7. Раз-/разо-/рас-

The prefix раз- (разо-; рас- before unvoiced consonants) may indicate that the action uncovers or undoes something, e.g.

развора́чивать or развёртывать/разверну́ть	*to unfold, unwrap*
развя́зывать/развяза́ть	*to untie*
разгружа́ть/разгрузи́ть	*to unload*
раскрыва́ть/раскры́ть	*to open* (wide), *reveal, disclose*

Examples:

Ребёнок развора́чивал свои́ пода́рки.
The child was unwrapping its presents.
Он развя́зывает шнурки́.
He is untying his shoe-laces.
Порто́вые рабо́чие разгружа́ют кора́бль.
The dockers are unloading the ship.

§8. С-/со-

The prefix с- (со-) has several functions apart from those given in 47.6 above, including the following.

i. It commonly implies joining, linking, e.g.

свя́зывать/связа́ть	*to tie together, connect, link, unite*
соединя́ть/соедини́ть	*to unite, join*

Examples:

Э́ти собы́тия те́сно свя́заны друг с дру́гом.
These events are closely linked to one another.
Автостра́да соединя́ет Ло́ндон с Би́рмингемом.
A motorway links London to Birmingham.

ii. When attached to the indeterminate verbs of motion the prefix с- may give a perfective verb which indicates that the subject moved in one direction and then back again (see 45.3.iii above).

This use of с- with the indeterminate verbs of motion needs to be carefully distinguished from the use of с- with those same verbs in its directional meaning of *down* or *off*. The verb сходи́ть, for example, may be a perfective (with imperfective ходи́ть) meaning *to walk somewhere and back*, or it may be an imperfective (with perfective сойти́) meaning *to walk down/off*. In the case of the verb бе́гать (*to run*), the two meanings are distinguished by stress: сбе́гать is the perfective form meaning *to run somewhere and back*, while сбега́ть (perfective сбежа́ть) is an imperfective meaning *to run down*.

§9. У-

The prefix у- also has a number of functions and meanings besides its directional meaning, including the following.

i. Like о- (see 48.9.i above) it is often used as a means of creating a verb from an adjectival root. Such verbs frequently have comparative meaning. Examples:

улучша́ть(ся)/улу́чшить(ся)	*to improve* (from лу́чший)
уменьша́ть(ся)/уме́ньшить(ся)	*to diminish, decrease* (from ме́ньший)
упроща́ть(ся)/упрости́ть(ся)	*to simplify/be simplified* (from просто́й)
ускоря́ть(ся)/уско́рить(ся)	*to speed up, accelerate* (from ско́рый)
ухудша́ть(ся)/уху́дшить(ся)	*to make worse/get worse* (from ху́дший)

Examples from the press:

За после́днее десятиле́тие креди́ты на образова́ние увели́чились вдво́е.
Over the last decade spending on education has increased twofold.
Жизнь фе́рмеров в после́дние го́ды уху́дшилась.
The life of the farmers has deteriorated in recent years.

ii. The prefix у- may also indicate removal or diminution, e.g.

уре́зывать/уре́зать	*to cut, reduce*
ушива́ть/уши́ть	*to take in* (clothes)

Examples:

Прави́тельство уре́зало ассигнова́ния на вы́сшее образова́ние.
The government has cut the funds for higher education.
Она́ похуде́ла и уши́ла свои́ пла́тья.
She has grown thinner and has taken in her dresses.

iii. Among the other less common meanings of the prefix у- one might note the sense of achievement in spite of opposition (e.g. устоя́ть, *to stand one's ground*); the indication of abundance (e.g. усыпа́ть/усы́пать, *to strew with*); and (usually with -ся, and often in a negative construction) to express fitting in, finding room, e.g. умеща́ться/умести́ться, *to fit in* (intrans.).

Exercises

A. *Translate into English and indicate the meaning or function of the prefix in the verbs in bold print:* (1) Ребя́та **помолча́ли**, пото́м **поговори́ли** ещё. (2) В гостя́х я **про́был** два часа́. (3) Росси́я бу́дет **пересма́тривать** догово́р с респу́бликой Коре́я. (4) Мы ви́дели большу́ю ба́нду хулига́нов, кото́рые разбива́ли витри́ны, гра́били магази́ны, **поджига́ли** автомоби́ли. (5) Он вы́шел без зо́нтика и **промо́к** до мо́зга косте́й. (6) Она́ повела́ ло́шадь в коню́шню, **погла́живая** её гри́ву. (7) ООН призыва́ет всех, кто вовлечён в вое́нные де́йствия, **приостанови́ть** их. (8) В учи́лище Ве́ра **прозанима́лась** то́лько год. (9) Репорта́жи, опублико́ванные в тече́ние э́того го́да в «Изве́стиях», впервы́е **припо́дняли** за́навес секре́тности, опу́щенный а́рмией и спецслу́жбами над той траги́ческой исто́рией. (10) По-ви́димому пчёлы мо́гут **предуга́дывать** землетрясе́ния. (11) Мы о́чень лю́бим свою́ рабо́ту. Но в свобо́дное вре́мя не ме́нее лю́бим **почита́ть** хоро́шую кни́гу, журна́л, газе́ту. (12) Го́род был зава́лен сне́гом. Дере́вья бы́ли толсты́ от и́нея. Бо́льше двухсо́т ме́тров нельзя́ бы́ло **пробежа́ть** по у́лице. (13) Ска́зки — э́то вели́кая литерату́ра, кото́рую чита́ем и **перечи́тываем** себе́ и де́тям. (14) Весь день больно́й **пролежа́л** в полусне́. (15) Тре́неры в на́шем футбо́ле на́чали **погова́ривать**, что су́дьи вымога́ют у них взя́тки. (16) Желе́зная доро́га **свя́зывает** э́ти города́. (17) Самолёт приземли́лся. Пассажи́ры **расстегну́ли** ремни́. (18) По́вар **пересоли́л** о́вощи. (19) Врач разгова́ривал с медсестро́й, вре́мя от вре́мени **погля́дывая** на пацие́нта. (20) Э́тот собо́р **устоя́л** при наше́ствии тата́р, не́ был разру́шен ни в го́ды пе́рвой мирово́й войны́, ни во вре́мя гражда́нской войны́.

B. *Translate into Russian:* (1) The government is reviewing its policy. (2) They rebuilt the city after the war. (3) The student is re-reading her essay. (4) The chef overcooked the meat. (5) They overestimate my abilities. (6) She had something to eat. (7) He whistled every now and again while he was working in the garden. (8) I foresee difficulties. (9) The door was ajar. (10) I stood in a queue for half an hour. (11) I let the cat out of the bag. (12) We unwrapped our presents. (13) I am trying to simplify this task. (14) The economic prospects are getting worse. (15) The number of pupils studying Russian in British schools is decreasing. (16) He opened the window a little to air the room. (17) After supper she sat in the dining-room for a while. (18) Soviet papers used to report that factories had overfulfilled their plans. (19) The demonstrators have set fire to government buildings. (20) The coup d'état accelerated the break-up of the Soviet Union.

LESSON 50

ASPECTUAL PAIRS

§1. Imperfective and perfective pairs
The vast majority of Russian verbs have distinct imperfective and perfective forms. The meaning and use of the different forms, and their relation to the tense system of English, will be dealt with in Lessons 52-54 below. This lesson and the following one examine the main ways in which the two members of a pair may differ from one another.

§2. Distinguishing features of aspectual pairs
The distinctions between the imperfective and perfective forms are of various types, viz.

i. a prefix may be added to many simple imperfective verbs to give a perfective, e.g. де́лать/сде́лать, *to do, make*;

ii. in many pairs the difference lies only in the ending and, consequently, conjugation: imperfectives end in -ать/ять and belong to conjugation 1a, while perfectives end in -ить and belong to the 2nd conjugation, e.g. реша́ть/реши́ть, *to decide, solve*; объясня́ть/объясни́ть, *to explain*;

iii. some imperfective verbs may be transformed by the use of the suffix -нуть into perfective verbs belonging to conjugation 1b, e.g. маха́ть/махну́ть, *to wave*;

iv. in the case of a few pairs the imperfective and perfective forms are based on quite different roots, e.g. брать/взять, *to take*;

v. in verbs of motion with a prefix the imperfective form is based on the indeterminate verb while the perfective form is based on the determinate form, e.g. входи́ть/войти́, *to enter*;

vi. in a small number of verbs the only distinction between imperfective and perfective forms in the infinitive is one of stress, though the two forms belong to different conjugations, e.g. отреза́ть (1a)/отре́зать (1b), *to cut off*;

vii. many perfective verbs which have a prefix may be lengthened by the insertion of the infix -ыва-/-ива- to give a secondary imperfective form, which will belong to the conjugation 1a, e.g. подпи́сывать/подписа́ть, *to sign*; рассма́тривать/рассмотре́ть, *to examine*;

viii. many other perfective verbs which have a prefix are lengthened by the addition of the infix -а- to the stem, whose final consonant is concealed in the perfective infinitive, to give a secondary imperfective form, which will belong to the conjugation 1a, e.g. зажига́ть/заже́чь, *to set light to*; привлека́ть/привле́чь, *to attract*.

It should be added that some verbs have only one form for both aspects, e.g. ра́нить, *to wound, injure*. Other verbs have only an imperfective form, e.g. сто́ить, *to cost, be worth*. A very small number of verbs have only a perfective form, e.g. очути́ться, *to find oneself*.

These various types of distinction between aspects will be dealt with in order below. This lesson will deal with aspectual pairs of types i-vi above. The following lesson will deal with pairs of types vii and viii and with those verbs which are unpaired.

§3. Formation of perfective verbs by the addition of a prefix to a simple verb

Most simple verbs without a prefix are imperfective, e.g. крыть, *to cover*; теря́ть, *to lose*; де́лать, *to do, make*; лгать, *to lie* (tell lies); петь, *to sing*; пря́тать, *to hide*; сле́пнуть, *to go blind*; ра́довать, *to gladden*; писа́ть, *to write*; рисова́ть, *to draw*; печь, *to bake*; по́ртить, *to spoil*; пуга́ть, *to frighten*; души́ть, *to stifle*.

The addition of a prefix to these imperfective forms renders them perfective. Various prefixes (most commonly по-, с-, о- [об-], на-, из- [ис-], за-) may be used in this way without changing the meaning of the verb except inasmuch as they give it perfective meaning, or, to put it another way, the prefixes themselves carry no meaning of their own in this context (contrast their use as modifiers of the meaning of verbs, as described in the preceding four lessons).

Note that simple verbs of all conjugations (1a, 1b with vowel stems, 1b with consonant stems, 2nd conjugation) are represented among the verbs which form their perfectives in this way, though the majority of such simple verbs belong to the first conjugation.

impf.	pf.	
крыть (1b)	покры́ть	*to cover*
теря́ть (1a)	потеря́ть	*to lose*
де́лать (1a)	сде́лать	*to make, do*
лгать (1b)	солга́ть	*to lie* (tell lies)
петь (1b)	спеть	*to sing*
пря́тать (1b)	спря́тать	*to hide*
сле́пнуть (1b)	осле́пнуть	*to go blind*
ра́довать (1b)	обра́довать	*to gladden*

писа́ть (1b)	написа́ть	*to write*
рисова́ть (1b)	нарисова́ть	*to draw*
печь (1b)	испе́чь	*to bake*
по́ртить (2)	испо́ртить	*to spoil*
пуга́ть (1a)	испуга́ть	*to frighten*
души́ть (2)	задуши́ть	*to stifle, strangle*

§4. Verbs with imperfective forms in -ать/-ять and perfectives in -ить
Verbs which have aspectual pairs of this type may or may not be derived from a prefixless simple verb. The pair проверя́ть/прове́рить, *to check*, for example, is based on the simple verb ве́рить, to which a prefix has been added, whereas the pair включа́ть/включи́ть, *to switch on*, *to include*, is not derived from any simple verb used without a prefix in the modern language. In a small number of verbs an aspectual pair in -ать/-ять and -ить is found in both the prefixless simple verb and in the derivative which does have a prefix, e.g. пуска́ть/пусти́ть, *to let* and отпуска́ть/отпусти́ть, *to let go, release*.

The imperfective forms in -ать/-ять in the aspectual pairs under consideration invariably belong to the conjugation 1a, while the perfective forms in -ить invariably belong to the 2nd conjugation. Thus:

i. pairs derived from a prefixless simple verb:

simple verb		derived pf.	derived impf.	
буди́ть	*to wake, rouse*	возбуди́ть	возбужда́ть	*to excite, stir*
ве́рить	*to believe*	уве́рить	уверя́ть	*to assure*
грузи́ть	*to load*	разгрузи́ть	разгружа́ть	*to unload*
дели́ть	*to divide, share*	отдели́ть	отделя́ть	*to separate*
крепи́ть	*to strengthen*	подкрепи́ть	подкрепля́ть	*to reinforce*
пра́вить	*to rule, drive*	напра́вить	направля́ть	*to direct*
сели́ть	*to settle*	пересели́ть	переселя́ть	*to resettle*
щеми́ть	*to press*	прищеми́ть	прищемля́ть	*to pinch, squeeze*

ii. pairs in which both forms bear a prefix and which are not based on a simple prefixless verb:

impf.	pf.	
включа́ть	включи́ть	*to switch on, include*
возвраща́ть	возврати́ть	*to return*
получа́ть	получи́ть	*to receive, obtain*
заряжа́ть	заряди́ть	*to load* (firearm)
вообража́ть	вообрази́ть	*to imagine*
выража́ть	вы́разить	*to express*

отличáть	отличи́ть	*to distinguish, single out*
отвечáть	отвéтить	*to reply*
побеждáть	победи́ть	*to defeat*

iii. pairs consisting of two prefixless simple forms and pairs consisting of these simple forms with prefixes:

impf.	pf.	
пускáть	пусти́ть	*to let*
отпускáть	отпусти́ть	*to let go*
спускáть	спусти́ть	*to lower*
решáть	реши́ть	*to decide, solve*
разрешáть	разреши́ть	*to permit*
ступáть	ступи́ть	*to step*
вступáть	вступи́ть	*to step in, enter*
поступáть	поступи́ть	*to enter* (e.g. university)
явля́ться	яви́ться	*to be*
объявля́ть	объяви́ть	*to announce, declare*
появля́ться	появи́ться	*to appear*

Note also the unusual pair покупáть/купи́ть, *to buy*. In other pairs based on the root -купáть/купи́ть, however, both forms bear a prefix, e.g. подкупáть/подкупи́ть, *to bribe, suborn* (see 49.3.iii above).

§5. Pairs including a perfective form with the suffix -нуть

i. Some verbs indicating state or change of state have imperfective forms in -ать and perfective forms in -нуть, e.g.

impf.	pf.	
погибáть	поги́бнуть	*to die, perish*
прилипáть	прили́пнуть	*to stick* (intrans.)
прокисáть	проки́снуть	*to turn sour*
промокáть	промóкнуть	*to get wet*

Of the same type but with a modified imperfective stem are derivatives of the simple verb сóхнуть, *to get dry*, e.g. высыхáть/ вы́сохнуть, *to dry up*. Note also вздыхáть/вздохнýть, *to sigh*. (See also 10.7 above on these verbs.)

ii. This suffix is also used to form perfective verbs with semelfactive meaning, i.e. denoting the performance of a single action, e.g.

impf.		pf.	
кричáть	*to shout*	кри́кнуть	*to give a shout*
стучáть	*to knock*	стýкнуть	*to give a knock*
толкáть	*to push*	толкнýть	*to give a push*

§6. Pairs of verbs from different roots

A few common verbs have forms from quite different roots for the two aspects:

impf.	pf.	
брать	взять	*to take*
говори́ть	сказа́ть	*to say*
класть	положи́ть	*to put*
лови́ть	пойма́ть	*to catch*

Note also the following pairs, in which the two forms have the same root but do not differ in accordance with the normal patterns and in which the imperfective form is reflexive whilst the perfective form is not:

impf.	pf.	
ложи́ться	лечь	*to lie down*
сади́ться	сесть	*to sit down*
станови́ться	стать	*to become*

Note also that the imperfective ло́паться, *to burst, split*, is reflexive whilst the perfective form, ло́пнуть, is not. (See also 14.8 above on these verbs.)

§7. Verbs of motion

In most verbs of motion with prefixes the imperfective verb consists of prefix + the indeterminate form (e.g. приходи́ть), whilst the perfective verb consists of prefix + determinate form (e.g. прийти́). (See 46.3 above on the modification of simple verbs of motion when prefixes are attached to them.)

Examples:

impf.	pf.	
входи́ть	войти́	*to enter*
взлета́ть	взлете́ть	*to fly up, take off*
вывози́ть	вы́везти	*to export*
догоня́ть	догна́ть	*to catch up with*
переводи́ть	перевести́	*to transfer, translate*
подполза́ть	подползти́	*to creep up to*
приноси́ть	принести́	*to bring*
разъезжа́ться	разъе́хаться	*to disperse* (intrans.)
убега́ть	убежа́ть	*to run away*

§8. Aspectual pairs in which imperfective and perfective forms are distinguished by stress

Derivatives of the simple 1b verbs ре́зать, *to cut*, and сы́пать, *to pour* (solids), *strew,* have imperfective and perfective forms which can only be distinguished by their stress in the infinitive, past tense, and past active participles. (In the present and future tenses, on the other hand, the forms are distinct, since the imperfectives belong to the conjugation 1a whereas the perfectives, like the simple verbs themselves, belong to conjugation 1b.) Thus:

impf.	(present tense/ 1st pers. sing.)	pf.	(future tense/ 1st pers. sing.)	
зареза́ть	зареза́ю	заре́зать	заре́жу	*to murder, knife*
отреза́ть	отреза́ю	отре́зать	отре́жу	*to cut off*
посыпа́ть	посыпа́ю	посы́пать	посы́плю	*to sprinkle*
рассыпа́ть	рассыпа́ю	рассы́пать	рассы́плю	*to spill, scatter*

Exercise

Give the perfective form of the following imperfective verbs: брать; ввози́ть; возража́ть, *to object*; выключа́ть, *to switch off*; выпуска́ть, *to let out*; забега́ть; заключа́ть, *to conclude, confine*; закрепля́ть, *to fasten, consolidate*; изобража́ть, *to depict*; класть; ложи́ться; нареза́ть, *to cut, slice;* опуска́ть, *to let down, lower, insert;* отправля́ть, *to send, dispatch*; отража́ть, *to reflect*; отходи́ть; петь; печь; погиба́ть; поража́ть, *to strike*; превраща́ть, *to convert, transform*; приводи́ть; приступа́ть, *to set about, get down to*; проявля́ть, *to show, manifest*; разделя́ть, *to divide, share*; разноси́ть, *to distribute*; разряжа́ть, *to unload* (firearm); станови́ться; убежда́ть, *to convince*; улета́ть, *to fly away.*

LESSON 51

ASPECTUAL PAIRS: INFIXES

§1. Formation of secondary imperfective verbs with the infix -ыва- / -ива-
In most instances a prefix attached to a verb does carry some meaning, or at least it modifies the meaning of the simple verb. When the prefix does carry meaning of its own or give the simple verb further meaning which needs to be preserved in an imperfective verb, then the secondary imperfective form is most commonly derived from the perfective by the insertion of an infix. In very many verbs this infix is -ыва- or -ива-. The resulting imperfective with -ыва- or -ива- belongs to the conjugation 1a, and is characterised by stress on the syllable immediately before the infix, e.g.

simple verb	pf. with prefix	secondary impf.	
вязáть	развязáть	развя́зывать	*to untie*
дéлать	передéлать	передéлывать	*to re-do*
дýмать	обдýмать	обдýмывать	*to think over*
игрáть	проигрáть	проúгрывать	*to lose* (game, etc.)
искáть	отыскáть	оты́скивать	*to find, track down*
писáть	подписáть	подпúсывать	*to sign*

In many instances an **o** in the root of the verb will change to an **a** in the imperfective form derived in this way. This is always the case if the root is unstressed and is very often the case too if the root is stressed, e.g.

i. with unstressed **o** in the root of the perfective:

simple verb	pf. with prefix	secondary impf.	
колóть	проколóть	прокáлывать	*to pierce, perforate*
копáть	подкопáть	подкáпывать	*to undermine*
мотáть	размотáть	размáтывать	*to unwind*
—	остановúть	останáвливать	*to stop*
смотрéть	рассмотрéть	рассмáтривать	*to examine*
сосáть	всосáть	всáсывать	*to suck in, absorb*
толкáть	столкнýться	стáлкиваться	*to collide*

ii. with stressed **o** in the root of the perfective:

simple verb	pf. with prefix	secondary impf.	
морóзить	заморóзить	заморáживать	*to freeze* (trans.)
рабóтать	зарабóтать	зарабáтывать	*to earn*

стро́ить	устро́ить	устра́ивать	*to arrange*
—	успоко́ить	успока́ивать	*to calm, assuage*

Note however that in some verbs a stressed **о** in the root of the perfective form remains **о** in the imperfective form, e.g. perfective with prefix озабо́тить has imperfective озабо́чивать, *to worry, concern*.

§2. Formation of secondary imperfective verbs with other infixes

i. Many imperfective forms can be derived from perfective verbs consisting of prefix + simple verb by means of the insertion of the infix -ва-. The perfectives from which imperfectives with the infix -ва- can be derived are based on a small number of 1a verbs in -еть and -уть (e.g. греть, *to warm*, and дуть, *to blow*) and on a much larger number of 1b verbs, including monosyllables in -ыть (e.g. мыть, *to wash*), monosyllables in -ить (e.g. пить, *to drink*); петь, *to sing*; жить, *to live*; быть, *to be*; плыть, *to swim*, and miscellaneous others. All the resultant imperfectives with the infix -ва- belong to the conjugation 1a, e.g.

simple verb	pf. with prefix	secondary impf.	
греть	согре́ть (1a)	согрева́ть	*to warm*
дуть	наду́ть (1a)	надува́ть	*to inflate, blow up*
мыть	умы́ть (1b)	умыва́ть	*to wash*
крыть	закры́ть (1b)	закрыва́ть	*to close, shut*
рыть	зары́ть (1b)	зарыва́ть	*to bury*
бить	разби́ть (1b)	разбива́ть	*to break, smash*
вить	разви́ть (1b)	развива́ть	*to develop*
лить	нали́ть (1b)	налива́ть	*to pour*
петь	напе́ть (1b)	напева́ть	*to sing* (a melody)
жить	пережи́ть (1b)	пережива́ть	*to live through, endure*
быть	забы́ть (1b)	забыва́ть	*to forget*
плыть	всплыть (1b)	всплыва́ть	*to surface, come to light*
деть	наде́ть (1b)	надева́ть	*to put on* (clothing)
—	застря́ть (1b)	застрева́ть	*to get stuck*

Also with imperfectives with the infix -ва- are derivatives of дать, *to give*; знать, *to know*; and стать, *to become*, e.g.

simple verb	pf. with prefix	secondary impf.	
дать	изда́ть (1b)	издава́ть	*to publish*
знать	призна́ть (1b)	признава́ть	*to admit*
стать	встать (1b)	встава́ть	*to get up*

Note however that these imperfective forms derived from дать, знать, and стать lose the infix -ва- in their present tense (e.g. издаю́, издаёшь, etc.; see 9.2 above).

ii. Many secondary imperfective forms are derived from perfective verbs in -зти, -зть, -сти, -сть, -чь with the help of the infix -а-, e.g. from perfectives such as подмести́, *to sweep up*; соскрести́, *to scrape off*; напа́сть, *to attack*; привле́чь, *to attract;* помо́чь, *to help*; зажёчь, *to set light to*; подстри́чь, *to trim, clip*.

All of these perfectives have imperfective forms in -а́ть, which belong to the conjugation 1a. The consonant which precedes this ending in the imperfective is that consonant with which the stem of the perfective future ends (see 11.8-14 above). Thus:

simple verb	pf. with prefix	secondary impf.	
грызть	перегры́зть	перегрыза́ть	*to gnaw through*
трясти́	потрясти́	потряса́ть	*to shake, stun*
мести́	подмести́	подмета́ть	*to sweep up*
—	изобрести́	изобрета́ть	*to invent*
скрести́	соскрести́	соскреба́ть	*to scrape off*
пасть	напа́сть	напада́ть	*to attack*
"	пропа́сть	пропада́ть	*to be missing, vanish*

In verbs in -чь, which have two consonants in their present/future tense stem, it is the consonant with which the stem of the first-person singular and the third-person plural forms end that occurs in the secondary imperfective form, e.g.

simple verb	pf. with prefix	secondary impf.	
влечь	привле́чь	привлека́ть	*to attract*
сечь	отсе́чь	отсека́ть	*to cut off*
течь	уте́чь	утека́ть	*to flow away, leak*
мочь	помо́чь	помога́ть	*to help*
—	пренебре́чь	пренебрега́ть	*to neglect*
жечь	зажёчь	зажига́ть	*to set light to*
стричь	подстри́чь	подстрига́ть	*to trim* (by cutting)

Derivatives of the simple verb есть, *to eat*, form imperfectives with a stem in д, e.g. проеда́ть/прое́сть, *to corrode*.

Derivatives of красть, *to steal,* have imperfectives in -кра́дывать, e.g. вкра́дываться/вкра́сться, *to steal in, creep in*; прокра́дываться/про-кра́сться, *to steal by, steal past.*

Similarly there are a number of imperfective derivatives of класть, *to put*, in -кла́дывать, though it should be noted that the perfectives are based on the root -ложи́ть, e.g. вкла́дывать/вложи́ть, *to invest*;

закла́дывать/заложи́ть, *to put behind, lay* (foundation); скла́дывать/сложи́ть, *to pile, add, fold.*

Note also that derivatives of the verbs of motion везти́, *to take* (by transport); вести́, *to lead*; нести́, *to carry*, do not form their imperfectives in this way (see 50.7 above).

iii. Secondary imperfectives derived from those 1b verbs which have stems in -м- or -н- (see 11.3 and 11.5 above; e.g. жать, *to squeeze*; нача́ть, *to begin*; жать, *to reap*; мять, *to crumple*; and verbs based on the root -нять [see 10.6 and 11.3 above]) are formed with the infix -а- preceded by -им- and -ин- respectively, and also belong to the conjugation 1a, e.g.

simple verb	pf. with prefix	secondary impf.	
жать	пожа́ть	пожима́ть	*to press, squeeze*
"	сжать	сжима́ть	*to compress, clench*
—	нача́ть	начина́ть	*to begin*
жать	пожа́ть	пожина́ть	*to reap*
мять	размя́ться	размина́ться	*to limber up*
—	заня́ть	занима́ть	*to occupy, engage*
—	подня́ть	поднима́ть	*to lift, raise*
—	поня́ть	понима́ть	*to understand*
—	снять	снима́ть	*to take off*

iv. Secondary imperfectives derived from 1b verbs in -ере́ть (see 11.6 above) and of the simple verb брать are also formed with the help of the infix -а-, which in these verbs is preceded by -ир-, e.g.

simple verb	pf. with prefix	secondary impf.	
—	умере́ть	умира́ть	*to die*
—	запере́ть	запира́ть	*to lock*
тере́ть	стере́ть	стира́ть	*to wipe off*
брать	вы́брать	выбира́ть	*to choose*
"	собра́ть	собира́ть	*to gather, collect*
"	убра́ть	убира́ть	*to remove, take away, clear away*

§3. Unpaired verbs with imperfective and perfective meaning

There are a number of verbs which have only one form, which may be used with either imperfective or perfective meaning. Most of these verbs end in -овать. Some are of Slavonic origin, e.g.

веле́ть	*to order, command*
жени́ться	*to get married* (of man) [1]

1 pf. пожени́ться in sense of *to get married* (of a couple).

испо́льзовать	*to use, utilise*
иссле́довать	*to investigate, examine*
казни́ть	*to execute*
ра́нить	*to wound*
рассле́довать	*to look into, hold an inquiry into*
роди́ть	*to give birth*[2]
роди́ться	*to be born*[2]

2 But there is also impf. рожда́ть(ся).

The majority of these verbs, though, are of fairly recent foreign origin, e.g.

атакова́ть	*to attack*
гаранти́ровать	*to guarantee*
импорти́ровать	*to import*
конфискова́ть	*to confiscate*
организова́ть	*to organise*
стабилизи́ровать	*to stabilise*
экспорти́ровать	*to export*

The tendency to distinguish between aspects by the use of distinct forms, however, results in the formation of (i) some imperfectives of verbs in -овать by means of the use of the infix -ыва- (e.g. pf. арестова́ть > impf. apecто́вывать, *to arrest*) and (ii) perfectives of verbs in -овать by means of the use of various prefixes (e.g. pf. проиллюстри́ровать from impf. иллюстри́ровать, *to illustrate*; pf. сфотографи́ровать from impf. фотографи́ровать, *to photograph*).

§4. Unpaired verbs with imperfective form only

These verbs denote processes or conditions which are not the outcome of an action and are not associated with a particular stage in the process, and are therefore incapable of having perfective meaning, e.g.

зави́сеть (от + gen.)	*to depend on*
зна́чить	*to mean*
нужда́ться (в + prep.)	*to be needy, be in need (of)*
обоня́ть	*to smell* (trans.)
ожида́ть	*to expect*
отсу́тствовать	*to be absent*
подража́ть (+ dat.)	*to imitate*
походи́ть (на + acc.)	*to resemble**
предви́деть	*to foresee*
предчу́вствовать	*to have a presentiment*
преоблада́ть	*to prevail*

* But note the homonym походи́ть used as a perfective verb [по + ходи́ть] in the meaning *to walk around for a while.*

преслéдовать	*to pursue, persecute*
присýтствовать	*to be present*
разговáривать (с + instr.)	*to talk (to), converse (with)*
содержáть	*to keep, support, contain*
сожалéть	*to regret*
соотвéтствовать (+ dat.)	*to correspond (to)*
состоя́ть (из + gen./в + prep.)	*to consist (of/in)*
состязáться (с + instr.)	*to compete (with)*
сочýвствовать (+ dat.)	*to sympathise (with)*
стóить	*to cost, be worth*
ухáживать (за + instr.)	*to court, look after, tend*
учáствовать (в + prep.)	*to participate (in)*

§5. Unpaired verbs with perfective form only

These verbs, which are not numerous, denote an action which is quickly completed, or the moment of action, or a quick transition to another state, or the result of an action, e.g.

опóмниться	*to come to one's senses, collect oneself*
очнýться	*to regain consciousness, come to oneself*
очутиться	*to find oneself*
ри́нуться	*to rush, dash*
состоя́ться	*to take place*
стать	when this verb means *to begin*
хлы́нуть	*to gush, pour, surge*

Exercise

Give the imperfective forms of the following perfective verbs: вовлéчь, *to drag in, involve*; вы́грызть, *to gnaw out*; вы́играть, *to win* (game); вы́течь, *to flow out*; завязáть, *to tie up*; записáть, *to note down*; избрáть, *to elect*; обня́ть, *to embrace*; обрабóтать, *to work up, process*; одéть, *to dress*; остáться, *to remain*; отвлéчь, *to distract, divert*; отдáть, *to give back*; откры́ть, *to open, discover*; отперéть, *to unlock*; перегрéть, *to overheat*; передýмать, *to change one's mind*; перемотáть, *to rewind*; пересéчь, *to cut across, intersect*; пересмотрéть, *to review*; перестрóить, *to rebuild*; поддéлать, *to falsify, forge*; поджéчь, *to set light to*; подобрáть, *to pick, select*; приня́ть, *to accept, receive*; приобрести́, *to acquire*; продáть, *to sell*; раздéть, *to undress*; сбить, *to knock down*; слить, *to pour together, fuse*; смести́, *to sweep off*; смыть, *to wash off*; стрясти́, *to shake off*; уби́ть, *to kill*; узнáть, *to recognise, find out.*

LESSON 52

ASPECT AND TENSE

§1. Introductory

For practical purposes one can draw a basic distinction in usage between the two aspects which is quite straightforward, and it is this basic distinction that is examined in this lesson.

However, it is useful also to bear in mind the same sort of distinction as that which exists between the determinate and indeterminate verbs of motion (see 45.1-3 above). That is to say, one form (the perfective verb, like the determinate verb of motion) has a clear or marked meaning, while the other (the imperfective, like the indeterminate verb of motion) is used to convey a whole range of meanings that fall outside the scope of the marked form. This distinction between the aspects will be examined further in the following lesson.

It should be emphasised at the outset that aspectual usage is one of the areas of Russian grammar in which it is difficult to formulate firm rules. While the guidance given in this and the following lesson generally holds good, apparent exceptions will frequently be found.

§2. The relationship between English tenses and Russian aspects

English, like other Western European languages such as French, Italian and Spanish, has a complex system of verb forms which enables the speaker to present past, present and future actions in numerous ways, e.g.

past perfect:	*I had read*
past perfect continuous:	*I had been reading*
past simple:	*I read*
past continuous:	*I was reading*
past habitual:	*I used to read*
present perfect:	*I have read*
present perfect continuous:	*I have been reading*
present simple:	*I read*
present continuous:	*I am reading*
future perfect:	*I shall have read*
future simple:	*I shall read*
future continuous:	*I shall be reading*

This range of forms enables the speaker to denote the aspect of an action (perfect, simple or continuous) as well as the tense (past, present or future).

Russian has past, present and future tenses, but the aspect of the actions is conveyed first and foremost by choice of the appropriate member of an aspectual pair rather than by a complex system of tense endings and auxiliary forms of the sort available in the Western European languages.

§3. Aspect and tense or mood

Verbs of both aspects have six indicative forms with endings dependent on person (1st person singular, etc.; e.g. читáю, прочитáю), four past tense forms with endings dependent on gender (masculine, etc.; e.g. читáл, прочитáл), and imperative forms (e.g. читáй, прочитáй).

Note that the indicative form of the perfective verb (e.g. прочитáю) will as a rule have future meaning *(I shall read)*.

Note too that there is also an imperfective future, which consists of an appropriate form of the future tense of the verb *to be* (i.e. бýду, бýдешь, бýдет, бýдем, бýдете, бýдут) + imperfective infinitive (e.g. читáть).

§4. Basic use of the perfective

The perfective verb has the function of presenting a single action in its totality. It should therefore be used as a rule if the speaker is referring to an action that has been or will be successfully completed, e.g.

Он прочитáл кни́гу. *He read/has read/had read the book.*
Он прочитáет кни́гу. *He will read the book.*

Note that in the second example above the perfective has future meaning. The perfective may not as a rule have present meaning, since actions in the present are by their nature incomplete.

Many adverbs or adverbial expressions encourage (if they do not oblige) the use of a perfective verb, e.g. вдруг, *suddenly*; неожи́данно, *unexpectedly*; совсéм, *quite, completely*; срáзу, *immediately*; and expressions of time with за + accusative, e.g. он написáл письмó за оди́н день, *he wrote the letter in a day.*

The perfective will commonly be used where an action has some result or where the action belongs in a past or future sequence, because each action in a sequence is complete before the next action takes place, e.g. онá встáла, умы́лась, одéлась, и вы́шла, *she got up, washed, got dressed, and went out.*

Consider the following fable by Tolstoy in which perfective verbs denote completed actions in a narrative sequence:

Однáжды, когдá лев спал, мышь **пробежáла** по егó тéлу. Лев **проснýлся**, и **поймáл** её. Мышь **стáла** проси́ть, чтóбы лев **отпусти́л**

её. Она́ **сказа́ла**: «Е́сли ты меня́ отпу́стишь, и я тебе́ когда́-нибудь **помогу́**». Лев **засмея́лся** и **отпусти́л** мышь. Пото́м охо́тники **пойма́ли** льва́ и **привяза́ли** его́ верёвкой к де́реву. Мышь **услы́шала** льви́ный рёв, **прибежа́ла**, **перегры́зла** верёвку и **сказа́ла**: «По́мнишь, ты смея́лся надо мной. А тепе́рь ты ви́дишь, что и мышь мо́жет помо́чь льву́».
One day, when a lion was sleeping, a mouse ran over its body. The lion woke up and caught it. The mouse started to plead with the lion to let it go. It said: 'If you let me go I shall help you one day'. The lion burst out laughing and let the mouse go. Then some hunters caught the lion and tied it to a tree with rope. The mouse heard the lion's roar, ran up, gnawed through the rope and said: 'Do you remember, you laughed at me. But now you see that even a mouse may help a lion'.

§5. Basic uses of the imperfective

It is possible for practical purposes to define two main, but actually quite distinct, functions of the imperfective.

i. To denote past, present, or future action which is incomplete, in the process of taking place, e.g.

   Он чита́л кни́гу. — *He was reading a book.*
   Он чита́ет кни́гу. — *He is reading a book.*
   Он бу́дет чита́ть кни́гу. — *He will be reading a book.*

   Imperfective verbs naturally refer to past or future actions which take place concurrently with other actions or which are interrupted by other actions (and the action which interrupts will generally be denoted by a perfective verb), e.g.

   Она́ чита́ла кни́гу, пока́ её мать гото́вила на ку́хне.
   She was reading/read a book while her mother was cooking in the kitchen.
   Она́ бу́дет чита́ть кни́гу, пока́ её мать бу́дет гото́вить на ку́хне.
   She will read/will be reading a book while her mother cooks in the kitchen.
   Она́ чита́ла кни́гу, когда́ её мать вошла́.
   She was reading a book when her mother came in.
   Она́ бу́дет чита́ть кни́гу, когда́ её мать войдёт.
   She will be reading a book when her mother comes in.

ii. To denote repeated or frequent action in the past, present or future. Many adverbs and adverbial expressions encourage the use of an imperfective verb with frequentative meaning, e.g. вре́мя от вре́мени, *from time to time*; всегда́, *always*; иногда́, *sometimes*; ка́ждый год, *every year*; ка́ждый день, *every day*; мно́го раз, *many times*; не раз, *more than once*; постоя́нно, *constantly*; ча́сто, *often*; and other expressions indicating periods of time. Examples from the press:

Такси́сты всегда́, да́же в стро́гие времена́, бра́ли с иностра́нцев валю́ту.
Taxi-drivers always, even in strict times, took foreign currency from foreigners.
Иногда́ шеф приноси́л де́ньги, рубле́й 50-100, я дава́л распи́ску в получе́нии.
Sometimes the chief would bring money, 50-100 roubles, [and] I would sign a receipt for them.
Он был хи́ппи, его́ не раз сажа́ли в психу́шку.
He was a hippie, more than once they put him in a psychiatric hospital.
Оди́н фе́рмер постоя́нно подозрева́л в нече́стности свои́х рабо́тников-африка́нцев: в разгово́ре с ним они́ опуска́ли глаза́, не смотре́ли в лицо́, как бу́дто зна́ли за собо́й вину́.
One [South-African] *farmer constantly suspected his African workmen of dishonesty: in conversation with him they would lower their eyes and would not look him in the face, as if they knew they were guilty.*
Две неде́ли ве́тер дул в сто́рону Го́меля, Могилёва, Ми́нска. Две неде́ли он рассе́ивал опа́сные радионукли́ды над деревня́ми и города́ми.
For two weeks the wind blew in the direction of Gomel, Mogilev, and Minsk. For two weeks it scattered dangerous radionuclides over villages and towns.
Рабо́тали бра́тья так, что их де́ти спра́шивали у мам, куда́ пропа́ли па́пки.
The brothers worked so [hard] that their children would ask their mums where their dads had got to.

Note that in all tenses (past, present and future) the same imperfective aspect may bear two meanings (firstly, incomplete action; secondly, repeated action) which in English are conveyed by separate tenses (firstly, *was reading, is reading, will be reading*; and secondly, *read, reads, will read*).

Consider the use of imperfective verbs, in the two different functions described, in the following passage by Tolstoy. The Roman figures in brackets after the verbs in the past tense indicate which of the two functions of the imperfective described above (incomplete action and repeated action) obtains in each particular case.

Два челове́ка шли (i) вме́сте по доро́ге, и ка́ждый нёс (i) на плеча́х свою́ но́шу. Оди́н челове́к нёс (i), не снима́я, всю доро́гу, а друго́й ча́сто остана́вливался (ii), снима́л (ii) но́шу, и сади́лся (ii) отдыха́ть. Но он до́лжен был вся́кий раз опя́ть поднима́ть (ii) но́шу на пле́чи.

И тот челове́к, кото́рый снима́л (ii) но́шу, уста́л бо́льше, чем тот, кото́рый нёс (i), не снима́я.
Two people were walking together along a road, and each was carrying a burden on his shoulders. One person was carrying [his burden] the whole way without putting it down, but the other one frequently stopped, took off the burden and sat down to rest. But the latter had each time to raise the burden up on to his shoulders again. And the person who [repeatedly] put down the burden got tired more quickly than the one who carried it without putting it down.

§6. The present perfect continuous tense

A present tense is used in Russian to render the English present perfect continuous, i.e. to denote an action which began in the past and is still continuing, e.g.

Я пять лет изуча́ю ру́сский язы́к.
I have been studying Russian for five years.
О́коло тридцати́ лет ведёт он переда́чу «Споко́йной но́чи, малыши́!»
He has been doing the programme 'Good Night Children!' for about thirty years. (Press)

§7. The use of the future tense in subordinate clauses

It should be noted that a future tense is used in Russian in certain contexts where English uses a present tense.

After conjunctions such as е́сли and когда́ a future tense must be used in Russian if the action clearly is yet to take place, e.g.

Е́сли вы прочита́ете э́ту кни́гу, вы поймёте его́ взгля́ды.
You will understand his views if you read this book
Е́сли ты меня́ отпу́стишь, и я тебе́ когда-нибудь помогу́.
If you let me go I shall help you one day. (From the Tolstoy fable quoted in §4 above)
Когда́ он придёт, мы поговори́м об э́том.
We shall talk about this when he arrives.

§8. Choice of tense in reported speech

Russian verbs used in reported speech are put in the tense which would have been used in the original statement or question. This usage differs from English usage. Compare for example the tenses used in the reported speech in the following Russian and English sentences:

Я сказа́л ему́, что я живу́ [imperfective present] в Ло́ндоне.
I told him that I lived [past simple] *in London.*

Он сказа́л, что он придёт [perfective future].
He said that he would come [conditional].
Он спроси́л, изуча́ю [imperfective present] ли я ру́сский язы́к.
He asked whether I was studying [past continuous] *Russian.*

Note that in reported questions *whether* is rendered by ли and that the Russian word order, with inversion of subject and predicate, is the order used in the original question (just as the tense is the tense used in the original question). The last of the three examples above illustrates the point.

The following examples from the press provide further illustration of the Russian use of tense in reported speech:

Она́ спроси́ла, зна́ю ли я учени́цу на́шей шко́лы по фами́лии Га́ек.
She asked whether I knew a pupil of our school by the name of Gaek.
Спроси́ла, согла́сен ли я.
She asked whether I agreed.
Прие́хавшие сапёры убеди́лись, что ми́на не взорвётся.
The sappers who had arrived convinced themselves that the mine would not explode.

§9. Summary

The following table summarises what are perhaps the most common relationships between Russian aspectual forms and English tenses. Note though that it would be quite wrong to suppose that the Russian aspectual form may only be rendered in English by the tense given here. The English forms *I read* (past) and *I have read*, for example, might equally be used in certain contexts where Russian has the imperfective чита́л (see e.g. 53.4 below).

tense	impf.		pf.	
past	чита́л =	*I was reading* *I used to read* *I have been reading* (if the action is now complete) *I had been reading*	прочита́л =	*I read* *I have read* *I had read*
present	чита́ю =	*I read* *I am reading* *I have been reading* (if the action is still going on)		

future

бу́ду чита́ть =	*I shall be reading* *I shall read* (repeatedly) *I am going to read*	прочита́ю = *I shall read*

Exercises

A. *Choose the appropriate form from the aspectual pair in brackets to complete the meaning of the following sentences:* (1) Они́ ти́хо (бесе́довали/побесе́довали), как вдруг (раздава́лся/разда́лся) взрыв. (2) Ты бу́дешь (де́лать/сде́лать) всё, что я попрошу́. (Отвеча́ть/Отве́тить) на все вопро́сы, кото́рые зада́м. (3) Я объясни́л, почему́ я (приходи́л/пришёл). Он (вздыха́л/вздохну́л) и (пожима́л/пожа́л) мне ру́ку. (4) Он не раз (подчёркивал/подчеркну́л), что бу́дущее фина́нсовой по́мощи на́шему госуда́рству зави́сит от хо́да рефо́рм. (5) (Конча́лась/Ко́нчилась) Оте́чественная война́ с Герма́нией, (начина́лась/начала́сь) «холо́дная» с неда́вними сою́зниками. (6) В метро́ люблю́ (чита́ть/прочита́ть) Пу́шкина. (7) В э́то вре́мя мы ре́дко (испы́тывали/испыта́ли) нужду́. (8) Жена́ запла́кала. Он (гляде́л/погляде́л) на неё, (подходи́л/подошёл) к ней и (целова́л/поцелова́л) её в го́лову. (9) Она́ вре́мя от вре́мени (шепта́ла/прошепта́ла) себе́ «Бо́же мой! Бо́же мой!» (10) Он иногда́ (приходи́л/пришёл) домо́й по́сле полу́ночи. (11) Ве́тер всё вре́мя (уси́ливался/уси́лился). (12) За полго́да она́ си́льно (худе́ла/похуде́ла). (13) Всё быстре́е (пролета́ли/пролете́ли) облака́ над на́ми. (14) Они́ смотре́ли, как он спуска́лся с горы́, как постепе́нно в темноте́ (исчеза́ла/исче́зла) его́ фигу́ра. (15) У роди́телей ча́сто быва́ете? Стара́юсь (приезжа́ть/прие́хать) как мо́жно ча́ще. (16) Ми́ссис Ки́ннок нема́ло возде́йствовала на формирова́ние полити́ческих взгля́дов своего́ му́жа. Она́ до́лго (сохраня́ла/сохрани́ла) ле́вую ориента́цию. (17) Он э́то ча́сто (повторя́л/повтори́л) в ра́зные го́ды, что умрёт в том же во́зрасте, в како́м у́мер его́ оте́ц. (18) Все э́ти го́ды ре́йтинг програ́ммы (возраста́л/возро́с), а техни́ческие сре́дства (убыва́ли/у́были). (19) Меня́ всегда́ (поража́ло/порази́ло) оби́лие газе́т в магази́нах на у́лицах, ска́жем, Стокго́льма, Хе́льсинки. (20) Е́сли в Москве́ ра́ньше существова́ли райо́ны, где ре́дко (угоня́ли/угна́ли) автомоби́ли, то тепе́рь таки́е «бе́лые» места́ с ка́рты столи́цы (исчеза́ли/исче́зли).

B. *Translate into English:* (1) Бо́лее тридцати́ лет занима́ется он изуче́нием приро́ды ту́ндры. (2) Вот уже́ че́тверть ве́ка рабо́таю в МГУ. (3) Англи́йским языко́м она́ занима́ется с пелёнок. (4) Она́ всю жизнь живёт в Москве́. (5) Депута́том я рабо́таю год. (6) Я сказа́л А́нне, что я позвоню́ ей ве́чером. (7) Она́ сказа́ла мне, что хо́чет пойти́ на конце́рт. (8) Серге́й спроси́л меня́, куда́ я иду́. (9) Та́ня спроси́ла его́, когда́ он придёт. (10) Продавщи́ца отве́тила мне, что в магази́не уже́ нет хле́ба. (11) Он спроси́л её, ви́дела ли она́ но́вую пье́су. (12) Я спроси́л его́, давно́ ли изуча́ет англи́йский язы́к. (13) Врач спроси́л меня́, хорошо́ ли себя́ чу́вствую. (14) Преподава́тельница спроси́ла студе́нтов, чита́ли ли они́ э́ту кни́гу. (15) Мы спроси́ли его́, получи́л ли он на́ше письмо́.

C. *Translate into Russian:* (1) She was writing a letter. (2) I shall read this book. (3) He got up, got dressed and went out. (4) On Sundays he used to read the newspapers. (5) I bought a new hat. (6) He sat down and went to sleep. (7) He often went to sleep after dinner. (8) I was cooking the supper when you came in. (9) They are building a new house. (10) They build hundreds of houses each year. (11) I was closing the door when suddenly the postman arrived. (12) What will you be doing when I come home? (13) Do you know whether she is at home today? (14) He asked me whether I spoke Russian. (15) We wanted to find out whether the professor would give his lecture today. (16) I have been working in France for two years. (17) He was ironing his shirts all evening. (18) He ironed all his shirts in ten minutes. (19) Sometimes he would call on us after work. (20) He called on me unexpectedly.

LESSON 53

ASPECTS: FURTHER POINTS ON USAGE

§1. Verbs requiring an imperfective infinitive

There are a number of verbs which require any infinitive which follows them to be used in the imperfective aspect. These verbs essentially indicate the stage an action has reached (e.g. *to begin, to continue, to stop, to finish*) and the action denoted by the infinitive therefore cannot in this context be seen in its totality.

The following Russian verbs (arranged with the verbs which relate to the beginning of actions first and with those that relate to the finishing of actions last) invariably require an imperfective infinitive after them:

начина́ть/нача́ть	*to begin, to start*
стать	(when this perfective verb means *to begin*)
принима́ться/приня́ться	*to set about*
научи́ться	*to learn* (to do sthg.)
полюби́ть	*to grow fond* (of doing sthg.)
привыка́ть/привы́кнуть	*to get used* (to doing sthg.)
продолжа́ть*	*to continue*
конча́ть/ко́нчить	*to finish*
броса́ть/бро́сить	(when this verb means *to give up, abandon*)
перестава́ть/переста́ть	*to stop* (doing sthg.)
надоеда́ть/надое́сть	*to grow tired* (of doing sthg.; used impersonally)
отвыка́ть/отвы́кнуть	*to get out of the habit* (of doing sthg.)
устава́ть/уста́ть	*to tire* (of doing sthg.)

* The perfective form продо́лжить is rarely used except in the sense of *to prolong*, and will be followed by a verbal noun rather than an infinitive, e.g. мы продо́лжили обсужде́ние, *we carried on the discussion.*

The following examples illustrate the use of the imperfective infinitive after these verbs. (The examples in this and the next lesson include a number from the works by Pulkina and Rassudova cited on p.ix.)

Нéрвы москвичéй от непреры́вной канонáды начинáют **сдавáть.**
The nerves of the Muscovites are beginning to give way under the incessant bombardment. (Press)
Мышь стáла **просúть,** чтóбы лев отпустúл её.
The mouse started asking the lion to let it go. (Tolstoy; quoted in 52.4 above)
Мéстный набóрщик привы́к **набирáть** механúчески.
The local type-setter had got used to setting the type mechanically. (Press)
Нам надоéло **читáть** газéты.
We are tired of reading the papers.
Фéликс Светов перестáл **печáтаться** и замолчáл.
Feliks Svetov ceased to be published and fell silent. (Press)
Онú не уставáли **напоминáть** об э́тих собы́тиях.
They did not tire of mentioning these events.

Note that the verb which indicates the stage the action has reached may be of either aspect. Thus in the above examples the verbs *to begin, to get used to*, etc. are used in imperfective forms in some instances (начинáют, уставáли) and in perfective forms in others (стáла, привы́к). Choice of aspect for the verb indicating the stage the action has reached is determined by the general considerations set out in the previous lesson and in other sections of this lesson. It is only the following infinitive which must always be imperfective.

§2. Verbs requiring a perfective infinitive

A much smaller number of verbs require any infinitive used after them to be in the perfective aspect, notably:

забы́ть	*to forget* (to do sthg.)
остáться	*to remain* (to be done)
удáться	*to succeed in, manage* (used impersonally)
успéть	*to have time to, manage* (in the sense of *to have time to*)

Examples:

Он забы́л **опустúть** письмó в почтóвый я́щик.
He forgot to post the letter.
Ей остáлось тóлько **наклéить** мáрку на конвéрт.
It remained only for her to stick a stamp on the envelope.
Сегóдня я не успéл **зайтú** к ним, зайдý зáвтра.
I did not have time to call in on them today, I'll call tomorrow.

§3. Use of the imperfective to denote attempt or non-achievement of goal

Because the perfective verb indicates that an action has been or will be carried through to completion, it follows that actions which have not come to fruition must be described by the imperfective. The imperfective may therefore be used, in single-instance contexts, to tell us that an agent is working towards a certain goal, or striving for it, but that at the point to which the verb relates he or she has not yet achieved that goal.

This use of the imperfective is well illustrated by another fable by Tolstoy in which a deer who has been admiring his antlers and ruing the fact that his legs are so thin and unattractive finds himself chased by a lion:

> Вдруг вы́скочил лев и бро́сился на оле́ня. Оле́нь пусти́лся скака́ть по чи́стому по́лю. Он уже́ **убега́л** от льва, но когда́ прибежа́л в лес, то запу́тался рога́ми за су́чья, и лев схвати́л его́. Тогда́ оле́нь и говори́т: «Глу́пый я! Ду́мал, что но́ги пло́хи и то́нки, а они́ **спаса́ли** меня́. Ра́довался, что рога́ хоро́шие, а из-за них поги́б».
> *Suddenly a lion leapt out and rushed at the deer. The deer set off at a gallop over the open field. He was getting away from the lion, but when he came to a forest he got caught up in the boughs by his antlers and the lion seized him. Then the deer said: 'I was stupid! I thought that my legs were ugly and thin, but they were saving me. I was glad that my antlers were handsome, but because of them I am done for'.*

In some cases the sense of striving implicit in a Russian imperfective will have to be rendered in English by the inclusion of some verb such as *to try*, as in the following examples (taken from the works by Forsyth and Rassudova cited on p.ix.):

> Войска́ четы́ре дня **бра́ли** го́род, а не взя́ли его́.
> *The troops tried for four days to capture the town, but they did not succeed in taking it.*
> У него́ бы́ло напряжённое лицо́: он **вспомина́л**, где и когда́ он ви́дел э́того челове́ка.
> *He had a strained look on his face: he was trying to recall where and when he had seen this person.*

In other cases one might have to translate the two aspects of the Russian verb by quite different English verbs in order to preserve the distinction between the meaning of striving or non-achievement implicit in the imperfective, on the one hand, and the meaning of achievement of one's objective implicit in the perfective, on the other. Examples:

impf.		pf.	
сдава́ть экза́мен	*to sit/take an exam*	сдать экза́мен	*to pass an exam*
держа́ть экза́мен	*to sit/take an exam*	вы́держать экза́мен	*to pass an exam*
дока́зывать	*to contend, maintain*	доказа́ть	*to prove*

Example from the press:

> Я **доказывала**, что, как любой человек, могу забыть. Он говорил, что у меня хорошая память.
> *I contended that like any human being I could forget [things]. He said* [in refutation] *that I had a good memory.*

Consider also the following example from the sports page of 'Izvestiya':

> Он **бил** и не забил пенальти.
> *He took the penalty but did not score.*

§4. Use of the imperfective for simple statements of fact
It is arguable that the perfective aspect of the Russian verb, denoting as it does actions which are seen as complete, is the aspect which is felt to have clear and precise meaning. The imperfective verb, on the other hand, is capable of various functions. It may be used not only to describe actions which are seen as incomplete or which are repeated (as described in 52.5 above) but also, *faute de mieux*, simply to convey other meanings which fall outside the scope of the perfective verb.

Among these further functions of the imperfective is simple statement of fact. An imperfective verb is commonly used in contexts which at first sight might appear to require a perfective verb (i.e. to denote a single completed action) if the speaker is primarily interested not in the perfective nature of the action but in the fact or possibility that some action of a particular sort has taken place. Consider the following examples:

> Спасибо, я уже **пил** чай.
> *Thank you, I have already had some tea.*
> Вы читали «Преступление и наказание»?
> *Have you read 'Crime and Punishment'?*
> После взрыва в московском метро, когда погибли люди, в основном дети, на Западе появилась статья журналиста Виктор Луи. Он **писал**, что взрыв, возможно, произвели диссиденты.
> *After the explosion in the Moscow underground, in which people died, mainly children, an article by the journalist Victor Louis appeared in the West. He wrote that dissidents may have caused the explosion.* (Press)
> Вчера по радио **передавали**, что сегодня будет снег.
> *They said on the radio yesterday that there would be snow today.*
> Три года назад мы **рассказывали** с экрана о том, как...
> *Three years ago we told the story on the screen of how...*(Press)

In all of the above examples the verb refers to a single completed action in the past, but an imperfective verb is preferred to the perfective that might be expected because in all instances it is quite immaterial whether the action has been completed or not. The important factor is that some drinking has taken place or some reading or writing or broadcasting has been done.

It is natural that in sentences in which the imperfective verb is used with the function of simple statement of fact the focus of attention should often be the subject and/or object rather than the verb itself, e.g.

> Толсто́й писа́л «Войну́ и мир».
> *Tolstoy wrote 'War and Peace'.*

The important information in this statement is that Tolstoy was the author of 'War and Peace', not that he eventually finished writing that novel. Contrast the use of the perfective verb in statements in which it is important to show that some writing was completed:

> До 1825 [ты́сяча восемьсо́т два́дцать пя́того го́да] Бесту́жев **написа́л** не́сколько рабо́т в ду́хе романти́зма.
> *By 1825 Bestuzhev had written several works in the spirit of Romanticism.* (Soviet encyclopedia)
> Он на́чал писа́ть. К сентябрю́ **написа́л** пе́рвые гла́вы.
> *He began to write. By September he had finished the first chapters.* (Press)
> Спаси́бо, что вы **написа́ли** в Моссове́т в мою́ защи́ту.
> *Thank you for writing to Mossovet* [the Moscow Soviet] *in my defence.* (Press)
> Она́ **написа́ла** письмо́ отцу́, но забы́ла опусти́ть его́ в почто́вый я́щик.
> *She wrote a letter to her father but forgot to post it.*

In the first two examples above the perfective verb tells us that something was achieved by a certain date. In the third example there is the sense of something useful having been done. In the fourth example a sequence of actions is described and it must be made clear that the writing was completed before something else was done.

§5. Verbs infrequently used in the perfective

Several common verbs which do have both imperfective and perfective forms tend to occur in the imperfective rather than the perfective even when they denote a single completed action.

The perfective forms of за́втракать, *to have breakfast*; обе́дать, *to have dinner*; у́жинать, *to have supper* (поза́втракать, пообе́дать, поу́жинать, respectively) are rarely used unless the action is one of a sequence.

Note also that the perfective forms of ви́деть, *to see*, and слы́шать, *to hear* (уви́деть and услы́шать respectively) are used much more narrowly than

English tenses that one would normally expect to be rendered in Russian by perfective verbs (e.g. *saw, have seen*, etc.), and tend to refer to the beginning of a perception, e.g.

> Как-то, входя́ в магази́н, она́ уви́дела бегу́щего с па́чкой де́нег, услы́шала кри́ки.
> *Once, on entering a shop, she saw a man running off with a packet of money and she heard cries.* (Press)

Contrast the use of the imperfective:

> Я ви́дел но́вый фильм Куроса́вы.
> *I have seen Kurosawa's new film.*

The imperfective verbs ви́деть and слы́шать may even mean *to be able to see* and *to be able to hear* respectively. Examples:

> Из своего́ окна́ он ви́дел мо́ре.
> *He could see the sea from his window.*
> Мы сиде́ли в одно́м из после́дних рядо́в и пло́хо слы́шали то, что говори́л докла́дчик.
> *We were sitting in one of the rows furthest back and could not hear properly what the speaker was saying.*

Finally, contrast the use of the imperfective and perfective forms in the following example:

> Снача́ла я ничего́ не ви́дел вдали́, но пото́м уви́дел ма́ленькую чёрную то́чку.
> *At first I could not see anything in the distance, but then caught sight of a tiny black dot.*

§6. Annulled action

A further function of the imperfective verb is to denote an action which has been completed but whose effect is no longer felt because some other action has nullified it, e.g.

> Он открыва́л окно́.
> *He opened the window* [but now it has been closed again].
> Она́ брала́ кни́гу в библиоте́ке.
> *She took a book out of the library* [but now she has returned it].
> Он выходи́л.
> *He went out* [and came back again].

The use of the imperfective to denote annulled actions is particularly common with verbs of motion.

The use of the imperfective in such circumstances really enables the speaker to describe not one but two actions (in the first example above, for instance, the opening and the closing of the window). If on the other hand the speaker wishes to describe an action whose effects are still felt (i.e. the opening of a window which remains open), or to present the action as one of a series, then the perfective verb is required. Contrast the following statements, which incorporate perfective verbs, with the first two (otherwise identical) statements given above:

> Он откры́л окно́.
> *He opened the window* [and it is still open, or it remained open while other things were done].
> Она́ взяла́ кни́гу в библиоте́ке.
> *She took a book out of the library* [and still had it out at the time of speaking, or did other things before returning it].

The use of the imperfective to denote annulled action, and the contrasting use of the perfective to denote action whose results are still apparent, should not seem alien to English speakers, since the English past simple tense and the present perfect tense may be juxtaposed with the same effect. The statement *I opened the window,* for example, may tell us that the window was open for a while but that it is now shut again (compare imperfective открыва́л), whereas the statement *I have opened the window* tells us that the window has been opened and remains open (compare perfective откры́л).

§7. Use of imperfective to express time spent doing something

Although the point has implicitly been made in 52.5.i above, it is worth mentioning here that the imperfective may be used in contexts where the amount of time spent on something or the amount of time it takes to do something is being described, e.g.

> Она́ два часа́ реша́ла э́ту пробле́му.
> *She spent two hours solving this problem.*
> Он дво́е су́ток е́хал в Сиби́рь.
> *It took him two days to travel to Siberia.*

Exercises

A. *Choose the form from the aspectual pair in brackets which is correct in the context:* (1) Ситуа́ция в регио́не продолжа́ет (остава́ться/оста́ться) взрывоопа́сной. (2) С нача́ла пятидеся́тых годо́в положе́ние на́чало (изменя́ться/измени́ться) к лу́чшему. (3) Я отвы́к (встава́ть/встать) ра́но. (4) Она́ с де́тства научи́лась (игра́ть/сыгра́ть) на пиани́но. (5) Он полюби́л (гуля́ть/погуля́ть) по па́рку по́сле обе́да. (6) Во мно́гих города́х представи́телям ме́стной администра́ции удало́сь (угова́ривать/уговори́ть) авиадиспе́тчеров отказа́ться от попы́тки парализова́ть возду́шное движе́ние в стране́. (7) Обы́чно роди́тели начина́ют (забо́титься/позабо́титься) о здоро́вье ребёнка то́лько тогда́, когда́ он заболе́ет. (8) Нам пока́ удаётся (сде́рживать/сдержа́ть) на́тиск СПИ́Да. (9) Че́стно говоря́, я переста́л (чита́ть/прочита́ть) газе́ты. (10) В ха́рьковском автомагази́не на́чали (продава́ть/прода́ть) теле́ги. (11) Она́ успе́ла (писа́ть/написа́ть) ма́тери. (12) Я забы́л (загля́дывать/загляну́ть) в химчи́стку. (13) Оте́ц игра́л на бая́не. Он-то и стал (обуча́ть/обучи́ть) меня́, как то́лько я подросла́, игре́ на э́том музыка́льном инструме́нте. (14) В э́то вре́мя большо́е коли́чество люде́й э́того зна́ка пройду́т испыта́ние на про́чность, и далеко́ не все Козеро́ги бу́дут спосо́бны (держа́ть/вы́держать) э́тот косми́ческий экза́мен. (15) О ма́ссовом исхо́де гра́ждан неме́цкой национа́льности из Росси́и «Изве́стия» уже́ (писа́ли/написа́ли). (16) Вы (чита́ли/прочита́ли) рома́ны Распу́тина? (17) Она́ (писа́ла/написа́ла) статью́ и уе́хала в о́тпуск. (18) Я (ви́дел/уви́дел) това́рища и пошёл ему́ навстре́чу. (19) Как то́лько я (слы́шал/услы́шал) звоно́к, я сра́зу же снял телефо́нную тру́бку. (20) Мы сиде́ли в парте́ре и хорошо́ (ви́дели/уви́дели) сце́ну. (21) Я вы́шел в сад и (слы́шал/услы́шал) пе́ние птиц. (22) Ты (слы́шал/услы́шал), что он сказа́л? (23) Я посла́л отцу́ письмо́, что́бы он (приезжа́л/прие́хал) к нам в го́сти. (24) Почему́ карти́на виси́т кри́во? Ты (снима́л/снял) её? (25) Това́рищ (заходи́л/зашёл) ко мне, но меня́ не́ было до́ма.

B. *Translate into Russian:* (1) He began to write. (2) They got used to arriving home late. (3) She finished getting dressed. (4) He continued to read the newspaper. (5) She stopped reading. (6) They got tired of listening to the radio. (7) Have you read Pasternak's poetry? (8) I have seen that film. (9) She had supper. (10) Our Russian friend came to Britain last year [and has now gone home again]. (11) I want to leave the library [and come back again]. (12) I want to leave the library and go to the cinema. (13) When he caught sight of her he raised his hat. (14) Who wrote 'Dead Souls'? (15) Dostoevsky did not write his major novels until after his exile in Siberia. (16) Could you see the sea from your room in the hotel? (17) He has forgotten to buy bread. (18) It remained for her to sign the letters. (19) Have you had lunch? (20) For several hours he tried to solve the problem.

LESSON 54

USE OF ASPECT IN NEGATIVE EXPRESSIONS

§1. Negated verbs in the past tense

An imperfective verb should be used to denote complete absence of a particular action. The statement мы не встреча́лись, for example, would mean *we have not met.*

A perfective verb should be used, on the other hand, to indicate that an action was not performed on a specific occasion, e.g. мы не встре́тились, *we did not meet*. (Note that the same distinction may be conveyed in English by the use of different tenses, *we have not met* and *we did not meet* respectively.) The negated perfective may also mean that the subject was not able to carry out an action or failed to do something which it was intended to do.

Contrast the following sets of examples (some of which are taken from Rassudova, see p.ix.):

i. complete absence of action (imperfective):

Мно́гие все семь ме́сяцев не выходи́ли из до́ма.
Many people did not come out of their houses the whole seven months. (Press)
Це́лыми дня́ми он не подходи́л к столу́.
For days on end he would not come to the table [to eat]. (Press)
Позо́рную свою́ та́йну я не открыва́л никому́.
I have not revealed my shameful secret to anyone. (Press)

ii. non-performance on a specific occasion, or inability to carry out an action or failure to carry out intention (perfective):

Он не реши́л э́ту зада́чу.
He could not solve this problem.
Звоно́к буди́льника не разбуди́л его́, так кре́пко он спал.
The alarm-clock did not wake him, so soundly was he sleeping.
Он до́лжен был прийти́, но не пришёл.
He was due to come but he did not come.
— Ты купи́л пода́рок до́чке? — Нет, не купи́л, не нашёл ничего́ подходя́щего.
'Have you bought a present for your daughter?' 'No, I haven't, I did not find anything suitable.'

§2. Prohibition versus impossibility
Modal constructions with the meaning *may not* or *should not* are followed by imperfective verbs, whereas constructions meaning *cannot* are rendered by perfective forms. Contrast for example the following statements involving the use of нельзя́:

> Нельзя́ тут переходи́ть [impf.] доро́гу.
> *One must not cross the road here* [because e.g. there is no crossing and one may be fined].
>
> Нельзя́ тут перейти́ [pf.] доро́гу.
> *One cannot cross the road here* [because e.g. there is too much traffic or the road is up and it is dangerous].

The following sets of examples (some of which are taken from Pulkina and Rassudova; see p.ix) further illustrate the distinction:

i. prohibition (imperfective):

> В ко́мнату нельзя́ входи́ть в пальто́.
> *One must not enter the room in one's overcoat.*
> Не сле́дует доверя́ть таку́ю отве́тственную рабо́ту новичку́.
> *One should not entrust such responsible work to a novice.*
> Зама́лчивать не име́ете пра́ва.
> *You do not have the right to remain silent.* (Press)

ii. impossibility (perfective):

> Нельзя́ отня́ть у люде́й их взгля́ды.
> *One cannot take people's views away from them* [although everything else, such as their freedom and property, can be taken away]. (Press)
> До утюга́ нельзя́ дотро́нуться: тако́й он горя́чий.
> *You can't touch the iron: it's too hot.*
> На э́тот вопро́с невозмо́жно отве́тить?
> *Is it impossible to answer this question?* (Press)

§3. Dissuasion, inadvisability versus persuasion, advisability
Many verbs or expressions require any following infinitive, if it is negated, to be imperfective. Among the verbs in this category are those which express:

i. a speaker's attempt to dissuade someone from doing something;

ii. advice or a request or exhortation that something not be done;

iii. a decision, promise or intention not to do something.

Examples (some from Pulkina and Rassudova), arranged in the broad categories listed above:

> Он уговори́л меня́ не **остава́ться.**
> *He persuaded me not to stay.*
>
> Все сове́туют тебе́ не **соглаша́ться** на э́то предложе́ние.
> *Everybody advises you not to agree to this proposal.*
> Врач посове́товал больно́му не **принима́ть** снотво́рного.
> *The doctor advised the patient not to take a sleeping tablet.*
> Председа́тель предложи́л не **зака́нчивать** пре́ния.
> *The chairman proposed that discussion not be brought to an end.*
>
> Коали́ция реши́ла не **наступа́ть** на столи́цу.
> *The coalition decided not to attack the capital.* (Press)
> Я обеща́л не **возвраща́ться** сего́дня домо́й до пяти́ часо́в.
> *I promised not to return home before five o'clock today.*
> Преподава́тель наме́рен не **увели́чивать** коли́чества заня́тий в неде́лю.
> *The teacher intends not to increase the number of classes a week.*

The verb *to dissuade* itself, отгова́ривать/отговори́ть, also requires a following infinitive to be imperfective, e.g.

> Оте́ц отговори́л сы́на **меня́ть** профе́ссию.
> *The father dissuaded his son from/talked his son out of changing his profession.*

If on the other hand verbs such as угова́ривать/уговори́ть, сове́товать/посове́товать, предлага́ть/предложи́ть, проси́ть/попроси́ть, реша́ть/реши́ть are followed by a verb that is not negated, then the following infinitive may be of either aspect, depending on the usual considerations concerning prolongation or frequency of the action. That is to say a perfective infinitive will be required if the action is performed on a single occasion, but an imperfective infinitive will be required if the action is recurrent, as the following examples from Pulkina make clear:

> Он уговори́л меня́ оста́ться [pf.].
> *He persuaded me to stay.*
> Врач посове́товал больно́му приня́ть [pf.] снотво́рное.
> *The doctor advised the patient to take a sleeping tablet.*
> Я обеща́л верну́ться [pf.] домо́й к пяти́ часа́м.
> *I promised to be back home by five o'clock.*
> Я обеща́л всегда́ возвраща́ться [impf.] домо́й к пяти́ часа́м.
> *I promised always to be back home by five o'clock.*

§4. Phrases expressing inexpediency

There are a number of such phrases, which also require a following infinitive to be imperfective, e.g.

не сто́ит *it is not worth*
не́зачем *there is no need to/no point in*
бесполе́зно *it is useless to*
вре́дно *it is harmful to*

Examples from Pulkina and Rassudova:

Не сто́ит ждать его́, он придёт о́чень по́здно.
It's not worth waiting for him, he'll arrive very late.
Не сто́ит смотре́ть э́тот фильм: он неинтере́сный.
It's not worth seeing this film; it isn't interesting.
Не́зачем объясня́ть э́то так подро́бно, это лёгкий материа́л.
There is no need to explain this in such detail; it's easy material.
Бесполе́зно учи́ть его́ пе́нию: у него́ о́чень плохо́й слух.
It's useless teaching him to sing: he's got a very bad ear [for music].
Тебе́ вре́дно кури́ть.
Smoking is bad for you.

§5. Negative imperatives

Note that imperfective verbs are also used to convey prohibitions in negative imperatives (or negative infinitives), whilst perfective verbs in negative imperatives convey warnings. Contrast, for example, the prohibitions не уходи́те, *don't go away*, and не входи́ть в пальто́, *don't come in with your coat on*, with the warning не упади́те!, *don't fall over!* (See also 43.6 and 7 above on this subject.)

Exercises

A. *Choose the form from the aspectual pair in brackets which is correct in the context:* (1) Я никогда́ не (писа́л/написа́л) в газе́ту, но сейча́с про́сто не могу́ молча́ть. (2) Он до́лго не (отвеча́л/отве́тил) на мой вопро́с. (3) Цивилиза́цию нельзя́ (сменя́ть/смени́ть) так же бы́стро и легко́, как назва́ние Ленингра́да. (4) (Возвраща́ть/Верну́ть) уваже́ние к своему́ госуда́рству нельзя́ обеща́ниями, кля́твами и́ли бронемаши́нами. (5) Я рекоменду́ю всем предпоче́сть меню́ с высо́ким содержа́нием овоще́й и фру́ктов и с минима́льным коли́чеством жиро́в. Не сто́ит та́кже (увлека́ться/увле́чься) спиртны́м. (6) На́ше прави́тельство вме́шивается в те вопро́сы, в кото́рые ни в ко́ем слу́чае не должно́ (вме́шиваться/вмеша́ться). (7) Нельзя́ (говори́ть/сказа́ть), что он трудолюби́в. (8) Нам ну́жно попридержа́ть свой язы́к, не (вступа́ть/вступи́ть) в деба́ты, не (входи́ть/войти́) в конфронта́цию. (9) Она́ не (приходи́ла/пришла́) во́время. (10) Вам не сле́дует сли́шком широко́ (распуска́ть/распусти́ть) свои́ кры́лья, (возбужда́ть/возбуди́ть) оппоне́нтов. (11) Вам сле́дует быть внима́тельным к свои́м пла́нам, це́лям, и не (расска́зывать/рассказа́ть) о них да́же друзья́м. (12) Он мно́го рабо́тал и ему́ нельзя́ бы́ло (уезжа́ть/уе́хать) домо́й в о́тпуск. (13) Мне ка́жется, что про Вели́кую Оте́чественную войну́ ка́ждую неде́лю (пока́зывать/показа́ть) по телеви́дению не на́до. (14) Стара́йтесь не (вступа́ть/вступи́ть) ни в каки́е конфли́кты. (15) Предста́вим, что во вре́мя забасто́вки авиадиспе́тчеров кто-то не (мог/смог) прилете́ть на по́хороны ма́тери и́ли не (привози́л/привёз) во́время ребёнка на лече́ние. (16) Мили́ция сове́тует автомобили́стам не (брать/взять) пассажи́ров. (17) Не сто́ило бы (извеща́ть/извести́ть) об э́том мир. (18) На́ше пра́вило: не (открыва́ть/ откры́ть) дверь незнако́мым лю́дям, не установи́в пре́жде, кто и́менно. (19) (Де́лать/сде́лать) э́того не сто́ит. (20) Не сле́дует (оставля́ть/оста́вить) на виду́ у случа́йных посети́телей це́нные ве́щи, дороги́е карти́ны, шкату́лки...

B. *Translate into Russian:* (1) We waited for a long time but they did not come. (2) This student never got up before eleven o'clock. (3) She advised me not to go out without a hat. (4) You should not get off the bus while it is still going. (5) One cannot swim across the river; it's too dangerous. (6) He persuaded his father to call a doctor. (7) He persuaded his father not to call a doctor. (8) I promise not to be late. (9) One cannot imagine such a terrible disaster. (10) One must not swear at other drivers.

LESSON 55

CONDITIONAL SENTENCES

Conditional sentences in Russian are of two types, depending on whether the speaker means that in certain circumstances (a) something will/will not happen or (b) something might happen. The following two sections outline verbal usage in the protasis (the subordinate clause which contains the condition, usually introduced by е́сли, *if*) and in the apodosis (the main clause, which states the consequence) in both types of conditional sentence.

§1. Real conditional sentences
In conditional sentences of the first type, in which the speaker is saying that given certain conditions a particular consequence definitely did/does/will or did not/does not/will not follow, a verb in the past, present or future tense (depending on the context) is used in each clause. Examples from the press:

> Е́сли на́ши шко́льные уче́бники не отврати́ли [pf. past] нас от Пу́шкина, то как же силён Пу́шкин!
> *If our school textbooks have not put us off Pushkin, then how strong Pushkin is!*
> Е́сли кто-то ду́мает [impf. present], что ры́нок реши́т всё, то э́то оши́бка.
> *If anyone thinks the market will solve everything, then that is a mistake.*
> Е́сли Ю́жная А́фрика потеря́ет [pf. future] свой суверените́т над Уо́лвиш-Бей, она́ потеря́ет [pf. future] контро́ль над са́мым ва́жным по́ртом за́падного побере́жья на ю́ге А́фрики.
> *If South Africa loses its sovereignty over Walvis Bay it will lose control of the most important port on the west coast of southern Africa.*
> Тегера́н бу́дет [future] гото́в помо́чь в освобожде́нии за́падных зало́жников, е́сли США на де́ле отка́жутся [pf. future] от вражде́бных де́йствий в отноше́нии Ира́на.
> *Tehran will be prepared to help with the freeing of western hostages if the USA actually refrains from hostile actions towards Iran.*
> Я счита́ю так: е́сли мы нала́дим [pf. future] ры́нок земли́, то ключ ко всем про́чим пробле́мам бу́дет на́йден.
> *I think this: if we put the land market in order then the key to all other problems will be found.*

It is important to note that a future tense is used in the protasis in Russian (see потеря́ет in the third example above, отка́жутся in the fourth, нала́дим in the last) when the verb denotes an event that has yet to take place. Contrast this usage with the English use of the present tense in such clauses (see also 52.7 above).

§2. Hypothetical conditional sentences

In conditional sentences of the second type, in which the speaker is saying that given certain hypothetical conditions some consequence would/would not follow or would have/would not have followed, both the protasis and the apodosis must have a verb in the conditional mood. This mood is rendered in Russian simply by the appropriate form of the past tense (masculine, feminine, neuter or plural) together with the unchangeable particle бы. Examples from the media:

> Е́сли бы рабо́ты на́чались во́время, то расхо́ды бы́ли бы гора́здо ни́же.
> *If work had begun on time* [but it did not], *then the cost would have been much lower.* (Press)
> Е́сли бы перестро́йка начала́сь сра́зу по́сле войны́, то мы, запу́ганные соотечественники, не́ были бы раски́даны по бе́лу све́ту.
> *If perestroika had begun straight after the war* [but it did not] *then we, intimidated fellow countrymen, would not have been scattered through the wide world.* (Press)
> Всё, о чём вы пи́шете, е́сли бы не происходи́ло у нас на глаза́х, мо́жно бы́ло бы приня́ть за абсу́рд.
> *Everything that you write about, if it were not happening before our very eyes* [but it is], *could be taken to be absurd.* (Press)
> Как бы вы отнесли́сь к тому́, е́сли ваш четырёхле́тний ребёнок вдруг бы пропе́л таку́ю пе́сенку?
> *How would you react if your four-year-old child suddenly sang a song like that?* (Press)
> Е́сли бы экспериме́нт прошёл успе́шно, то учёные смогли́ бы получи́ть све́дения о про́филе ве́рхних слоёв земно́й атмосфе́ры.
> *If the experiment had been successful* [but it was not], *then scientists would have been able to get information about the upper layers of the Earth's atmosphere.* (TV)

Note that conditional sentences of this type may relate to past, present or future time, and only from the context will it be clear which meaning is intended.

Note also the position of the particle бы. In the protasis бы almost always follows е́сли (and it may be contracted to б). In the apodosis бы generally follows the verb in the past tense. However, it may also follow some other word in the clause to which one intends to give emphasis, e.g. я бы э́того не сде́лал, *I would not have done that.* (This example also shows that a protasis may be lacking altogether.)

§3. Use of imperative forms in the protasis

In conditional sentences of the second, hypothetical, type the protasis may also be rendered with the use of a second-person singular imperative in place of éсли + verb in past tense + бы. Example from the press:

> В Ни́не само́й умерла́ худо́жница. Живи́ она́ в други́х усло́виях, отда́й её роди́тели в худо́жественную шко́лу, худо́жник и состоя́лся бы.
> *In Nina herself the artist died. Had she lived in other conditions, had her parents sent her to art school, she would indeed have become an artist.*

§4. Further points relating to both types of conditional sentence

Note also that in both types of conditional sentence:

i. it is essential in Russian to separate the protasis from the apodosis by a comma (see all the examples in §§1-3 above);

ii. the apodosis may be introduced by то (or тогда́), just as the apodosis may be introduced by *then* in English, provided that it follows the protasis and does not precede it (see the majority of the examples in §§1 and 2 above).

§5. Further conditional conjunctions

In addition to е́сли Russian has the following conjunctions which may express condition:

е́сли не	*unless*
е́сли то́лько	*provided that*
при усло́вии, что	*on condition that*
раз	*if*

Examples:

> Я не сдам экза́мен, е́сли не помо́жешь мне.
> *I shan't pass the exam unless you help me.*
> Я опублику́ю статью́, е́сли то́лько вы одо́брите её.
> *I shall publish the article provided that you approve it.*
> Я вам дам мою́ ру́чку при усло́вии, что вы за́втра возврати́те её.
> *I shall give you my pen on condition that you return it tomorrow.*
> Раз вы бу́дете в Москве́, зайди́те к нему́.
> *If you are going to be in Moscow, call in on him.*

Exercises

A. *Translate into English:* (1) Е́сли вы не понима́ете, я вам объясню́. (2) Е́сли за́втра бу́дет хоро́шая пого́да, мы пойдём в зоопа́рк. (3) Мне бы́ло бы ле́гче, е́сли бы я знал, почему́ она́ ушла́. (4) Е́сли ве́чером ты бу́дешь до́ма, я зайду́ к тебе́. (5) Я вы́йду, е́сли ты не переста́нешь крича́ть. (6) Дава́й пойдём в бассе́йн, е́сли у тебя́ бу́дет свобо́дное вре́мя. (7) Е́сли вы до́лго уезжа́ете из до́ма, сле́дует отключи́ть телефо́н. (8) Е́сли бы вы отве́тили на мой вопро́с, я была́ бы о́чень благода́рна. (9) Е́сли ны́нешнее прави́тельство оста́нется у вла́сти, Росси́я ста́нет на грань траге́дии. (10) Е́сли таки́е явле́ния бу́дут распространя́ться, то нас мо́гут ожида́ть ху́дшие времена́. (11) Намно́го бы́ло бы ле́гче, е́сли бы лю́ди помога́ли бли́жнему пережи́ть беду́. (12) Е́сли бы я был трудолюби́вым, то сиде́л бы, как все норма́льные лю́ди, и занима́лся бы одни́м де́лом. (13) В реа́льности, хоти́м мы того́ и́ли нет, есть мужска́я и же́нская роль, и тре́тьей не дано́. Е́сли э́то изме́нится, мы мно́гое потеря́ем. (14) Е́сли ве́рить э́тому фи́льму, то в пе́рвые послевое́нные го́ды де́ти из де́тских домо́в росли́ в бо́лее челове́чной атмосфе́ре, чем сейча́с. (15) Дойди́ войска́ до це́нтра го́рода, то они́ по всей вероя́тности уничто́жили бы не́сколько зда́ний истори́ческого значе́ния.

B. *Translate into Russian:* (1) If she comes home before six o'clock I shall not go out. (2) If I had five pounds I would buy that book. (3) If I were rich I would buy a new car. (4) If I have a lot of money in a year's time I shall buy that house. (5) I would go mad if the children shouted all day long. (6) He would not go away if you asked him to stay. (7) I would not play football if I had a headache. (8) I shall not go to the cinema if you do not come with me. (9) I would not go to the cinema if you wanted to stay at home. (10) Were you to explain it to me slowly then I am sure I would understand.

LESSON 56

THE SUBJUNCTIVE MOOD

§1. Form of the subjunctive

As well as forming the conditional mood, the past tense of the verb + the particle бы renders the subjunctive in Russian. There are no sets of distinctive verbal endings or different subjunctive tenses of the sort found in, for example, French, Italian, Spanish. As in these Western European languages, though, the subjunctive in Russian may be used in concessive clauses and in subordinate clauses after verbs of wishing, ordering, permitting, doubting, and fearing and after various negative antecedents.

§2. Concessive clauses

These are clauses introduced by *whoever, whatever, whichever, however, wherever, whenever*, etc. and they may be translated into Russian by the appropriate pronoun (кто, что, како́й, как, где, куда́, когда́, etc.) in the form required by the context and followed by the particle бы + ни + verb in past tense. Note that as with conditional sentences in which бы is used, so in such concessive clauses too a verb accompanied by this particle may refer to past, present or future actions. Examples from the media:

Кем бы пото́м они́ ни ста́ли, а приви́тое чу́вство красоты́ от них никуда́ не уйдёт.
Whoever they may become later on, the sense of the beautiful which has been inculcated in them will never leave them. (Press)
Я счита́ю, что про́шлое непреме́нно на́до бере́чь, како́е бы плохо́е оно́ ни́ было.
I think the past should definitely be preserved however bad it might have been. (Press)
Всем наро́дам СССР, всем гра́жданам, како́й бы национа́льности они́ ни́ были и где бы они́ ни прожива́ли, гаранти́рованы ра́вные права́ и возмо́жности.
All peoples of the USSR, all citizens, of whatever nationality they may be and wherever they may reside, are guaranteed equal rights and opportunities. (Press)
Где бы мы ни находи́лись, на свои́ слёты собира́емся ежего́дно.
Wherever we are/may be we gather each year for our get-togethers. (Press)
Подо́бные де́йствия недопусти́мы, где бы э́то ни́ было.
Such actions are inadmissible anywhere [lit. *wherever it might be*]. (TV)

Note the expressions как бы то ни́ было, *be that as it may*, and во что бы то ни ста́ло, *at all costs/at any price*.

Note too that concessive clauses may also be translated by the use of the appropriate pronoun + ни + verb in the appropriate tense. Example from the press:

> Что ни говори́те, друзья́, а прия́тно поро́й встре́тить для себя́ неожи́данное там, где, каза́лось бы, никаки́х откры́тий быть не мо́жет.
> *Whatever you say/say what you will, friends, it is nice sometimes to encounter the unexpected in places where it would seem there could be no discoveries.*

It should also be remembered that *whatever, wherever, whenever*, etc. do not invariably introduce concessive clauses. They may merely impart emphasis, as in the question *wherever have you been?*, in which case the emphatic particle же might be used: где же ты был?

§3. Exhortation

The particle бы may also be used, with a verb in the past tense, to express an exhortation or gentle command or the desirability of some action. As in conditional sentences and concessive clauses, the verb in the past tense, accompanied by бы, may refer to past, present or future action. Examples:

> Вы бы помогли́ ему́.
> *You should help him/should have helped him.*
> «Отку́да нам знать, как составля́ется догово́р об аре́нде?» — уста́ло се́рдится...«Вот присла́ли бы нам из Москвы́ образе́ц!»
> *'How are we to know how a rent agreement is drawn up?' he snaps wearily. 'They should have sent us a model from Moscow!'* (Press)
> А пока́ о́чень хоте́лось бы, что́бы у люде́й не исся́кла ве́ра в рефо́рмы.
> *For the time being one really wishes people's faith in the reforms would not dry up.* (Press)

§4. Wishing

After verbs of wishing the subordinate clause should be introduced by что́бы (a coalescence of что + бы) and the verb in the subordinate clause should be in the past tense, e.g. я хочу́, что́бы вы пошли́ туда́ сего́дня, *I want you to go there today.* (Compare French *Je veux que vous y alliez aujourd'hui.*) Examples from the press:

> Я хочу́, что́бы на́ши де́ти и вну́ки, е́сли они́ по кро́ви свое́й ру́сские, зна́ли наш родно́й язы́к.
> *I want our children and grandchildren, if they are of Russian blood, to know our native language.*

Понима́ете, жена́ — о́чень каприз́ная да́ма, и мне не хоте́лось бы, что́бы она́ была́ в ку́рсе на́ших дел.
My wife's a very capricious woman, you understand, and I don't want her to know what we're up to.
Мы бу́дем моли́ться, что́бы э́то вели́кое начина́ние получи́ло дальне́йшее разви́тие.
We shall pray that this great undertaking [perestroika] *may develop further.*

See also the use of что́бы after хоте́лось бы in the last example in §3 above.

§5. Commanding and permitting

After verbs of commanding, permitting, etc. the subjunctive may also be used, e.g.

Он приказа́л, что́бы я вы́шел из ко́мнаты.
He ordered me to leave the room.
Капита́н веле́л, что́бы солда́т застрели́л демонстра́нта.
The captain ordered the soldier to shoot the demonstrator.
Мы сказа́ли, что́бы де́вушка принесла́ хле́б.
We told the waitress to bring some bread.

It is important to note though that subjunctive constructions in such sentences are only alternatives to the use of an object and verb in the infinitive, and indeed the latter, simpler, construction is more common. Thus the English sentences in the examples above might also have been rendered thus: он приказа́л мне вы́йти из ко́мнаты; капита́н веле́л солда́ту застрели́ть демонстра́нта; and мы сказа́ли де́вушке принести́ хлеб respectively.

§6. Doubting

After verbs of doubting, used affirmatively, and after verbs of thinking or declaring, used negatively, a subjunctive may also be used, e.g.

Я сомнева́юсь, что́бы он пришёл.
I doubt whether he would have come/will come.
Я не ве́рил, что́бы он пришёл.
I did not believe he would have come/would come.

When the verbs in the subordinate clause refer to events in the future, though, then the verb may be in the future tense and the clause will be introduced by что. Thus in the above examples the second of the two possible English meanings in each case might have been rendered я сомнева́юсь, что он придёт and я не ве́рил, что он придёт.

§7. Fearing

After verbs of fearing two constructions are possible. They may be followed by (i) a negative subjunctive (i.e. a negative verb in the past tense in a clause introduced by чтóбы or как бы; compare French *je crains qu'il ne vienne*), or (ii) a verb in the future tense in a clause introduced by что, e.g.

> Я боюсь, чтóбы (or как бы) он не пришёл
>
> or
>
> Я боюсь, что он придёт.

Both sentences mean *I am afraid he may come*, though the first construction may imply more doubt as to whether the feared event will take place.

When it is feared that something may not happen, then only the second construction is possible. Thus the sentence *I was afraid he would not come* may only be rendered by я боялся, что он не придёт. A further example from the press:

> Я так боялся, что меня не выберут.
> *I was so afraid that they would not elect me.*

§8. Negative antecedent

The subjunctive must also be used after a negative antecedent which has the effect of making the statement in the subordinate clause contrary to fact, e.g. я не встречáл рýсского человéка, котóрый так хорошó знáл бы английский язык, *I have not met a Russian who knew English so well.* (Compare French *je n'ai rencontré aucun russe qui connaisse si bien l'anglais.*) Example from the press:

> Я не дýмаю, чтóбы ктó-нибудь мог чётко ответить на вопрóс.
> *I don't think that anyone could give a clear answer to the question.*

§9. То, чтóбы

Note also the use of чтóбы after an appropriate form of то in sentences which would be rendered in English by a gerundial form of the verb (i.e. a verb in *-ing*), e.g.

> Все мы заинтересóваны в том, чтóбы принять наилýчшие решéния.
> *We all have an interest in taking the best decisions.* (Press)

Exercises

A. *Translate into English:* (1) Хочу́, чтобы вы бы́ли счастли́вы. (2) Роди́тели хотя́т, чтобы я рабо́тал врачо́м. (3) Дми́трий сказа́л мне, чтобы я купи́л ему́ биле́т. (4) Я хоте́л бы, чтобы прави́тельство не соверша́ло очеви́дных оши́бок. (5) Где бы он ни́ был, у него́ сра́зу же появля́лись друзья́. (6) Мы о́чень хоте́ли, чтобы вы получа́ли газе́ты без переры́ва. Но, увы́! По́чта оказа́лась сильне́е нас. (7) Я э́то переживу́, как бы тру́дно ни́ было. (8) Норве́жские рыбаки́ потре́бовали, чтобы в стране́ была́ со́здана незави́симая слу́жба, кото́рая регуля́рно проверя́ла бы рыболо́вные ба́нки на радиоакти́вность. (9) Хочу́ всю жизнь выпи́сывать ваш журна́л, ско́лько бы он ни сто́ил. (10) Я за то, чтобы телекомпа́нии бы́ли в ка́ждом кру́пном го́роде. (11) Отве́ты на на́ши анке́ты прихо́дят отовсю́ду, из всех сувере́нных госуда́рств, каку́ю бы поли́тику их ли́деры ни проводи́ли. (12) Поуча́ствовала бы в ко́нкурсе «Са́мый смешно́й день в жи́зни». Почему́? Надое́ло говори́ть о це́нах, об очередя́х. (13) Я не хоте́л бы, чтобы моя́ жизнь была́ свя́зана с же́нщиной, кото́рая ниче́м не занима́ется. (14) О́чень хоте́лось бы, чтобы мне написа́л како́й-нибудь весёлый, не злой челове́к. (15) Я бою́сь, что у мое́й до́чки мо́жет разви́ться ко́мплекс неполноце́нности. (16) Дай Бог, чтобы твоя́ жена́ тебя́ люби́ла да́же ни́щим! (17) Нельзя́ допусти́ть, чтобы не́нависть и вражда́ доста́лись в насле́дство на́шим де́тям и вну́кам. (18) Она́ бесконе́чно чи́стит, мо́ет, полиру́ет, гото́вит обе́д из пяти́ блюд и тре́бует, чтобы муж всё э́то оцени́л. (19) Во всех газе́тах призыва́ют чита́телей писа́ть, но с огово́ркой: «Ру́кописи не рецензи́руются и не возвраща́ются». А сде́лать бы наоборо́т. (20) Мы открыва́ем для себя́ но́вые страни́цы второ́й мирово́й войны́, други́ми глаза́ми перечи́тываем ста́рые. Но как бы го́рьки они́ ни́ были, неизме́нно святы́м остаётся в се́рдце и па́мяти День Побе́ды.

B. *Translate into Russian:* (1) People pay attention to him whatever he says. (2) Whatever you might think of him, he is intelligent. (3) Whichever channel you switch on the news is the same. (4) Wherever she sat she found it difficult to see the stage. (5) Whoever you speak to will say the same. (6) Such people are useful wherever they live. (7) Whatever are you doing? (8) I am against capital punishment, however legitimate it might seem in some circumstances. (9) I want you to buy me a new shirt. (10) I do not want her to know what I am doing. (11) He was afraid she would be late. (12) He told me to come in. (13) They should have told us about that. (14) The police require you to fill in a form. (15) I doubt whether she would have believed you. (16) I want my daughter to study music. (17) I am afraid he will not tell me that. (18) Do you want me to buy you a new dictionary? (19) I should like to read your book. (20) The workers demanded that measures be taken to improve safety in the factory.

LESSON 57

FORMATION AND USE OF GERUNDS

§1. Formation of gerunds from imperfective verbs
The imperfective gerund, corresponding to an English gerund in *-ing* (e.g. *starting*), denotes an incomplete action.

The stem from which the imperfective gerund is formed is the same as the stem for the present tense of the verb, and may be found by removing the last two letters from the third-person plural form. To this stem is added -я, e.g.

impf. infin.		3rd pers. pl.	stem	impf. gerund
начина́ть	*to begin*	начина́ют	начина-	начина́я
теря́ть	*to lose*	теря́ют	теря-	теря́я
владе́ть	*to master*	владе́ют	владе-	владе́я
кома́ндовать	*to command*	кома́ндуют	команду-	кома́ндуя
жить	*to live*	живу́т	жив-	живя́
терпе́ть	*to endure*	те́рпят	терп-	те́рпя
приходи́ть	*to arrive*	прихо́дят	приход-	приходя́

§2. Verbs with stem in a sibilant
In the case of verbs whose stem ends in one of the sibilants **ж, ч, ш, щ**, the spelling rule (see 1.4 above) necessitates the use of -а rather than -я as the ending, e.g.

impf. infin.		3rd pers. pl.	stem	impf. gerund
держа́ть	*to hold*	де́ржат	держ-	де́ржа
стуча́ть	*to knock*	стуча́т	стуч-	стуча́
дыша́ть	*to breathe*	ды́шат	дыш-	ды́ша

§3. Verbs in -ава́ть
Verbs ending in -ава́ть and belonging to the type 1b with vowel stems and stressed endings (see 9.2 above) do not form their gerunds from the stem of the 3rd person plural, but reinstate the infinitive stem, e.g.

infin.		impf. gerund
дава́ть	*to give*	дава́я
продава́ть	*to sell*	продава́я
узнава́ть	*to find out*	узнава́я
вставáть	*to get up*	встава́я

§4. Gerund of быть

The gerund of быть is бу́дучи.

§5. Gerund of imperfective reflexive verbs

In reflexive verbs the particle -ся is modified to -сь (as it is after a vowel in the present/future tense of reflexive verbs), e.g.

infin.		impf. gerund
умыва́ться	*to get washed*	умыва́ясь
интересова́ться	*to be interested in*	интересу́ясь
сме́яться	*to laugh*	сме́ясь
боя́ться	*to fear*	боя́сь

§6. Imperfective verbs which do not have a gerund

Note that quite a large number of imperfective verbs are not capable of forming a gerund, or at least their gerund is rarely, if ever, used, e.g.

i. verbs of the conjugation 1b which have infinitives in -зать or -сать but stems in ж or ш respectively, e.g. вяза́ть, *to tie*; ма́зать, *to smear*; писа́ть, *to write*; чеса́ть, *to comb*;

ii. verbs which do not have a vowel in their present-tense stem (most of these belong to the 1b conjugation), such as бить, *to strike*; вить, *to wind*; лить, *to pour*; пить, *to drink*; шить, *to sew*; жать, *to press* and *to reap*; мять, *to crumple*; рвать, *to tear*; ждать, *to wait*; слать, *to send*; тере́ть, *to rub*;

iii. verbs of the conjugation 1b in -чь, e.g. течь, *to flow*; бере́чь, *to guard*; стричь, *to cut* (hair);

iv. verbs of the conjugation 1b which have an infinitive in -нуть, e.g. ги́бнуть, *to perish*; гло́хнуть, *to go deaf*; ки́снуть, *to go sour*; сле́пнуть, *to go blind*, etc.;

v. miscellaneous common verbs, notably бежа́ть, *to run*; гнить, *to rot*; драть, *to tear*; е́хать, *to go* (by transport); звать, *to call*; лезть, *to climb*; петь, *to sing*.

In many cases, however, it is possible to form a gerund from an imperfective verb from the same root which has the same or a related meaning, e.g. причёсывать (instead of чеса́ть), налива́ть (instead of лить), ожида́ть (instead of ждать), посыла́ть (instead of слать), вытира́ть (instead of тере́ть), погиба́ть (instead of ги́бнуть), which all form gerunds in the normal way.

§7. Смотре́ть and хоте́ть

Gerunds cannot be formed from the imperfective verbs смотре́ть, *to look at,* and хоте́ть, *to want*, and gerunds from гляде́ть and жела́ть (гля́дя and жела́я) are used instead. The expressions несмотря́ на + accusative and хотя́, which are of gerundial origin, mean *in spite of* and *although* respectively.

§8. The meaning of the imperfective gerund

The imperfective gerund describes action which is taking place at the same time as the action described by the main verb in the sentence. This action must be incomplete, and it must be simultaneous with the action described by the main verb. Examples:

> Сою́зные войска́ на́чали осторо́жное продвиже́ние к це́нтру, ме́дленно подавля́я очаги́ сопротивле́ния ира́кского гарнизо́на.
> *Allied troops began a careful advance towards the centre, slowly suppressing the centres of resistance of the Iraqi garrison.* (Press)
> Отступа́я, ира́кская а́рмия оста́вила столи́цу без воды́.
> *Retreating, the Iraqi army left the capital without water.* (Press)
> Рабо́тая на фе́рме, я могу́ сказа́ть, что э́то жу́ткий физи́ческий труд, от кото́рого во́ешь по ноча́м.
> *Working on a farm I can say that this is terrible physical labour which makes one howl at night.* (Press)
> Слу́шая ра́дио и чита́я газе́ты, мо́жно узнава́ть, что̀ происхо́дит в ми́ре.
> *One can find out what is happening in the world by listening to the radio and reading the newspapers.*
> Обогрева́я страну́, они́ не чу́вствуют, что страна́ забо́тится о них.
> *Although they heat the country they* [workers in power stations] *don't feel that the country cares about them.* (TV)

Imperfective gerunds are used in the following public notices:

> Уходя́, гаси́те свет.
> *Turn out the light when you leave.*
> Опуска́я письмо́, прове́рьте нали́чие и́ндекса.
> *Check the code when you post your letter.*

Note the following points about the use of imperfective gerunds:

i. the subordinate clause containing the gerund must be separated from the main clause by a comma;

ii. the main verb may be in the past, present or future tense;

iii. imperfective gerunds may translate English expressions such as *by doing* or *although they do* as well as simply *doing* or *while doing*;

iv. the subject of the main verb must be the same as the subject of the gerund. In all the above examples it is the same agent who is carrying out both actions described in the sentence. If the subject of the verb in the subordinate clause is not the same as the subject of the verb in the main clause, then a gerund cannot be used in the subordinate clause. The sentence *While she reads the text I write out the words I don't know*, for example, must be translated thus: Пока́ она́ чита́ет текст, я выпи́сываю незнако́мые слова́.

§9. Set expressions

Many imperfective gerunds have become established in the language as set expressions, e.g.

невзира́я на + acc.	*regardless of*
не поклада́я рук	*indefatigably*
пра́вду говоря́	*to tell the truth*
принима́я во внима́ние	*taking into account*
су́дя по + dat.	*judging by*

Example from the press:

Ра́ньше хорони́ли ма́ло, и су́дя по замшéлым креста́м, до́лго лю́ди жи́ли.
In earlier times there were fewer burials, and judging by the moss-covered crosses [in the graveyards] *people lived for a long time.*

Some gerunds have become established in the language as adverbial expressions, e.g. лёжа, *lying*; мо́лча, *silently*; си́дя, *sitting*; сто́я, *standing*. The stress in these forms is on a different syllable from the syllable on which it falls in the 3rd person plural and on which it would therefore normally fall in the gerund. (Change of stress is a common phenomenon in Russian when a word becomes a different part of speech, e.g. when a gerund becomes an adverb as in the above examples.)

There are a few other adverbial expressions which are also of gerundial origin but which end in -учи or -ючи (the Old Russian gerundial endings), e.g. кра́дучись, *stealthily*; умéючи, *skilfully*; жить припева́ючи, *to live in clover.*

§10. Formation of gerunds from perfective verbs

The perfective gerund, which corresponds to an English expression of the sort *having done*, describes an action which has been completed. The gerund of the majority of perfective verbs is formed by replacing the final -л of the masculine form of the past tense with -в, e.g.

infin.		past tense, masc.	pf. gerund
прочита́ть	*to read*	прочита́л	прочита́в
потеря́ть	*to lose*	потеря́л	потеря́в
покрасне́ть	*to blush*	покрасне́л	покрасне́в
откры́ть	*to open*	откры́л	откры́в
встать	*to get up*	встал	встав
вы́пить	*to drink*	вы́пил	вы́пив
написа́ть	*to write*	написа́л	написа́в
проколо́ть	*to puncture*	проколо́л	проколо́в
потяну́ть	*to pull*	потяну́л	потяну́в
нача́ть	*to begin*	на́чал	нача́в
почи́стить	*to clean*	почи́стил	почи́стив
полете́ть	*to fly*	полете́л	полете́в
постоя́ть	*to stand*	постоя́л	постоя́в
помолча́ть	*to be silent*	помолча́л	помолча́в

The ending -вши is also found, but is archaic.

§11. Perfective gerunds in -ши and -я

Most perfective verbs which do not form their past tense by adding л to the final vowel of the infinitive stem are capable in theory of forming gerunds by adding the suffix -ши to the final consonant of the masculine form of the past tense. Thus дости́гнуть, *to reach, attain*, (past tense, masculine дости́г) would have gerund дости́гши. However, gerunds in -ши are considered archaic, and although they may occasionally be encountered they are not commonly used. They may nowadays be replaced, in some verbs with an irregular past tense, by the normal type of perfective gerund in -в (e.g. привы́кнув, from привы́кнуть, even though the past tense of this verb is привы́к).

The gerund of those perfective verbs of motion of the determinate category which have infinitives in -ти is formed by attaching -я to the stem of the future tense, e.g.

infin.		pf. gerund
войти́	*to enter*	войдя́
привести́	*to bring*	приведя́
вы́везти	*to export*	вы́везя
унести́	*to carry away*	унеся́

Such forms do occur in the modern literary language. Theoretically it is possible to form gerunds of this type from other perfective verbs in -сти (e.g. приобретя́, *having acquired*, from приобрести́) and from some second-conjugation verbs (principally verbs which denote taking up a position; e.g. облокотя́сь, *having propped oneself up on one's elbows*, from облокоти́ться; прислоня́сь, *having leaned*, from прислони́ться) as well, but such forms are rarely used.

§12. Gerunds of perfective reflexive verbs

Reflexive verbs which are perfective form their gerunds by adding the suffix -шись to the final в, e.g.

pf. infin.	past tense, masc.	pf. gerund
верну́ться *to return*	верну́лся	верну́вшись
заинтересова́ться *to get interested in*	заинтересова́лся	заинтересова́вшись

§13. The meaning of the perfective gerund

The perfective gerund describes action which has taken place before the action described by the main verb. The action described by the perfective gerund must be completed. Examples:

Сде́лав свой докла́д, он пото́м отвеча́л на вопро́сы.
Having given his report he then replied to questions. (Press)
Подойдя́ побли́же, те ста́ли разма́хивать бе́лым фла́гом и поднима́ть ру́ки.
Having come a little closer they started waving a white flag and raising their hands. (Press)
Они́ попроси́ли воды́ и, получи́в её, ра́достно ста́ли крича́ть: «Джордж Буш!»
They asked for some water, and having received it, started joyfully shouting 'George Bush!' (Press)
Негра́мотный молодо́й челове́к, просиде́в здесь три-четы́ре го́да, вы́йдет, по-пре́жнему не уме́я чита́ть.
An illiterate young man, having spent three or four years here in prison, will come out as before unable to read. (Press)
Нельзя́ уходи́ть, не заплати́в.
One mustn't go without paying.

Note the following points about the use of perfective gerunds:

i. the subordinate clause containing the gerund must be separated from the main clause by a comma;

ii. the action described by the main verb in the sentence is not necessarily in the past; it may even be in the future. The crucial point is that as a rule it takes place after the action described by the gerund has been completed;

iii. a perfective gerund used in a negative construction may translate an English phrase with the meaning *without having done*;

iv. as with the imperfective gerund, the subject of the main verb must be the same as the subject of the gerund. If the action in the subordinate clause and the action in the main clause are being carried out by different subjects, then a gerund cannot be used.

§14. Set expressions

A few perfective gerunds, particularly gerunds in -я, have become established in the language as set expressions, e.g.

немно́го погодя́	*a little later*
подбоче́нившись	*with hands on one's hips*
сиде́ть сложа́ ру́ки	*to sit around idly* (lit. *with arms folded*)
спустя́ рукава́	*in a slipshod fashion*

Exercises

A. *Give the gerund of the following imperfective verbs:* ввози́ть, иска́ть, конча́ть, наде́яться, объясня́ть, организова́ть, открыва́ть, открыва́ться, переставá́ть, плати́ть, помога́ть, признава́ть, принима́ть, приходи́ть, продава́ть, разгова́ривать, слу́шать, слы́шать, спуска́ть, эксплуати́ровать.

B. *Complete the following sentences using a gerund of the imperfective verb in brackets if it is possible to do so in the context. If an imperfective gerund may not be used then put the verb in the form required by the context.* (1) (Говори́ть) о це́лях своего́ визи́та, Е́льцин вы́делил четы́ре основны́х моме́нта. (2) Мы вновь и вновь просма́тривали видеоза́пись, (сра́внивать) её с информа́цией, полу́ченной в хо́де предыду́щих полётов. (3) Увлека́юсь Львóм Толсты́м. Но (быть) в Москве́, не смогла́ попа́сть в музе́й вели́кого писа́теля — закры́т. (4) Знамени́тые ру́сские мецена́ты приобрета́ли карти́ны, ру́кописи, произведе́ния иску́сства, а зате́м передава́ли свои́ колле́кции музе́ям, (де́лать) их всео́бщим достоя́нием. (5) Жирино́вский объяви́л, что ста́вит це́лью воссозда́ние Росси́и в преде́лах Росси́йской импе́рии, (включа́ть) По́льшу и Финля́ндию. (6) (Начина́ть) со второ́й неде́ли октября́, внима́тельнее отнеси́тесь к своему́ здоро́вью. (7) По́мните, что окружа́ющие лю́ди име́ют пра́во на своё со́бственное мне́ние. (Забыва́ть) об э́том, вы риску́ете быть постоя́нно вовлека́емыми в конфли́кты. (8) Как нахо́дят доро́гу пти́цы, (отправля́ться) в тёплые края́? (Пролета́ть) ты́сячи киломе́тров днём и но́чью, в непого́ду и нена́стье, они́ никогда́ не теря́ют ку́рса. (9) (Испо́льзовать) э́ти сове́ты, вы смо́жете избежа́ть дистре́сса, а зна́чит, стать хозя́ином со́бственной судьбы́. (10) Госуда́рство не позволя́ло мили́ции эффекти́вными спо́собами боро́ться с престу́пностью, (отка́зывать) ей в за́работках, техни́ческих сре́дствах, в автомоби́лях, да́же в бензи́не.

C. *Give the gerund of the following perfective verbs:* вы́полнить, засмея́ться, нали́ть, объедини́ться, объясни́ть, откры́ть, позво́лить, посла́ть, потолсте́ть, придержа́ться, прие́хать, прийти́, приколо́ть, принести́, приня́ть, прода́ть, протяну́ть, сесть, убеди́ться, умы́ть.

D. *Complete the following sentences using a gerund of the perfective verb in brackets if it is possible to do so in the context. If a perfective gerund may not be used then put the verb in the form required by the context.* (1) (Закóнчить) э́тот небольшóй эксперимéнт, мы продóлжили разговóр в лаборатóрии. (2) (Постро́ить) сáмый большóй в странé стадиóн в Лужникáх, Ники́та Хрущёв егó назвáл и́менем Лéнина. (3) Читáтели, вероя́тно, пóмнят весёлую англи́йскую пéсенку о дóме, котóрый (постро́ить) Джек. (4) А какóв Олéг Константи́нович на сáмом дéле? Об э́том вы узнáете, (прочитáть) интервью́, опубликóванное в нáшей газéте. (5) В му́зыке романти́зма, пожáлуй, артисти́ческие кáчества Э.Анжапари́дзе раскрывáются я́рче всегó, и телезри́тели смóгут их оцени́ть, (прослу́шать) в её исполнéнии баллáды Ф.Шопéна. (6) Когдá мы (прощáться) с президéнтом, он попроси́л задержáться. (7) Я вообщé-то никогдá не писáл на телеви́дение, но сегóдня, (уви́деть) вáшу передáчу, прóсто не смог не написáть — так онá меня́ заинтересовáла. (8) Получи́ть каталóг книг вы мóжете, (вы́слать) конвéрт с указáнием тóчного обрáтного áдреса по слéдующему áдресу. (9) (Подня́ться), в состоя́нии шóка Алексáндр Мень напрáвился к своему́ дóму, у порóга котóрого скончáлся от потéри крóви. (10) — Гóсподи, благослови́, — сказáла, (перекрести́ться), однá из монáхинь.

E. *Translate into Russian, using gerunds where possible:* (1) While reading the letter from my brother I thought about my parents. (2) While the teacher was talking the pupils were writing in their exercise-books. (3) While returning from the university I met him in the street. (4) While she was opening the window someone came into the room. (5) Having written the letter I went to the post office. (6) Having had supper she went into the lounge to watch television. (7) Having watched the film I decided to read the book again. (8) On receiving the letter he answered it. (9) If you haven't understood the question you can't answer it. (10) You mustn't leave without saying goodbye. (11) Not knowing my address she can't write to me. (12) While working on his book the writer visited the library every day. (13) Having given me the money she went away. (14) Judging by what I have read in the papers the shop will open tomorrow. (15) Having got dressed he went downstairs. (16) Having become interested in science she started visiting exhibitions. (17) Taking everything into consideration the book is a good one. (18) Having heard the news he immediately turned off the radio. (19) He played football in spite of the fact that he had stomach-ache. (20) They worked tirelessly.

LESSON 58

FORMATION AND USE OF PRESENT AND PAST ACTIVE PARTICIPLES

§1. Formation of present active participles

These participles, which have the meaning *who / which is doing*, describe actions which are incomplete, and they may therefore be formed from imperfective verbs only.

The stem for the present active participle may be found by removing the final -т of the 3rd person plural of the present tense, and to this stem is added the suffix -щий, e.g.

impf. infin.		3rd pers. pl.	pres. act. part.
покупáть	*to buy*	покупáют	покупáющий
мыть	*to wash*	мóют	мóющий
организовáть	*to organise*	организýют	организýющий
вставáть	*to get up*	встаю́т	встаю́щий
пить	*to drink*	пьют	пью́щий
писáть	*to write*	пи́шут	пи́шущий
идти́	*to go*	идýт	идýщий
нести́	*to carry*	несýт	несýщий
красть	*to steal*	крадýт	крадýщий
мести́	*to sweep*	метýт	метýщий
везти́	*to convey*	везýт	везýщий
печь	*to bake*	пекýт	пекýщий
говори́ть	*to speak*	говоря́т	говоря́щий
стоя́ть	*to stand*	стоя́т	стоя́щий
лежáть	*to lie*	лежáт	лежáщий
кончáться	*to finish* (intrans.)	кончáются	кончáющийся
интересовáться	*to be interested in*	интересýются	интересýющийся

§2. Declension and use of present active participles

The active participles decline like adjectives of the type хорóший, óбщий, that is to say they have masculine, feminine and neuter forms, nominative, accusative, genitive, dative, instrumental and prepositional forms, and singular and plural forms.

The reflexive particle always remains -ся in present active participles, even when it is preceded by a vowel, as it is for example in the masculine genitive singular form (интересýющегося), the feminine nominative and accusative singular forms (интересу́ющаяся, интересу́ющуюся respectively), the neuter nominative and accusative singular forms (интересу́ющееся), and the nominative and accusative plural forms (интересу́ющиеся).

The present active participle corresponds exactly to a phrase consisting of кото́рый + present indicative, and should not be used unless it could be replaced by such a phrase. It must agree in gender, case and number with the noun in the main clause which is the subject of the action described by the participle. Examples from the press:

> Докуме́нты, подтвержда́ющие [= кото́рые подтвержда́ют] э́тот факт, бы́ли на́йдены в архи́вах США.
> *Documents confirming this fact were found in US archives.*
> Ма́лая часть от э́тих затра́т могла́ бы реши́ть серьёзные пробле́мы, стоя́щие [=кото́рые стоя́т] пе́ред челове́чеством, осо́бенно пе́ред развива́ющимися стра́нами [= стра́нами, кото́рые развива́ются].
> *A small part of this outlay could solve the serious problems confronting mankind, particularly [those confronting] the developing countries.*
> дире́ктор по иссле́дованиям ча́стной вашингто́нской иссле́довательской организа́ции, занима́ющейся [= кото́рая занима́ется] стра́нами восто́чного бло́ка
> *the research director of a private Washington organisation which studies the countries of the eastern bloc*
> Для нерабо́тающих пенсионе́ров [= пенсионе́ров, кото́рые не рабо́тают], студе́нтов дневны́х отделе́ний, получа́ющих [= кото́рые получа́ют] стипе́ндию, безрабо́тных, живу́щих [= кото́рые живу́т] на посо́бия, же́нщин, находя́щихся [= кото́рые нахо́дятся] в о́тпуске по ухо́ду за детьми́, предусмо́трена компенса́ция в разме́ре 85 [восьми́десяти пяти́] рубле́й в ме́сяц.
> *For pensioners who are not working, students at day release centres who are receiving a grant, unemployed people who are living on benefit, [and] women who are off work looking after children, provision is made for compensation [at the rate] of 85 roubles a month.*

Note the agreement between the participle and the noun to which it refers in each example, and note also that it is necessary to separate the main clause from the subordinate clause containing the participle by a comma.

The active participles, which are of Old Church Slavonic origin, are literary in tone, and are not widely used in conversation, where the relative clause with кото́рый prevails, but they are used very widely indeed in literature of every description.

§3. Present active participles in set expressions

A large number of present active participles, however, have established themselves in the language with adjectival or nominal meaning, and these may be used in conversation as well as in writing, e.g.

блестя́щий	*brilliant*
бу́дущий	*future*
веду́щий	*leading*
выдаю́щийся	*conspicuous, outstanding*
жела́ющий	*person who wants* (to do sthg.)
куря́щий	*smoker*
млекопита́ющее	*mammal*
мо́ющие сре́дства	*detergents*
настоя́щий	*real, present*
начина́ющий	*beginner*
небью́щийся	*unbreakable*
некуря́щий	*non-smoker*
отта́лкивающий	*repellent*
пи́шущая маши́нка	*typewriter*
подходя́щий	*suitable*
потряса́ющий	*staggering, tremendous*
предстоя́щий	*impending*
предыду́щий	*preceding*
пресмыка́ющееся	*reptile*
руководя́щий	*leading, governing*
сле́дующий	*following*
слу́жащий	*white-collar worker*
теку́щий	*current*
трудя́щийся	*(manual) worker*
угрожа́ющий	*threatening, menacing*
успока́ивающее сре́дство	*sedative*
цвету́щий	*flourishing*

Some participles have combined with other words to form new adjectives, e.g.

болеутоля́ющий	*analgesic*
вездесу́щий	*ubiquitous, omnipresent*
всемогу́щий	*omnipotent*
душераздира́ющий	*heart-rending*

§4. Old Russian participial forms in -чий

Alongside the active participles in -щий there also exist some in -чий which are of Old Russian origin and which now have a purely adjectival function. They suggest that the object is characterised by or inclined to some quality or action, e.g.

бродя́чий	*wandering, vagrant*	
жгу́чий	*hot, smarting*	(жгу́чий вопро́с, *burning question*)

колю́чий	*prickly, thorny*	(колю́чая про́волока, *barbed wire*)
лету́чий	*flying, fleeting*	(лету́чая мышь, *bat*)
могу́чий	*mighty, powerful*	
певу́чий	*melodious*	
сидя́чий	*sitting, sedentary*	
стоя́чий	*standing, stagnant*	
ходя́чий	*walking, popular, current*	

Note also горя́чий, *hot*, and горю́чий, *combustible*.

These forms with purely adjectival meaning should not be confused with the active participles from the same verbs (бродя́щий, жгу́щий, etc.).

§5. Formation of past active participles

These participles fulfil a similar function to the present active participles, but they refer to past actions, and since these may be complete or incomplete past active participles may be formed from either perfective or imperfective verbs.

The past active participle is formed where possible by replacing the final -л of the masculine form of the past tense of a verb with the suffix -вший, e.g.

infin.		past tense, masc.	past act. part.
покупа́ть (impf.)	*to buy*	покупа́л	покупа́вший
купи́ть (pf.)	*to buy*	купи́л	купи́вший
мыть (impf.)	*to wash*	мыл	мы́вший
умы́ть (pf.)	*to wash*	умы́л	умы́вший
организова́ть (impf. and pf.)	*to organise*	организова́л	организова́вший
встава́ть (impf.)	*to get up*	встава́л	встава́вший
встать (pf.)	*to get up*	встал	вста́вший
писа́ть (impf.)	*to write*	писа́л	писа́вший
написа́ть (pf.)	*to write*	написа́л	написа́вший
говори́ть (impf.)	*to speak*	говори́л	говори́вший
сказа́ть (pf.)	*to tell*	сказа́л	сказа́вший
стоя́ть (impf.)	*to stand*	стоя́л	стоя́вший
конча́ться (impf.)	*to finish*	конча́лся	конча́вшийся
ко́нчиться (pf.)	*to finish*	ко́нчился	ко́нчившийся

§6. Past active participles of verbs with irregular past tense

Verbs which have a past tense whose masculine form ends in a consonant other than -л form their past active participle by adding the suffix -ший to the final consonant of that form, e.g.

infin.		past tense, masc.	past act. part.
нести́ (impf.)	*to carry*	нёс	нёсший
понести́ (pf.)	*to carry*	понёс	понёсший
везти́ (impf.)	*to convey*	вёз	вёзший
печь (impf.)	*to bake*	пёк	пёкший
умере́ть (pf.)	*to die*	у́мер	у́мерший
дости́гнуть (pf.)	*to attain*	дости́г	дости́гший

Verbs with infinitives in -сти and which have a stem in **д** or **т**, and идти́ and all its derivatives, which have a stem in **д**, retain this consonant, in place of the final -л of the past tense, and then add -ший. In such verbs **ё** changes to **е**, e.g.

infin.		past tense, masc.	past act. part.
вести́ (impf.)	*to lead*	вёл	ве́дший
ввести́ (pf.)	*to introduce*	ввёл	вве́дший
изобрести́ (pf.)	*to invent*	изобрёл	изобре́тший
идти́ (impf.)	*to go*	шёл	ше́дший
пойти́ (pf.)	*to go*	пошёл	поше́дший
прийти́ (pf.)	*to come*	пришёл	прише́дший

However, many past active participles of this sort (e.g. пёкший and изобре́тший in the lists above), though possible theoretically, are unlikely to be encountered in modern Russian.

§7. Declension and use of past active participles

The past active participles decline in exactly the same way as the present active participles, i.e. like adjectives of the type хоро́ший.

As in the present active participles, the reflexive ending -ся never changes, even if it occurs after a vowel as in e.g. the masculine genitive singular form ко́нчившегося.

The past active participles correspond to a phrase of the sort кото́рый + past tense, e.g.

реша́вший	=	кото́рый реша́л
реши́вший	=	кото́рый реши́л
покупа́вший	=	кото́рый покупа́л
купи́вший	=	кото́рый купи́л

Like the present active participles they must agree in gender, case and number with the noun to which they refer, and the subordinate clause in which they occur must be separated from the main clause by a comma. Examples from the press:

Но, к сожале́нию, нет ещё адеква́тной реа́кции на возни́кшую ситуа́цию [= ситуа́цию, кото́рая возни́кла].
But unfortunately there is still not an adequate reaction to the situation which has arisen.
Авто́бус, вёзший [= кото́рый вёз] госте́й на сва́дьбу, упа́л с моста́ че́рез ре́чку. Об э́той траге́дии, случи́вшейся [= кото́рая случи́лась] в Башки́рии, сообща́ет со́бственный корреспонде́нт «Изве́стий» А. Зино́вьев.
A bus which was taking guests to a wedding fell off a bridge over a stream. 'Izvestiya''s own correspondent A.Zinoviev reports on this tragedy, which happened in Bashkiriya.
Знамени́тый «Тита́ник» постро́или на бе́лфастской ве́рфи, счита́вшейся [= кото́рая счита́лась] тогда́ одно́й из лу́чших в ми́ре.
The famous 'Titanic' was built in the Belfast shipyard which was at that time considered one of the best in the world.
Вот и вся исто́рия о ру́сском америка́нце, о челове́ке, верну́вшемся [= кото́рый верну́лся] на ро́дину свои́х пре́дков и заслужи́вшем [= кото́рый заслужи́л] пра́во стать её граждани́ном.
That is the whole story about a Russian American, about a man who returned to the land of his forefathers and who earned the right to become its citizen.

§8. Past active participles in set expressions

Like the present active participles the past active participles have a literary flavour. Some of them too though have become established in the language in an adjectival or nominal meaning, e.g.

бы́вший	*former, ex-*
неуда́вшийся	*unsuccessful, failed*
проше́дший	*past, last* (проше́дшее вре́мя, *past tense*)
сумасше́дший	*mad(man)*

Exercises

A. *Give the present active participle of:* бормота́ть, брать, взлета́ть, волнова́ть, вяза́ть, достига́ть, есть, е́хать, жать (to press), жать (to reap), запира́ть, импорти́ровать, коло́ть, корми́ть, крыть, лгать, лежа́ть, лить, ложи́ться, маха́ть, моло́ть, ненави́деть, пересма́тривать, петь, подпи́сывать, проверя́ть, слабе́ть, снима́ть, спать, устава́ть.

B. *Give the past active participle of:* ждать, закры́ть, занима́ться, лови́ть, оде́ть, отнима́ть, поги́бнуть, пойма́ть, по́льзоваться, поня́ть, привле́чь, провести́, пройти́, проколо́ть, раздева́ться, свя́зывать, сшить, убеди́ть, чеса́ть, эксплуати́ровать.

C. *The following sentences have been taken from the press but have been rewritten with a phrase containing кото́рый + verb in the present or past tense in place of a present or past active participle. Restore the participles in the form in which they would have occurred in the given context.* (1) По́сле ма́ссовых увольне́ний, кото́рые прошли́ во второ́м кварта́ле э́того го́да, а́рмия «ли́шних люде́й» в бы́вшей ГДР соста́вила 1068 миллио́нов челове́к. (2) Полузащи́тник сбо́рной кома́нды ФРГ, Ло́тар Матте́ус, кото́рый выступа́ет за мю́нхенскую «Бава́рию», попа́л под подозре́ние поли́ции как возмо́жный член террористи́ческой организа́ции. (3) В Гре́ции подгото́влен законопрое́кт, кото́рый предусма́тривает национализа́цию 130 ты́сяч гекта́ров земли́, кото́рая принадлежи́т це́ркви. (4) Для пассажи́ров обы́чного («экономи́ческого») кла́сса, кото́рые отправля́ются по са́мым популя́рным авиатра́ссам, наприме́р в Нью-Йо́рк и́ли Сингапу́р, це́ны то́же вы́росли на два́дцать проце́нтов. (5) По разли́чным да́нным, от 50-100 ты́сяч дете́й и подро́стков в во́зрасте 5-17 лет, кото́рые потеря́ли роди́телей и́ли ушли́ из до́ма, бродя́жничают по у́лицам Ме́хико. (6) Фи́рма «Ла́твияс на́фта», кото́рая занима́ется прода́жей нефтепроду́ктов на террито́рии респу́блики, отмени́ла с 1 а́вгуста тало́ны на бензи́н. (7) Раке́та была́ вы́пущена с самолёта-бомбардиро́вщика, кото́рый принадлежи́т ВВС Югосла́вии. (8) Когда́ сня́ты прегра́ды, кото́рые разделя́ли наро́ды, лю́ди пыта́ются лу́чше узна́ть друг дру́га. (9) В Казахста́не состоя́лся пе́рвый междунаро́дный музыка́льный марафо́н «Го́лос А́зии», кото́рый собра́л азиа́тских исполни́телей поп- и рок-му́зыки. (10) Причёску вам сде́лают африка́нские мастера́. В сало́не рабо́тают то́лько нигери́йцы, кото́рые специа́льно прие́хали для э́того в Москву́. (11) Продолжа́ем расска́з об иностра́нных фи́рмах, кото́рые развора́чивают свою́ де́ятельность на ру́сском ры́нке. (12) Сле́довало бы изучи́ть о́пыт други́х стран, пре́жде всего́ восто̀чноевропе́йских, кото́рые то́же страда́ют от уте́чки мозго́в. (13) В переда́че речь пойдёт о де́тях «из проби́рки». В на́шей стране́ ребя́т, кото́рые родили́сь таки́м о́бразом, пока́ совсе́м немно́го — не хвата́ет ну́жных лека́рств, диагности́ческой аппарату́ры. (14) Вы посети́те де́тскую карти́нную галере́ю, кото́рая откры́лась в далёком Владивосто́ке. (15) «Ка́бельное телеви́дение» со́здано Гостелера́дио год наза́д и уже́ изве́стно зри́телям ка́бельных сете́й страны́ свои́ми програ́ммами, кото́рые включа́ют зарубе́жные и оте́чественные фи́льмы, мультфи́льмы, развлека́тельные переда́чи.

D. *Translate into Russian:* (1) This organisation helps people who are looking for work. (2) They are trying to define the causes which make people become criminals. (3) The scientist who discovered that law was a brilliant man. (4) Everyone was talking about the event which took place at the station yesterday. (5) She writes about the problems which have arisen as a result of the reunification of Germany. (6) I am reading a book which deals with the development of the revolutionary movement in Russia. (7) The policeman went up to the lorry that had stopped outside the shop. (8) A lot of people who are interested in photography belong to this club. (9) He works in a factory which is situated in the centre of town. (10) I did not pay any attention to the man who was sitting in the corner.

LESSON 59

FORMATION OF PRESENT AND PAST PASSIVE PARTICIPLES

Russian has both present and past passive participles (e.g. чита́емый and прочи́танный respectively). The present passive participles are relatively infrequently used, although they are becoming increasingly common in contemporary journalism. The past passive participles are very frequently encountered, and their formation and use give greater difficulty.

This lesson deals with the formation of the present passive participles (and with their limited use) and with the formation of the past passive participles. The following lesson deals with the use of the past passive participles and with the various other means of rendering the passive voice in Russian.

§1. Formation of present passive participles

These participles are generally formed from imperfective verbs by adding the ending -ый to the first-person plural form, e.g.

рассма́тривать *to examine*	рассма́триваем	рассма́триваемый *being examined*
организова́ть *to organise*	организу́ем	организу́емый *being organised*
люби́ть *to love*	лю́бим	люби́мый *being loved*

Verbs with an infinitive ending in -ава́ть, though, have present passive participles in -ава́емый, e.g. дава́ть, *to give*, has дава́емый, *being given*.

A few verbs ending in -ём in the 1st person plural have a present passive participle in -о́мый, e.g. вести́, *to lead*, has ведо́мый, *being led*. However, some of the participles of this type that are theoretically possible are in practice most unlikely to be encountered, e.g. несо́мый, *being carried*, from нести́.

Many verbs are not capable of forming a present passive participle, e.g. брать, *to take*; класть, *to put*; петь, *to sing*; писа́ть, *to write*; and the monosyllabic verbs in -ить such as пить, *to drink*.

§2. Use of present passive participles

These participles do have short forms, like the past passive participles, but are hardly ever used predicatively. They are used attributively, in the written language, to describe something that is being done, and like the past passive participles they must agree in gender, case and number with the noun they qualify. Examples from the press:

> ма́ссовая безрабо́тица и порожда́емые е́ю отча́яние и гнев
> *mass unemployment and the despair and anger generated by it*
> Заде́ржаны ли́ца, подозрева́емые в уча́стии в ма́ссовых беспоря́дках.
> *People are being detained who are suspected of participation in mass disturbances.*
> В кри́зисной ситуа́ции, созда́вшейся вокру́г америка́нских зало́жников, уде́рживаемых мусульма́нскими экстреми́стскими группиро́вками в Лива́не, впервы́е появи́лись про́блески наде́жды.
> *For the first time rays of hope have appeared in the critical situation surrounding the American hostages who are being held by Muslim extremist groups in Lebanon.*
> Сего́дня ка́ждый седьмо́й компью́тер, поставля́емый в Росси́ю, произво́дится на предприя́тиях «Ви́про».
> *Today every seventh computer supplied to Russia is produced in a Vipro factory.*

However, the main use of the present passive participles is in expressions in which they have become fixed in the language, e.g.

ископа́емое	*mineral, fossil*
люби́мый	*beloved, favourite*
незабыва́емый	*unforgettable*
незави́симый	*independent*
обвиня́емый	*defendant, the accused*
пуленепробива́емый	*bullet-proof*
рекоменду́емый	*recommended*
сгора́емый	*inflammable, combustible*
уважа́емый	*respected, dear* (as formal term of address in letters)

There are also many negative adjectives in the language, which although derived from perfective verbs are modelled on the imperfective passive participle. These forms signify that something will not be done and correspond to English adjectives prefixed with *in-* / *un-* and ending in *-able* / *-ible*. Examples:

необъясни́мый	*inexplicable*
непобеди́мый	*invincible*
неудержи́мый	*irrepressible*
неутоми́мый	*indefatigable*
неуязви́мый	*invulnerable*

§3. Formation of past passive participles

As a general rule these participles may only be formed from verbs which are:

i. perfective, since they denote actions which have been completed;

ii. transitive (i.e. capable of governing a direct object), e.g. прочита́ть, *to read*; умы́ть, *to wash*, but not встать, *to get up*; постоя́ть, *to stand for a while*. They cannot therefore be formed from reflexive verbs, since in these verbs the reflexive particle -ся itself fulfils the function of a direct object.

There are basically three types of past passive participle in Russian:

i. participles in which the ending -ый is added to the final **т** of the infinitive;

ii. participles in which the ending -нный is added to the final **а** or **я** of the verbal stem, giving a participle in -анный or -янный;

iii. participles in which the ending -енный (or under stress -ённый) is added to a stem ending in a consonant.

These types of past passive participle will be dealt with in order below.

§4. Past passive participles in -тый

The following types of verb form their past passive participle in this way.

i. Verbs derived from a monosyllabic simple verb in -ить, e.g.

pf. infin.		past pass. part.	
разби́ть	*to break, smash*	разби́тый	*broken, smashed*
вы́пить	*to drink*	вы́питый	*drunk*
сшить	*to sew*	сши́тый	*sewn*

ii. Verbs derived from a monosyllabic simple verb in -ыть, e.g.

закры́ть	*to close*	закры́тый	*closed, shut*
умы́ть	*to wash*	умы́тый	*washed*
подры́ть	*to undermine*	подры́тый	*undermined*

But not e.g. завы́ть, *to howl*, because this verb is intransitive and therefore incapable of forming a past passive participle.

iii. Verbs derived from a monosyllabic simple verb in -еть, e.g.

оде́ть	*to dress*	оде́тый	*dressed*
разде́ть	*to undress*	разде́тый	*undressed*
спеть	*to sing*	спе́тый	*sung*

iv. Verbs in -ере́ть, e.g.

запере́ть	*to lock*	за́пертый	*locked*
отпере́ть	*to unlock*	о́тпертый	*unlocked*
стере́ть	*to wipe off*	стёртый	*wiped off, erased*

Note that in these verbs the final -е- of the infinitive form is lost in the participle and that the stress moves one syllable forward in the participle, and that in verbs derived from тере́ть this shift results in the transformation of е to ё.

v. Verbs in -оть, e.g.

проколо́ть	*to puncture*	проко́лотый	*punctured*
смоло́ть	*to grind*	смо́лотый	*ground*

Note that in these verbs too the stress in the participle moves one syllable forward.

vi. Verbs in -уть, e.g.

разду́ть	*to inflate*	разду́тый	*inflated*
протяну́ть	*to stretch*	протя́нутый	*stretched*
упомяну́ть	*to mention*	упомя́нутый	*mentioned*

Note that in these verbs too the stress moves forward one syllable, unless it would fall on the prefix as a consequence of such a shift.

vii. Verbs in -ать and -ять which in their indicative forms have a stem in м- or н- (see 10.6 and 11.3 and 11.5 above), e.g.

взять	(1st pers. sing. возьму́)	*to take*	взя́тый	*taken*
нача́ть	(1st pers. sing. начну́)	*to begin*	на́чатый	*begun*
приня́ть	(1st pers. sing. приму́)	*to receive*	при́нятый	*received*

Note that in these verbs too the stress moves one syllable forward, and may fall on the prefix.

§5. Past passive participles in -анный and -янный

The vast majority of verbs with an infinitive in -ать or -ять belong in this category, no matter what stem they have in the indicative. Thus:

прочита́ть	*to read*	прочи́танный	*read*
взволнова́ть	*to agitate*	взволно́ванный	*agitated*
написа́ть	*to write*	напи́санный	*written*
связа́ть	*to connect*	свя́занный	*connected*
вспаха́ть	*to plough*	вспа́ханный	*ploughed*

отыска́ть	*to track down*	оты́сканный	*tracked down*
прода́ть	*to sell*	про́данный	*sold*
задержа́ть	*to delay, detain*	заде́ржанный	*delayed, detained*
потеря́ть	*to lose*	поте́рянный	*lost*

Note that with these verbs too the stress moves one syllable forward unless it would fall on the prefix as a consequence of such a shift (though in compounds of дать it does fall on the prefix, e.g. про́данный from прода́ть).

§6. Past passive participles in -енный and (under stress) -ённый
This category includes many 1b verbs with consonant stems and all second-conjugation verbs with a consonant stem other than those in -ать.

1b verbs in -чь (see 11.13-14) which have two stems in their present/future tense (a velar in the 1st person singular and 3rd person plural, and a sibilant in the remaining persons) have a stem in the sibilant in the past passive participle.

It is important to note that the participles in this category embody any of the irregularities (epenthetic -л- or consonant change) which affect the 1st person singular of the indicative of second-conjugation verbs (see 12.6-8).

The stress in participles of this category generally falls on the same syllable as in the 2nd person singular of the indicative. In other words those verbs in this category which have stress on the stem in the 2nd person singular have a participle in -енный, while those which have stress on the ending in the 2nd person singular have a participle in -ённый. Thus:

infin.	1st pers. sing.	2nd pers. sing.	past pass. part.
ввести́ *to introduce*	введу́	введёшь	введённый *introduced*
принести́ *to bring*	принесу́	принесёшь	принесённый *brought*
смести́ *to sweep off*	смету́	сметёшь	сметённый *swept off*
ввезти́ *to import*	ввезу́	ввезёшь	ввезённый *imported*
заже́чь *to set light to*	зажгу́	зажжёшь	зажжённый *set alight*
испе́чь *to bake*	испеку́	испечёшь	испечённый *baked*
реши́ть *to decide*	решу́	реши́шь	решённый *decided*
заморо́зить *to freeze*	заморо́жу	заморо́зишь	заморо́женный *frozen*

укра́сить *to adorn*	укра́шу	укра́сишь	укра́шенный *adorned*
встре́тить *to meet*	встре́чу	встре́тишь	встре́ченный *met*
почи́стить *to clean*	почи́щу	почи́стишь	почи́щенный *cleaned*
просвети́ть *to enlighten*	просвещу́	просвети́шь	просвещённый *enlightened*
поста́вить *to put*	поста́влю	поста́вишь	поста́вленный *placed*
покорми́ть *to feed*	покормлю́	поко́рмишь	поко́рмленный *fed*
купи́ть *to buy*	куплю́	ку́пишь	ку́пленный *bought*

Perfective verbs ending in -дить which have an imperfective in -ждать (e.g. освободи́ть, imperfective освобожда́ть) have the consonant combination -жд- in their past passive participle, even though this combination is not present in the 1st person singular of the perfective:

освободи́ть *to free*	освобожу́	освободи́шь	освобождённый *freed*

A few 1b verbs have a past passive participle in unstressed -енный even though they have a stressed ending in the 2nd person singular, e.g.

найти́ *to find*	найду́	найдёшь	на́йденный *found*
укра́сть *to steal*	украду́	украдёшь	укра́денный *stolen*

Note also the forms уви́денный from уви́деть, *to see*, and съе́денный from съесть, *to eat up*.

§7. Adjectives in -еный and -ёный

There are a number of words which are in origin past passive participles, but which are formed from simple imperfective verbs, have only one -н- in their ending, and have an adjectival use. Most of these words are culinary terms. Examples:

варёный	*boiled*
жа́реный	*roast, fried, grilled*
золочёный	*gilded*
копчёный	*smoked*
па́реный	*steamed*
печёный	*baked*
рифлёный	*corrugated*

ру́бленый	*minced*
солёный	*salted*
сушёный	*dried*
тушёный	*braised*
учёный	*learned person, scientist, scholar*

Note also the past passive participle ра́неный, *wounded*, which may also be used as a noun with the meaning *a casualty*, and which is from the biaspectual verb ра́нить.

Past passive participles of the normal type may exist alongside the forms given above, e.g. сва́ренный, *boiled*, from свари́ть, *to boil*, посо́ленный, *salted*, from посоли́ть, *to salt*.

§8. Words of participial origin

Many words used as adjectives or nouns are past passive participles in origin, e.g.

да́нные	*data*
изби́тый	*hackneyed*
ограни́ченный	*limited*
определённый	*definite*
рассе́янный	*distracted*

Exercise

Give the past passive participle of the following verbs: воплоти́ть (impf. воплоща́ть), вы́брать, вы́везти, вы́двинуть, заказа́ть, заня́ть, извле́чь, изуми́ть, испо́ртить, наня́ть, напра́вить, обогати́ть (impf. обогаща́ть), обра́довать, око́нчить, останови́ть, отрази́ть, переоде́ть, перечи́слить, погуби́ть, подави́ть, поня́ть, порва́ть, предста́вить, прекрати́ть (impf. прекраща́ть), пригото́вить, призна́ть, провести́, протере́ть, расколо́ть, сбить, скрыть, слить, смыть, убеди́ть (impf. убежда́ть), удиви́ть.

LESSON 60

USE OF PAST PASSIVE PARTICIPLES AND OTHER RENDERINGS OF THE PASSIVE

§1. Use of long forms of past passive participles

These participles, which correspond to English participles of the type *read, written, washed*, etc., decline in exactly the same way as adjectives of the type но́вый, and if used in the long form must agree in gender, case and number, as adjectives do, with the noun they qualify. The clause in which they occur corresponds exactly to a clause with кото́рый and must be marked off from the main clause by commas. Examples:

Письмо́, напи́санное ва́шим отцо́м, лежи́т на столе́.
The letter written by your father is on the table.
Я чита́ю кни́гу, напи́санную ва́шим отцо́м.
I am reading the book written by your father.
В э́том магази́не не совсе́м обы́чный для Ве́нгрии подбо́р това́ров: овсяны́е хло́пья, фрукто́вые и овощны́е со́ки, дже́мы, пригото́вленные без примене́ния консерва́нтов и иску́сственных краси́телей.
In this shop there is a selection of goods [that is] not very usual for Hungary: oat flakes, fruit and vegetable juices, jams made without the use of preservatives or artificial colouring. (Press)
В А́нглии существу́ют да́же прию́ты для ко́шек, лишённых хозя́йской любви́ и ла́ски.
In England there are even homes for cats deprived of an owner's love and affection [lit. *caress*]. (Press)

§2. Formation and use of short past passive participles

The past passive participles also have four indeclinable short forms (masculine, feminine, neuter, and plural), as do most adjectives, e.g.

long form of past pass. part.	masc. short form	fem. short form	neut. short form	pl. short form
откры́тый	откры́т	откры́та	откры́то	откры́ты
прочи́танный	прочи́тан	прочи́тана	прочи́тано	прочи́таны
поте́рянный	поте́рян	поте́ряна	поте́ряно	поте́ряны
поста́вленный	поста́влен	поста́влена	поста́влено	поста́влены
принесённый	принесён	принесена́	принесено́	принесены́
решённый	решён	решена́	решено́	решены́

Note that in all past passive participles in -нный only one -н- survives in the short form, and that the short forms of participles in -ённый are always stressed on the ending, with the result that in the feminine, neuter and plural short forms ё has been transformed to е.

The short form of the past passive participle cannot be used unless the participle is used predicatively (i.e. unless some part of the verb *to be* comes between the noun and the participle qualifying it). However, if the participle is used predicatively then it must be in the short form. Compare, for example, the following sentences:

> Магнитофо́ны, сде́ланные в Япо́нии, дёшевы.
> *Tape-recorders made in Japan are cheap.*
>
> Те магнитофо́ны бы́ли сде́ланы в Япо́нии.
> *Those tape-recorders were made in Japan.*

In the first sentence the long form of the participle must be used, because the participle is used attributively (i.e. in an adjectival phrase describing the tape-recorders). In the second sentence, on the other hand, the participle is used predicatively (i.e. part of the verb *to be* separates the noun *tape-recorders* from the participle *made*), and the short form must therefore be used.

Note that the verb *to be* is not necessarily stated in the Russian (e.g. магази́н откры́т, *the shop is open*, where the verb *to be* is understood).

Further examples:

> Президе́нт США Дж. Буш в телеобраще́нии к стране́ заяви́л о том, что Куве́йт освобождён.
> *The President of the USA, George Bush, announced in a television address to the country that Kuwait had been liberated.* (Press)
> Зда́ние опеча́тано.
> *Building sealed.* (Public notice)
> Тепе́рь и в Душанбе́ введена́ тало́нная систе́ма.
> *A system of rationing has now been introduced in Dushanbe as well.* (Press)
> Посо́л был ра́нен в но́гу.
> *The ambassador was wounded in the leg.* (TV)
> До́ма телефо́н давно́ был отключён.
> *The telephone at home had been cut off long ago.* (Press)
> Кровь была́ пролита́.
> *Blood was shed.* (TV)
> Бы́ли обсуждены́ после́дние серьёзные собы́тия в стране́.
> *The latest serious events in the country were discussed.* (TV)
> Дома́ здесь бы́ли постро́ены на́спех сра́зу по́сле войны́.
> *The houses here were built hastily immediately after the war.* (Press)

§3. Avoidance of passive: use of active voice

Although passive participles are widely used in speech, they belong first and foremost to the written language. In speech their use may often be avoided by turning the sentence round in order to make possible the use of a verb in the active voice. Thus in the third example in §2 above one might just as well have said в Душанбе́ ввели́ тало́нную систе́му, *they have introduced rationing in Dushanbe*. In the fifth example one might likewise say давно́ отключи́ли телефо́н, *they cut off the telephone long ago*. Indeed in speech these active constructions, being easier to use, are more common than the passive constructions widely found in the press.

The same tendency to avoid the passive is found in English; compare for example the passive construction *our telephone has been cut off* with the active construction *they've cut off our telephone*. In both Russian and English the active variant involves the use of an unspecified *they* as the subject of the verb. (French and German achieve the same result with the third-person singular pronouns *on* and *man* respectively.) Note though that in Russian the pronoun они́ is not included in such constructions.

Further examples:

> Постро́или но́вое кино́ в це́нтре го́рода.
> *They've built a new cinema in the town centre/A new cinema has been built in the town centre.*
> Закры́ли доро́гу.
> *They've closed the road/The road has been closed.*
> Отложи́ли конфере́нцию.
> *They've postponed the conference/The conference has been postponed.*
> Отвезли́ его́ в больни́цу.
> *They've taken him to hospital/He's been taken to hospital.*

In many passive sentences, of course, the agent is named, e.g. э́та кни́га была́ напи́сана Достое́вским, *this book was written by Dostoevsky*. Such sentences too may be rendered with an active verb instead of a passive participle, e.g. э́ту кни́гу писа́л Достое́вский (on use of the imperfective here, see 53.4 above). Note, though, that Russian generally preserves the word order of the passive construction, with the named agent following the verb. Further examples:

> Э́тот зако́н ввели́ консерва́торы.
> *This law was introduced by the Conservatives.*
> Аме́рику откры́л Колу́мб.
> *America was discovered by Columbus.*
> Его́ уби́ли партиза́ны.
> *He was killed by guerrillas.*
> Её арестова́ла мили́ция.
> *She was arrested by the police.*

The Russian case system usually precludes any possible confusion as a result of the inverted word order in such constructions.

§4. Use of reflexive verbs in passive sense

A passive construction in English is very commonly rendered by a reflexive verb in Russian. This is particularly the case if the verb that is to be used is imperfective and if the subject is inanimate. Such constructions may be couched in past, present and future tenses. Examples from the press:

> Заво́д во Флори́де стро́ится совме́стно сове́тским и америка́нским предприя́тиями.
> *A factory in Florida is being built jointly by Soviet and American enterprises.*
> Зна́ние и уме́ние — э́то то́же това́р, кото́рый покупа́ется и продаётся.
> *Knowledge and skill is also a commodity that is bought and sold.*
> Хлорфторуглеро́ды испо́льзуются и на ли́ниях по изготовле́нию компью́теров.
> *CFCs are used on computer production lines as well.*
> На го́рных доро́гах устана́вливаются экологи́ческие патру́ли.
> *On the mountain roads ecological patrols are being set up.*
> Ры́ночные отноше́ния бу́дут стро́иться в на́шей стране́ (и в Москве́ то́же) ещё до́лгие, до́лгие го́ды.
> *Market relations will be built in our country (and in Moscow too) over many long years to come.*

§5. Impersonal constructions describing natural phenomena

Finally it is worth mentioning a curious Russian construction which is used when the effects of some natural force (e.g. snow, water, wind) are being described and which may generally be rendered in English by means of a passive construction. Take for example the statement доро́гу занесло́ сне́гом, which may be translated *the road is snowed up* or *the road is blocked with snow.* Literally the Russian is saying *it* [i.e. some impersonal phenomenon, some force of nature] *has blocked the road with snow.*

This construction is analogous to the active construction involving the use of a third-person plural verb form (e.g. *they have cut off the telephone*) illustrated in §3 above, the only differences being that the subject is now some force of nature and that the instrument used by that force (e.g. snow) has to be specified. Further examples, from Pulkina (see p.ix):

> Водо́й зали́ло луга́.
> *The meadows were flooded with water.*
> Ве́тром сорва́ло кры́шу.
> *The roof was torn off by the wind.*

Exercises

A. *Complete the following sentences by inserting a past passive participle of the verb or verbs in brackets in the form required by the context.* (1) Э́та инициати́ва прави́тельства была́ (поддержа́ть) во мно́гих райо́нах страны́. (2) Преступле́ние бы́ло (соверши́ть) во вто́рник ве́чером, за дво́е су́ток до того́, как труп был (обнару́жить). (3) В результа́те перестре́лки че́тверо престу́пников бы́ли (уби́ть) и тро́е (арестова́ть). (4) Це́рковь (отдели́ть) у нас от госуда́рства. (5) В тот ве́чер был оди́н из пра́здников — годовщи́на подписа́ния ми́рного догово́ра, (заключи́ть) в пе́рвую мирову́ю войну́. (6) Была́ (реконструи́ровать) дрена́жная систе́ма анса́мбля, (очи́стить) водосто́чные коло́дцы. (7) В тот день дом был (запо́лнить) до преде́ла. (8) В Моско́вском информацио́нном це́нтре на Смоле́нском бульва́ре прошла́ вы́ставка персона́льных компью́теров, (предста́вить) америка́нскими и япо́нскими фи́рмами. (9) В 1908 году́ начала́сь реставра́ция монасты́рских фре́сок, одна́ко не была́ (зако́нчить) из-за вспы́хнувшей в 1914 году́ войны́. (10) В реда́кции накопи́лось мно́го пи́сем с вопро́сами, (адресова́ть) люби́мому певцу́. (11) Монасты́рь был (основа́ть) в 1398 году́. (12) В на́шей стране́ уже́ (опубликова́ть) произведе́ния Га́лича, Бро́дского, Аксёнова, Войно́вича и други́х. (13) Худо́жественный теа́тр, (основа́ть) Станисла́вским и Немиро́вичем-Да́нченко, получи́л неожи́данно для них сами́х и́мя Го́рького. (14) Сгуща́ется полити́ческая и вое́нная обстано́вка в райо́не Перси́дского зали́ва, (вы́звать) агре́ссией Ира́ка про́тив сувере́нного Куве́йта. (15) Шло постепе́нное разруше́ние э́той жемчу́жины ру́сского зо́дчества. Огра́да во мно́гих места́х была́ (проби́ть) и (разру́шить), кры́ша (сорва́ть), око́нные стёкла (вы́бить).

B. *Translate into Russian:* (1) The resolution was accepted. (2) St Petersburg was founded by Peter the Great. (3) The impression made by this event was profound. (4) The measures taken by the government were useless. (5) The plan presented at the meeting is a good one. (6) The idea developed in this article is banal. (7) The flowers picked last week have already faded. (8) The documents signed by the minister were sent to the embassy. (9) Her face, reflected in the mirror, turned pale. (10) The car stolen on Wednesday was found on Saturday. (11) His name was among those listed in the newspaper. (12) The sum spent on education in 1973 was much greater. (13) A new member of parliament was elected. (14) In the course of the first five-year plan many new factories were built. (15) These questions are going to be discussed constantly. (16) He knew where the keys were kept. (17) This novel was written by Lermontov. (18) She was respected by everybody. (19) He was killed by guerrillas. (20) This decision was taken by the prime minister. (21) She was arrested yesterday. (22) I was blown off the roof by a strong wind. (23) The library is closed. (24) The door is locked. (25) The book was published yesterday.

LESSON 61

TRANSLATION OF THE VERB *TO BE*

Translation of the verb *to be* into Russian gives rise to some difficulty. Indeed the frequency of the use of the verb in English is one of the chief obstacles among advanced students to the writing of idiomatic Russian. This lesson examines the very numerous verbs to which Russian resorts in sentences in which an English-speaker might comfortably use some part of the verb *to be*. However, this list does not exhaust the subject, for there are many contexts in which a concept that could be formulated in English with the help of the verb *to be* would be expressed in Russian in quite a different way.

§1. Быть

The verb быть has no present tense in modern Russian, although it does have future forms (бу́ду, бу́дешь, бу́дет, бу́дем, бу́дете, бу́дут), past forms (был, была́, бы́ло, бы́ли), imperative forms (будь and бу́дьте), a gerund (бу́дучи), and active participles (бу́дущий and бы́вший).

There are two remnants in the modern language of the present tense which this verb once had, namely есть (the old third-person singular form; cf. English *is*, French *est*, German *ist*, Italian *è*, Spanish *es*), and суть (the old third-person plural form; cf. French *sont*, German *sind*, Italian *sono*, Spanish *son*). In the modern language есть means *there is, there are,* but it may still be used in the sense of *is* in a very restricted way (see §13 below). As a verbal form суть may still be found in definitions in a scientific style; more commonly though суть is a feminine noun meaning *essence, gist,* and it occurs in the phrase суть де́ла, *the heart of the matter.*

The verb быть is used very much less frequently than the verb *to be* in English, and in idiomatic Russian many other verbs will be used in its place where English would use some form of the verb *to be*. In the sections which follow the Russian alternatives and their precise individual meanings are given.

It should however be emphasised that there do remain many contexts in which it is correct to use быть, and there follow a few examples of its contemporary use (or of its omission, indicated by a dash, if the present tense is understood) in the press:

Его́ вес — о́коло четырёх килогра́ммов.
His [a baby's] *weight is about four kilogrammes.*

Террито́рия Ли́хтенштейна — 157 [сто пятьдеся́т семь] квадра́тных киломе́тров.
The territory of Liechtenstein is 157 square kilometres.
Сейча́с преде́льно разрешённая ско́рость движе́ния по шоссе́ — 130 [сто три́дцать] киломе́тров в час, по автодоро́ге — 90 [девяно́сто].
At present the maximum permitted speed for traffic is 130 kilometres an hour on the motorway and 90 on the main road.
Э́то была́ бы лока́льная война́ с глоба́льными после́дствиями.
This would be a local war with global consequences.
Пози́ции в э́тих вопро́сах должны́ быть я́сными и твёрдыми.
One's positions in these matters must be clear and firm.

Note that in all the above examples the verb *to be* has the function of introducing a simple definition of the subject.

Note also that when some form of быть does actually appear in the Russian its complement, if it is a noun, will in the modern language almost always be in the instrumental case, except in constructions with э́то (see 27.5).

§2. Быва́ть

When the verb *to be* in English has habitual or frequentative meaning then быва́ть may be used in Russian. This verb does have a present tense, and it belongs to conjugation 1a. Examples from the press:

Все мужчи́ны о́строва отправля́ются на рабо́ту в Сингапу́р и́ли Мала́йзию, и быва́ют до́ма лишь на крупне́йшие мусульма́нские пра́здники.
All the men on the island set off to work in Singapore or Malaysia and are at home only for the main Muslim holidays.
Нача́льник тюрьмы́ ча́сто у него́ быва́л.
The prison governor often came to see him.
Быва́ют ситуа́ции, когда́ дарёному коню́ необходи́мо загляну́ть в зу́бы.
There are situations in which it is essential to look a gift horse in the mouth.

§3. Явля́ться/яви́ться and представля́ть собо́й

These verbs may be used as substitutes for быть. Both may be used when the complement defines the subject, as will be seen in the examples below, and both are literary rather than colloquial.

With явля́ться/яви́ться one noun must be in the nominative case and the other must be in the instrumental case. It is the noun denoting the broader of the two concepts that should be put in the instrumental case, while the noun denoting the more specific concept, the precise thing on which the speaker wishes to concentrate, will be in the nominative. Or to put it another way, the noun in the instrumental tells us what sort of thing the specific noun in the nominative is. Thus in the statement са́мой оригина́льной ча́стью кни́ги явля́ется пе́рвая глава́ (*the most original part of the book is the first chapter*), the *first chapter* is the specific thing on which the sentence focuses, while the phrase *the most original part* tells us what sort of thing that chapter is.

It follows from what has been said that such relatively vague words as исто́чник, *source*; перспекти́ва, *prospect*; попы́тка, *attempt*; причи́на, *reason, cause*; пробле́ма, *problem*; результа́т, *result*; сле́дствие, *consequence*; часть, *part*, will often be found in the instrumental case when явля́ться/яви́ться is used.

As far as word order is concerned, in practice the noun in the nominative will often come at the end of its clause in Russian, because the word at the end of a clause will carry special weight, and it will be on precisely this word that the speaker wishes to concentrate attention. Note though that the choice as to which noun should be put in which case does not actually hinge on word order.

Examples from the media:

> Э́тот инциде́нт не явля́ется ава́рией.
> *This* [nuclear] *incident is not an accident.* (TV)
> Основны́ми исто́чниками облуче́ния персона́ла на я́дерных реа́кторах явля́ются проду́кты корро́зии металли́ческих пове́рхностей труб.
> *The products of the corrosion of the metallic surfaces of the pipes are the fundamental sources of irradiation of personnel at nuclear reactors.* (Press)
> Наси́лие пра́вого то́лка про́тив госуда́рства явля́ется реа́льной перспекти́вой.
> *Right-wing force against the state is a real possibility.* (Press)
> Кусо́чки берли́нской стены́ продаю́тся упако́ванными в паке́ты, в коро́бках, с сертифика́тами, подтвержда́ющими, что они́ действи́тельно явля́ются ча́стью той са́мой берли́нской стены́.
> *Little pieces of the Berlin Wall are being sold in packets and in boxes, with certificates confirming that they are indeed a part of that very Berlin Wall.* (Press)
> Состоя́вшиеся в Дама́ске перегово́ры яви́лись очередно́й попы́ткой найти́ «ара́бское реше́ние» конфли́кта в Зали́ве.
> *The talks which took place in Damascus were the latest attempt to find an 'Arab solution' to the Gulf conflict.* (Press)

With представля́ть собо́й, which is much less common than явля́ться, the complement will be in the accusative case. Examples from the press:

> Э́ти материа́лы, кото́рые стано́вятся радиоакти́вными во вре́мя рабо́ты реа́ктора, представля́ют собо́й обы́чные при́меси в леги́рующих элеме́нтах ста́ли.

These materials, which become radioactive while the reactor is in operation, are the usual admixtures in the alloying elements of steel.

Поня́ть Минздра́в мо́жно, когда́ он тре́бует элемента́рных све́дений о препара́те: что он собо́й представля́ет, как и когда́ его́ принима́ть.

One can understand the Ministry of Health when it requires elementary information about a [medicinal] preparation: what it is, how and when it should be taken. (Press)

§4. Стать

This perfective verb is sometimes used as an apparent synonym for яви́ться. Examples from the press:

Причи́ной катастро́фы ста́ли техни́ческие непола́дки.

Technical malfunctions were the cause of the disaster.

Закры́тие ба́зы ста́ло одно́й из составны́х часте́й програ́ммы по сокраще́нию ассигнова́ний на оборо́ну.

The closure of the base was one of the components of a programme of defence cuts.

Провозглаше́ние стра́нами За́пада програ́ммы оказа́ния по́мощи Росси́и на о́бщую су́мму 24 миллиа́рда до́лларов ста́ло серьёзным подкрепле́нием для Е́льцина.

The announcement by Western countries of a 24-billion dollar aid programme to Russia has greatly strengthened Yeltsin's position [lit. *was a serious reinforcement for Yeltsin*].

§5. Заключа́ться and состоя́ть

When *to be* means *to consist in* then one of the verbs заключа́ться or состоя́ть may be used. In this meaning these verbs will be followed by в + prepositional case. Examples from the press:

Одна́ из гла́вных причи́н недово́льства лицеи́стов заключа́ется в том, что они́ обеспоко́ены свои́м бу́дущим.

One of the main causes of the lycée pupils' discontent is that they are worried about their future.

Пока́ ещё не я́сно, в чём бу́дет заключа́ться возмо́жная по́мощь Ира́на в урегули́ровании конфли́кта.

It is not yet clear what Iran's possible help in resolving the conflict will be.

Преиму́щество хлорфторуглеро́дов пе́ред други́ми вещества́ми состои́т в том, что они́ не горю́чи, не токси́чны и нейтра́льны.

The advantage of CFCs over other substances is that they are not inflammable, not toxic, and neutral.

Отве́т состои́т в том, что́бы держа́ть войска́ в гото́вности.

The answer is to keep troops in readiness.

§6. Составля́ть/соста́вить

When the verbs *to constitute* or *to amount to* can be used in place of *to be* then the verb составля́ть/соста́вить may be used in Russian. It is followed by the accusative case and is particularly common in statistical contexts. Examples from the press:

Конфли́кты косну́лись тех райо́нов, где лю́ди не́которых национа́льностей составля́ют меньшинство́.
The conflicts have touched regions where people of certain nationalities are a minority.
В сле́дующие 15 [пятна́дцать] лет америка́нские инвести́ции соста́вят 5-10 [пять-де́сять] миллиа́рдов до́лларов.
Over the next 15 years American investment [in the Soviet economy] *will be 5-10 billion dollars.*
Температу́ра реа́ктора к моме́нту ги́бели подло́дки составля́ла о́коло 70 [семи́десяти] гра́дусов.
The temperature of the reactor at the moment the submarine was destroyed was about 70 degrees.

This verb is particularly common in the phrases составля́ть/соста́вить часть, *to be a part of*, and составля́ть/соста́вить исключе́ние, *to be an exception*, e.g.

Уо́лвиш-Бей составля́ет часть Ю́жной А́фрики.
Walvis Bay is part of South Africa. (Press)

§7. Находи́ться

When the verb *to be* in English describes the position or location of places, people or things, then находи́ться (perfective form not applicable in this sense) should be used in Russian. Examples from the media:

Но ведь и никако́й америка́нский штат не нахо́дится так бли́зко к на́шим грани́цам, как Аля́ска.
But no American state is so close to our borders as Alaska. (Press)
Президе́нт находи́лся в Крыму́ на о́тдыхе.
The president was on holiday in the Crimea. (TV)
На его́ борту́ нахо́дится груз шри-ланки́йского ча́я.
On board [a ship] *is a cargo of Sri-Lankan tea.* (Press)

Находи́ться may also translate some part of the verb *to be* when state or condition is being described. Examples from the press:

Тепе́рь ба́за нахо́дится под контро́лем гре́ческих ВМС [вое́нно-морски́х сил].
The base is now under the control of the Greek navy.
Вновь вы́делился в ряда́х белоголубы́х И́горь Доброво́льский, находя́щийся сейча́с в хоро́шей фо́рме.

Igor Dobrovolsky, who is currently in good form, again stood out in the ranks of the blue-and-whites [a football team].
Радиоаппарату́ра находи́лась в отли́чном состоя́нии.
The radio equipment was in excellent condition.

The past passive participle располо́жен (fem. располо́жена, neut. располо́жено, pl. располо́жены) may also be used if geographical situation is being described, e.g.

Тру́дно найти́ хоть одного́ мужчи́ну в деревня́х индонези́йского о́строва Бавеа́н, кото́рый располо́жен в 120 [ста двадцати́] киломе́трах к се́веру от Я́вы.
It is hard to find a single man in the villages of the Indonesian island of Bawean, which is situated 120 kilometres north of Java. (Press)

§8. Стоя́ть, лежа́ть, сиде́ть
When the verb *to be* means *to be standing, to be lying,* or *to be sitting,* then стоя́ть, лежа́ть, сиде́ть respectively should be used, e.g.

Буты́лка стои́т на столе́.
The bottle is on the table.
Кни́га лежи́т на столе́.
The book is on the table.
Ко́шка сиди́т на полу́.
The cat is on the floor.

Note that лежа́ть is used of people being in hospital. Thus: он лежи́т в больни́це, *he is in hospital.*

Note also that сиде́ть is used of people or animals being in a place of confinement. Thus уби́йца сиди́т в тюрьме́, *the murderer is in prison,* and лев сиди́т в клётке, *the lion is in a cage.* Note also the expression сиде́ть до́ма, *to stay at home.*

§9. Прису́тствовать
When *to be* means *to be present* then прису́тствовать should be used, e.g.

Он прису́тствовал на заседа́нии.
He was at the meeting.

§10. Рабо́тать, служи́ть
When *to be* means *to work as, serve as/in,* then рабо́тать or служи́ть may be used, after both of which the noun denoting position will be in the instrumental case, e.g.

Потóм в Калифóрнии семь лет он рабóтает лётчиком-испытáтелем.
Then for seven years he was a test pilot in California. (Press)
Он слýжит в áрмии.
He is in the army.

§11. Стóить

When *to be* means *to be worth, to cost*, then стóить should be used, e.g.

Э́та кни́га стóит дéсять рублéй.
This book is ten roubles.

§12. Приходи́ться

When *to be* means *to fall on* (of dates) or to stand in a certain relationship to (of kinship), then приходи́ться (the perfective is inapplicable in this sense) should be used, e.g.

В э́том годý Пáсха прихóдится на пя́тое апрéля.
This year Easter is on 5 April.
Он мне прихóдится племя́нником.
He is my nephew.

§13. Есть

When the subject and complement are the same then *is* may be rendered by есть. Examples from the press:

В ти́трах мнóжество имён, и кто есть кто — покá неясно.
There is a multitude of names in the titles, and it is not clear so far who is who.
Скóлько десятилéтий кря́ду мы тверди́м вослéд Ки́плингу: Зáпад есть Зáпад, а Востóк есть Востóк.
How many decades in succession have we been repeating after Kipling that East is East and West is West.

§14. Существовáть

Note also the use of the verb существовáть, *to exist.* Examples from the press:

В любóй странé существýет раздéльное разви́тие нарóдов.
In any country there is a separate development of peoples [from article about apartheid].
В услóвиях повы́шенной концентрáции воéнной си́лы, крáйней неприя́зни и подозри́тельности конфликтýющих сторóн существýет как бы риск самовозгорáния.

In conditions where military forces are highly concentrated and the sides in conflict are in a state of extreme hostility and suspicion there is potentially a risk of self-combustion.

§15. Имéться

When *to be* means *to be available*, or when *there is* refers to the availability of some facility, then имéться should be used, e.g.

В гóроде имéется кинó.
There is a cinema in the town.
По имéющимся дáнным...
According to such information as there is... (Press)

§16. Состоя́ться

This verb means *to take place*, and may on occasion be used to translate *there was/there will be*, e.g.

В пресс-цéнтре МИД состоя́лась пресс-конферéнция.
There was a press conference in the press centre of the Ministry of Foreign Affairs. (Press)

Note that состоя́ться is a perfective verb and therefore refers to past or future events. This verb should not be confused with the non-reflexive состоя́ть, which is dealt with in §5 above.

§17. Use of *to be* for emphasis

In English statements of the sort *it is in the country that he feels happiest, it was then that he understood what had happened, it was in Paris that he met her,* the function of the verb *to be* is merely to lend emphasis to the word that follows.

This construction should be rendered in Russian not by some verb corresponding to the English verb *to be* but by the use of word order which draws attention to the word it is wished to emphasise, so that the Russian has one clause fewer than the English. Thus the last example in the previous paragraph might be rendered я её в Пари́же встрéтил, or в Пари́же я её встрéтил.

Exercises

A. *Insert in the space provided in the following sentences the verb which you consider most appropriate from among those examined in the lesson above. In some sentences there is more than one correct choice. Put any words in brackets in the case dictated by your choice of verb.* (1) Эпицéнтр землетрясéния ... в 600 километрах на юго-востóк от Тегера́на. (2) (Отсу́тствие) питьево́й воды́ ... сего́дня (причи́на) восьми́десяти проце́нтов всех боле́зней. (3) Мать ... (сто́рож) в моско́вском кинотеа́тре. (4) Ча́стный се́ктор колхо́за приноси́л хозя́йству свы́ше десяти́ проце́нтов от о́бщей при́были, кото́рая ... 19 миллио́нов рубле́й. (5) На борту́ самолёта ... офице́ры прави́тельственной а́рмии, афга́нские бе́женцы, верну́вшиеся из Ира́на, и други́е пассажи́ры. (6) Что́бы никого́ не оби́деть, не бу́дем называ́ть фами́лий уча́стников. Кто ... (кто), вы са́ми уви́дите. (7) ... ли бог? (8) Го́род ... на берегу́ реки́. (9) Ложь ... (ложь). (10) Хотя́ о́бщая су́мма америка́нских ассигнова́ний на разве́дывательную де́ятельность де́ржится в секре́те, как ста́ло изве́стно из не́которых исто́чников, она́ ... о́коло тридцати́ миллиа́рдов до́лларов. (11) (Существова́ние) тако́й систе́мы се́льского хозя́йства ... (исто́чник) кру́пных социа́льно-экономи́ческих пробле́м. (12) Лю́ди везде́ хотя́т ... (лю́ди). (13) В э́том го́роде ... оди́н из после́дних музе́ев, име́ющих отноше́ние к и́мени Ста́лина. (14) Э́та кни́га ... в библиоте́ке. (15) О́бщий годово́й дохо́д семьи́ — 100.000 рубле́й. (Основна́я до́ля) в нём ... (зарпла́та) Влади́мира Алексе́евича. (16) (Еди́нственные конкуренто-спосо́бные това́ры, произведённые) на́шей страно́й, ... не (телеви́зоры) и (видеомагнитофо́ны), а (автома́ты) и (та́нки). (17) Сре́дняя производи́тельность труда́ рабо́чего в Белару́си ... всего́ 41 проце́нт от производи́тельности труда́ неме́цкого рабо́чего. (18) Еле́на ча́сто по служе́бным дела́м ... в Москве́. (19) Пробле́ма ... (то), что ещё поднима́ется инфля́ция. (20) Она́ ... по ше́ю в воде́.

B. *Translate into Russian:* (1) The main difficulty is lack of funds. (2) Politicians are part of a closed system. (3) This enormous project is a reworking of pages from another book. (4) Examples of other sources of his art are paintings and postcards. (5) Oil is the main subject on the agenda. (6) He is in my view the best writer of his generation. (7) The ostrich is a bird. (8) He is the French ambassador in Washington. (9) A mistake is a mistake. (10) It was then that I understood he was mad. (11) The patient's weight is seventy kilogrammes. (12) The population of London is over ten million. (13) The monument is near the station. (14) How many passengers were on board the plane? (15) The talks are an attempt to find a peaceful solution to the problem.

LESSON 62

ADVERBS AND ADVERBIAL PHRASES

Adverbs are words which modify the meaning of verbs, adjectives or other adverbs, e.g. *he is speaking* ***quietly****; a* ***slightly*** *sad expression; she was walking* ***quite quickly****.*

While most adverbs in Russian are formed from adjectives by means of one of the suffixes -о, -е, or -и, there are also many which are made up in some other way.

§1. Adverbs in -о

Adverbs of this type are formed from adjectives with a hard stem and from present and past passive participles or adjectives derived from them, e.g.

adj.	adv.	
бы́стрый	бы́стро	*quickly*
гро́мкий	гро́мко	*loudly*
прия́тный	прия́тно	*pleasantly*
стро́гий	стро́го	*strictly*
ти́хий	ти́хо	*quietly*
неизмери́мый	неизмери́мо	*immeasurably*
взволно́ванный	взволно́ванно	*agitatedly*
неожи́данный	неожи́данно	*unexpectedly*

Some adjectives with a stem in a sibilant also have adverbs in -о́, but this ending must be stressed in accordance with the spelling rule in 1.5 above, e.g. горячо́, *hotly.*

Note that in some adverbs end stress results in the change of ё into е, e.g.

тёмный	темно́	*darkly*
тёплый	тепло́	*warmly*

§2. Adverbs in -е

Adverbs of this type are formed from most adjectives with a soft stem (-ний) and from adjectives derived from present active participles in -щий, e.g.

adj.	adv.	
кра́йний	кра́йне	*extremely*
блестя́щий	блестя́ще	*brilliantly*

Note though that some adjectives in -ний have adverbs in -o, e.g.

adj.	adv.	
да́вний	давно́	*a long time ago*
по́здний	по́здно	*late*
ра́нний	ра́но	*early*

The adjective и́скренний, *sincere*, may have either и́скренне or и́скренно.

§3. Adverbs in -и

Adverbs of this type are formed from adjectives in -ский and -ско́й, and from the few adjectives in -цкий, e.g.

adj.	adv.	
дру́жеский	дру́жески	*amicably*
мастерско́й	мастерски́	*in a masterly way*
молоде́цкий	молоде́цки	*spiritedly*

§4. Adverbs of the type по-ру́сски

Adverbs of manner are also formed with по and the suffix -и from adjectives ending in -ский and -цкий, e.g.

по-де́тски	*like a child*
по-дру́жески	*in a friendly way*
по-дура́цки	*like a fool*

When formed from adjectives denoting nationality adverbs of this type may indicate use of a given language, e.g.

(говори́ть)	по-англи́йски	*(to speak)*	*English*
	по-ара́бски		*Arabic*
	по-испа́нски		*Spanish*
	по-италья́нски		*Italian*
	по-кита́йски		*Chinese*
	по-неме́цки		*German*
	по-ру́сски		*Russian*
	по-туре́цки		*Turkish*
	по-францу́зски		*French*
	по-япо́нски		*Japanese*

Note though that whereas adverbs of this type are used after говори́ть, *to speak*; понима́ть, *to understand*; and писа́ть, *to write*, after знать, *to know;* изуча́ть, *to study*; and преподава́ть, *to teach*, on the other hand, accusative phrases (англи́йский язы́к, ара́бский язы́к, etc.) are used.

Adverbs of manner are formed in a similar way, by means of the preposition по and the suffix -и, from soft adjectives in -ий (see 29.1 above), e.g.

по-во́лчьи	*like a wolf*
по-коша́чьи	*like a cat*
по-челове́чьи	*like a human being*

§5. Adverbs derived from preposition + short adjective

In Old Russian short adjectives, as well as long adjectives, had case endings. Remnants of the declension of short adjectives are seen in many modern Russian adverbs which consist of a preposition and a short masculine or neuter adjective in an appropriate case, e.g. издалека́, *from afar*, which consists of the preposition из + a genitive short form of the adjective далёкий.

Several prepositions and cases are represented among such adverbs, particularly на and за + accusative, до, из, с + genitive, по + dative, and в and на + prepositional. In some instances such adverbs are invariably or commonly combined with a particular verb. Examples:

надо́лго	*for a long time*
нале́во	*to the left*
напра́во	*to the right*
задо́лго	*long (before)*
за́живо погребённый	*buried alive*
за́ново	*anew*
раскалённый добела́	*white-hot*
" докрасна́	*red-hot*
и́здавна	*for a long time*
и́зредка	*now and then*
сле́ва	*on the left*
слегка́	*slightly*
смо́лоду	*in one's youth*
сно́ва	*again*
спра́ва	*on the right*
понемно́гу	*little by little*
вполне́	*fully, entirely*
путеше́ствовать налегке́	*to travel light*
наравне́ с + instr.	*on a level with*

§6. Adverbs derived from preposition + long adjective

A few compound adverbs consist of a preposition and an adjective in the long form in an appropriate case. Thus in a few adverbs в is combined with a feminine accusative singular form, e.g. яйцо́ вкруту́ю, *hard-boiled egg*. However, the most numerous adverbs in this category are adverbs of manner which consist of по and a neuter dative singular form of the long adjective. Note that these adverbs are hyphenated. Examples:

по-другóму	*in a different way*
одéтый по-зи́мнему	*dressed in winter clothes*
одéтый по-лéтнему	*dressed in summer clothes*
по-нóвому	*in a new fashion*
по-прéжнему	*as before*
по-своéму	*in one's own way*
по-стáрому	*as of old*

This category of adverb includes the expressions по-мóему, по-твóему, по-нáшему, по-вáшему (*in my/your/our/your opinion*).

§7. Adverbs derived from preposition + noun

There are also many compound adverbs which consist of a preposition and a noun in an appropriate case. The prepositions most commonly found in such combinations are в and на + accusative, but за and под + accusative, до, из, от, с + genitive, к and по + dative, за + instrumental, and в and на + prepositional, among others, are also found. In some instances the preposition remains separate from the noun and thus forms an adverbial phrase. Many of these adverbs are commonly found in combination with a particular verb or noun. Examples:

вверх	*upwards*
вниз	*downwards*
внутрь	*inwards*
вперёд	*forwards*
засти́гнуть врасплóх	*to catch unawares*
вслух	*aloud*
навéрх	*upstairs* (motion)
навы́ворот	*inside out, the wrong way round*
навы́нос	*for consumption off the premises*
вы́вернуть наизнáнку	*to turn inside out*
наконéц	*finally*
наоборóт	*on the contrary*
на рéдкость	*uncommonly*
натощáк	*on an empty stomach*
за грани́цу	*abroad* (motion)
вы́йти зáмуж	*to get married* (of woman)
подря́д	*running, in a row*
без огля́дки	*without looking back, carelessly*
говори́ть без ýмолку	*to talk incessantly*
дóнизу	*to the bottom*
и́здали	*from afar*
óтроду	*from birth*
сначáла	*at first*
срáзу	*at once*
кстáти	*by the way, incidentally*
раздели́ть пополáм	*to divide in half*

за́мужем	*married* (of a woman)
за грани́цей	*abroad* (location)
вме́сте	*together*
внача́ле	*at first, in the beginning*
внизу́	*below, downstairs*
внутри́	*inside* (location)
впереди́	*in front*
впосле́дствии	*subsequently*
наверху́	*above, upstairs*
на днях	*the other day, any day now*
накану́не	*on the eve*

Some of the expressions in the list above may serve not only as adverbs but also as prepositions e.g. внутрь, внутри́, впереди́, all of which take a genitive case (see 22.3 and 22.11 above).

§8. Adverbial expressions in the instrumental case

Some nouns used in the instrumental case, without any preposition, serve as adverbs of manner or time, e.g. шёпотом, *in a whisper*; весно́й, *in spring* (see 26.3-4 above). In some instances the noun from which the adverb is originally derived is no longer used in its own right in the modern language, as is the case with пешко́м, *on foot*.

§9. Adverbs derived from numerals

Some adverbial expressions are derived from numerals, e.g. впервы́е, *for the first time*; одна́жды, *once*.

Note also the forms вдво́е, *double*, *twice as much*; втро́е, *three times*, etc.; and the forms вдвоём, *two together*, *as a pair*; втроём, *three together*, etc.

§10. Some common adverbs

There follows a list of other common adverbs of time, place and quantity or degree which have not been dealt with elsewhere.

i. Adverbs of time:

вдруг	*suddenly*
во́время	*in time*
всегда́	*always*
вчера́	*yesterday*
до́лго	*a long time*
ежедне́вно	*daily*
ежего́дно	*annually*
за́втра	*tomorrow*
иногда́	*sometimes*

ны́не	*nowadays*
позавчера́	*the day before yesterday*
по́сле	*afterwards*
послеза́втра	*the day after tomorrow*
пре́жде	*before*
ра́ньше	*earlier*
сего́дня	*today*
сейча́с	*now*
тепе́рь	*now*
тогда́	*then, at that time*
уже́	*already*

ii. Adverbs of place:

везде́	*everywhere*
всю́ду	*everywhere*
далеко́	*far off*
до́ма	*at home*
здесь	*here*
отсю́да	*from here, hence*
отту́да	*from there, thence*
сюда́	*here* (expressing motion), *hither*
там	*there*
туда́	*there* (expressing motion), *thither*
тут	*here*

iii. Adverbs of quantity or degree:

весьма́	*very, highly*
во́все не	*not at all*
дово́льно	*fairly, rather, quite*
доста́точно	*enough*
едва́	*hardly, barely, scarcely*
е́ле	*barely, only just*
лишь	*only*
о́чень	*very*
почти́	*almost*
ро́вно	*exactly, precisely*
сли́шком	*too (much)*
соверше́нно	*absolutely, completely*
совсе́м	*quite, entirely, altogether*
то́лько	*only*

Exercises

A. *Give the adverb derived from the following adjectives or participles:* гру́стный, зве́рский, изли́шний, истери́ческий, кре́пкий, ло́вкий, ме́дленный, мя́гкий, не́жный, незави́симый, плохо́й, прекра́сный, ре́дкий, свобо́дный, споко́йный, траги́ческий, угрожа́ющий, хи́трый, че́стный, шу́мный.

B. *Complete the following sentences by providing the appropriate adverb or phrase. Note the position of the adverbs in the Russian sentences.* (1) Она́ (brilliantly) зна́ет ру́сский язы́к. (2) Он говори́т (Arabic). (3) (In my opinion) вы пра́вы. (4) Я пое́хал (abroad). (5) Мы пи́шем (Chinese). (6) Она́ пошла́ (upstairs). (7) Мы (early) встаём. (8) Они́ (late) ложа́тся спать. (9) Он говори́т (Japanese). (10) Они́ живу́т (abroad). (11) Мы (for a long time) зна́ем друг дру́га. (12) Он говори́л (in a whisper). (13) Почему́ ты чита́ешь (aloud)? (14) Заключённые счита́ли, что они́ бы́ли (alive) погребены́. (15) Пойдём (together). (16) Там мо́жно покупа́ть пи́во (to take away). (17) (Finally) маши́на останови́лась. (18) Я сове́тую тебе́ не пить во́дку (on an empty stomach). (19) Я ви́дел его́ (the other day). (20) Они́ раздели́ли торт (in half). (21) (Suddenly) разда́лся крик. (22) Э́то (extremely) неудо́бно. (23) Она́ (in a masterly way) вы́полнила свои́ обя́занности. (24) Хо́лодно на у́лице. Одева́йтесь (in winter clothes). (25) Блаже́н, кто (in his youth) был мо́лод. (26) Мы заживём (like human beings), полу́чим свобо́ду вы́бора рабо́ты, учёбы, ме́ста жи́тельства, судьбы́! (27) Да́же пограни́чники, с кото́рыми я встре́тился в междунаро́дном аэропорту́ «Шереме́тьево», вели́ себя́ (in a different way). (28) Мне о́чень прия́тно, что в Росси́и (as before) все зна́ют и лю́бят Ле́рмонтова. (29) Премьер-мини́стр (as before) наме́рен продолжа́ть ли́нию своего́ прави́тельства в сфе́ре оборо́ны. (30) Всё остаётся (as of old).

LESSON 63

COORDINATING CONJUNCTIONS AND TRANSLATION OF *ALSO*

§1. Types of conjunction

Conjunctions may be divided into two broad types: coordinating conjunctions and subordinating conjunctions. Coordinating conjunctions (e.g. *and*, *but*) link two similar parts of a sentence or parts of a compound sentence, e.g. *He went out and ran to the bus stop*. Subordinating conjunctions (e.g. *because*) link a subordinate clause to a main clause and define the relationship between the two, e.g. *He ran to the bus stop because he was late*.

Coordinating conjunctions may be connective (e.g. *and*), adversative (e.g. *but*), or disjunctive (e.g. *or*). These will be dealt with in this lesson. Subordinating conjunctions may be causal (e.g. *because*), temporal (e.g. *when*), purposive (e.g. *in order that*), resultative (e.g. *so that*), concessive (e.g. *although*), comparative (e.g. *as though*), or conditional (e.g. *if*). Conditional subordinating conjunctions have been dealt with in 55 above. The most common subordinating conjunctions of the remaining types are dealt with in the following lesson.

§2. Connective coordinating conjunctions

и	*and*
а	*and*
не то́лько...но и	*not only...but also*
как...так и	*as well as*

Examples:

война́ и мир
war and peace
Вот ваш па́спорт, а вот ва́ша ви́за.
Here's your passport, and here's your visa.
Он купи́л не то́лько но́вый телеви́зор, но и холоди́льник.
He bought not only a new television but also a refrigerator.
Как консерва́торы, так и лейбори́сты одобря́ют э́ти ме́ры.
Labour Party members as well as Conservatives approve of these measures.

On further uses of и see §6 below.

§3. Adversative coordinating conjunctions

а	*but*
но	*but*
всё же	*nevertheless, all the same*
одна́ко	*however*

Examples:

Пора́ уходи́ть, а я не хочу́.
It's time to go, but I don't want to.
Я согла́сен с ва́ми, но что нам де́лать?
I agree with you, but what are we to do?
Маши́на была́ ему́ не по карма́ну, но он всё же купи́л её.
He couldn't afford the car, but he bought it all the same.
Он всё объясни́л; одна́ко я не по́нял.
He explained everything; however, I didn't understand.

Although in many contexts either а or но may be used, а is required in the following circumstances.

i. After a negative when there is strong adversative meaning (i.e. not *this* but *that*), or in other words when two things are mutually exclusive, e.g.

   Она́ не до́ма, а на рабо́те.
   She is not at home but at work.
   Э́то произведе́ние не о́пера, а бале́т.
   This work is not an opera but a ballet.

ii. Before the pronoun сам when the actions of two subjects are being contrasted, e.g.

   Все други́е пассажи́ры вы́шли, а я сам оста́лся в ваго́не.
   All the other passengers got out, but I myself remained in the carriage.

Note also the expression а вдруг, which means *suppose, what if,* e.g.

А вдруг авто́бус не придёт?
Suppose the bus doesn't come?
А вдруг она́ под сле́дствием?
Suppose she is under surveillance? (Press)

§4. Disjunctive coordinating conjunctions

и́ли	*or*
ли́бо	*or*
то...то	*now...now*

Examples:

> Я приду́ за́втра и́ли послеза́втра.
> *I shall come tomorrow or the day after tomorrow.*
> То снег идёт, то дождь.
> *Now it's snowing, now it's raining.*

The conjunction ли́бо is synonymous with и́ли, but is less frequently used.

§5. Translation of *also*

The use of та́кже and то́же, which are not always interchangeable, gives some difficulty (to Russians as well as foreigners). Whereas та́кже may be used in most circumstances, the range of meaning of то́же is more limited. In brief, то́же may be used if an additional subject is performing the same action (e.g. *I am going to the cinema; he is also going to the cinema*). Та́кже must be used, on the other hand, if a single subject is performing an additional action (e.g. *I am going to the cinema and I am also calling on my parents*), or performing an action that affects an additional object (e.g. *I am going to the cinema and I am also going to the theatre*).

The following article from the press reminds native speakers of this distinction.

> Предста́вьте себе́, что ваш друг собира́ется в кино́ и спра́шивает вас, не хоти́те ли вы пойти́ вме́сте с ним. Вы счита́ете, что э́то хоро́шая иде́я, и говори́те ему́: «Я то́же пойду́». И вы идёте в кино́. А по доро́ге ваш друг расска́зывает вам, что он уже́ сего́дня побыва́л в музе́е и на вы́ставке. Он говори́т так: «Я уже́ сего́дня был в музе́е и то́же на вы́ставке».
>
> Стоп! Мы с ва́ми два ра́за встре́тили сло́во «то́же», кото́рое бли́зко по значе́нию к сло́ву «и». Но пра́вильно ли мы употреби́ли э́то сло́во в обо́их слу́чаях?
>
> Ока́зывается, нет. И здесь есть ра́зница. В пе́рвом приме́ре ваш това́рищ и вы (два субъе́кта) идёте в кино́ (ва́ше де́йствие напра́влено на оди́н объе́кт: кино́). В э́том слу́чае употребле́ние сло́ва «то́же» пра́вильно: ваш това́рищ и вы то́же идёте в кино́ (в литерату́ре как сино́ним мо́жет выступа́ть сло́во «та́кже»).
>
> Во второ́м слу́чае де́йствие ва́шего това́рища (оди́н субъе́кт) бы́ло напра́влено на два объе́кта (музе́й и вы́ставка). Ме́жду слова́ми «музе́й» и «вы́ставка» сло́во «то́же» употребля́ться не мо́жет. Здесь необходи́мо испо́льзовать сло́во «та́кже», кото́рое ча́сто употребля́ется вме́сте со сло́вом «а»: «а та́кже». Ваш това́рищ до́лжен был сказа́ть: «Я уже́ сего́дня был в музе́е, а та́кже на вы́ставке».
>
> Ита́к, отноше́ния ме́жду двумя́ субъе́ктами, де́йствие кото́рых напра́влено на оди́н объе́кт, соединя́ем сло́вом «то́же», а отноше́ния ме́жду двумя́ объе́ктами — сочета́нием «а та́кже».

Imagine that your friend is planning to go to the cinema and asks you whether you want to go with him. You think this is a good idea and you say to him, 'I'll come too [тóже]'. And you go to the cinema. But on the way your friend tells you that he has already been to the museum and to an exhibition today. He says, 'I have already been to the museum today and to an exhibition too [тóже]'.

Stop! We have twice met the word 'too' [тóже] which is close in meaning to the word 'also' [и]. But have we used this word correctly in both cases?

As it happens, no. There is a difference here. In the first example your friend and you (two subjects) are going to the cinema (your action is directed at one object, the cinema). In this case the use of the word 'тóже' is correct: your friend and you 'тóже' are going to the cinema (in literature the word 'тáкже' may be used as a synonym).

In the second case the action of your friend (one subject) was directed at two objects (the museum and the exhibition). The word 'тóже' cannot be used between the words 'museum' and 'exhibition'. Here one must use the word 'тáкже', which is often used together with the word 'a': 'a тáкже'. Your friend should have said, 'I have already been to the museum and also [a тáкже] the exhibition today'.

So, relations between two subjects whose action is directed at one object we link with the word 'тóже', whereas relations between two objects we link with the combination 'a тáкже'.

§6. Use of и in the sense of *also, too, as well, either*

In many cases the conjunction и is used in the sense of *also, too, as well.* The following examples from the press make this usage clear:

Коротковóлновые потóки сóлнечной радиáции вы́зовут рáзного рóда мутáции у живóтных и растéний, приведýт к увеличéнию рáковых заболевáний. Произойдýт и глобáльные изменéния клúмата.
Short-wave streams of solar radiation will cause various mutations in animals and plants and will lead to an increase in cancerous illnesses. Global changes of climate will also occur.

Тревóгу по пóводу сохранéния живóй прирóды на Британских островáх бьют и рядовы́е консервáторы.
Rank-and-file Conservatives too are sounding the alarm about nature conservation in the British Isles.

Недáвно над Антаркти́дой обнарýжена дырá размéром почти́ в дéсять миллиóнов квадрáтных километров. Наблюдáется уменьшéние озóнового слóя и над мнóгими гýсто населёнными райóнами планéты.
A hole almost ten million square kilometres in size was recently discovered over the Antarctic. The reduction of the ozone layer is being observed over many densely populated regions of the planet as well.

In clauses with a negative verb и may have the meaning *either*, e.g.

> М. Тэ́тчер, пра́вда, не объясни́ла, почему́ у́ровень инфля́ции подня́лся сейча́с до 5,9 [пяти́ це́лых и девяти́ деся́тых] проце́нта. В её ре́чи о побе́дах то́ри не нашла́ ме́ста и пробле́ма безрабо́тицы.
> *M[argaret] Thatcher, it is true, did not explain why the level of inflation has now risen to 5.9 per cent. In her speech about the Tories' triumphs the problem of unemployment did not find a place either.* (Press)

Exercise

Supply the correct word or words (та́кже, а та́кже, то́же) to complete the following sentences or passages: (1) Жена́ лю́бит му́зыку. Я ... люблю́ му́зыку. (2) Он подари́л мне кни́ги, ... самова́р. (3) Я интересу́юсь литерату́рой, ... теа́тром. (4) Ка́ждый уро́к на пять мину́т прерыва́ется му́зыкой — вре́мя физкульту́ры и эмоциона́льной разря́дки для дете́й. И для учи́теля ... (5) Росси́я ока́жет по́мощь Таджикиста́ну в формирова́нии национа́льных вооружённых сил. Росси́я и Таджикиста́н ... подписа́ли соглаше́ние, согла́сно кото́рому одна́ росси́йская диви́зия оста́нется на террито́рии Таджикиста́на. (6) Я до сих пор по́мню, как оте́ц с ма́терью сказа́ли нам, де́тям: «Людьми́ бу́дьте! Сде́лает вам челове́к зло, а вы добро́м отвеча́йте. Он поймёт и тогда́ ... добро́м отве́тит.» (7) Руководи́тели сосе́дних с Кита́ем стран никогда́ не забыва́ют о территориа́льных тре́бованиях Кита́я, ... о том, что он ощуща́ет себя́ вели́кой держа́вой, име́ющей пра́во на влия́ние в регио́не. (8) Франсуа́ Миттера́н заяви́л, что не ви́дит бо́лее подходя́щей фигу́ры на пост президе́нта Камбо́джи, кро́ме при́нца Си́анука. Он ... обрати́л внима́ние при́нца на то, что мирова́я обще́ственность отряди́ла больши́е си́лы на урегули́рование вооружённого конфли́кта в Камбо́дже. (9) Мы сохраня́ем па́мятники старины́. Ру́сская пля́ска тако́й же па́мятник, сохранённый в века́х! И ру́сская пе́сня ... (10) Пе́ред отлётом из США ли́дер босни́йских се́рбов Р.Ка́раджич встреча́лся с С.Вэ́нсом и Д.О́уеном. 11 февраля́ Вэнс и О́уен встре́тились ... с руководи́телями делега́ции босни́йских мусульма́н.

LESSON 64

SUBORDINATING CONJUNCTIONS

§1. The distinction between prepositions and conjunctions

Some English words (e.g. *after, before, since*) may function either as prepositions or conjunctions. When they are prepositions they are followed by a noun, pronoun or verbal noun, e.g. *after dinner, before us, since graduating*. When they are conjunctions they introduce a subordinate clause, e.g. *after I had had dinner; before I went out; since I graduated.*

In Russian the two functions, prepositional and conjunctional, are distinguished. The English words *after*, *before*, and *since* must be rendered in Russian as по́сле, до, с respectively when they are prepositions (по́сле у́жина, до нас, с оконча́ния университе́та; see 21.3, 22.5, 22.11). When on the other hand these words are conjunctions they must be translated by the phrases given in this lesson.

Note that in Russian subordinate clauses must be marked off from main clauses by a comma, which in some instances is usually placed within the conjunctional phrase, e.g. с тех пор, как, *since*.

The lists of conjunctions of various sorts which follow are very selective.

§2. Causal subordinating conjunctions

потому́ что	*because*
так как	*since, as* (in causal meaning)
и́бо	*for* (bookish in tone)

Examples:

Я тороплю́сь, потому́ что опа́здываю.
I am hurrying because I am late.
Так как он пришёл ра́но, он вошёл в зал ожида́ния.
As he arrived early he went into the waiting room.

§3. Temporal subordinating conjunctions

едва́...как	*scarcely, barely, no sooner...than*
как то́лько	*as soon as*

когда́	*when*
ка́ждый раз, когда́	*whenever*
пока́	*while*
пока́ не	*until*
по́сле того́, как	*after*
до того́, как	*before*
пре́жде чем	*before*
пе́ред тем, как	*just before*
с тех пор, как	*since* (temporal)

Note that these conjunctions, unlike their English equivalents, require a verb in the future tense if they do indeed refer to a future action. In English we use the present tense of verbs in the subordinate clause in sentences such as *We shall have supper as soon as you* ***arrive***, and *When you* ***finish*** *the book we shall go out*, even though the action indicated by the verbs in bold print is not yet taking place. In Russian, though, these verbs would be rendered by the perfective future forms придёте and ко́нчите respectively.

Examples:

Едва́ она́ пришла́ домо́й, как её муж вы́шел.
She had barely come home when her husband went out.
Как то́лько го́сти приду́т, мы вы́ключим телеви́зор.
As soon as the guests come we shall turn off the television.
Когда́ он вошёл в ко́мнату, все замолча́ли.
When he entered the room everyone fell silent.
Ка́ждый раз, когда́ мы встре́чаемся, он говори́т о свое́й бы́вшей жене́.
Whenever we meet he talks about his former wife.
По́сле того́ как она́ вы́шла из ко́мнаты, все на́чали говори́ть о ней.
After she had left the room everybody started talking about her.
Мы израсхо́довали мно́го де́нег на ремо́нт до́ма до того́, как нам удало́сь прода́ть его́.
We spent a lot of money on repairs to the house before we managed to sell it.
Пре́жде чем мы встре́тимся с ним, я хочу́ поговори́ть с ва́ми.
Before we meet him I want to have a talk with you.
Води́тель вы́скочил из каби́ны пе́ред тем, как грузови́к загоре́лся.
The driver leapt out of the cab just before the lorry burst into flames.
Я зна́ю их с тех пор, как мы поступи́ли в университе́т.
I have known them since we entered university.

The conjunction пока́ is always followed by an imperfective verb; пока́ не, on the other hand, must be followed by a perfective. Examples:

Пока́ он чита́л газе́ту, мы слу́шали ра́дио.
While he was reading the newspaper we listened to the radio.
Мы сиде́ли у него́ до́лго, пока́ не принесли́ протоко́лы на́ших допро́сов.
We sat in his room for a long time until they brought the transcript of our interrogations. (Press)

Как is used instead of когда́ to render *when* in sentences whose main clause has a negative verb which indicates that a period of time had not elapsed or a distance had not been covered before the action in question was interrupted, e.g.

Не прошло́ и двух мину́т, как он повтори́л свою́ оши́бку.
Not two minutes had passed when he made the same mistake again.
Маши́на не прошла́ и одного́ киломе́тра, как опя́ть слома́лась.
The car had not gone a kilometre when it broke down again.

Как is also used to render *before* after не успе́ть, *not to have time to*, e.g. он не успе́л закры́ть дверь, как тро́нулся по́езд, *he didn't have time to close the door before the train started moving.*

§4. Purposive subordinating conjunctions

что́бы	*in order that, so that*
для того́, что́бы	*in order that, so that*
с тем, что́бы	*with a view to*

Note that что́бы must be followed by an infinitive or by a verb in the past tense; it cannot be followed by a verb in the present tense or the future. Examples:

Я объясня́ю э́то, что́бы вы не повтори́ли свою́ оши́бку.
I am explaining this so that you should not repeat your mistake.
Я приглаша́ю вас с тем, что́бы предста́вить вам на́шего иностра́нного го́стя.
I'm inviting you with a view to introducing our foreign guest to you.

§5. Resultative subordinating conjunctions

так что	*so that*
до того́, что	*to a point where*

Examples:

Автóбус сломáлся, так что онú опоздáли.
The bus broke down so that they were late.
Он до тогó замёрз, что чуть не ýмер.
He got so frozen he almost died.

§6. Concessive subordinating conjunctions

хотя́	*although*
тогдá как	*while, whereas*
несмотря́ на то, что	*in spite of the fact that*

Examples:

Хотя́ инфля́ция и снижáется, правúтельство снóва повышáет подохóдный налóг.
Although inflation is coming down the government is again raising income tax.
На сéвере хóлодно зимóй, тогдá как на юге тепло́.
In the north it is cold in winter, whereas in the south it is warm.
Тормозá не рабóтают несмотря́ на то, что механик обслужúл их вчерá.
The brakes aren't working in spite of the fact that the mechanic serviced them yesterday.

§7. Comparative conjunctions

как	*as, like*
бýдто	*as if, as though*
слóвно	*like, as if, as though*
тóчно	*as if, as though*
так же... как	*as...as*

Examples:

бéлый как снег
white as snow
Он пришёл с такúм вúдом, бýдто всю ночь не спал.
He arrived looking as if he had not slept all night.
Он плáвает слóвно рыба.
He swims like a fish.
Онá ведёт себя́ тóчно сумасшéдшая.
She is behaving like a madwoman.
Онá так же умнá, как и её брат.
She is as clever as her brother.

Exercise

Translate into Russian: (1) He played the piano while his brother was working. (2) You will probably read the paper while I am cooking supper. (3) I shall read until we go to bed. (4) We shall be at home until the play begins. (5) He stayed in the library until his friend came. (6) Before you cook supper we shall watch the news on television. (7) We shall be at home until six o'clock. (8) After lunch we usually rest. (9) After you had gone we had lunch. (10) I have been unemployed since I saw you in February. (11) He had barely left the room when she began to cry. (12) As soon as the match had finished we went home. (13) The car was going slowly because there was a lot of traffic. (14) He did not go out as he had a headache. (15) Do a bit of work now so that you should be free this evening. (16) He made the same mistake in spite of the fact that I had explained this grammatical rule to him many times. (17) The younger brother is very hard-working, whereas the elder one is lazy. (18) I shall buy a refrigerator although I have not got much money. (19) I am going to bed early because I have got flu. (20) I rang the cinema in order to find out when the film begins.

English-Russian vocabulary

The vocabulary does not include words which are specifically dealt with in the lesson to which an exercise relates.

The Russian words given here are suitable as a translation of the English words when they are used with the sense they have in a given exercise in this book. They may not be suitable as a translation of the English words when those words occur in other contexts.

The imperfective member of an aspectual pair of verbs is invariably given first. If only one form is given it is imperfective unless otherwise stated. Only the masculine nominative singular form of adjectives and the nominative form of the pronouns is given.

Verbs in -ать and -ять are of conjugation 1a (see Lesson 7), and verbs in -ить are of the second conjugation unless otherwise indicated. In the case of verbs of conjugation 1b and second-conjugation verbs which have some irregularity in the 1st person singular or which undergo some change of stress within the present/future tense, the first- and second-person singular forms (or where appropriate third-person forms) are given in brackets.

If a noun undergoes a change of stress in its declension this change is indicated by (a) inclusion in brackets of the genitive singular form of nouns which have end stress in all forms except the nominative singular, or (b) inclusion of several forms where the pattern is more complex.

The phrase *as in* used in parentheses indicates that a word is not specifically dealt with in a lesson but behaves in the same way as other words which are dealt with there.

ability	спосо́бность (fem.)
able: to be able	мочь (могу́, мо́жешь; 13.4)
about	о + prep. (15.15)
abroad	за грани́цу (motion); за грани́цей (location)
academy	акаде́мия
to accept	принима́ть/приня́ть (приму́, при́мешь)
accident	ава́рия, несча́стный слу́чай
achievement	достиже́ние
actor	актёр
address	а́дрес (5.1.iii)
advantage	преиму́щество
advice	сове́т
to advise	сове́товать (сове́тую, сове́туешь)/ посове́товать + dat. (24.1)

afford: see 25.4

Afghanistan	Афганиста́н
afraid: to be afraid	боя́ться (бою́сь, бои́шься) + gen. (20.1)
after	по́сле + gen. (22.11)
again	опя́ть, сно́ва
against	про́тив + gen. (22.9); о + acc. (18.2)
against: to have sthg. against	име́ть (име́ю, име́ешь) что-нибудь про́тив + gen.
age	во́зраст
age (epoch)	эпо́ха
agenda	пове́стка дня
ago	тому́ наза́д
agreement	согла́сие
ahead	вперёд (motion)
air	во́здух
to air	прове́тривать/прове́трить
airport	аэропо́рт (15.13)
alcohol	алкого́ль (masc.)
all	весь (35.5)
almost	почти́; with verb чуть не
already	уже́
always	всегда́
ambassador	посо́л (3.1)
American	америка́нский
among	среди́ + gen. (22.10)
and	и
animal	живо́тное (16.2,29.5)
annexe	пристро́йка
another	друго́й
to answer (letter, question)	отвеча́ть/отве́тить (отве́чу, отве́тишь) на + acc. (17.5)
apology	извине́ние
appetite	аппети́т
April	апре́ль (masc.)
architecture	архитекту́ра
to argue	спо́рить/поспо́рить
to arise	возника́ть/возни́кнуть (возни́кну, возни́кнешь; 13.7)
arm	рука́ (acc. sing. ру́ку, nom./acc. pl. ру́ки, dat. pl. рука́м, etc.)
armed forces	вооружённые си́лы
arms	ору́жие (sing.)
army	а́рмия
around	по + dat. (25.1)
to arrest	аресто́вывать/арестова́ть (аресту́ю, аресту́ешь)
arrival	прие́зд, прибы́тие
to arrive (by transport)	приезжа́ть/прие́хать (прие́ду, прие́дешь)

to arrive (on foot)	приходи́ть (прихожу́, прихо́дишь)/ прийти́ (приду́, придёшь; 13.6)
art	иску́сство
article	статья́ (6.12)
as well	и (see 63.6)
ashamed	сты́дно + dat. (23.6)
to ask (to make request)	проси́ть (прошу́,про́сишь)/попроси́ть
to ask (question)	спра́шивать/спроси́ть (спрошу́, спро́сишь)
asleep: to fall asleep	засыпа́ть/засну́ть (засну́, заснёшь)
at home	до́ма
at last	наконе́ц
attack	ата́ка
to attack	напада́ть/напа́сть (нападу́, нападёшь; 13.5) на + acc. (17.5)
attempt	попы́тка
to attend (lecture)	посеща́ть/посети́ть (посещу́, посети́шь)
attitude	отноше́ние
audience	зри́тели (pl.; acc./gen. pl. зри́телей)
August	а́вгуст
aunt	тётя (6.9)
author	а́втор
autumn	о́сень (fem.)
to await	ждать (жду, ждёшь) + acc. or gen. (20.3)
away from	от + gen. (21.2)
back (adj.)	за́дний (28.7)
bad	плохо́й
banal	бана́льный
bankruptcy	банкро́тство
barrel	бо́чка (as in 6.1)
to be	быть (10.10, 27.5, 61.1)
to be at home	сиде́ть до́ма
beautiful	краси́вый
to become	станови́ться (становлю́сь, standо́вишься)/ стать (ста́ну, ста́нешь) (27.6)
bed: to go to bed	ложи́ться/лечь (ля́гу, ля́жешь) спать
beer	пи́во
before	до + gen. (22.5); пе́ред + instr. (26.8)
to begin	начина́ть(ся)/нача́ть(ся) (начну́, начнёшь)
beginning	нача́ло
behind	за + acc. (motion; 18.1.i); за + instr. (position; 26.5)
to believe	ве́рить/пове́рить + dat. (20.2)
to believe in	ве́рить/пове́рить в + acc. (17.3)
to belong to (club, society)	принадлежа́ть (принадлежу́, принадлежи́шь) к + dat. (25.6)
best	лу́чший
between	ме́жду + instr. (26.6)

bicycle	велосипе́д
big	большо́й
bird	пти́ца
birthday	день рожде́ния
bit: to do a bit of work	порабо́тать
black	чёрный
blouse	блу́зка
to blow off	сдува́ть/сдуть (сду́ю, сду́ешь)
blue	си́ний, голубо́й (light blue)
board	доска́ (acc. sing. до́ску, nom./acc. pl. до́ски, dat. pl. доска́м, etc.)
board: on board	на борту́
book	кни́га
border	грани́ца
boring	ску́чный
to borrow	занима́ть/заня́ть (займу́, займёшь)
bottle	буты́лка, буты́лочка
bottle (for scent)	флако́н
box	коро́бка (as in 6.1), я́щик
boy	ма́льчик
braggart	хвасту́н (хвастуна́, etc.)
brandy	конья́к (коньяка́, etc.)
brave	хра́брый
bread	хлеб
to break	лома́ть/слома́ть
to break (crockery, glass, etc.)	разбива́ть/разби́ть (разобью́, разобьёшь)
breakfast	за́втрак
break-up	распа́д
breather: to take a breather	передохну́ть (pf.; передохну́, передохнёшь)
briefcase	портфе́ль (masc.)
bright	я́ркий
to bring (by carrying)	приноси́ть (приношу́, прино́сишь)/ принести́ (принесу́, принесёшь; 13.3)
to bring (by transport)	привози́ть (привожу́, приво́зишь)/ привезти́ (привезу́, привезёшь; 13.3)
Britain	Брита́ния
British	брита́нский
broad	широ́кий
brother	брат (5.4)
to build	стро́ить/постро́ить
building	зда́ние
bus	авто́бус
to buy	покупа́ть/купи́ть (куплю́, ку́пишь)
cabin	каби́на
calculation	подсчёт

to call on	заходи́ть (захожу́, захо́дишь)/зайти́ (зайду́, зайдёшь; 13.6) к + dat.; загля́дывать/загляну́ть (загляну́, загля́нешь) к + dat.
to call (out)	вызыва́ть/вы́звать (вы́зову, вы́зовешь)
can	мочь (могу́, мо́жешь; 13.4)/смочь
can (to know how to)	уме́ть (уме́ю, уме́ешь)/суме́ть
can (impers.)	мо́жно (23.4)
candidate	кандида́т
cannot: see *to be able*	
cannot: one cannot	нельзя́ (23.4)
canteen	столо́вая (29.5)
capital	столи́ца
capital punishment	сме́ртная казнь
captain	капита́н
car	маши́на, автомоби́ль (masc.)
carriage	ваго́н
case	чемода́н
case (instance)	слу́чай
cashier	касси́рша
cat	ко́шка (6.1)
to catch	лови́ть (ловлю́, ло́вишь)/пойма́ть
cathedral	собо́р
cause	причи́на
centre	центр
chair	стул (5.4)
chairman	председа́тель (masc.)
to change	изменя́ть(ся)/измени́ть(ся) (изменю́, изме́нишь)
to change (transport)	переса́живаться/пересе́сть (пересяду, пересядешь; 13.5) на + acc.
channel (on TV)	програ́мма
The Channel	Ла-Ма́нш
chapter	глава́ (nom./acc. pl. гла́вы, etc.)
character (in play)	лицо́ (16.2)
cheap	дешёвый
to check	проверя́ть/прове́рить
cheek	щека́ (acc. sing. щёку, nom./acc. pl. щёки, gen. pl. щёк, dat. pl. щека́м, etc.)
cheese	сыр (nom./acc. pl. сыры́, etc.)
chef	по́вар (5.1.iii)
chemist	хи́мик
chemist's (shop)	апте́ка
'The Cherry Orchard'	«Вишнёвый сад» (15.13)
child	ребёнок (4.4)
children	де́ти (5.11)
Chinese	кита́йский
to choose	выбира́ть/вы́брать (вы́беру, вы́берешь)

Christmas	Рождество́
church	це́рковь (fem.; 5.9)
cigarette	сигаре́та
cinema	кино́ (indecl.)
circumstance	обстоя́тельство
city	го́род (5.1.iii)
class	класс
classroom	аудито́рия
clear	я́сный
clever	у́мный
climate	кли́мат
clock	часы́ (3.2)
to close	закрыва́ть/закры́ть (закро́ю, закро́ешь)
closed	закры́тый
clothes	оде́жда (sing. only)
club	клуб
coffee	ко́фе (masc.; indecl.)
cold	холо́дный
cold: it is cold	хо́лодно
colour	цвет (5.3)
to come (by transport)	приезжа́ть/прие́хать (прие́ду, прие́дешь)
to come (on foot)	приходи́ть (прихожу́, прихо́дишь)/ прийти́ (приду́, придёшь; 13.6)
to come in	входи́ть (вхожу́, вхо́дишь)/войти́ (войду́, войдёшь; 13.6)
comfortable	удо́бный
Common Market	О́бщий ры́нок (ры́нка, etc.; 15.8)
communism	коммуни́зм
company	компа́ния
complex	сло́жный
to condemn	осужда́ть/осуди́ть (осужу́, осу́дишь)
condition	усло́вие
conduct	поведе́ние
conference	конфере́нция
to consider	счита́ть/счесть (сочту́, сочтёшь; 13.5) (27.6)
constantly	постоя́нно
to consult	сове́товаться (сове́туюсь, сове́туешься)/ посове́товаться с + instr. (26.10)
to continue	продолжа́ть/продо́лжить (53.1)
to cook	гото́вить (гото́влю, гото́вишь)/ пригото́вить
cooking	ку́хня
copy (of book)	экземпля́р
corner	у́гол (3.1)
corridor	коридо́р

to cost	сто́ить
to count	счита́ть/посчита́ть
country (as opposed to town)	дере́вня (gen. pl. дереве́нь, dat. pl. деревня́м, etc.)
country (native land)	ро́дина
coup d'état	госуда́рственный переворо́т
course: in the course of	в тече́ние + gen.
coward	трус
crack	щель (fem.; gen. pl. щеле́й, dat. pl. щеля́м, etc.)
criminal	престу́пник
to cross	переходи́ть (перехожу́, перехо́дишь)/ перейти́ (перейду́, перейдёшь; 13.6)
crowd	толпа́ (nom./acc. pl. то́лпы, etc.)
to cry	пла́кать (пла́чу, пла́чешь)/запла́кать
Cuba	Ку́ба
cup	ча́шка (6.1)
custom	обы́чай
customs	тамо́жня (6.10)
to cut	ре́зать (ре́жу, ре́жешь)/поре́зать
to cut off	отреза́ть/отре́зать (отре́жу, отре́жешь)
Cyprus	Кипр
Czechoslovakia	Чехослова́кия
dangerous	опа́сный
dangerous: it is dangerous	опа́сно
daughter	дочь (4.2), до́чка (as in 6.1)
day	день (masc.; 3.1)
'Dead Souls'	«Мёртвые ду́ши»
to deal with	рассма́тривать/рассмотре́ть (рассмотрю́, рассмо́тришь)
dean	дека́н
December	дека́брь (masc.; декабря́, etc.)
to decide	реша́ть/реши́ть
decision	реше́ние
to define	определя́ть/определи́ть
delicate	то́нкий, делика́тный
demonstrator	демонстра́нт
Denmark	Да́ния
dentist	зубно́й врач (врача́, etc.)
to develop	развива́ть/разви́ть (разовью́, разовьёшь)
development	разви́тие
dictionary	слова́рь (masc.; словаря́, etc.)
to die (of natural causes)	умира́ть/умере́ть (умру́, умрёшь; 13.8)
to die (to perish)	погиба́ть/поги́бнуть (поги́бну, поги́бнешь; 13.7)
difficult	тру́дный
difficult: it is difficult	тру́дно

difficulty	тру́дность (fem.)
dining-room	столо́вая (29.5)
dinner: to have dinner	обе́дать/пообе́дать
dirty	гря́зный
disadvantage	недоста́ток (недоста́тка, etc.)
disaster	катастро́фа
discipline	дисципли́на
to discover	открыва́ть/откры́ть (откро́ю, откро́ешь)
to discuss	обсужда́ть/обсуди́ть (обсужу́, обсу́дишь)
disease	заболева́ние
dish	блю́до
dishes (crockery)	посу́да
to do	де́лать/сде́лать
doctor	врач (врача́, etc.)
document	докуме́нт
dog	соба́ка
Don	Дон (15.13)
door	дверь (fem.; gen. pl. двере́й, dat. pl. дверя́м, etc.)
Dostoevsky	Достое́вский
doubt	сомне́ние
down	по + dat. (25.1)
downstairs	вниз
draught	сквозня́к (сквозняка́, etc.)
dress	пла́тье (6.7)
drink	напи́ток (напи́тка, etc.)
to drink	пить (пью, пьёшь)/вы́пить
driver	води́тель (masc.)
to drop	роня́ть/урони́ть
drunk (person)	пья́ница (masc. and fem.)
each	ка́ждый
early (adj.)	ра́нний (28.7)
early (adv.)	ра́но
to earn	зараба́тывать/зарабо́тать
earth	земля́ (nom./acc. pl. зе́мли, gen. pl. земе́ль, dat. pl. зе́млям, etc.)
Easter	Па́сха
eastern	восто́чный
easy	лёгкий
easy: it is easy	легко́
to eat	есть (12.10, 13.5)
economic	экономи́ческий
education	образова́ние
elder	ста́рший (31.3)
to elect	избира́ть/избра́ть (изберу́, изберёшь)
elephant	слон (слона́, etc.)

embassy	посо́льство
end	коне́ц (3.1)
enemy	враг (врага́, etc.)
engineer	инжене́р
England	А́нглия
Englishman	англича́нин (4.3)
enormous	огро́мный
to enter (educational institution)	поступа́ть/поступи́ть (поступлю́, посту́пишь) в + acc. (17.3)
entrance	вход
especially	осо́бенно
essay	сочине́ние
Ethiopia	Эфио́пия
even	да́же
evening	ве́чер (5.1.iii)
event	собы́тие
every	ка́ждый
everybody	все (pl. of весь; 35.5)
everything	всё (neut. sing. of весь; 35.5)
examination	экза́мен
example	приме́р
exception	исключе́ние (26.5)
excursion	экску́рсия
exercise	упражне́ние
exercise-book	тетра́дь (fem.)
exhibition	вы́ставка
exile	ссы́лка
exit	вы́ход
expensive	дорого́й
experience	о́пыт
expert	экспе́рт
to explain	объясня́ть/объясни́ть
explanation	объясне́ние
to express	выража́ть/вы́разить (вы́ражу, вы́разишь)
expression	выраже́ние
face	лицо́
fact	факт
fact: the fact that	то, что
factory	фа́брика, заво́д (15.8)
faculty	факульте́т (15.8)
to fade	блёкнуть (блёкну, блёкнешь; 13.7)/поблёкнуть; (of flowers) увяда́ть/увя́нуть
to fall ill	заболе́ть (заболе́ю, заболе́ешь) (pf.)
family	семья́ (nom./acc. pl. се́мьи, gen. pl. семе́й, dat. pl. се́мьям, etc.)

far from	далекó от + gen.
farmer	фéрмер
fashionable	мóдный
father	отéц (3.1)
favourable	благоприя́тный
February	феврáль (masc.; февраля́, etc.)
to feed	корми́ть (кормлю́, кóрмишь)/покорми́ть
feeling	чу́вство
few (not many)	мáло + gen. (19.2)
few: a few	немнóго (19.2)
field	пóле (nom. pl. поля́, etc.)
fifteen	пятнáдцать + gen. pl.
to fill in (form)	заполня́ть/запóлнить
film	фильм
to find	находи́ть (нахожу́, нахóдишь)/найти́ (найду́, найдёшь; 13.6)
to find (to come across)	заставáть (застаю́, застаёшь)/застáть (застáну, застáнешь)
to find it + adj.	находи́ть (нахожу́, нахóдишь)/найти́ (найду́, найдёшь; 13.6) + instr. of adj. (27.6)
to find out	узнавáть (узнаю́, узнаёшь)/узнáть
finger	пáлец (3.1)
to finish	кончáть(ся)/кóнчить(ся)
first	пéрвый
fish	ры́ба
fist	кулáк (кулакá, etc.)
five	пять + gen. pl.
five-rouble note	пятёрка
five-year plan	пятилéтка
flat	кварти́ра
flock (of sheep)	отáра
flower	цветóк (5.3)
flu	грипп
flu: I have flu	я заболéл(а) гри́ппом
to fly	летéть (лечу́, лети́шь)/полетéть or летáть (45)
fog	тумáн
fool	дурáк (дуракá, etc.)
football	футбóл
football (adj.)	футбóльный
footballer	футболи́ст
forces (armed)	вооружённые си́лы
foreign	инострáнный
foreigner	инострáнец (инострáнца, etc.)/инострáнка
forest	лес (5.1.iii)
to forget	забывáть/забы́ть (забу́ду, забу́дешь)
form (piece of paper)	бланк
forty	сóрок + gen. pl.

to found	осно́вывать/основа́ть (осную́, оснуёшь)
France	Фра́нция
free	свобо́дный
French	францу́зский
French (language)	францу́зский язы́к (языка́, etc.)
Frenchwoman	францу́женка
fresh	све́жий
Friday	пя́тница
friend	друг (5.5), подру́га
front (adj.)	пере́дний (28.7)
front (military)	фронт
funds	ассигнова́ния (neut. pl.)
Gagarin	Гага́рин (as in 4.7)
gang	ша́йка (6.3)
garage	гара́ж (гаража́, etc.)
garden	сад (nom. pl. сады́, etc.; 15.13)
generation	поколе́ние
generous	ще́дрый
Germany	Герма́ния
get: you get (answer in sum)	будет, получа́ется
to get	получа́ть/получи́ть (получу́, полу́чишь)
to get dressed	одева́ться/оде́ться (оде́нусь, оде́нешься)
to get off	сходи́ть (схожу́, схо́дишь)/сойти́ (сойду́, сойдёшь; 13.6) с+ gen.
to get out	выходи́ть (выхожу́, выхо́дишь)/вы́йти (вы́йду, вы́йдешь; 13.6) из + gen.
to get up	встава́ть (встаю́, встаёшь)/встать (вста́ну, вста́нешь)
girl	де́вушка (as in 6.1)
girl (little girl)	де́вочка (6.1)
to give	дава́ть (даю́, даёшь)/дать (12.10)
to give (lecture)	чита́ть/прочита́ть
to give up	броса́ть/бро́сить (бро́шу, бро́сишь)
given	при + prep. (15.17)
glass (for brandy, etc.)	рю́мка (as in 6.1)
glass (material)	стекло́
glue	клей
to go (by transport)	е́хать (е́ду, е́дешь)/пое́хать or е́здить (е́зжу, е́здишь) (45)
to go (of means of transport)	идти́ (идёт, иду́т; 13.6) or е́хать (е́дет, е́дут) (44.3)
to go (on foot)	идти́ (иду́, идёшь; 13.6)/пойти́ (пойду́, пойдёшь) or ходи́ть (хожу́, хо́дишь) (45)
to go away (by transport)	уезжа́ть/уе́хать (уе́ду, уе́дешь)
to go away (on foot)	уходи́ть (ухожу́, ухо́дишь)/уйти́ (уйду́, уйдёшь; 13.6)

to go from (of means of transport)	идти́ (идёт; 13.6)/пойти́ (пойдёт), отходи́ть (отхо́дит)/отойти́ (отойдёт; 13.6)
to go in	входи́ть (вхожу́, вхо́дишь)/войти́ (войду́, войдёшь; 13.6)
to go out	выходи́ть (выхожу́, выхо́дишь)/вы́йти (вы́йду, вы́йдешь; 13.6)
to go to bed	ложи́ться (ложу́сь, ложи́шься)/лечь (ля́гу, ля́жешь; 13.4) спать
to go to sleep	засыпа́ть/засну́ть (засну́, заснёшь)
to go up to	подходи́ть (подхожу́, подхо́дишь)/ подойти́ (подойду́, подойдёшь; 13.6) к + dat.
Gogol	Го́голь (masc.)
good	хоро́ший
goodbye: to say goodbye to	проща́ться/попроща́ться or прости́ться (прощу́сь, прости́шься) с + instr. (26.10)
government	прави́тельство
government (adj.)	прави́тельственный
grain	зерно́
grammatical	граммати́ческий
great	вели́кий
greater	бо́льше
group	гру́ппа
guerrilla	партиза́н (6.4)
hair	во́лосы (pl.; gen. pl. воло́с, dat. pl. волоса́м, etc.)
half an hour	полчаса́ (in oblique cases получа́са)
hand	рука́ (acc. sing. ру́ку, nom./acc. pl. ру́ки, dat. pl. рука́м, etc.)
handwriting	по́черк
to hang (intrans.)	висе́ть (вишу́, виси́шь)
hangover: with a	с похме́лья
to happen	происходи́ть (происхо́дит)/произойти́ (произойдёт; 13.6)
happy	счастли́вый
hard-working	приле́жный
harmful	вре́дный для + gen.
hat	шля́па
to hate	ненави́деть (ненави́жу, ненави́дишь)
to have	у + gen. (21.4); име́ть (име́ю, име́ешь)
he	он
head	голова́ (acc. sing. го́лову, nom./acc. pl. го́ловы, gen. pl. голо́в, dat. pl. голова́м, etc.)
head-ache: I have/had a head-ache	у меня́ боли́т/боле́ла голова́
headmaster	дире́ктор (5.1.ii) (шко́лы)
health	здоро́вье
hear	слы́шать (слы́шу, слы́шишь)/услы́шать
heart	се́рдце (nom./acc. pl. сердца́, gen. pl.

	сердéц, dat. pl. сердцáм, etc.)
hearth	камúн
heavy	тяжёлый
hello: to say hello to	здорóваться/поздорóваться с + instr. (26.10)
to help	помогáть/помóчь (помогý, помóжешь; 13.4) + dat. (24.1)
help: cannot help	не мочь (могý, мóжешь; 13.4) не + infin.
her	её (34.2, 35.2)
here (location)	здесь, тут
hero	герóй
herself: see 34.3-4	
high	высóкий
him	егó, etc. (34.2)
his	егó (34.2, 35.2)
history	истóрия
to hit	ударя́ть/удáрить
to hold up	задéрживать/задержáть (задержý, задéржишь)
hold-up	задéржка
home: at home	дóма
home(wards)	домóй
honey	мёд
hostel	общежúтие
hot (of weather)	жáркий
hot (to the touch)	горя́чий
hotel	гостúница
hour	час (15.13; nom./acc. pl. часы́, etc.)
house	дом (5.1.iii)
how	как
how many	скóлько + gen. (19.2)
how much	скóлько + gen. (19.2)
humour	ю́мор
hundred	сто + gen. pl.
hundred (collective)	сóтня (39.3)
hunger	гóлод
hunter	охóтник
husband	муж (5.5)
I	я
ice	лёд (льда, etc.; 15.13)
idea	идéя (6.11)
idol	кумúр
if	éсли
ill	больнóй
ill: to fall ill	заболéть (заболéю, заболéешь) (pf.)
illegible	неразбóрчивый
illness	болéзнь (fem.)

to imagine	представля́ть/предста́вить (предста́влю, предста́вишь) себе́
immediately	сра́зу
to import	ввози́ть (ввожу́, вво́зишь)/ввезти́ (ввезу́, ввезёшь; 13.3)
important	ва́жный, значи́тельный
impracticable	нереа́льный
impression: to make an impression	производи́ть (произвожу́, произво́дишь)/произвести́ впечатле́ние на + acc.
to improve	улучша́ть(ся)/улу́чшить(ся)
in	в + prep. (15.1-3) or acc. (17.2.i); че́рез + acc. (18.8.ii); под + instr. (26.9)
inexplicable	необъясни́мый
influence	влия́ние
information	информа́ция
inhabitant	жи́тель (masc.)
insect	насеко́мое (16.2, 29.5)
instance	слу́чай
institute	институ́т
intelligent	у́мный; short forms умён, умна́, etc.
interested: to be/become interested in	интересова́ться (интересу́юсь, интересу́ешься)/заинтересова́ться + instr. (27.4)
interesting	интере́сный
interpreter	перево́дчик
into	в + acc.
invincible	непобеди́мый
to invite	приглаша́ть/пригласи́ть (приглашу́, пригласи́шь)
inwards	внутрь
Irina	Ири́на
to iron	гла́дить (гла́жу, гла́дишь)/погла́дить
it	он, она́, оно́, etc. (34.1)
its	его́, её
Ivan	Ива́н
Ivanov	Ива́но́в (as in 4.7)
January	янва́рь (masc.; января́, etc.)
jeans	джи́нсы (pl.; gen. pl. джи́нсов)
job	рабо́та
joy	ра́дость (fem.)
juice	сок
July	ию́ль (masc.)
June	ию́нь (masc.)
just (only)	то́лько
just: to have just	то́лько что
to keep	храни́ть
to keep doing sthg.	всё + impf. verb (35.5)

to keep to	держа́ться (держу́сь, де́ржишься) + gen. (20.2)
key	ключ (ключа́, etc.)
Kiev	Ки́ев
to kill	убива́ть/уби́ть (убью́, убьёшь)
to kill (cattle)	забива́ть/заби́ть (забью́, забьёшь)
kilogramme	килогра́мм
kilometre	киломе́тр
kind	до́брый, любе́зный
kiss	поцелу́й
to kiss	целова́ть (целу́ю, целу́ешь)/поцелова́ть
kitchen	ку́хня (6.10)
knife	нож (ножа́, etc.)
to know	знать
kopeck	копе́йка (6.3)
Labour Party	Лейбори́стская па́ртия
lack	недоста́ток (недоста́тка, etc.), нехва́тка
ladder	ле́стница
lake	о́зеро (nom../acc pl. озёра, etc.)
land	земля́ (nom./acc. pl. зе́мли, gen. pl. земе́ль, dat. pl. зе́млям, etc.)
language	язы́к (языка́, etc.)
last (final)	после́дний (28.7)
last (past)	про́шлый
last: at last	наконе́ц
last week	на про́шлой неде́ле
last year	в про́шлом году́
late (adj.)	по́здний (28.7)
late (adv.)	по́здно
late: to be late	опа́здывать/опозда́ть
latest	после́дний (28.7)
to laugh	смея́ться (смею́сь, смеёшься)/ засмея́ться
law	зако́н
lawyer	адвока́т
lazy	лени́вый
to learn	учи́ться/научи́ться + dat. of subject learned (24.2)
to leave (to abandon)	покида́ть/поки́нуть (поки́ну, поки́нешь)
to leave (to go away from)	уходи́ть (ухожу́, ухо́дишь)/уйти́ (уйду́, уйдёшь; 13.6) от + gen.
to leave (to go out of)	выходи́ть (выхожу́, выхо́дишь)/вы́йти (вы́йду, вы́йдешь; 13.6) из + gen.
to leave (to move off from)	отходи́ть (отхожу́, отхо́дишь)/отойти́ (отойду́, отойдёшь; 13.6) от + gen.
lecture	ле́кция
lecturer	преподава́тель (masc.)

left-hand	ле́вый
legitimate	зако́нный
Leningrad	Ленингра́д
Lermontov	Ле́рмонтов
lesson	уро́к
let (3rd pers. imp.)	пусть (43.8)
letter	письмо́ (nom./acc. pl. пи́сьма, gen. pl. пи́сем, dat. pl. пи́сьмам, etc.)
library	библиоте́ка
to lie (to be lying)	лежа́ть (лежу́, лежи́шь)
to like	люби́ть (люблю́, лю́бишь), нра́виться/понра́виться (23.7)
line	ли́ния
lion	лев (3.1)
list	спи́сок (спи́ска, etc.)
to list	перечисля́ть/перечи́слить
to listen to	слу́шать/послу́шать + acc.
literature	литерату́ра
to live	жить (живу́, живёшь)
to lock	запира́ть/запере́ть (запру́, запрёшь; 13.8)
London	Ло́ндон
long	дли́нный
long: a long time	до́лго
to look	вы́глядеть (вы́гляжу, вы́глядишь; 27.6)
to look at	смотре́ть (смотрю́, смо́тришь)/посмотре́ть на + acc. (17.5)
to look for	иска́ть (ищу́, и́щешь; 20.3)
lorry	грузови́к (грузовика́, etc.)
to lose	теря́ть/потеря́ть
to lose (to be deprived of)	лиша́ться/лиши́ться + gen. (20.2)
lot: a lot (of)	мно́го + gen. (19.2)
lounge	гости́ная (29.5)
to love	люби́ть (люблю́, лю́бишь)
low	ни́зкий
Lukashin	Лука́шин (as in 4.7)
lunch	обе́д
lunch: to have lunch	обе́дать/пообе́дать
lung	лёгкое (29.5)
mad	сумасше́дший
mad: to go mad	сходи́ть (схожу́, схо́дишь)/сойти́ (сойду́, сойдёшь; 13.6) с ума́
madman	сумасше́дший (as in 29.5)
magazine	журна́л
main	гла́вный
major	крупне́йший
to make (to compel)	вынужда́ть/вы́нудить (вы́нужу, вы́нудишь)
to make (mistake)	де́лать/сде́лать

man	мужчи́на (masc.), челове́к (6.4)
man: old man	стари́к (старика́, etc.)
manager	дире́ктор (5.1.ii), ме́неджер
many	мно́го + gen. (19.2)
March	март
market	ры́нок (ры́нка, etc.;15.8)
to master	владе́ть (владе́ю, владе́ешь)/овладе́ть + instr. (27.1)
match (game)	матч
mathematics	матема́тика
May	май
me	меня́, etc. (34.1)
mean	скупо́й
to mean (to intend to say)	хоте́ть (12.10) сказа́ть
measure	ме́ра
meat	мя́со
medical	медици́нский
medicine	лека́рство
to meet (to become acquainted with)	знако́миться (знако́млюсь, знако́мишься)/ познако́миться с + instr. (26.10)
to meet (by arrangement)	встреча́ться/встре́титься с + instr.
to meet (by chance)	встреча́ть/встре́тить (встре́чу, встре́тишь)
meeting (encounter)	встре́ча
meeting (formal)	заседа́ние
member	член
metre	метр
mewing	мяу́канье
midday	по́лдень (gen. sing. полу́дня, dat. sing. полу́дню, etc.)
mile	ми́ля
milk	молоко́
million	миллио́н + gen. pl.
mine	мой (35.1)
minister	мини́стр
minute	мину́та
mirror	зе́ркало
miser	скупе́ц (скупца́, etc.)
mistake	оши́бка (as in 6.1)
modern	совреме́нный
Monday	понеде́льник
money	де́ньги (pl.; gen. pl. де́нег, dat. pl. деньга́м, etc.)
month	ме́сяц
monument	па́мятник
more than	бо́льше чем or бо́льше + gen.
morning	у́тро (gen. sing. утра́ in expressions of time; also по утра́м)

morning: in the morning	у́тром
Moscow	Москва́
Moscow (adj.)	моско́вский
mother	мать (fem.; 4.2)
mountain	гора́ (acc. sing. го́ру, nom./acc. pl. го́ры, dat. pl. гора́м, etc.)
mouse	мышь (fem.; gen. pl. мыше́й, dat. pl. мыша́м, etc.)
mouth	рот (as in 3.1; see also 15.13)
to move off (of means of transport)	отходи́ть (отхо́дит)/отойти́ (отойдёт; 13.6)
movement	движе́ние
Mrs	госпожа́
much	мно́го + gen.
much (with comparative)	гора́здо
mum	ма́ма
museum	музе́й
mushroom	гриб (гриба́, etc.)
music	му́зыка
must: we/you must	мы/вы должны́
must: one/you must not	нельзя́ (23.4, 54.2)
my	мой (35.1)
name	и́мя (neut.; 4.1)
navy	вое́нно-морско́й флот
near	бли́зко от + gen.
neck	ше́я
neighbour	сосе́д (5.8)
never	никогда́ не
new	но́вый
news	изве́стия (neut. pl.)
news: piece of news	но́вость (fem.)
newspaper	газе́та
nice (of food)	вку́сный
Nikitin	Ники́тин (as in 4.7)
nine	де́вять + gen. pl.
north	се́вер (15.10)
not	не
not far from	недалеко́ от + gen.
not only...but also	не то́лько.... но и
to notice	замеча́ть/заме́тить (заме́чу, заме́тишь)
novel	рома́н
novelist	романи́ст
November	ноя́брь (masc.; ноября́, etc.)
Novosibirsk	Новосиби́рск
now	тепе́рь, сейча́с
nowadays	ны́не
number	число́ (nom./acc. pl. чи́сла, gen. pl. чи́сел, dat. pl. чи́слам, etc.)

obvious	очеви́дный
October	октя́брь (masc.; октября́, etc.)
o'clock	час (40.2)
off	с + gen. (21.3)
often	ча́сто
oil	нефть (fem.)
old	ста́рый
old man	стари́к (старика́, etc.)
old woman	стару́ха
older	ста́рше + gen.
on	на + prep. (15.7) or acc. (17.4.i)
on time	во́время
one	оди́н (37.2)
to open	открыва́ть(ся)/откры́ть(ся) (откро́ю, откро́ешь)
orange	апельси́н
to order (to book, reserve)	зака́зывать/заказа́ть (закажу́, зака́жешь)
to order (to command)	прика́зывать/приказа́ть (прикажу́, прика́жешь) + dat. (24.2)
organisation	организа́ция
ostrich	стра́ус
other	друго́й
ought	сле́дует (23.7)
our	наш (35.1)
out of	из + gen. (21.1)
outside	о́коло + gen. (22.8), пе́ред + instr. (26.8)
over	свы́ше+ gen. (22.11)
overcoat	пальто́ (indecl.)
to overcook	перева́ривать/perевари́ть (переварю́, перева́ришь)
to overfulfil	перевыполня́ть/перевы́полнить
own	свой (35.3), со́бственный
Oxford (adj.)	о́ксфордский
page	страни́ца
painting	карти́на
pale	бле́дный
paper	бума́га
paper (newspaper)	газе́та
parent	роди́тель (masc.)
Paris	Пари́ж
park	парк
parliament	парла́мент
party	па́ртия
to pass (also of time)	проходи́ть (прохожу́, прохо́дишь)/ пройти́ (пройду́, пройдёшь; 13.6)
passenger	пассажи́р

Pasternak	Пастерна́к
path	тропи́нка, доро́жка
patient	больно́й (29.5), пацие́нт
paw	ла́па, ла́почка
to pay	плати́ть (плачу́, пла́тишь)/заплати́ть
to pay attention to	обраща́ть/обрати́ть (обращу́, обрати́шь) внима́ние на + acc.
peaceful	ми́рный
pear	гру́ша
peasant	крестья́нин (4.3)
pen	ру́чка (as in 6.1)
penguin	пингви́н
people	лю́ди (gen. люде́й, dat. лю́дям, instr. людьми́, prep. лю́дях)
performance	спекта́кль (masc.)
period	пери́од
person	челове́к (6.4, 41.4.ii)
to persuade	угова́ривать/уговори́ть
Peter the Great	Пётр (Петра́, etc.) Вели́кий
petrol	бензи́н
Petrov	Петро́в (as in 4.7)
philosopher	фило́соф
photography	фотогра́фия
piano (grand)	роя́ль (masc.)
piano (upright)	пиани́но (indecl.)
to pick (flower)	срыва́ть/сорва́ть (сорву́, сорвёшь)
to pick (to select)	подбира́ть/подобра́ть (подберу́, подберёшь)
picture	карти́на
piece	кусо́к (3.1)
pilot	пило́т, лётчик
plan	план
plane	самолёт
plank	доска́ (acc. sing. до́ску, nom./acc. pl. до́ски, gen. pl. досо́к, dat. pl. доска́м, etc.)
plant	расте́ние
plate	таре́лка (6.1)
play	пье́са
to play (a game)	игра́ть в + acc. (17.3)
to play (a musical instrument)	игра́ть на + prep. (15.12)
to play a role	игра́ть роль (fem.)
player	игро́к (игрока́, etc.)
pleasant	прия́тный
please	пожа́луйста
pocket	карма́н
poet	поэ́т
poetry	стихотворе́ния (neut. pl.)
police	мили́ция

policeman	милиционе́р
policy	поли́тика
politician	полити́ческий де́ятель (masc.)
poor	бе́дный
pop music	популя́рная му́зыка
Popov	Попо́в (as in 4.7)
popular	популя́рный
population	населе́ние
porter	носи́льщик
portion	по́рция
position	положе́ние
post office	по́чта (15.8)
postcard	откры́тка (as in 6.1)
postman	почтальо́н
potatoes	карто́шка (sing. only)
pound	фунт
pram	(де́тская) коля́ска
present (gift)	пода́рок (пода́рка, etc.)
to present (plan)	представля́ть/предста́вить (предста́влю, предста́вишь)
pretty	хоро́шенький, краси́вый
price	цена́ (acc. sing. це́ну, nom./acc. pl. це́ны, etc.)
prime minister	премье́р-мини́стр
probably	вероя́тно, наве́рно
problem	пробле́ма
to produce	производи́ть (произвожу́, произво́дишь)/ произвести́ (произведу́, произведёшь; 13.5)
produced	произведённый
professor	профе́ссор (5.1.ii)
profound	глубо́кий
programme	програ́мма
project	прое́кт
to promise	обеща́ть/пообеща́ть
prospect	перспекти́ва
to prove (to turn out to be)	ока́зываться/оказа́ться (окажу́сь, ока́жешься)
publicly	публи́чно
to publish	публикова́ть (публику́ю, публику́ешь)/ опубликова́ть
punishment	наказа́ние
pupil	учени́к (ученика́, etc.)
to put (in lying position)	класть (кладу́, кладёшь; 13.5)/ положи́ть (положу́, поло́жишь)
to put (in standing position)	ста́вить (ста́влю, ста́вишь)/поста́вить
to put in jeopardy	ста́вить (ста́влю, ста́вишь)/поста́вить под угро́зу

queen	королéва
question	вопрóс
queue	óчередь (fem.; gen. pl. очередéй, dat. pl. очередя́м, etc.)
quick	бы́стрый
quiet	ти́хий
quiet (taciturn)	молчали́вый
radio	рáдио (indecl.)
rain: it rains	дождь идёт
to raise	поднимáть/подня́ть (подниму́, подни́мешь)
rank	ранг, чин (nom./acc. pl. чины́, etc.)
to reach	достигáть/дости́гнуть (дости́гну, дости́гнешь; 13.7) + gen. (20.2)
to read	читáть/прочитáть
reader	читáтель (masc.)
to receive	получáть/получи́ть (получу́, полу́чишь)
recession	спад
recognition: beyond recognition	до неузнавáемости
red	крáсный
to reflect	отражáть/отрази́ть (отражу́, отрази́шь)
refrigerator	холоди́льник
to report	сообщáть/сообщи́ть
to require	трéбовать (трéбую, трéбуешь)/ потрéбовать + gen. (20.2)
to reread	перечи́тывать/перечитáть
reservoir	водохрани́лище
resolution	резолю́ция
resources	срéдства (neut. pl.)
to respect	уважáть
to rest	отдыхáть/отдохну́ть (отдохну́, отдохнёшь)
restaurant	рестор́ан
result	результáт
result: as a result of	в результáте + gen.
to return (intrans.)	возвращáться/верну́ться (верну́сь, вернёшься)
return journey	обрáтный путь (4.6)
reunification	воссоединéние
revolution	револю́ция
revolutionary (noun)	революционéр
revolutionary (adj.)	революциóнный
reworking	перерабóтка
rich	богáтый
right (answer, etc.)	прáвильный
right (of person)	прáвый (30.5.i)
to ring	звони́ть/позвони́ть (person) + dat. (24.2); (institution) в + acc.

river	река́ (nom./acc. pl. ре́ки, dat. pl. ре́ка́м, etc.)
road	доро́га
roof	кры́ша
room	ко́мната
room (in hotel)	но́мер (5.1.iii)
rose	ро́за
rouble	рубль (masc.; рубля́, etc.)
round	кру́глый
row	ряд (15.13; nom./acc. pl. ряды́, etc.)
rule	пра́вило
to run	бежа́ть (12.10)/побежа́ть or бе́гать (45)
Russia	Росси́я
Russian	ру́сский
Russian (language)	ру́сский язы́к (языка́, etc.)
sack	мешо́к (мешка́, etc.)
sad	гру́стный, печа́льный
sadly	гру́стно, печа́льно
safety	безопа́сность (fem.)
to sail	плыть (плыву́, плывёшь)/поплы́ть or пла́вать (45)
St Petersburg	Санкт-Петербу́рг
same	тот же (35.4)
satisfied	дово́льный; short forms дово́лен, дово́льна, etc (30.5.i)
Saturday	суббо́та
saucepan	кастрю́ля
to say	говори́ть/сказа́ть (скажу́, ска́жешь)
school	шко́ла
science	нау́ка
scientific	нау́чный
scientist	учёный (29.5)
sea	мо́ре (nom./acc. pl. моря́, etc.)
to see	ви́деть (ви́жу, ви́дишь)/увидеть
to seem	каза́ться (кажу́сь, ка́жешься)/показа́ться
to sell	продава́ть (продаю́, продаёшь)/прода́ть (as in 12.10)
to send	посыла́ть/посла́ть (пошлю́, пошлёшь)
sense (of humour)	чу́вство (ю́мора)
September	сентя́брь (masc.; сентября́, etc.)
serious (acute)	о́стрый
service (attention, e.g. in restaurant)	се́рвис
service (facility)	слу́жба
seven	семь + gen. pl.
seventy	се́мьдесят + gen. pl.
several	не́сколько + gen. (19.2)
she	она́

sheet (of paper)	лист (листа́, etc.)
ship	кора́бль (masc.; корабля́, etc.)
shirt	руба́шка (as in 6.1)
shoe	ту́фля (gen. pl. ту́фель)
to shoot (elephant)	убива́ть/уби́ть (убью́, убьёшь)
shop	магази́н
short	коро́ткий
should	сле́дует, сле́довало бы (23.7)
to shout	крича́ть (кричу́, кричи́шь)
to show	пока́зывать/показа́ть (покажу́, пока́жешь)
shower	душ
Siberia	Сиби́рь (fem.)
side	сторона́ (acc. sing. сто́рону, nom./acc. pl. сто́роны, gen. pl. сторо́н, dat. pl. сторона́м, etc.)
sight: at first sight	на пе́рвый взгляд
to sign	подпи́сывать/подписа́ть (подпишу́, подпи́шешь)
to sing	петь (пою́, поёшь)/спеть
single: not a single	ни оди́н...не
sister	сестра́ (nom. pl. сёстры, acc./gen. pl. сестёр, dat. pl. сёстрам, etc.)
to sit (to be sitting)	сиде́ть (сижу́, сиди́шь)
to sit down	сади́ться (сажу́сь, са́дишься)/сесть (ся́ду, ся́дешь; 13.5)
situated: to be situated	находи́ться (нахо́дится)
situation	ситуа́ция
six	шесть + gen. pl.
six o'clock	шесть часо́в
slice	ломо́ть (masc.; ломтя́, etc.)
slightest	мале́йший
slow	ме́дленный
slowly	ме́дленно
small	ма́ленький, небольшо́й
to smoke	кури́ть (курю́, ку́ришь)
smoking	куре́ние, кури́ть
snake	змея́ (nom. pl. зме́и, acc./gen. pl. змей, dat. pl. зме́ям, etc.)
snow	снег
social	социа́льный
sofa	дива́н
soldier	солда́т (6.4)
solution	реше́ние
to solve	реша́ть/реши́ть
some	не́который, изве́стный
someone	кто-нибудь, кто-то (36.6)
sometimes	иногда́

son	сын (5.5)
source	исто́чник
south	юг (15.10)
Soviet	сове́тский
Soviet Union	Сове́тский Сою́з
space	ко́смос
Spain	Испа́ния
Spanish	испа́нский
Spanish (language)	испа́нский язы́к (языка́, etc.)
to speak (to)	говори́ть (с + instr.)
to speak Russian	говори́ть по-ру́сски
specialist	специали́ст
spectator	зри́тель (masc.)
to spend (money)	тра́тить (тра́чу, тра́тишь)/истра́тить
to spend (money, official)	расхо́довать (расхо́дую, расхо́дуешь)/ израсхо́довать
to spend (time)	проводи́ть (провожу́, прово́дишь)/ провести́ (проведу́, проведёшь; 13.5)
spider	пау́к (паука́, etc.)
spoon	ло́жка (as in 6.1)
spring	весна́
square	пло́щадь (fem.; gen. pl. площаде́й, dat. pl. площадя́м, etc.)
stadium	стадио́н
stage (in theatre)	сце́на
to stand	стоя́ть (стою́, стои́шь)
standard	у́ровень (masc.; у́ровня, etc.)
standard of living	жи́зненный у́ровень (у́ровня, etc.)
to start	начина́ть/нача́ть (начну́, начнёшь), стать (ста́ну, ста́нешь; 53.1)
station	вокза́л, ста́нция
to stay	остава́ться (остаю́сь, остаёшься)/ оста́ться (оста́нусь, оста́нешься)
to stay at home	сиде́ть (сижу́, сиди́шь) до́ма
to steal	красть (краду́, крадёшь; 13.5)/укра́сть
stomach-ache: he has stomach-ache	у него́ боли́т желу́док
stop	остано́вка
to stop (to come to a halt)	остана́вливаться/останови́ться (остановлю́сь, остано́вишься)
storm	гроза́ (nom./acc. pl. гро́зы, etc.)
story	расска́з
street	у́лица
strict	стро́гий
to strike (of clock)	бить (бьёт)/проби́ть
to stroll	гуля́ть/погуля́ть
strong	си́льный
strong (of drink, organism)	кре́пкий
student	студе́нт/студе́нтка

to study	изуча́ть/изучи́ть (изучу́, изу́чишь)
style	стиль (masc.)
subject (on agenda)	вопро́с
success	успе́х
such	тако́й (36.4)
suddenly	вдруг
sugar	са́хар
suit	костю́м
suitcase	чемода́н
sullen	угрю́мый
sum	су́мма
summer	ле́то (nom./acc. pl. лета́; 41.4.i)
sun	со́лнце
Sunday	воскресе́нье
supper	у́жин
supper: to have supper	у́жинать/поу́жинать
to supply	снабжа́ть/снабди́ть (снабжу́, снабди́шь)
support	подде́ржка
sure	уве́рен, уве́рена, etc.
swallow	ла́сточка (6.1)
to swear at	руга́ть/вы́ругать на + acc.
sweet	конфе́та
sweet (adj.)	сла́дкий
to swim	плыть (плыву́, плывёшь)/поплы́ть or пла́вать (45)
to swim across	переплыва́ть/переплы́ть (переплыву́, переплывёшь)
to switch on	включа́ть/включи́ть
system	систе́ма
table	стол (стола́, etc.)
tail	хвост (хвоста́, etc.)
to take	брать (беру́, берёшь)/взять (возьму́, возьмёшь)
to take (to lead)	вести́ (веду́, ведёшь; 13.5)/повести́ or води́ть (вожу́, во́дишь) (45)
to take (decisions, measures)	принима́ть/приня́ть (приму́, при́мешь)
to take off	взлета́ть/взлете́ть (взлечу́, взлети́шь)
to take out	вынима́ть/вы́нуть (вы́ну, вы́нешь)
to take place	случа́ться/случи́ться
talent	тала́нт
talented	тала́нтливый
to talk	говори́ть/поговори́ть
talkative	болтли́вый, разгово́рчивый
talks	перегово́ры (pl.; 3.2)
tall	высо́кий
task	зада́ча

taste	вкус
tasty	вку́сный
Tatyana	Татья́на
taxi	такси́ (neut.; indecl.)
tea	чай (19.3)
teacher	учи́тель (masc.; 5.2)
team	кома́нда
to tear out	вырыва́ть/вы́рвать (вы́рву, вы́рвешь)
telegram	телегра́мма
to telephone	звони́ть/позвони́ть (24.2)
television (medium)	телеви́дение
television (set)	телеви́зор
to tell	говори́ть/сказа́ть (скажу́, ска́жешь)
ten	де́сять + gen. pl.
tennis	те́ннис
terrible	ужа́сный
Thames	Те́мза
than	чем or gen. case (31.2, 32.8)
to thank	благодари́ть/поблагодари́ть
that (demonstrative)	тот (35.4)
that (relative)	что (36.2)
that (this, it)	э́то
theatre	теа́тр
theft	кра́жа
their	их, свой (35.2-3)
them	их, etc. (34.1-2)
theme	те́ма
then (at that time)	тогда́
then (next)	пото́м
theory	тео́рия
there (motion)	туда́
there are	есть
there is	есть
there was	бы́ло
there were	бы́ли
there will be	бу́дет, бу́дут
they	они́
thick (dense)	густо́й
to think	ду́мать
third	тре́тий (29.1)
thirty	три́дцать + gen. pl.
this	э́тот (35.4)
this afternoon	сего́дня по́сле обе́да
this evening	сего́дня ве́чером
this morning	сего́дня у́тром
thought	мысль (fem.)
thousand	ты́сяча + gen. pl.
three	три + gen. sing.

ticket	билéт
tiger	тигр
time	врéмя (neut.; 4.1)
time (occasion)	раз (6.4)
time: it is time to	порá + infin.
time: on time	вóвремя
tired: to be tired of	надоедáть/надоéсть (12.10; as in 13.5; see also 23.7)
tobacco	табáк (табакá, etc.)
today	сегóдня
together with	вмéсте с (+ instr.)
tomorrow	зáвтра
tonight	сегóдня вéчером
tonne	тóнна
too (excessively)	слúшком
top	верх (loc. на верхý)
to touch	дотрáгиваться/дотрóнуться (дотрóнусь, дотрóнешься) до + gen.
tourist	турúст
towards	к + dat. (25.6)
tower	бáшня (6.10)
town	гóрод (5.1.iii)
toy	игрýшка (as in 6.1)
traffic	движéние
train	пóезд (5.1.iii)
tram	трамвáй
travel	поéздки (pl.; gen. pl. поéздок)
to travel	éхать (éду, éдешь)/поéхать or éздить (éзжу, éздишь) (45)
to travel (if distance defined)	проéхать (pf.; проéду, проéдешь)
tree	дéрево (5.4)
troops	войскá (neut. pl.; gen. pl. войск)
to try	пытáться/попытáться, старáться/постарáться
Turgenev	Тургéнев
to turn off	выключáть/вы́ключить
to turn pale	бледнéть (бледнéю, бледнéешь)/побледнéть
twenty	двáдцать + gen. pl.
twenty-four-hour period	сýтки (pl.; 3.2)
twenty-six	двáдцать шесть + gen. pl.
two	два (masc.), две (fem.) + gen. sing.
typical of	типúчный для + gen.
umbrella	зóнтик
uncle	дя́дя (masc.; 6.9)
unclear	нея́сный
under	под + acc. (18.4.i) or instr. (26.9)

to understand	понима́ть/поня́ть (пойму́, поймёшь)
unemployed	без рабо́ты
unexpectedly	неожи́данно
unfavourable	неблагоприя́тный
ungainly	неуклю́жий
university	университе́т
until: not...until	то́лько
to upset	опроки́дывать/опроки́нуть (опроки́ну, опроки́нешь)
Urals	Ура́л (15.10)
urgent	сро́чный
us	нас, etc. (34.1)
useful	поле́зный
useless	бесполе́зный
usually	обы́чно, обыкнове́нно
vase	ва́за
version	ве́рсия
very	о́чень
victory	побе́да
view: in my view	на мой взгляд
village	дере́вня (gen. pl. дереве́нь, dat. pl. деревня́м, etc.)
visa application form	ви́зовая анке́та
to visit	посеща́ть/посети́ть (посещу́, посети́шь)
vodka	во́дка
voice	го́лос (5.1.iii)
Volga	Во́лга
to vote	голосова́ть (голосу́ю, голосу́ешь)/ проголосова́ть
to wait	ждать (жду, ждёшь)/подожда́ть
waiter	официа́нт
to wake up	просыпа́ться/просну́ться (просну́сь, проснёшься)
to walk	идти́ (иду́, идёшь; 13.6)/пойти́ (пойду́, пойдёшь) or ходи́ть (хожу́, хо́дишь) (45)
to walk past	проходи́ть (прохожу́, прохо́дишь)/ пройти́ (пройду́, пройдёшь; 13.6) ми́мо + gen.
wall	стена́ (acc. sing. сте́ну, nom./acc. pl. сте́ны, dat. pl. стена́м, etc.)
to want	хоте́ть (12.10)/захоте́ть
war	война́ (nom./acc. pl. во́йны, etc.)
warm	тёплый
to wash (window)	мыть (мо́ю, мо́ешь)/вы́мыть
Washington	Вашингто́н
to watch	смотре́ть (смотрю́, смо́тришь)/ посмотре́ть

water	вода́ (acc. sing. во́ду, nom./acc. pl. во́ды, dat. pl. вода́м, etc.)
way: on the way home	по доро́ге домо́й
we	мы
weak	сла́бый
wealthy	бога́тый
to wear (clothes): see 15.5	
to wear (habitually)	носи́ть (ношу́, но́сишь)
weather	пого́да
Wednesday	среда́ (acc. sing. сре́ду, nom./acc. pl. сре́ды, dat. pl. среда́м, etc.)
week	неде́ля
to weigh (intrans.)	ве́сить
weight	вес
well known	изве́стный
what	что
when	когда́
where	где
which	кото́рый (36.3.i, 36.3.iii)
while	пока́
whisper	шёпот
to whisper	шепта́ть (шепчу́, ше́пчешь)/прошепта́ть
white	бе́лый
who	кто (36.1, 36.3.i, 36.3.iii)
whole	весь (35.5), це́лый
why	почему́
wide	широ́кий
wife	жена́ (nom. pl. жёны, acc./gen. pl. жён, dat. pl. жёнам, etc.)
wind	ве́тер (3.1)
window	окно́ (nom./acc. pl. о́кна, gen. pl. о́кон, dat. pl. о́кнам, etc.)
wine	вино́ (nom./acc. pl. ви́на, etc.)
winter	зима́ (acc. sing. зи́му, nom./acc. pl. зи́мы, etc.)
with	с + instr. (26.10)
withdrawal	ухо́д
without	без+ gen. (22.1)
woman	же́нщина
wood	лес (5.1.iii, 15.13)
word	сло́во (nom./acc. pl. слова́, etc.)
work	рабо́та
to work	рабо́тать
to work on	рабо́тать над + instr. (26.7)
worker	рабо́тник
worker (manual)	рабо́чий (29.5)
worthless: is worthless	ничего́ не сто́ит
to write	писа́ть (пишу́, пи́шешь)/написа́ть
writer	писа́тель (masc.)

wrong (answer, etc.)	непра́вильный
wrong (of person)	непра́вый
yacht	я́хта
year	год (41.4.i)
year: in a year's time	че́рез год
years of age	лет (23.3; see also 41.4.i)
yesterday	вчера́
you	ты, вы, etc. (34.1)
young	молодо́й
younger	мла́дший
your	твой, ваш (35.1)
youth	ю́ность (fem.), мо́лодость (fem.)
zoo	зоопа́рк

Index of English prepositions

After prepositions which are capable of governing only one case the case in question is not given in this index.

about	насчёт, 22.11; о(б) + prep., 15.15; о́коло, 22.8, 41.1; про, 18.5; с + acc., 18.6
above	над, 26.7
according to	по + dat., 25.1
across	че́рез, 18.8.i
adjacent to	при, 15.17
after	за + acc., 18.1.iv; за + instr., 26.5; по + prep., 15.16; по́сле, 22.11
against	о + acc., 18.2; про́тив, 22.9
along	вдоль, 22.11; по + dat., 25.1
amid, among	среди́, 22.10
apart from	кро́ме, 22.11; поми́мо, 22.11
apropos of	по по́воду, 22.11
around	о́коло, 22.8
as far as	до, 22.5
at	в + acc., 17.2.iii, 40.2.i-ii; в + prep., 15.2-3, 15.8, 15.11, 15.13, 40.2.iii, 40.2.vi; за + acc., 18.1.v; за + instr., 26.5; по + dat., 25.1; у, 21.4; *without preposition in expressions of time*, 40.2.iv
at the time of	при, 15.17
attached to	при, 15.17
away from	от, 21.2; с + gen., 21.3
because of	вслéдствие, 22.11; из-за, 22.6
before	до, 22.5; пе́ред, 26.8
behind	за + acc., 18.1.i; за + instr., 26.5; позади́, 22.11
below, beneath	под + instr., 26.9
besides	кро́ме, 22.11; поми́мо, 22.11
between	мéжду, 26.6
beyond	за + acc., 18.1.i, 18.1.iv; за + instr., 26.5
by	во́зле, 22.11; за + acc., 18.1.vi; к, 25.6; на + acc., 17.4.v; о́коло, 22.8; по + dat., 25.1; у, 21.4
by means of	посрéдством, 22.11; путём, 22.11
concerning	о(б) + prep., 15.15; про, 18.5; относи́тельно, 22.11
contrary to, despite	вопреки́, 25.7
down	по + dat., 25.1; с + gen., 21.3
during	за + acc., 18.1.iii
except	кро́ме, 22.11

Index of Russian words and morphemes

Omitted from this index are Russian words given in lists of:

nouns with a mobile vowel (3.1)
nouns with plural form only (3.2)
indeclinable nouns (3.3)
masculine nouns with plural in -á (5.1)
nouns requiring insertion of **о** or **е** in the genitive plural (6.1)
nouns combined with на + prepositional in the meaning *in* or *at* (15.8, 15.10-11)
nouns with locative singular in -ý/-ю́/-и́ (15.13-14)
nouns followed by к (25.6)
common adjectives in -ний (28.7)
adjectives used as nouns (29.5)
adjectives requiring insertion of vowel in masculine short form (30.2)
present active participles used as set expressions (58.3)
adverbs of the type по-ру́сски which denote knowledge of a language (62.4)
adverbs consisting of a preposition and short adjectival form (62.5)
adverbs consisting of a preposition and noun (62.7)
common adverbs of time, place, and quantity or degree (62.10.i-iii)

Where reference is made to sections dealing with aspectual pairs, only the imperfective member of the pair is given in the following list, unless the perfective member is based on a different root (as for example in the case of the pair брать/взять). Forms which are perfective only are indicated as such. Reference is not made to the very numerous verbs which exemplify the use of prefixes in Lessons 46-9, since these are arranged in alphabetical order within the lessons themselves.

Position of stress is not indicated in this index.

Index of grammatical subjects

Current and forthcoming titles in the BCP Russian Language series

First Russian Vocabulary (key to the Russian Texts Series), P. Waddington
A Guide to Essay Writing in Russian, Svetlana and Stephen le Fleming
Modern Russian: An Advanced Grammar Course, Derek Offord
The New Russia: Readings on Russian Culture, Nijole White
Russian by Subjects (a classified vocabulary), P. Waddington
Russian Etymological Dictionary, Terence Wade
Russian for Business Studies, Svetlana le Fleming
What's in a Russian Word?, Ian Press